GENDER IN HISTORY

Series editors:
Pam Sharpe, Patricia Skinner and Penny Summerfield

The expansion of research into the history of women and gender since the 1970s has changed the face of history. Using the insights of feminist theory and of historians of women, gender historians have explored the configuration in the past of gender identities and relations between the sexes. They have also investigated the history of sexuality and family relations, and analysed ideas and ideals of masculinity and femininity. Yet gender history has not abandoned the original, inspirational project of women's history: to recover and reveal the lived experience of women in the past and the present.

The series Gender in History provides a forum for these developments. Its historical coverage extends from the medieval to the modern period, and its geographical scope encompasses not only Europe and North America but all corners of the globe. The series aims to investigate the social and cultural constructions of gender in historical sources, as well as the gendering of historical discourse itself. It embraces both detailed case studies of specific regions or periods, and broader treatments of major themes. Gender in History titles are designed to meet the needs of both scholars and students working in this dynamic area of historical research.

Artisans of the body in early modern Italy

D0145362

Manchester University Press

ARTISANS
OF THE BODY
IN EARLY MODERN
ITALY
IDENTITIES, FAMILIES
AND MASCULINITIES

⇒ Sandra Cavallo ⇐

Manchester University Press
Manchester and New York

distributed exclusively in the USA by Palgrave

Translated from an unpublished manuscript by Liz Heron and Sandra Cavallo

The right of Sandra Cavallo to be identified as the author of this work has been asserted by her in accordance with the Copyright, Designs and Patents Act 1988.

Published by Manchester University Press
Oxford Road, Manchester M13 9NR, UK
and Room 400, 175 Fifth Avenue, New York, NY 10010, USA
www.manchesteruniversitypress.co.uk

Distributed in the United States exclusively by
Palgrave Macmillan, 175 Fifth Avenue,
New York, NY 10010, USA

Distributed in Canada exclusively by
UBC Press, University of British Columbia, 2029 West Mall,
Vancouver, BC, Canada V6T 1Z2

British Library Cataloguing-in-Publication Data is available

Library of Congress Cataloging-in-Publication Data is available

ISBN 978 0 7190 8151 4 paperback

First published by Manchester University Press in hardback 2007

This paperback edition first published 2010

Printed by Lightning Source

Contents

List of plates

List of figures

List of tables

Acknowledgements

Many friends and colleagues, both in England and Italy, have given me encouragement and have generously discussed with me the idea and contents of the book. It is impossible to remember them all but I especially wish to thank Margaret Pelling and Patrick Wallis. In the later stages the project has benefited in particular from the advice and criticism of Clare Coope, Pene Corfield, Ida Fazio, Daniela Lombardi, Cathy McClive, Michael Eve, Liz Heron, Franco Ramella, Raffaella Sarti, Tessa Storey and Andrew Wear, who discussed with me the structure of the book or read drafts of individual chapters. I am also grateful for the insightful comments made by the anonymous readers at Manchester University Press. My gratitude to the Wellcome Trust, which supported research for this project in the early stages. My greatest debt is to my husband Marco Buttino who read and commented upon each of the several drafts of the book and gave me much support.

Parts of Chapter five and seven have already appeared in my article 'Métiers apparentés: barbiers-chirurgiens et artisans du corps à Turin (XVIIe–XVIIIe siècle)', *Histoire Urbaine*, n.15 Avril 2006, pp. 27–48 and in the chapter 'L'importanza della "famiglia orizzontale" nella storia della famiglia Italiana', in Ida Fazio and Daniela Lombardi (eds) *Generazioni. Legami di parentela tra passato e presente* (Viella, Rome 2006), pp. 69–92. I am grateful to the editors of these publications and to the publishers for permission to reprint this material.

List of abbreviations

AAT: Archivio Arcivescovile di Torino
  18.1.1–6: parish of SS. Simone e Giuda, *Liber status animarum*, 1648–1728.
  18.2.6: parish of S. Pietro del Gallo, *Baptizatorum liber*, 1678–99.
  18.2.10: parish of S. Pietro del Gallo, *Matrimoniorum liber*, 1619–77.
  18.2.11: parish of S. Pietro del Gallo, *Matrimoniorum liber*, 1654–1729.
  18.2.14: parish of S. Pietro del Gallo, *Mortuorum liber*, 1654–84.
  18.2.15: parish of S. Pietro del Gallo, *Mortuorum liber*, 1684–1715.
  18.4.6: parish of SS. Processo e Martiniano, processicoli matrimoniali, 1665–67.
  18.4.8: parish of SS. Processo e Martiniano, processicoli matrimoniali, 1689–95.
  18.4.12: parish of SS. Processo e Martiniano, processicoli matrimoniali, 1723–31.
ACT: Archivio del Comune di Torino.
AOSG: Archivio dell'Ospedale S. Giovanni.
Art. 530: AST, s.r., Camerale, Art. 530, *Consegna degli individui di Torino*, 1705.
AST, s.I: Archivio di Stato di Torino, sezione prima.
AST, s.r.: Archivio di Stato di Torino, sezioni riunite.
Borelli: G. B. Borelli, *Editti antichi e nuovi dei Sovrani Principi della Real Casa di Savoia* (Turin, 1681).
BSBS: *Bollettino Storico Bibliografico Subalpino*.
Consegna dei Francesi 1690: AST, sez.I, Provincia di Torino, m. 4° fasc. 20, *Consegna dei Francesi*, 1690.
Contadoria Generale: AST, s.r., Ministero della Guerra, *Contadoria Generale*, 24 vols, 1588–1688.
De' Tumori: *Chirurgia Teorico-Pratica di Paolo Bernardo Calvo Chirurgo Colleggiato in Torino. Trattato primo De' Tumori* (Turin, 1702).
Delle Ferite: *Chirurgia Teorico-Pratica di Paolo Bernardo Calvo Chirurgo Colleggiato in Torino. Trattato delle Ferite* (Turin, 1712).
Duboin: F. A. Duboin, *Raccolta per ordine di materia delle leggi, editti, manifesti ecc.*, 23 vols (Turin, 1818–69).
Guardie del Corpo di S.M.: AST, s.r., Ministero della Guerra, Ruoli di Rivista, *Guardie del Corpo di S.M. 1696–1846*.
Ins.: AST, s.r., *Insinuazione di Torino*.
OSML: Archivio dell'Ospedale dei SS. Maurizio e Lazzaro.
PCF: AST, s.r., Patenti Controllo Finanze.
'Registro delli chirurghi ... di Torino': AST, s.r., I Archiviazione. *Speziali, Fondighieri e Chirurghi*, m. 1, 'Registro delli chirurghi e barbieri della presente città di Torino che hanno fatto fede delle patenti di loro costituzione', 1695.
'Registro delli ... cirugici e barbieri ... della Provincia di Torino': AST, s.r., I Archiviazione. *Speziali, Fondighieri e Chirurghi*, m. 1, 'Registro delli speciari,

cirugici e barbieri delle Terre della Provincia della presente Città', 1695.

'Memorie per il regolamento': 'Memorie per il regolamento... raccolte per comando di Madama reale l'anno 1679', in Duboin, vol. 8, pp. 111 ff.

Regie Patenti e Commissioni: Ministero della Guerra, *Regie Patenti e Commissioni*, 1714–42.

Rollo dei Francesi ... 1704: *Rollo dei Francesi habitanti in Torino li 4 Agosto 1704* in AST, s.I, Provincia di Torino, m. 4, fasc. 20.

'Stato de' Cerusici e Flebotimisti': Archivio Storico dell'Università di Torino, 'Stato de' Cerusici e Flebotomisti descritti per ordine di provincie', c.1730.

'Stato dei negozianti e artisti ... 1742': 'Stato dei negozianti e artisti della presente città, 1742' in AST, s.r., I Archiviazione, Commercio e manifatture, m.1.

'Ticheta': AST, sez. I, Cerimoniale, Cariche di Corte, m.1, unnumbered and undated file, 'Ticheta, o sia forma e modo col quale intendiamo debban servire li nostri Gentiluomini di Camera et altri dipendenti'.

'Vercelli': AST, s.r., I Archiviazione. *Speziali, Fondighieri e Chirurghi*, m.2, 'Vercelli', 1695.

Introduction

This study examines the role of the many different artisans involved in various aspects of the care, comfort and appearance of the body in seventeenth- and early eighteenth-century Italy: barbers, surgeons, jewellers, tailors, wigmakers and perruquiers, perfumers and upholsterers. In so doing it brings to light the strong cultural affinities and social links which existed between them and which have hitherto largely been unrecognised. The connections between these occupational groups emerged, unexpectedly, in the course of a study of early modern barber-surgeons and have led me to shift the focus of attention from a single occupation to a full sector of the artisan world, for which I have coined the term 'artisans of the body'.

Surgeons acquired new prestige and visibility in the medical field in this period, thanks in particular to the central role they came to play in hospitals and in military health care. However, an exclusive focus on the medical activities of surgeons has led scholars to neglect other important aspects of their practice. The baroque age also witnessed a considerable increase in demand for services concerned with the hygiene, beauty and general well-being of the body. Boosted by the concentration of the elites into towns, the rise of an urban genteel society and its rituals encouraged the expansion of a culture of appearances together with the professional activities related with its maintenance. The repercussions of these processes on the experience of being a surgeon were significant: on the one hand, tasks related to decorum and beautification came to play a central role in the identity of many such practitioners; on the other hand, strong ties developed at both a cultural and social level between barber-surgeons and other craftsmen concerned with the body. These links have been overlooked by a history of medicine too focused on tracing the 'medicalisation' of the occupation in this period and its emancipation from activities which have been seen as purely aesthetic; and, more generally, by a history of work, trades and professions aimed primarily at identifying the growing distance between contiguous occupations within a narrative of increased specialisation.

Recent conceptualisations of identity have moved away from this 'discontinuist' perspective, which systematically stresses differences and contrasts rather than nuances and continuities between social groups, identities and cultural attitudes.[1] In line with this trend the present study concentrates instead on overlaps between the spheres of activity of barber-surgeons and those in adjacent occupations, in the attempt to make sense of the tendency, often remarked upon by social historians, of some trades to cluster in unexpected ways. Why, for example, are barber-surgeons frequently associated with jewellers or with upholsterers? To grasp the points of contact that existed, at the time, between activities which now appear unrelated we need to adopt an anthropological perspective and explore the conceptual basis of this professional cluster. Barbers' tracts and surgical treatises, court regulations, health advice books and other texts documenting the characteristics of individual professional cultures have therefore been employed to recreate the meaning that these occupations had for contemporaries. This investigation highlights the unity of discourse then current between ideas of health, hygiene, appearance and comfort (chapters 2–3). Inspired by some of the ideas formulated by Pierre Bourdieu, this study stresses the cultural rather than economic or practical links between apparently distant trades.[2]

At the same time it is suggested here that cultural and professional ties were closely intertwined with social and kinship ties. While scholars of the medical occupations have normally limited their attention to the professional activities of medical practitioners,[3] my focus extends to the social, public and family life of barber-surgeons and to the ways in which these spheres interacted with their professional experience (chapters 4–7). Concentrating on one specific case, that of Turin, and using biographical analysis as its method, this study builds a wide-ranging picture of these practitioners and the world to which they belonged. It considers the surgeons' family experience, the nature of their relationship with parents, kin and neighbours, the characteristics of their life cycle, as well as issues of property, consumption and material culture. How common was the father-to-son transmission of trade? What role did mothers, wives and sisters play in the reproduction of this occupational milieu? How significant were bonds of biological kinship and how did they compare with relations created through marriage or with relationships with neighbours? In addressing these sorts of questions the study throws new light on crucial aspects of the experience of the urban middling sorts (or at least on one component of it), a section of the population which has received increased scholarly attention in England but which has been overlooked in works concerned with early modern Italy and continental Europe more generally.[4]

The focus on crafts concerned with appearance makes Turin particularly appropriate as the principal setting for this study. As capital of the dukedom of Savoy,[5] it was the seat of a baroque court, and thus it gives us the opportunity to examine in detail developments that were simultaneously taking place elsewhere in Europe, and to which early modern historians are now giving increasing attention: changes in fashion, the expansion of court life, the emergence of a new kind of gentleman no longer conforming to military ideals, and defined by luxury consumption, comfort and a genteel style of living that call for new types of services for the body.[6] The period more specifically under consideration in this study runs roughly from the mid-seventeenth century, the moment from which the first listings of barber-surgeons active in the city survive, to the 1720s, when reforms of the university were introduced that, according to the traditional periodisation, transformed the figure of the surgeon, relocating his professional training from the workshop to the university and giving a theoretical dimension to his eminently practical skills. This, it is argued, led to the legitimisation of the surgeon's competence to treat internal as well as external diseases and turned him into a general practitioner.[7] In reality, notwithstanding these reforms, no radical change came about in the professional status of the Turin surgeon, at least as far as its institutional definition was concerned.[8] Morever, as we shall see, thanks to a range of exceptions and exemptions, even decades after the introduction of these provisions, surgeons who had no university training continued to practise without difficulty.

The period under consideration also saw a significant development of medical structures: the two major hospitals in the city were enlarged and doubled their capacity, the municipal medical service expanded considerably and so did health provision for the army; in addition, new possibilities for the employment of barber-surgeons arose at court. These developments provided many new settings for surgical practice and corresponding opportunities for training young surgeons. There were, however, several other aspects of the transformation of Turin that had an impact on the experience of barber-surgeons in this period. Between 1620 and 1730 the city expanded and changed both physically and socially. Its walls were extended three times in this period, its population increased considerably and its trades, especially the luxury crafts, boomed. A myriad of private palaces was commissioned both by the long-established nobility, which was moving in to take up stable residence in the city, and by the newly ennobled families and the merchant and financial class flourishing around the court. The court of Savoy had been located in Turin ever since the official entry of the dukes in 1563. But it was only from the 1630s, under the regency of Madama Cristina, the sister of Louis XIII of France, that it began to expand considerably, on the model of the French court, both in terms of the functions and number of court employees. Among these we will encounter a significant number of barber-surgeons and other artisans of the body: the analysis of their positions and roles at court will provide a valuable insight into the features of this occupational milieu.

The nature of this study has obviously changed considerably in the course of research. I embarked on an investigation of an occupational group, barber-surgeons, and found myself instead exploring an occupational milieu, that of artisans of the body. Moreover, my interest in an occupation and on patterns of behaviour that were to some degree shared and collective has gradually given way to an in-depth study of single individuals that provides a better measure of the range of possibilities available to a surgeon living at this time. How did this change of perspective come about? In these introductory pages it seems worth retracing the steps that have gradually led to a redefinition of questions, sources and ways of looking at them.

Barber-surgeons have been surprisingly neglected in the social history of early modern medicine, and so my decision to focus on them arose initially from the wish to redress an imbalance in the historiography. With the exception of Toby Gelfand's book (now out of print), tracing the institutional history of Paris surgeons in the context especially of hospital medicine in the seventeenth and eighteenth centuries, and Margaret Pelling's important articles, offering a broader perspective on the professional experience of barber-surgeons in sixteenth- and seventeenth-century England, recent studies on medical practitioners have given scant attention to surgeons.[9] As has occurred in the case of studies of early modern France and England, historians of the medical profession in early modern Italy have tended to focus on the figures of the charlatan and the learned physician.[10] More recently scholarly interest has extended to the apothecary, who is seen as playing a crucial role in the commercialisation of medical remedies that was already underway in sixteenth-century Italy.[11] And yet, as David Gentilcore acknowledges, 'The barber, bloodletter or phlebotomist was the most common sort of medical practitioner'.[12] In my study of hospitals and other charitable institutions in early modern Turin I had indeed come across surgeons much more frequently than physicians, apothecaries or charlatans. As in France and in England, it was they who ran the hospitals, at least from the time of their major expansion in the third quarter of the seventeenth century, with the assistance of a slew of 'young surgeons' (rather like journeymen) whom we find from the 1670s regularly spending a phase of their training in these institutions.[13] It is surgeons again, and the members of one family in particular (the Vernas and their kin), who are at the centre of the conflict between the principal hospital of the city and the University 'reformers' in the 1730s. Moreover, the so-called Surgeons of the Poor were the key implementers of the massive system of medical outdoor relief that for nearly a century remained at the heart of municipal intervention to assist the labouring poor.[14]

The surgeon therefore appears as the dominant figure within the city's medical provision.[15] It should be noted however that the evidence on which I was basing my observations was different from the sources employed in other studies of medical practitioners in early modern Italy. In Turin there were no surviving records of the activities of the College of Physicians and of the Protophysician's board (*Protomedicato*) studied by Gianna Pomata for Bologna and by David Gentilcore for the Kingdom of Naples.[16] These were the organs with authority over medical matters in their remit was not just the prerogative of granting the licence to practise medicine but also the legal power to prosecute those accused of illicit practice or malpractice. The material documenting the activities of these bodies is obviously prescriptive and judicial in nature, consisting of regulations, court depositions and denunciations, and therefore gives special visibility to some figures of practitioner to the detriment of others: that is (rather than surgeons) to physicians – who embodied the role of arbiters in the court proceedings and frequently prompted lawsuits against irregular practitioners – and to 'charlatans' and other unofficial healers, who represented the most frequently investigated group of practitioners.[17] Moreover, a focus on the activities of medical tribunals can give the impression that the authorities succeeded effectively in enforcing hard and fast distinctions between the therapeutic duties of different categories of practitioners.[18] Those who were summoned to court were accused of trespassing beyond the professional demarcation established by ordinances in medical matters, but how exceptional were they? Clearly, such documentation tends to depict as marginal and deviant practices that were perhaps fairly common, such as practising without a licence or the use of internal medicine by barber-surgeons. But to what extent were the dichotomies internal-external, manual-intellectual, learned-empirical which informed prescriptive definitions of the respective domains of physicians, surgeons and barbers reflected in daily practice? An analysis of the lawsuits alone does not suffice to clear up this question; to gain an insight into ordinary medical practice we need to adopt another viewpoint.

The absence of the canonical sources in the case of Turin has encouraged me to turn to material as yet underused, such as popular literature on how to maintain health and printed works produced by ordinary surgeons and barbers, as a means of inquiry into their practice and mindset. In addition, the possibility of developing a detailed biographical study of Turin's barber-surgeons has enabled me to shift the emphasis away from legal prescription and the control exercised over medical practice 'from above'. Stress is laid instead on the strategies for self-fashioning through which practitioners presented and defined themselves in everyday life, and on the unofficial mechanisms through which access to independent practice and the provision of medical services on the market were limited 'from below'. Thus this study brings about a change in perspective: my sources give only scattered information on how barber-surgeons were examined and licensed but they have much to say on how they talked about the licence and what social value it had outside the courtroom. The evidence does not allow for an institutional history of the occupation in Turin: only two documents, dated 1660 and 1676, have survived which signal the existence of a professional association of barber-surgeons in the city (this will be examined in chapter 2). How continuous the presence of this body was is however unknown. Sparse evidence suggests that its members were involved in the issuing of licences to practise but we have no direct documentation illustrating the role and activities of the company. The attention in this study shifts therefore from the corporate structure of the occupation and its regulatory and representative bodies (guilds, colleges, *Protomedicati*), to the informal grouping of these practitioners, be it founded on local or kinship ties. My sources have also allowed me to give unprecedented attention to the various stages of the career path: to training, not so much in terms of guild prescriptions but rather in the context of family and kinship relationships; to the figure of the 'young surgeon' that turns out to be central to surgical practice in this period; to the organisation of work inside and outside the barber-surgeon's shop, and to the nature of the rapport between colleagues and between masters and young surgeons.

From the very start, the relationship between work and career, on the one hand, and family and kinship ties on the other, emerged as a central feature of my investigation. This subject has hitherto been addressed mainly in relation to the patrician and mercantile groups of the Renaissance and early modern period, but not with reference to artisan and professional groups. The centrality of this link was obvious in the surgeons I already knew about, such as Alberto Verna and his descendants, who ran the city's principal hospital for generations. The dynastic character of their professional power alerted me about the significance of the transmission of professional knowledge and positions within the family. But the unconventional nature of the succession also urged me to consider the occupations carried out within the wider kinship network (including the connections made through marriage) and not simply the relationship between the trade of a father and that of his sons: Alberto Verna's position in the hospital was in fact inherited by a nephew of his, Evasio, then by a young cousin of the latter and then by Evasio's son-in-law.

Initially, I addressed these questions from a perspective of collective biography and I sought out the sources that provided a communal portrait of the surgeons' professional and family experience. Available to me were two extraordinarily rich sources that seemed ideal for my purposes. First, the 1705 census of the population of Turin, which gave the composition of the domestic unit and detailed the name and age of its members and their relationship to the head of household, recording also the house and city block (*Cantone*) where they lived. Second, there was a survey carried out ten years earlier (1695) of all barber-surgeons in Turin, licensed and unlicensed, which gave information about the stages in their past professional career, the date of the licence (if held), and frequently recorded the location of the shop within the city. Together with the lists of practitioners of surgery, compiled, for various reasons, in the years 1660, 1690, 1705, during the 1730s and in 1742, these enabled me to trace the continuity of surnames over time, and thus dynastic ascendancy within the occupation. And yet the apparent richness of this material was, on closer scrutiny, misleading. The population census gave only limited indications about the relationship between family and career: it provided a snapshot of the domestic unit at a certain date, but it did not reveal how long the couple in question had been married, whether this was a first marriage, how many children the surgeon had had, how many had already left home and what they did. The census lacked depth and on its own supplied information that was ambiguous and hard to interpret. Further difficulties arose from my attempt to trace the typical career of a surgeon: to offer one example, I could match up the information from the population census with that from the occupational surveys in order to explore the relationship between age, the granting of a licence and the start of independent practice. But although in many cases this procedure highlighted similar trajectories and age patterns, there was also much variation across both extremes of the spectrum: some practitioners took up the licence at seventeen or eighteen, others were over thirty and after decades of independent practice did not yet hold it! In short no consistent profile emerged for this occupational group. At this point, I could have confined myself to the average, excluding the exceptions, in order to plot the trajectory of a 'typical' surgeon, or I could aim to provide a more realistic picture which accommodated the range of situations encountered.[19] My concern has therefore been to pinpoint the professional and social practices that were recurring features of this occupational milieu, while refraining from suggesting some falsely uniform picture that would deny subjectivity and variety.

These considerations led me to opt for a biographical approach. This meant gathering whatever information could be found that concerned my practitioners in the different archives of the city: from the various kinds of notarial deeds in which the individual could be involved, to the births, deaths and marriages relating to him in the parish registers that have survived, to evidence about surgeons' appointments found in hospital records, or in municipal, court and military records. Cross-referenced, and used with the census data and the professional records I have already mentioned, this wealth of evidence gave the members of the Verna dynasty – to take one example – depth and a history, documenting their origins and their economic and social rise, their most significant professional and family connections and the milieus in which they moved. Biographical studies have generally taken prominent practitioners as their subject, whereas here it was a matter of reconstructing the life trajectories of ordinary surgeons who happened to have played a part in the life of the city and its people. For each one of the eighty-eight surgeons included in the 1695 survey I therefore put together as much material as was possible. Of course, their biographies vary in completeness and this generally rules out any statistical conclusions, something that is in any case alien to the approach taken in this study, which aims to emphasise the variety of solutions adopted for often common problems.[20] However, for some thirty barber-surgeons the reconstruction of their life story is fairly complete.

It should be stressed that the Turin sources make it possible to develop biographical research on ordinary people to an extent that is usually impossible. Uniquely in Italy, indexes for notarial deeds are available in Turin in alphabetical order, and we should remember how wide-ranging these documents are. In the Italian states a great many issues were put in the hands of a notary: notarial records therefore include not just marriage contracts and wills but papers relating to the entrusting of orphans to guardians, deeds of emancipation (an extremely useful source for studying relationships between generations), the constitutions and dissolutions of professional societies, settlements of inheritance disputes, divisions between heirs, and proxies, purchases and loans, and so forth. Even though these legal documents are not the only source on which this study is based, they have certainly been a key one.

Biographical analysis confirmed and amplified my impression of the significance of family ties in all aspects of a surgeon's experience, including the professional sphere. On the one hand, it shed light on the constant presence of kin in the life of the individual, suggesting the need to take account of a family that went beyond the household of cohabitants as gathered by the census, and therefore to overcome the distinction between family and kinship that is still central in many studies. But there was a further aspect: biographical analysis highlighted the extension of bonds of kinship and made me realise that many individuals I had initially thought of as unconnected to one another, not related but belonging to other 'families', were in fact kin. The tie of kinship was often rendered invisible by a difference in surnames: the individuals in question were not just fathers, sons, brothers, uncles or nephews through the father's line, but brothers-in-law, fathers-in-law, uncles of a wife, cousins or nephews through the female line. What emerged therefore were the limitations of the patrilineal understanding of the family and the need to adopt a bilateral reconstitution of family ties that considered not just those given by the same surname but also those formed by marriage. Although it has been recognised that making kinship synonymous with a shared surname 'poses significant methodological problems', this is the approach normally pursued in studies of the role of kinship in Renaissance and early modern Italy.[21] Usually, the focus of analysis has been neither the conduct of all those who are in fact related, nor the 'active' kinship network, in other words the web of relatives with whom there are frequent interactions. Rather, attention has centred on the actions of one section of the group of relatives: those who bear the same surname, in order to find some unifying thread that would explain their conduct in the form of a collective biography.[22] This is clearly a representation of kinship that bears little resemblance to real life, one that takes for granted that a shared surname is a fundamental principle of association and that patrilineal ties are more significant than those with relations who might well be blood relatives and even be close in degree of kinship but have different surnames.[23] Moreover, the important distinction between 'active' kinship ties and 'latent' or potential ties, those that can be traced through genealogical reconstruction but play no significant role in the individual's life, has not been translated into research practice.[24] A number of scholars have pointed to the importance of matrilineal ties in the transmission of inheritance, the political role of affinal relations and the bilateral nature of bonds of affection.[25] James Grubb in particular has stressed 'the frequency, intensity and variety of relations with marital kin' and exposed the limits of the vertical view of the patrician family in studies of the Italian Renaissance.[26] And yet these considerations frequently remain no more than a marginal corrective to a substantially patrilineal view of kinship in the early modern period. There are no examples to date of studies that develop a thorough reconstitution of kinship, taking all the ties into account, whether biological or affinal, patrilineal or matrilineal, cognatic or agnatic. By placing the individual at the centre of the analysis, and inquiring which family ties truly mattered to him or her within the whole kinship group, I hope to offer a more effective view of the role of kinship. Emphasis is shifted therefore in this study from kinship as a predefined entity to the dynamics by means of which each individual *created* his or her own nucleus of significant ties within those potentially available to him, negotiating between individual aspirations and projects and biological and ideological constraints.

Another unexpected element that the biographies brought to light was represented by the kinds of figures who appeared repeatedly in the social and family relationships of my barber-surgeons. Friends and kin were sometimes other surgeons but rarely physicians or apothecaries; they were mostly artisans and, in addition, they were from a limited range of occupations. The outlines of what I expected would be a group defined by the common medical occupation were therefore fading; the biographical study of barber-surgeons was introducing me much more into the world of artisans, and to a specific sector of this world. This posed the problem of the surgeon's identity, his social placing. Which milieu was he part of? How far did he belong in the medical community? And why did he tend to associate with particular occupations? These questions could be tackled through an in-depth study of surgeons' networks that paid attention to parties in contracts and financial transactions, to the witnesses to their legal acts and those for whom they themselves acted as witnesses, to those who stood as guarantors for them and as proxies, in other words those they trusted and relied on. By this point however I was no longer simply studying the surgeons but a social environment, barber-surgeons and their social relationships: whom they married and to whom they were related, with whom they worked, and those with whom they maintained close social, economic and professional relationships. Thus the focus of this study became an occupational milieu, that precisely of 'artisans of the body', rather than a single occupation and the questions pursued concern the ways in which this social space was organised. Biography here was understood as a study of society centred on the individual or, in more technical terms as ego-centred network analysis, as a way – in other words – of exploring the nature and boundaries of social aggregations outside predefined categories and groups (occupations for example) and of posing the question of how and why people come together.[27]

The biographical approach also adds a new dimension to the study of early modern masculine identities, which hitherto has largely relied on prescriptive literature and judicial sources. Biographies bring us into contact with ordinary lives that are often remote from the ideals celebrated in conduct books and likewise from behaviour that was judged to be deviant and became the object of judicial prosecutions. The fundamental contribution of this approach is that it applies to the male experience analytical perspectives that are usually associated with the practice of women's history: attention to the life cycle, to the age category, to marital state and to the parental role. Looking at the age of barber-surgeons, for example, has proved a key analytical tool in my study: it threw new light on the relationships between master and pupil, and, more generally, made it possible to reconsider the way in which youth during this period has been described, and how the various ages of man – youth, adulthood, old age – were perceived.

Attention to the male life cycle has also enabled me to verify the importance of demographic detail in the analysis of individual and family histories; increasingly seen as the preserve of historical demographers, this perspective has unjustly fallen out of favour in mainstream social history. And yet, paying attention to the number of children in a family, their age and sex, whether married or still a parental responsibility, or asking about how much impact the deaths of family members had on the opportunities open to an individual, has made it possible to identify important distinctions in male experience, thus avoiding the risk of talking about 'men' as some uniform category. Moreover, a concern with demographic events has shed light on phenomena to which little attention has hitherto been given: the extent of bachelorhood, or the number of couples without children, as well as the frequency and significance among these social groups of experiences such as the premature loss of a father or of both parents, the brief duration of many marriages and the remarriage of widowed males. The analysis therefore emphasises the variety of ways of being a man in the early modern period, but it also suggests new strategies for reading and understanding this variety (chapters 8–10). On the one hand, it draws attention to the existence of different legal traditions that, in various parts of Europe, established distinctive patterns for the acquisition of male independence. On the other hand, it is suggested that – as in the case of feminine models – ideals and practices of masculinity varied in different confessional contexts.

The book begins by problematizing the place that surgeons occupy in the professional environment (chapters 2–3). Using an array of divergent sources, from surgical and barber tracts to medical orders, from court regulations to the professional definitions (and self-definitions) employed in everyday life to label practitioners, it challenges and redesigns, both at practical and theoretical level, the boundaries that are often said to demarcate the respective professional domains of surgeons, physicians and barbers (chapters 1–2). At the same time this section highlights the strong connections that existed between the duties of barber-surgeons and a number of non-medical occupations concerned with the ornament and comfort of the body (chapter 3). The analysis of kinship ties shows that these connections were also replicated in kin networks, suggesting that 'artisans of the body' represented a social as well as an occupational milieu. Chapters 4–8 develop further the analysis of the social and professional world of barber-surgeons, making fully evident the implications of specific patterns of marriage and kinship formation for work opportunities and careers. Chapter 4 discusses the place that barber-surgeons occupied in the social landscape, exploring their lifestyle, material culture and patterns of property and comparing their salaries to those of physicians. With what groups did they share their social aspirations? Chapter 5 then examines the composition of their social, economic and professional networks. It considers in particular the opportunities for work partnerships created by inter-trade marriage and the role of age peer groups in the professional experience of artisans of the body. The age category is a key tool, in this section, to grasp the significance of kinship ties and the relationship between family and work. Chapter 6 deals with the contexts in which the acquisition of professional knowledge and skills took place. It outlines the specific features of the organisation of labour and of the reproduction of the trade, paying special attention to the many-sided figure of the 'young surgeon'. Chapter 7 reconsiders the meaning of marriage for artisans of the body and provides new evidence for documenting the contribution of wives, daughters, mothers and sisters to the workshop and to other settings where the trade was carried out. Finally, chapter 8 reassesses the authority attributed to the father in accounts of the early modern family along with the significance of patrilineal transmission and explores the alternative ways through which professional resources were handed down. Chapters 9–10 analyse the implications that the specific configuration of the father-son relationship, combined with the features of the labour market discussed above, had for the construction of personal and professional respectability. Chapter 9 examines how the legal subordination to the father could be negotiated and questions the universality of marriage as prime criterion for the achievement of full masculine status. Finally, chapter 10 questions the identification of the unlicensed with the 'irregular' practitioner common in accounts of the medical profession and explores the strategies adopted by both licensed and unlicensed practitioners for constructing professional credibility. The book moves therefore from the professional sphere to the domestic and familial and back again, in the attempt to show the close interconnection between these far from separate areas of artisan experience.

Notes

1 For a critique of the discontinuist analytical approach, in relation however to ethnological thinking, see J.-L. Amselle, *Logiques Métisses. Anthropologie de l'Identité en Afrique et Ailleurs* (Paris, 1990). More specifically, on the identity of early modern medical practitioners, M. Pelling, 'Medical practice in early modern England. Trade or profession?', in W. Prest (ed.), *The Professions of Early Modern England* (New York, 1987).

2 I refer in particular to the distinction between economic capital and cultural capital formulated in many works but especially in his *Distinction: A Social Critique of the Judgement of Taste* (London, 1984).

3 A unique exception, for a slightly earlier period, is represented by Françoise Lehoux's study of marriage, property and housing patterns of Parisian physicians: F. Lehoux, *Le Cadre de Vie des Médecins Parisiens aux XVIe et XVIIe Siècles* (Paris, 1976). The study however does not investigate the relationship between professional and private life.

4 Notable exceptions, in the case of France, are represented by J. Hardwick, *The Practice of Patriarchy: Gender and the Politics of Household Authority in Early Modern France* (University Park, 1998) and C. Dolan, *Le Notaire, la Famille et la Ville (Aix-en-Provence à la fin du XVIe siècle)* (Toulouse, 1998). On England, see among others J. Barry and C. Brooks (eds), *The Middling Sort of People: Culture, Society, and Politics in England, 1550–1800* (Basingstoke, 1994); M. Hunt, *The Middling Sort: Commerce, Gender and the Family in England 1680–1780* (Berkeley, 1996); and the overview by H. R. French, 'The search for the middle sort of people 1600–1800', *Historical Journal*, 43:1 (2000).

5 The Duke of Savoy obtained the title of King of Sicily in 1713 (then of Sardinia from 1720), as a result of the Peace of Utrecht. After this date he will therefore be referred to as His Majesty.

6 For significant examples of this trend see M. Belfanti and F. Giusberti (eds), *La Moda. Storia d'Italia Annali 9* (Turin, 2003); G. Vigarello, 'S'exercer, jouer', in *Histoire du Corps, vol. 1. De la Renaissance aux Lumières* (Paris, 2005), especially pp. 235–80; C. Lanoe, 'Les jeux de l'artificiel. Culture, production et consommation des cosmétiques à Paris sous l'Ancien régime, XVIe-XVIIIe siècles' (PhD thesis, Université Paris I, 2003).

7 D. Carpanetto, *Scienza e Arte del Guarire. Cultura, Formazione Universitaria e Professioni Mediche a Torino tra Sei e Settecento* (Turin, 1998), especially pp. 198–209.

8 The 'patents' obtained by surgeons in the wake of the reforms was inferior to the 'degree' conferred to physicians and in other faculties: Duboin, vol. 14, p. 730, n.1. Carpanetto, *Scienza*, p. 207.

9 T. Gelfand, *Professionalizing Modern Medicine: Paris Surgeons and Medical Science and Institutions in the Eighteenth Century* (Westport, Connecticut, 1980); M. Pelling, 'Occupational diversity: barber-surgeons and other trades, 1550–1640', *Bulletin of the History of Medicine*, 56 (1982); 'Compromised by gender: the role of the male medical

practitioner in early modern England', in H. Marland and M. Pelling (eds), *The Task of Healing. Medicine, Religion and Gender in England and the Netherlands, 1450–1800* (Rotterdam, 1996). See also Pelling's *The Common Lot. Sickness, Medical Occupations and the Urban Poor in Early Modern England* (London, 1998), which includes advanced versions of some of these pioneering works. Important insights into the professional experience of surgeons are also found in A. Wear, *Knowledge and Practice in English Medicine 1550–1680* (Cambridge, 2000), chapter 5 and L. McCray Beier, 'Seventeenth-century English surgery: the casebook of Joseph Binns', in C. Lawrence (ed.), *Medical Theory, Surgical Practice* (London, 1992).

10 David Gentilcore's *Healing and Healers in Early Modern Italy* (Manchester, 1998) devotes only five pages to barber-surgeons, many more to physicians and a full chapter to charlatans; G. Pomata, *Contracting a Cure: Patients, Healers and the Law in Early Modern Italy* (Baltimore, 1998). For an earlier period, see K. Park, *Doctors and Medicine in Early Renaissance Florence* (Princeton, NJ, 1985). On France, Laurence Brockliss and Colin Jones devote only a chapter of their monumental *The Medical World of Early Modern France* (Oxford, 1997) to surgeons. On England, see R. Porter, *Health for Sale. Quackery in England 1600–1850* (Manchester, 1989); H. Cook, *Trials of an Ordinary Doctor: Joannes Groenevelt in Seventeenth-Century London* (Baltimore, 1994) and *The Decline of the Old Medical Regime in Stuart London* (Ithaca, 1986); M. Pelling, *Medical Conflicts in Early Modern London. Patronage, Physicians and Irregular Practitioners 1550–1640* (Oxford, 2003). On charlatans in Europe, see also the articles in the recent *Cultural and Social History*, 3:3 (2006).

11 R. Palmer, 'Pharmacy in the republic of Venice in the sixteenth century', in A. Wear, R. K. French and I. M. Lonie (eds), *The Medical Renaissance of the Sixteenth Century* (Cambridge, 1985); D. Gentilcore, 'Apothecaries, 'charlatans', and the medical market-place in Italy, 1400–1750', in D. Gentilcore (ed.), *The World of the Italian Apothecary, Pharmacy in History*, 45:3 (2003).

12 Gentilcore, *Healing*, p. 74.

13 Gelfand, *Professionalizing*. On hospital surgeons in England see, among others, M. Fissell, *Patients, Power and the Poor in Eighteenth-Century Bristol* (Cambridge, 1991).

14 S. Cavallo, *Charity and Power in Early Modern Italy. Benefactors and their Motives in Turin 1564–1789* (Cambridge, 1995), pp. 208–14.

15 Another sphere in which barber-surgeons figure prominently is the courtroom where they are frequently summoned as experts: A. Pastore, *Il Medico in Tribunale: la Perizia Medica nella Procedura Penale di Antico Regime (sec. 16–18)* (Bellinzona, 1998); C. McClive, 'Bleeding Flowers and Waning Moons: A History of Menstruations in France, c.1495–1761' (PhD thesis, University of Warwick, 2004).

16 The legislation issued by both the *Protomedico* and the duke of Savoy in medical matters is however available in the collection of laws published by G. B. Borelli and F. A. Duboin.

17 Pomata, *Contracting*, p. 72.

18 *Ibid.*, pp. 62–5. A telling piece of evidence is that sentences were often very mild: *Ibid.*, pp. 81–3.

19 On the singularity of the biographical experience as opposed to its alleged exemplar character, see J. Revel, 'La storia come biografia', in F. Cigni and V. Tomasi (eds), *Tante Storie* (Milan, 2004), pp. 9 and 12.

20 For a classification of approaches to the study of biographies, see Revel, 'La storia',

p. 10; G. Levi, 'Les usages de la biographie', *Annales: Economies, Sociétés, Civilisations*, 44 (1989), pp. 1325–36.

21 'Too often not only the texts of the period (accounts of political struggles, chronicles) but also contemporary histories conclude on the basis of continuity of names that there was a continuity of factions, or conversely on the basis of changes of name that there was a remodeling of factions'. G. Delille, 'Marriage, faction and conflict in sixteenth-century Italy: an example and a few questions', in T. Dean and K. Lowe (eds), *Marriage in Italy 1300–1650* (Cambridge, 1998), pp. 161–3.

22 This analytical strategy has been formalised and hence made more evident in studies of the political use of kinship, see G. Levi, *Inheriting Power: The Story of an Exorcist* (Chicago, 1988); O. Raggio, *Faide e Parentele. Lo Stato Genovese Visto dalla Fontanabuona* (Turin, 1990); A. Torre, *Il Consumo di Devozioni. Religione e Comunità nelle Campagne dell'Antico Regime* (Venice, 1995).

23 It should be borne in mind that even the immediate kinship network of the individual is made up of people with a variety of surnames: all female blood relatives (daughters, sisters, nieces and grand-daughters, aunts), if married, have different surnames, and likewise all relatives acquired through the marriages of male members of the family.

24 D. Cressy, 'Kinship and kin interaction in early modern England', *Past and Present*, 113 (1986); see also chapter five n.5.

25 See for example S. Chojnacki, *Women and Men in Renaissance Venice. Twelve Essays on Patrician Society* (Baltimore, 2000); G. Calvi, *Il Contratto Morale. Madri e Figli nella Toscana Moderna* (Rome, 1994). For a helpful synthesis, see G. Pomata, 'Family and gender', in J. A. Marino (ed.), *Short Oxford History of Italy. Early Modern Italy 1550–1796* (Oxford, 2002).

26 J. S. Grubb, *Provincial Families of the Renaissance. Public and Private Life in the Veneto* (Baltimore, 1996), pp. 26–8.

27 On ego-centred or 'personal community' approaches to the study of social networks, see A. Plakans and C. Wheatherell, 'Household and kinship networks: the costs and benefits of contextualisation', *Continuity and Change*, 18 (2003), pp. 56–7.

1

The view of the body
of an ordinary surgeon

Bernardo Calvo and his writings

The image of the early modern surgeon offered by the professional regulations of the period is that of a medical practitioner who would treat solely those problems arising on the outside of the body, while its internal workings, being subject to the fluctuations of the humours, were the exclusive domain of the physician. This image has remained long unchallenged in accounts of the history of medicine. In the opinion of some authors it was primarily the diversity of therapeutic methods used rather than the disorders treated that distinguished the work of the surgeon from that of the physician;[1] legally, the surgeon could in fact prescribe only external remedies. Others have maintained that doctors and surgeons were treating two different types of disease: rheumatism, asthma, palsies, fevers, gouts and consumption in the former case; tumours, fractures, fistulae and stones in the latter.[2] In recent years this image has been greatly revised. Danielle Jacquart takes the view that the idea of the surgeon limiting himself to the treatment of external maladies, manual procedures and the application of topical remedies took shape only in the late eighteenth century: this reductive image of surgery was constructed through the negative opinion formulated by Quesnay in the *Encyclopédie*, which also doomed the achievements of medieval surgery to lasting oblivion.[3] Numerous studies have in fact shown how the figure of the 'doctor-surgeon', a kind of general practitioner, was relatively common in late medieval society. The learned surgeon who is well versed in Latin and equipped with an academic training, while himself being a prolific author of texts aiming to educate the more ignorant surgeon, is still a feature of the 1500s.[4]

The succeeding period has been given rather less scholarly attention. It is believed, however, that the divisions within the medical profession became polarised in the early modern age around the distinction between manual and intellectual skills. In the process, the figure of the learned surgeon began to disappear.[5] These changes are usually seen as being connected to the formation of professional guilds which became particularly effective in the sixteenth and seventeenth centuries.[6] As a corporate division takes shape between physicians, barber-surgeons and apothecaries we also witness the development of strictures which demarcate (albeit in a contradictory way) the spheres of competence of each group of practitioners, with the inside and the outside of the body taken as an indicator of occupational boundaries.[7] Moreover, this division brings with it a strong hierarchical element, not just at the level of the practice of medicine but of the supervision of such practice. On the one hand, the legislation in medical matters implicitly decrees surgery's subordination to medicine. In Paris for example, in 1505 barber-surgeons signed the first of several agreements with the faculty of medicine whereby they restricted themselves to the manual aspects of treatment, and confined themselves to treating patients only in the presence or on the command of doctors.[8] On the other hand, with the growth of centralised supervision of the exercise of medicine, colleges of physicians and, in Italy, Protophysicians, were assigned the task of inspecting the activities of all other practitioners (apothecaries, barbers, surgeons, empirics, midwives), examining them and granting them licences to practise.

Although in some cases the regulations were very biased, securing for physicians the right to practise every form of medicine,[9] in other situations they were more balanced: in Turin, they seemed more concerned to demarcate the boundaries between the respective domains of action of surgeons, physicians and apothecaries than to endow physicians with supreme power. The order not to 'undertake any function that belongs to the physician' by prescribing oral medication was certainly a persistent one in Savoy's legislation from 1568 onwards (then in 1676 and in 1709 it was also extended to barbers – which seems to suggest that the ban was broken even by those who were licensed as mere barbers).[10] And yet the surgeon's own territory was also protected: the ban on 'practising as a surgeon', which was directed at the apothecary, was repeated in all the medical ordinances from 1618 onwards.[11] Similarly, the surgeon's prerogatives over external remedies were protected, for the pharmacist was forbidden to dispense them without a prescription from the surgeon.[12]

The strengthening of corporate language and the divisions that emerge in the organisation of the medical profession has led commentators to conclude that 'the seventeenth century meant degradation as far as surgery was concerned'.[13] In this chapter I would like to re-examine the inferior status apparently accorded to surgery in the early modern period. The image of the subordination of surgeons to physicians comes to us through the powerful medium of the professional medical bodies which issued the regulations disciplining the practice of medicine and prosecuted those who violated these rules. However, the documentation produced by these professional bodies (colleges of physicians and Proto-medicati) only reflects the voice of the physician and his representation of the medical order. Can we really conclude that this view was dominant and shared by society at large? Can we be sure that ordinary people accepted the superiority of academic culture and did not appreciate the practical skills of the surgeons? Certainly, the superiority of non-manual work was to some extent interiorised even by the craftsman; but then, in all spheres of society, the manual/intellectual dycotomy coexisted and competed with other sets of values. It is therefore worth exploring alternative representations: what, for example, was the view of surgery proposed by the surgeons themselves? This perspective has rarely been taken into account.

I shall address these and other related issues by looking at the published works of one of the surgeons with whom this book is concerned. My analysis is based on two treatises, *De' Tumori* and *Delle Ferite*, published respectively in 1702 and 1711 by Paolo Bernardo Calvo, 'a member of the College of Surgeons in Turin', on two case histories (dated 1709 and 1711) annexed to the latter treatise, and on a third work published separately in the form of a letter in 1714.[14] My interest in Calvo's writings arises from the fact that he was a thoroughly unremarkable surgeon, though firmly rooted in the professional reality of Turin. Treatises on surgery have been attributed to that elite section of the profession which had also been trained in physic – those who have been defined 'learned surgeons' by historians of medicine in order to differentiate them from the majority who would have received a merely practical training.[15] It was therefore a surprise to me when I came across these published works authored by a surgeon who featured in my biographical index cards without anything else about him suggesting that he might have been at all exceptional.

It seems unlikely that Calvo might number among the learned surgeons of whom Vivien Nutton and others speak: the son of a surgeon, he seems to have received an ordinary training in barber surgeons' shops, and to have followed a normal artisanal career path. He was born in 1669 and, following his mother's death, was orphaned at the age of twelve when his father also died. As guardian for him and his sister, both of them minors, the father had chosen another surgeon, their neighbour Enrico Felice Stura, who was the elder brother to surgeon Matteo, with whom Calvo's father worked in partnership.[16] Thus it was in the Stura shop that the young Bernardo learned his trade and it was for his father's former partner, Matteo Stura, that he began working as a *Giovane* (a young surgeon).[17] The first time we come across him in the historical records is when at the age of twenty-five, and married some months since, he was fined for practising unlicensed in the San Gabriele *Cantone* together with another young surgeon, Bellino, for Matteo Stura, who, older and better established, was then municipal Surgeon of the Poor.[18] In mitigation, he says he goes no further than 'letting blood, applying cupping glasses, leeches and vesicatories' and that 'he intends to obtain the licence to practise on his own account the following Michaelmas'. Ten years later we find him with his own shop and residing with his wife, three young children and an apprentice in the same Cantone of San Gabriele were he had begun his career.[19] When another ten years have gone by, he turns out to be living there still and, besides being a surgeon, is a *Cantoniere*, which is to say he has a responsibility for public order on behalf of the municipality in the same Cantone where he lives and works.[20] The office was often associated with surgeons, as we shall see.

His activity therefore has a strongly local character, he practises for all his life in the small area of the city in which he was born.[21] Moreover, he does not seem to be known beyond the boundaries of the city, he has no famous correspondents, and even posthumously no one seems to have taken note of his writings; neither his name nor his works (with the exception of the letter to the more renowned doctor Fantoni) feature in the medical biographies of practitioners active in Piedmont compiled in the nineteenth century.[22] Even locally, he does not appear to stand out professionally: unlike some of the surgeons called upon for an opinion in the more difficult and controversial cases cited in his works, he seems not to have held any posts as a surgeon either in hospitals, at court or in the municipal medical service.[23] He was, admittedly, a member of the College of Surgeons (at least from 1702) but, as we shall observe below (chapter two), in this period the majority of surgeons active in the city seem to have been welcomed into its ranks. Yet the view of surgery emerging from his works is quite at odds with the orthodoxy expressed in the ordinances regulating the practice of medicine in the state. An analysis of his writings leads to a radical revision of the internal-external dichotomy, and of the related splits between intellectual and manual, theoretical and practical that have informed the enduring representation of the respective domains of the physician and the surgeon in the early modern period. What credit must we give to his writings? Do they express a minority view of surgery, and of whom are they representative? What relation do they have to the normal practice of surgery?

Calvo's works supply us with an opportunity to rethink the meaning of surgical tracts in this period. It has been maintained that the surgical literature published in the 1500s and early 1600s expresses a project of education for surgeons, and one aiming to unify surgery and physic, advanced by a handful of enlightened surgeons.[24] It would be hard to extend this interpretation to the works published by Calvo in the early 1700s: he does not write to educate, although, as we shall see, he takes issue with 'ignorant surgeons' who do not apply themselves to the study of the 'theoretical' and 'do not slake their thirst at the sea of anatomy'; but he writes rather to furnish a noble image of surgery, to say nothing of his own personal contribution to it.[25] Calvo's absence of academic background and his unremarkable professional standing testify to this being no purely elitist account. At the same time, the image of surgery presented in his writings, though idealised, is not so abstract and remote from common practice. Studying these kinds of surgical tract in a chapter significantly titled 'Surgery: the hand work of medicine', Andrew Wear has argued that works of this type 'were usually concerned with creating a learned surgery' and would therefore present 'surgery in a distorted light' especially so in their 'tendency to portray the surgeon as someone who theorises about the body, rather than just repairing it'.[26] As we shall see this approach is even more noticeable in the Italian material: here practical information and references to manual dexterity, given considerable weight in the treatises of English surgeons, are secondary to the display of theoretical knowledge about the working of the body and its anatomy; references to physical strength, as a desirable attribute of the surgeon, are all together absent. In what follows I would like to take these representational strategies seriously, as evidence of alternative ways of conceptualising surgical work. As we shall see, the views expressed in writings such as Calvo's make sense in terms of humoural physiology and expose the limitations of the legal representation of medical professional divisions, which appears inconsistent with widely shared theories of the body. Why should the surgeon confine himself to repairing the framework of the body as if its outside had no relation to its inside and what appears on the surface had no internal origin or implications? It is difficult to believe that this was the case if one considers that the separation between the outside and the inside of the body is alien to the theory of humours which, as many have suggested, was universally employed to describe the functioning of the body, by patients and practitioners alike.[27]

Moreover, a number of elements provide confirmation of the authenticity of the episodes reported by Calvo: his treatises are inhabited by flesh and blood human beings. The numerous case histories discussed refer to patients made recognisable, in a relatively small city, by the fact of being almost invariably quoted with names given in full and occupations mentioned. In one particular case, that relating to the 'extracting of a dead foetus through the navel', I have been able to verify the existence at that time of the patient being described and of her husband, the surgeon Alessandro Moran.[28] Likewise, the surgeons named obsequiously by Calvo, or else involved in one way or another in the cases he relates, are equally recognisable. They too do not figure among the practitioners celebrated in dictionaries of medical biography. However, these are very well known characters in the Turin context, and they emerge repeatedly in my biographical reconstruction. Some of them are endowed with a prestigious local reputation (Sebastiano Fassina, Alberto Verna, Domenico Deroy), which derives primarily from the surgical posts they occupy in the city; others are minor characters (Alessandro Moran, Giovanni Francesco Bellino, Giuseppe Deroy).[29] To some degree these figures are indeed an elite, but it is a professional elite, rather than the intellectual elite which is usually associated with the authorship of surgical tracts.

Although the question of the audience for these surgical treatises is a matter still to be addressed, it seems logical to see it as including the professional community to which the author belonged – those same surgeons and physicians cited time and again in his pages. Moreover, the strongly local aspect of Calvo's works in itself suggests that the representation of the surgeon emerging from them is consistent with the way in which many other Turin surgeons saw themselves and perceived their profession. Let us take a look at the contents of these writings.

The permeability of the body: external ailments, internal causes

Recent work has already partly modified the traditional view of surgery, which was strongly influenced by the institutional ordering of the medical professions; this has shown, at least with regard to seventeenth-century England, that surgery was not so crucially separated from medicine in epistemological terms. In her study of the English surgeon Binns, Lucinda Beier has argued that he violated the legal distinction between surgery and medicine on a daily basis; he prescribed internal medicines, because he shared the theoretical assumptions of the physician that any disorder could be corrected by re-establishing the balance of the humours. This is why Binns frequently employed purgatives and emetics, observeds the patients' bowel movements, treated the system as a whole rather than just the part, and was reluctant to use the knife, preferring gentler procedures.[30] Calvo's published works confirm these observations and, more generally, Andrew Wear's argument that surgeons 'viewed the body and its parts in much the same way as did physicians'.[31] However, the reassessment of what surgery was in this period can go even further, and include also a reconsideration of how it was understood: it was not just a matter of using internal therapies akin to those prescribed by the physician and of endorsing the theory of the body's humours. In the early 1700s Calvo actually gives an internal explanation for the ailments that appear on the body's surface, thereby ultimately invalidating the very notion of internal and external diseases. Tumours for example, regarded as a classic area for surgical intervention because they exhibit themselves on the surface, challenge this division: the tumour is described as an external manifestation of an internal disorder, at times provoked by 'wounds, dislocations, fractures and contusions', but nonetheless always having its immediate or initial cause in relation to the humours.[32] This means, Calvo explains, that every type of tumour takes its name from the dominant humour: 'erysipelatic phlegmon if the bile surpasses the blood, erysipelatoid oedema if the blood predominates', and so on, and can be traced to a different internal pathology. For example:

> in the view of Galen, Avicenna and others, the cause of the phlegmon is nothing but blood … the external causes are injuries and contusions. In the words of a modern observer, the phlegmon's accidental cause is to be identified in a more rapid flow of fluids: heated by a violent movement or exertion, the mass of blood … flows freely into even the smallest vessels, but when the movement ceases the blood cools down and the dense, viscous particles, being no longer able to flow on, cause obstruction and likewise expand outside the vessels.[33]

The correct diagnosis of tumours therefore requires the surgeon to have a knowledge of the internal workings of the body, something which Calvo makes a great show of possessing.

It would seem moreover that a great many internal 'disturbances' sooner or later are exhibited pathologically on the outside of the body: in his dedication to the reader Calvo maintains that there are at least 200 types of tumours (as has been noted, surgeons referred to every kind of swelling as a tumour).[34] Clearly, this inordinately increases the scope for surgical intervention.

The approach adopted nine years later in the treatise *Delle Ferite* seems no different. This is extensively concerned with 'compound injuries', which is to say those which have given rise to complications and whose treatment requires an understanding of the internal movement of humours which has caused the degeneration. For example:

The inflammation is produced by a building up of fluids on the affected part; when these find their customary pathway obstructed they cease to flow and they stagnate. Pain arises from the irregular movement of the spirits in the flow to the part and their flowing back towards the brain. The convulsion or spasm occurs either because of the copious and irregular building up of the fluids and the spirits in the motor fibres or else their great effusion. Gangrene stems from the dissipation or concentration of the particles which feed the blood and which are its life spirit, as well as from an obstruction or laceration of the nerves or from a coagulation and interruption of the blood's circulation.[35]

From the crucial role attributed to the alteration of the humours in causing external pathologies there also derives the need for the surgeon to be aware of the impact 'of the non-natural things' on the health of the patient.

It is the opinion of modern observers that there is a great abundance of different particles to be found in the fluids … the greater or lesser abundance of these same particles is due to the non-naturals, in particular to the quality of the air and of foods.[36]

For example, in the case of cancer:

The original causes are all those things which generate blood which is dry and melancholic, such as smoked meats, garlic, onions, pulses and late nights; the internal causes being the hot disturbance of the liver and the weakness of the spleen, the suppression of haemorrhoids and menses.[37]

Since it must act upon both the internal causes and the non-naturals, the treatment proposed by the surgeon will be wide-ranging and will therefore include prescriptions relating to the diet and the lifestyle the patient must adopt in order to promote a re-establishing of the balance of humours, the issue of blood and the purgatives which eliminate the harmful substances, and the various kinds of local and internal medicaments which will assist healing. The knife is only one component, not always a necessary one, and often the last line of treatment. In the case of the phlegmon, for example:

The suggested treatment is to prevent the humour from flowing in copious quantities to the part, evacuating the humour and correcting accidents. With a moderate diet and emissions of blood, through drainage or decongestants, unless there is any counter indication, forbidding it, and with internal laxatives, the first of these [objectives] will be achieved; attempts should be made to dissolve the tumour with local coolants and repellents, but not when it is at the critical stage, and when there is any sign of suppuration this must be encouraged with suppurants, then when the tumour is pierced the matter contained in it is drained, easing the pain with anodynes and coolants.[38]

It is clear that the surgeon employs the physician's entire therapeutic range besides his own. He is required in the first place to be able to intervene on the non-naturals: 'The happy outcome of any treatable injury depends not only on the skill of the man who operates but equally on the good use of the six non-natural things.'[39] Chapter three of the treatise *Delle Ferite*, for example, which extensively covers the non-naturals, suggests how the noxious effects of the air are particularly to be feared, and sometimes 'are the cause of alterations in the wound which are erroneously attributed to venereal disease, plethora, cacochimy … when instead it is merely a matter of having left the wound exposed'.

Diet in particular has a prominent place in the surgeon's concerns: it 'must be moderate … and yet it must be adequate to the person and their habits and here it is appropriate that the surgical rule (*economica chirurgica*) be very shrewd'.[40] It is striking in this passage that surgery is presented as the discipline that can master the logic of diet. The author then expounds upon the most suitable amount of rest and on the need to preserve the wounded patient from intense emotions – 'anger, melancholy and every other passion should be banished'.[41] The explanation for the danger represented by the passions relates of course to the humours and refers to the mind's capacity to influence corporeal processes, as occurs for example in the case of gangrene:

Gangrene also has its source in the passions of the mind, since it is from anger, melancholy and likewise from the love of Venus that irregular fermentations derive, whereby the salts change their nature and swell through the unaccustomed and violent correspondences that dispose them to become acid, acrid and corrosive.[42]

The use of pharmacological remedies is moreover quite legitimately a part of the surgeon's trade, and does not seem to be restricted to the physician. For example, certain ('vulnerary') potions, 'composed of: betony, or the roots of formentilla, fraxinella, angelica, lady's mantle, birthwort or other similar herbs which contain a great abundance of oil and salt particles', are recommended to be drunk for a wound.[43] And in the 'general treatment of tumours … the disease which is the related cause' is eliminated with the use of internal remedies to be employed, yet again, 'according to *the economy of surgery*' (my emphasis).[44] Calvo's treatises are crammed with pharmacological advice. He never puts forward his own medicines but displays his knowledge of both the qualities of the simples, classified according to the categories of the official pharmacopoeia, and the recipes for the compounds. The latter are usually drawn from the medical literature – 'the celebrated Muys says that the patient must take sixteen drops of this liquid three times a day in a decoction made with fir needles or spruce' – but sometimes there are also quack recipes recorded, like the 'elixir for constipation sold for a great price by a Frenchman to the King of Denmark'.[45]

As we have already seen, Calvo does not confine himself to prescribing local and external remedies as provided for by the regulations on the surgeon's duties, but he indicates medicaments to be administered in every possible variant: in the form of 'rubs and ointments', of oral remedies, of ablutions, drinks and enemas. Depending on the case in question, these various types of remedy are prescribed simultaneously or at different phases of the treatment.

We can see therefore how the distinction between internal and external not only fails to be applied to the maladies, but even to the remedies. Indeed, in the terms used by Calvo this distinction doesn't feature at all but is replaced by another one: therapies are classified according to the 'universal-local' dyad. Within this paradigm, interventions designed to modify the overall balance of the fluids are contrasted with those, implicitly of lesser value, which aim to heal a part of it: 'the progression of symptoms in serious injuries [is hindered] by diet, the letting of blood, purgatives and other *universals* in conjunction also with *locals* which by themselves alone would be nothing short of useless' (my italics).[46] It is clear that a classification which brings diet and oral remedies, theoretically the physician's prerogative, with blood-letting, a procedure exclusive to the surgeon, under the same category – 'universals' – would upset the allocation of therapies and areas of the body to different groups of practitioners.

The use of medications is constant and regularly goes hand-in-hand with surgical functions. For example, in removing foreign bodies, a specifically surgical task, the surgeon must whenever possible use poultices (supplying the recipes himself) in order to draw them out. Here, surgical and pharmacological techniques complement one another rather than being mutually exclusive. We learn for example that there are three types of suture ('flesh, with distinct and separate stitches; constrictive, with continuous stitches; attached, with distinct but discontinuous stitches') to be used on different wounds, but they are to be employed always in conjunction with pharmacological remedies which are 'tightening and glutinous'.[47] In many cases it is also possible to use alternative remedies to surgery in order to close the wound – what is called 'dry suture'; the recipe includes dragon's blood, gum, chalk, flour and the ubiquitous egg-white.

Calvo of course also discusses what we are used to regarding as surgical remedies in the true sense: he talks about types of dressing, cauterisation and ligature, and when these should be used;[48] he talks about amputation, terming it a 'ghastly operation' and about artificial limbs (the correct procedure for fitting them, what they should be like).[49] He talks about trepanning of the cranium in the case of internal injuries and specifies the kind of incision to be made in accordance with the size of the tumour.[50] But his disquisitions on the causes of various maladies and the medications best suited to treating them take up much more room than the space given over to the practical aspects of surgery. For example, there is no particular emphasis on the surgeon's dexterity, which is allegedly one of the cardinal attributes of the profession. Calvo actually asserts that 'hands without the aid of instruments and medicaments would be nothing short of useless'.[51] Moreover, in contrast with what this affirmation might suggest, the space dedicated to the surgeon's tools is also limited. Calvo defends the virtues of some surgical instruments (for example the superiority of some drills and scalpels in cranial trepanning, or of the curved needle in closure of the arteries) but often the instruments appear unworthy of any special mention. It is the talent of the surgeon that is highlighted rather than the quality of the surgeon's technology.

In Calvo's paradigm, therefore, the boundaries between medical and surgical practice fluctuate a good deal. The surgeon for example shares the physician's diagnostic expertise, and indeed he has an even greater range of means for assessing the ailment. The capacity for observation, usually associated with the practice of the physician, turns out to be an essential virtue of the surgeon, who must identify the type of tumour or internal injury out of an extremely broad spectrum. Calvo notably insists on the subtlety of this task: different types of tumour (or injury) have different causes and call for different treatments, so it is crucial to be able to distinguish them. To this end, visual observation is essential, but touch (which is not used by the physician), along with hearing and smell is a precious diagnostic tool for the surgeon. For example:

> the indications of erysipelas are a slight elevation and tension which on *touch* easily gives way to a great heat, extreme pain and a *colour* between redness and pallor, which immediately disappears and soon returns if constricted; the indications of the oedema are whiteness, indolence and a softness which easily gives way on touch and slowly becomes raised (my emphasis).[52]

> One can tell whether the injury is simple or compound from indications such as the *noise* made by the air coming out of the wound, from

the presence of haemorrhaging, and from symptoms such as the sensation of weight, difficulties in breathing, pain, tremors, syncope, cold sweats, and the quality of the blood coming out of the wound (my emphasis).[53]

The examination of injuries also serves to judge whether the blow has incurred any damage to the internal organs: therefore the surgeon must take stock of what is not visible, which is theoretically another prerogative of the physician. This is done partly through local observation accompanied by 'anatomical examination', which is to say investigation of the wound with 'a probe' [the stylet]; and partly by reconstructing the circumstances of the accident: 'the expert surgeon must ascertain the causes of the blow, whether it be with a sharp weapon, piercing or blunt, the force with which the blow was struck, or the height of the fall'. Questioning of the patient is therefore as crucial for the surgeon as it is for the physician. Likewise, for the surgeon, taking the pulse is also a valuable indicator of the patient's condition: 'it is a sign that death is not far away when blood pours out copiously along with a trembling of the whole body and when a drastic lowering of the pulse can be observed'.[54]

Quoting Hippocrates, Calvo argues that the basis of the 'noble art of Surgery' lies in 'preserving the health of man, safeguarding him from future illnesses, treating and healing those present ones'.[55] This is an extremely broad definition which goes well beyond the one supplied by the English surgeon James Cooke a decade or so earlier.[56] In Calvo's treatises the image of the surgeon is that of someone expert in every aspect of medicine: physiology and the pathology of the humours, the individual's constitution, diet and the non-naturals, and pharmacology. Equally important is 'theory', a term which designates the medical literature.

Theoretical versus practical medicine?

We have already seen how, in the discussion of the properties of medicaments, the importance of theoretical knowledge is continually reiterated. Calvo launches repeated salvoes against 'those who use them [medicines] because others are accustomed to... and follow like a blind man led by another who is blind, without studying the qualities, quantities and virtues of those same medicines'.[57] Implicit in these accusations is the superiority attributed to an approach supplying rational explanations of the therapies adopted, compared with a purely empirical approach. In other passages Calvo explicitly advocates the need for the surgeon to be educated in the texts of the medical tradition, and criticises those colleagues 'fond of idleness' who do not read but who confine themselves to practising and do not encourage their pupils to study. For example, speaking of trepanning of the cranium:

> Those who operate must avoid the dangers which are not infrequently encountered by those who have no theory to guide them but only the constant paltriness, indeed the blindness that is practice alone, carrying out such an important operation without the due reflections upon the necessity, manner and time for its performance.[58]

In fact, Calvo continually displays his own knowledge of the medical literature, at every turn quoting the opinions of the ancients (Galen, Hippocrates, Paulus Aegineta, Celsus) as well as the views of those he regards as 'the moderns'. These include names well known to us (such as Fallopius, Duverney, Paré, Chirac, Fabricius, Le Clerc) and also minor figures. These authors, whether well known or less known, classical and recent, seem all to be on the same level and are used indiscriminately as sources. In particular it does not appear that the ancients merit any special debt or greater trust. Only on one point are 'the moderns' repeatedly attacked: on the scepticism they display towards the use of purgatives and phlebotomy, which, they maintain, debilitate the injured person.[59] At first sight, this might seem a traditionalist retrogression in a work which presents the surgeon as dominating all the instruments of medicine. Yet it should not be forgotten that, as we have already observed, in Calvo's eyes bloodletting enjoys a status of thoroughgoing respect, possessing the dignity of a 'universal' therapy since it acts upon the movement of the fluids rather than just healing the locally diseased part.

In Calvo's treatises the emphasis is upon the necessity to determine the nature of the illness with certainty; only this kind of understanding can suggest the most suitable treatment. A great many pages are therefore devoted to disquisitions upon correct diagnosis, while the treatment is dealt with in somewhat general terms, and even when its practical aspects are dwelt upon it is not so much the dexterity of the hand which is praised as the capacity to decide whether it is necessary to have recourse to these means or not. This capacity is achieved through both theoretical study and the knowledge of anatomy gained in the practice of dissecting cadavers. Calvo acknowledges anatomy as having a crucial role, but more as an accessory which assists the surgeon's thinking about the body of the patient than as a source of manual expertise: 'it is what opens up the surgeon's way to diagnostic and prognostic indications, not merely for understanding the cause from the effect but in order, with anatomical knowledge, to anticipate the symptoms and predict their effects'.[60] Practical experience has a limited role by comparison with the theoretical.

We are a long way from that exaltation of the practical side of surgery and of manual skills which Wear encountered in the writings of seventeenth-century English surgeons.[61] Things have clearly changed. Calvo brings in numerous episodes drawn from his own surgical practice or that of his colleagues, but always when he is discussing an interpretation which is controversial in the literature. The description of a case allows him to take up a stance in a dispute in favour of one or another theory. For example, Calvo argues for the capacity of certain wounds to heal themselves, despite the contrary view of Hippocrates, Celsus and Avicenna, who see them as being fatal, and to this end he cites the case he had observed of a woman treated by his colleague Alberto Verna.[62] Calvo's opinion is not however presented as an original one; he restricts himself to corroborating an argument already upheld by an author. He is somewhat cautious and, since he makes no claims for miraculous methods and remedies that would liken him to some charlatan, he boasts no new discoveries or interpretations, instead remaining content with his ability to participate in the discussion between experts.

It is on the question of whether it is necessary to proceed to the trepanning of the cranium in order to extract 'intrusive blood' (cerebral haemorrhage) that Calvo brings in the greatest number of examples taken from his surgical practice. This technique, probably not very widely performed, is presented as if it were Calvo's speciality (he carried it out successfully even on an eight-year-old boy). In this case too the focus of the discussion turns on ascertaining whether it is necessary to proceed to trepanning, rather than on the procedure's technical aspects. The various cases are in fact all cited in support of the argument that 'indications can be misleading: there are fractures without symptoms and then there are fractures with cerebral lesions that heal without trepanation'.[63] It is therefore the surgeon's diagnostic qualities which are being celebrated rather than his practical skills:

> some days after the memorable liberation from siege of the royal city of Turin I had occasion to undertake numerous operations of trepanning, six of these being performed in one single day, and in different subjects with fractures I observed no variation in symptoms. These were treated by others as simple injuries but after having carried out a diligent examination of the damage I found intrusive blood in all of them.[64]

Calvo cites for example the case of Domenico Picco, who was fleeing pursuit at night when he fell and injured his face. The first surgeon to examine the patient initially deemed the accident a minor one, then, after Picco experienced fever, haemorrhaging and delirium, suggested that 'another surgeon' be called, namely Calvo, who overturned the diagnosis and launched 'a crusade' to persuade patient and family of the necessity to undertake trepanation.[65] What is clear in his account of this case is the wish to display that other virtue required of the good surgeon, over and above knowledge of anatomy and medical texts: decisiveness – the decisiveness to proceed undaunted to an unpopular operation when this proved necessary, challenging both the views of over-cautious or ignorant practitioners and the anxieties of patients and their families.

The multiple meanings of surgical tracts

The instance of trepanation also allows Calvo to illustrate the character traits as well as the intellectual gifts which are indispensable for the good surgeon: well-balanced resolve in decision-making, timeliness in taking action. These are traits which also have a bearing upon the construction of masculinity explored later in this book. It is impossible to avoid seeing in these and other passages the rhetoric of the surgeon as a brave and solitary warrior in his far-sightedness, vanquishing evil and willing to be associated, to this end, with techniques and instruments the mention and sight of which produce terror. As he says of amputation: 'Surgery is at its most compassionate when it shows itself to be cruel'.[66]

And yet, alongside this proposed image of heroism, the narrative also leaves room for the strategies of consensus enacted by surgeons when it came to the use of unusual and hazardous therapies. The principal instrument of this was consultation with other practitioners, which was used undoubtedly to win the patient's authorisation, but also, it can be argued, with an eye on safeguarding the surgeon's own professional integrity. Let us see how the case of Domenico Picco develops as Calvo sets out to perform a trepanation:

> to overcome the repugnance induced by the persuasions of the afore-mentioned surgeon, who because of being French had an opinion of his own, I took counsel more than once on the case, firstly with my colleague Giovanni Bellino … but some doubt remained about the necessity for the operation … [but since the symptoms persisted] I renewed my consultations, for had death occurred it would have been an unceasing reproach to me and then I myself well know that *had I not, I should have been accused with criticisms of carelessness for not using my skill to prevent it.* To this end I took counsel twice again with another expert called by the injured man's relatives, Carlo Giuseppe Deroy, who was of my opinion and the operation took place in his presence alone (my emphasis).[67]

In this passage the utter vulnerability of the surgeon's reputation stands out, this being subject to continuous scrutiny and exposed to manipulations.[68] The consultations serve to give public legitimacy to the surgeon's decisions and to protect him from possible future attacks by his clients and by the local medical community if things were to go wrong.[69]

It would seem that the publication of writings such as those we are examining fulfilled an analogous function. The account given of cases which refer to flesh and blood patients and practitioners, well known to the community in which these writings probably had the widest circulation, show us how much printed works aimed to protect the good name of the surgeon, discrediting negative rumours about the unconsidered nature of some of his decisions and resolving professional disputes. Indeed, Calvo's works are full of obscure (to us) references to conflicts, disagreements and enmities which must however have been grasped by local readers.[70] The remarks that have been made about another early modern literary genre, the artisan's autobiography, can well be applied to these writings: 'autobiographical writing served to settle accounts, file complaints, avenge insults (real or imagined), and generally to right wrongs – all not far from what Freud calls "motives of unpleasure".'[71]

So if we ask ourselves for what reason a surgeon, who by conventional parameters is relatively obscure, should take up the pen in the early 1700s and write a series of treatises and letters regarding the cases he has treated, there seem to be multiple answers. On the one hand these works must be read not as being aimed at a remote and impersonal medical readership but as engaging in dialogue with a well-known professional community and a local lay audience. They probably had an important promotional and protective role to play within the small world of their author. It is hard not to think for example that the printed letter addressed by Calvo to the physician Fantoni, about the 'extraction of a dead foetus through the navel' would have been intended to dispel the doubt that a fatal diagnostic and surgical error might have been committed upon the body of a woman who took some days to die in the wake of a bloody operation and who, incidentally, was herself the wife of a surgeon. The letter comes furnished with a reassuring reply from Fantoni and with another intervention also supporting Calvo from a physician in a nearby town, Paulo Agostino Luppi. Although these are presented in the terms of learned debates on the accuracy of the diagnosis, it seems clear that the publication of the case and of these professional opinions is aiming to give Calvo public absolution from implicit accusations of malpractice.[72]

On the other hand these works offer us an insight into how an ordinary practitioner like Calvo wished to represent his own profession at the start of the 1700s, and into the values which shaped the surgeon's professional identity in this period. Of course the writings in question should also be examined as part of a tradition of works on surgery from which they inherit thematic and narrative models. But the decision to emphasise certain aspects at the expense of others becomes quite clear if one goes on to consider the text in detail. Calvo's works do not share that aim of circulating knowledge and techniques identified by Nutton in the writings of the learned surgeons of the sixteenth century, nor the pride in manual skills highlighted by Wear in the works of the English surgeons of the following century. Stress is laid systematically on the superiority of theory over practice and on the reasoning powers required of the surgeon. We have observed the strength of Calvo's will to demonstrate the scope of the surgeon's knowledge, to prove that he knows the medical literature down to his fingertips and can expound with refinement on the distinctions between health disorders of similar appearance, that he knows the properties of medicines and how to administer them and is an expert in every domain of the physician's traditional competence. In his epistemology we have perceived that he overrides the very distinctions between internal and external diseases and therapies. I have suggested that these views are indicative of a lack of consensus about the principles underlying the legal/corporative demarcations which structure the medical profession; they highlight a tension between the voice of the physician and that of the surgeon which deserves further attention.

At the same time, these characteristics cannot but be a reflection of the esteem in which surgery is held at the start of the 1700s. In the quarter of a century since surgeons had taken charge of medical treatment in the army and navy, as well as provision for the very poor in the hospitals and, through the municipal medical service, in their homes, the dignity of the occupation had grown enormously. The surgeon increasingly fashions himself as a kind of general practitioner and the distinction between learned and unlearned surgeons is no longer so significant in this period; the former group was not any more an exclusive minority despite the fact that surgical education was still widely taking place outside the university. Calvo's treatises suggest that the idea and practice of surgery were being altered 'from below', well before the advent of the reforms of the 1720s and 1730s which have been credited for enhancing the status of the surgeon given that, on paper at least, they moved his education to the yniversity.[73] Although the information concerning a surgeon's education prior to the reform of the university of 1729 is extremely scant, it would seem that, already in the second half of the seventeenth century, his training was not strictly manual but had the advantage of theoretical components, a certain familiarity with medical texts and the opportunity to develop an increasingly intellectual approach to the occupation. The custom of attending university courses, especially the one in surgery, which, unlike the others, was held in the vernacular, had become relatively common. The fact that the obligation for surgeon's apprentices to attend 'the lecture in surgery ... at the university or the house of the reader', decreed in 1634 and confirmed in 1657, was not repeated in the successive medical ordinances suggests that this became standard practice in the following decades. In 1634, an attestation from the reader that the young man had attended the course and studied the subjects taught had already become a requirement for securing a licence to practise from the *Protomedico* (Protophysician).[74] Nor can it be ruled out that the private teaching of surgery, given on a fee-paying basis by the more eminent surgeons in their homes to small groups of students, might have become widespread in the early decades of the eighteenth century in Turin, just as it had in nearby France.[75] The complaint by the professor of surgery responsible for reforming the university that 'the surgeons of Turin hold schools in their shops and dissuade young men from going to the university' suggests this was so.[76] Too little is known at present of these independent forms of education, it is clear however that our understanding of the medical world and divisions within it has placed too much emphasis on universities as the only seats where an academic surgical education could be acquired. It is possible that this more composite training, which included attendance at the shop, at the university, at private lessons in the home of private tutors and, for many, hospital practice, explains a figure like Calvo and ways of exercising surgery in which theory and practice, manual operations and intellectual reflections do not appear as incompatible as it has often been assumed.

Finally there remains the author's subjectivity. I have found nothing in Calvo's life which might explain his prolific output as an author, a feature which seems at odds with the absence of any posts in the hospitals or at court. Numerous conjectures can be made: for example that the very lack of greater professional recognition impelled him to cultivate study and writing – the resentful and even violent tone to be found in his works whenever he refers to unnamed colleagues who are backward and ignorant, can lead one to think so. Certainly, his writings are an opportunity to exalt the superiority of his own diagnostic and prognostic talent by comparison with other practitioners. And yet his is not a protest against the medical community as a whole; many colleagues are praised and admired. Calvo does not therefore strike us as a marginal figure; he can of course be an unusually learned (and resentful) representative of the professional establishment, but he is a member of it to all intents and purposes; he seems to have good relations with many notable colleagues; and he seems also to be socially integrated into the Turin professional scene, for instance forging relationships with eminent practitioners in the city through godparenthood. However much the image of surgery offered by Calvo may be idealised, it cannot be a daydream entirely disconnected from the practice and perception of those like himself.

Notes

1 See for example Beier, 'Seventeenth-century English surgery', p. 54: 'Legally surgery was defined less by the disorders it treated than by its therapeutic methods'.

2 P. K. Wilson, *Surgery, Skin and Syphilis. Daniel Turner's London (1667–1741)* (Amsterdam, 1999), p. 59.

3 D. Jacquart, *La Médecine Médiévale dans le Cadre Parisien XIVe-XVe Siècle* (Paris, 1998), pp. 16–47; C. Rabier, 'Chirurgie', in D. Lecourt (ed.), *Dictionnaire de la Pensée Médicale* (Paris, 2004), pp. 231–7.

4 See the examples gathered for Venice and Feltre by Richard Palmer in 'Physicians and surgeons in sixteenth-century Venice', *Medical History*, 23 (1979); V. Nutton, 'Humanist surgery', in A. Wear, R. K. French and I. M. Lonie, *The Medical Renaissance of the Sixteenth Century* (Cambridge, 1985).

5 Pomata, *Contracting*, pp. 61–2; Wear, *Knowledge*, pp. 217–18. It seems significant for example that the academic surgeons of the Company of Saint Côme united with that of the ordinary barber-surgeons' company in 1655: Gelfand, *Professionalizing*, p. 24.

6 For France see the detailed reconstruction of this process of incorporation in Brockliss and Jones, *The Medical World*, chapter 3. For Italy, see the Bolognese case studied by Pomata, *Contracting*, especially pp. 69–72.

7 *Ibid.*, pp. 133–4.

8 Gelfand, *Professionalizing*, p. 22.

9 This is the case for Bologna and London: see Pomata, *Contracting*, p. 63; Wear, *Knowledge*, p. 217 and n. 20.

10 The ordinances 20 October 1568, 1 April 1618, 10 August 1657, 10 February 1660 are published in Borelli, pp. 966–97, and those of 3 March 1676 and 22 February 1709 in Duboin, vol. 10, pp. 85–7, 100.

11 'It will be prohibited to any apothecary to order or apply cupping glasses, or to carry out the surgeon's work, under penalty'. Borelli, p. 974, 1 April 1618.

12 The pharmacist was then for his part protected from the physician, who was repeatedly enjoined not to make medicines. See in particular the ordinances of 1676 and 1709 cited in n. 10.

13 Cited in Gelfand, *Professionalizing*, p. 22.

14 *De' Tumori; Delle Ferite; Lettera Istorica di Paolo Bernardo Calvo Chirurgo Colleggiato in Torino* (Turin, 1714).

15 Nutton, 'Humanist surgery'; Wear, *Knowledge*, pp. 212, 222; J. L. Fresquet Febrer, 'La práctica medica en los textos quirúrgicos espanoles en el siglo XVI', *Dynamis*, 22 (2002).

16 These biographical details are drawn from the notarial documents relating to Paolo Bernardo, to his father, and the Stura brothers: Ins. 1679, l. 3, c. 625; 1681, l. 4, c. 835; 1681, l. 7, c. 397; 1690, l. 4, vol. I, c. 45; 1694, l. 3, vol. II, c. 831.

17 Literally, 'youth'. The term describes a surgeon's assistant or journeyman. See chapter 6.

18 'Registro delli chirurghi ... di Torino', statement of Paolo Bernardo Calvo. A *Cantone* or *isola* was a group of adjacent houses marked out by three or four streets. The number of residents in each Cantone ranged from 100 to 300. In the last quarter of the seventeeenth century the city appeared divided into more than 120 Cantoni: F. Rondolino, *Vita Torinese durante l'Assedio (1703-1707)*, vo. 7 of Regia Deputazione di Storia Patria, *Le Campagne di Guerra in Piemonte (1703-8) e l'Assedio di Torino (1706)* (Turin, 1909), p. v.

19 Art. 530.

20 AST, s. I, *Provincia di Torino*, m.1, 'Cantonieri'. The duties of the *Cantoniere* will be discussed at length in chapter ten.

21 Even though he casually introduces a reference 'to the numerous observations I was able to garner in the course of my great travels even as far as the kingdoms ruled by the Turk'. *Delle Ferite*, p. 481. Here Calvo seems to be turning to a standard theme, the experience accumulated on exotic travels, which is characteristic of the way in which the authors of the books of secrets presented themselves in the sixteenth and early seventeenth centuries. William Eamon gives numerous examples of this in his *Science and the Secrets of Nature. Books of Secrets in Medieval and Early Modern Culture* (Princeton, 1994), particularly in chapter 4.

22 This is the *Lettera Istorica* 'in which he describes the extracting of a human foetus through the navel', mentioned in B. Trompeo, *Dei Medici e degli Archiatri dei Principi della Real Casa di Savoia* (Turin, 1857-58), p. 59.

23 Biographical research has brought no appointments to light. Moreover, it is unlikely that, if he had held any of these positions, these would not be mentioned in the presentation of the author in his printed works and in the notarial documents where he appears.

24 Nutton, 'Humanist surgery'; Wear, *Knowledge*, p. 211.

25 My approach in the reading of these works is similar to that adopted by Lianne McTavish in her analysis of early modern French obstetrical treatises. These, in her view, 'did far more than transmitting medical information': they outlined the characteristics of the 'admirable' midwife and man-midwife (L. McTavish, *Childbirth and the Display of Authority in Early Modern France* (Aldershot, 2005), pp. 14–15).

26 Wear, *Knowledge*, p. 211–12.

27 B. Duden, *The Woman Beneath the Skin* (Cambridge Massachusetts, 1991); Pomata, *Contracting*, pp. 129–39; Wear, *Knowledge*, especially chapter 3.

28 *Lettera Istorica*. On the frequent presence, in surgeons' books, of episodes from their own professional experience: see N. G. Siraisi, *Medieval and Early Renaissance Medicine. An Introduction to Knowledge and Practice* (Chicago, 1990), pp. 170–1.

29 Their names and their activities will crop up repeatedly in the course of this book. During his career Sebastiano Fassina held the posts of Surgeon to the Poor, Anatomist at the University, Surgeon to the Duke, His Majesty's Aide de Chambre, Surgeon General to the Army; Domenico Deroy was chief surgeon at the hospitals of San Giovanni, the Carità, and Santi Maurizio e Lazzaro, anatomical dissector at the University, and

army surgeon; Alberto Verna was chief surgeon at the hospital of San Giovanni and the Carità, anatomist at the University, Surgeon to the Princesses; Giovanni Francesco Bellino was Surgeon to the Poor and Surgeon to the Household of Madama Reale; Giuseppe Deroy was chief surgeon at the hospital of Santi Maurizio e Lazzaro; no posts emerge in the case of Alessandro Moran.

30 Beier, 'Seventeenth-century English surgery', pp. 54–5, 72–3.

31 Wear, *Knowledge*, p. 212.

32 *De' Tumori*, p. 2.

33 *Ibid.*, p. 9.

34 Beier, 'Seventeenth-century English surgery', p. 68.

35 *Delle Ferite*, p. 42.

36 *De' Tumori*, p. 9.

37 *Ibid.*, p. 41.

38 *Ibid.*, p. 9.

39 *Ibid.*, p. 21.

40 The term 'economica' is associated in this period with the rule of government, in particular with prudence, and is often used in relation to the careful administration of the household: see D. Frigo, *Il Padre di Famiglia* (Rome, 1985), pp. 65–7.

41 *Delle Ferite*, p. 23.

42 *Ibid.*, p. 63.

43 *Ibid.*, p. 22.

44 *De' Tumori*, cap. VII.

45 *Delle Ferite*, p. 89. Compound remedies are made up of vegetable, animal and mineral elements: cuttlefish bone, hare bristles, chimney soot, ashes of crayfish and squill, pulverised coral, hematite stone, aloe, vitriol, cobwebs, red sandalwood, incense, pomegranate rind, dragon's blood, bole armeniac. Many of these ingredients are much more banal than their names suggest: dragon's blood signifies common-or-garden tarragon and bole armeniac is a kind of clayey earth.

46 *Ibid.*, p. 36.

47 *Ibid.*, p. 33.

48 *Ibid.*, pp. 55, 70–1, 96–7.

49 *Ibid.*, pp. 91, 111–12.

50 *Ibid.*, p. 127.

51 *Ibid.*, p. 30.

52 *De' Tumori*, p. 16.

53 *Delle Ferite*, p. 15.

54 *Ibid.*, p. 15.

55 *De' Tumori*, p. 1.

56 Wear, *Knowledge*, p. 213.

57 *Delle Ferite*, p. 30.

58 *Ibid.*, p. 160.

59 *Ibid.*, pp. 72, 42–4.

60 *Ibid.*, p. 14. Anatomical knowledge is also essential to surgical techniques in order to avoid damaging the adjacent parts of the body.

61 Wear, *Knowledge*, pp. 212, 233.

62 *Delle Ferite*, p. 16.

63 *Ibid.*, p. 141.

64 *Ibid.*, p. 146.
65 *Ibid.*, p. 150.
66 *Ibid.*, p. 91.
67 *Ibid.*, pp. 148–50.
68 The public scrutiny to which practitioners were subjected and the role of tracts in providing a reassuring image of themselves is also a central theme in McTavish, *Childbirth*.
69 Wilson, *Surgery*, p. 47; Beier, 'Seventeenth-century English surgery', pp. 50–1.
70 On medical tracts as vehicles for the expression of professional rivalries: see McTavish, *Childbirth*, chapter five.
71 J. S. Amelang, *The Flight of Icarus. Artisan Autobiography in Early Modern Europe* (Stanford, 1998), p. 194.
72 *Lettera Istorica*, especially p. 15.
73 For example, D. Carpanetto, 'Gli studenti di chirurgia', in D. Balani, D. Carpanetto and F. Turletti, *La Popolazione dell'Università di Torino*, BSBS, 76 (1978). The university course in surgery was three years long and, from 1729, it became one of the requirements for securing authorisation to exercise the profession in the cities of the state 'on this side of the Mountains' (that is, in Piedmont); in Savoy and in the district of Nice, aspiring surgeons 'could study in their homes'. Moreover the regulations remained (perhaps deliberately) ambiguous about the training required for surgeons who did wish to practise in Piedmont but in the villages. Duboin, vol. 14, 'Regie Costituzioni', 20 August 1729, p. 733. The new rule did not affect the position of those already authorised to practise surgery: *ibid.*, 'Regolamento per l'Università', 20 September 1729, Capo 12, clause 13, p.645.
74 Orders of 2 November 1634, clause 9, and of 10 August 1657, clause 3, in Borelli, pp. 984, 993–4.
75 This phenomenon has been observed at the turn of the century in Paris and in other French university towns, Brockliss and Jones, *The Medical World*, pp. 509–12.
76 AST, s. I, Regie Università, m. II, fasc. 4, 'Progetti di regolamenti e provedimenti dell'Università di Torino', no date but presumably c. 1720.

2

Health, beauty and hygiene:
the broad domain of a barber-surgeon's duties

On Barbers

The art of these is in the selfsame way neat and clean. Since their end and purpose is the cleansing of the body, which is brought about by shaving, the trimming of hair, the washing and thorough buffing of those who have recourse to them, and their business can be set up with a very small expenditure given that the entire architecture of barbers is comprised in a basin, two razors, a lancet, a tenaculum, a pair of tongs, a comb, an earring, though not one that belonged to the Hunchback of Milan, two pairs of face towels, a sponge, a brazier with some coals, a bucket of lye and a small flask of rosewater for splashing faces with. Barbers are also used for blood-letting of the sick, and for applying cupping glasses, dressing wounds, giving enemas, extracting rotten teeth and other such things, so that their art, as Bernardino de Bistis says in his Rosary, is thereby inferior to the science of medicine.

[Tomaso Garzoni, *La piazza universale di tutte le professioni del mondo*, (Venice 1665. 1st edn. 1586)]

Hair, sweat and other kinds of 'excrements'

The picture of the surgeon that emerges from our discussion of Calvo's works has reduced considerably the distance that it is usually held to exist between surgeon and physician. We must now turn to another aspect of the image of the surgeon: the turbulence that allegedly characterised his relationship with the barber. Although the closeness between the duties of these two figures has frequently been observed, the history of medicine has for the most part described this pairing in negative terms. According to this view the association of surgery with hygienic and aesthetic services was regarded as degrading and undesirable by surgeons. Historians are eager to demonstrate the repeated attempts of the latter to separate from barbers and distance themselves from barbering and other body-care procedures. This tendency does not only dominate nineteenth-century accounts of the rise of surgery but is common also in recent historiography.[1] Gelfand for example specifies that in Paris barbers and surgeons combine forces again, after the decline of the academic surgeon, for purely economic reasons: in the 1600s few surgeons can make a living without also practising barbering, and in 1655 the two occupational communities also merge at institutional level.[2] Over the succeeding decades, however, we witness the surgeon's slow recovery for he distances himself from the barber once more. This happens through the gradual expansion of the surgeon's control over the hospital in the last quarter of the seventeenth century and a progressive 'medicalisation' of his activities. The process finally culminates in the partition of the barber-surgeons guild into two distinct occupational associations, something which becomes widespread in the course of the 1700s.[3] Once again, according to this narrative, a specialised elite develops within the surgical profession who refuses to perform the allegedly vile and servile procedures routinely carried out by the barber. Within this paradigm the activities of the barber are regarded as rudimentary, little related to medicine and devoid of dignity. But is it really true that the surgeon's association with hygienic practices was perceived as menial and diminishing? Were the barber's duties merely empirical and alien to any theoretical understanding of the body and of disease?

At a first glance the barber seems to be absorbed in duties which to the modern reader may appear purely aesthetic in nature and liken him more to the servant than to the medical practitioner, which is to say services concerning the hygiene of the body and the care for its appearance: cleaning nails, ears, teeth and pores, as well as washing, cutting, grooming and dressing beards and hair. In reality this distinction between the domain of appearances and that of health is misleading. The cleansing of the body was deemed to have an effect on health, rather than just being a matter of personal decorum. It was conducted with the aim of enabling the processing of waste products which lurked within the body and preventing these substances from becoming blocked and rotten inside, thus provoking pathologies of different kinds. Work produced over the last decade in this field has shown us the specificity of early modern understandings of physiological processes.[4] Two related aspects of these distinctive perceptions of the body deserve attention in this context: the fear of processes of internal corruption and the concept of the skin's permeability.

The danger of putrefaction spreading through the body is a crucial concern of early modern medicine. As Andrew Wear and Gianna Pomata have argued, this preoccupation explains the centrality of practices of evacuation in the therapeutics of the period: patients are purged, bled, made to vomit and sweat.[5] Techniques of bodily hygiene however, are not normally inscribed under the rubric of evacuative therapies; yet, I would suggest, they must be seen precisely in this light. Popular medical literature in the vernacular, such as the books of recipes and the collections of advice for maintaining health that become immensely popular from the mid-sixteenth century onwards, as well as occupational tracts for barbers, surgeons and apothecaries, place increasing emphasis on the removal of 'excrements' from the body.[6] The catalogue of these substances also lenghtens: the list now includes the 'coarseness of ears' (the *brutura delle orecchie*), understood to be putrified sweat retained in the depth of ears;[7] bad breath; the mouth and nose catarrhs; the filth that is expelled through the skin and is found on the scalp; and hair itself. Hair and beards are seen as the natural way through which the head purges itself:

> the hair are akin to lupins on the ground; for as when the lupins are sown, they purify the earth of all bad humours, so the hair upon the human body likewise expunge and relieve all the organs within and also the head of any unwanted coarseness.

The cutting of hair is therefore a procedure necessary for maintaining health given that 'a bushiness of hair' does not only produce a proliferation 'of vermin and filth' but the blocking of poisons to be expelled from the body: 'the small foramina in the skin having their opening obstructed, preventing and denying issue to the soot of dense vapours, so that the senses are gravely interfered with, the brain injured and the sensory faculties damaged.'[8] The head, seat of the brain, the centre of nervous faculties, is regarded as a particularly delicate part of the body, and one in which vaporous excrements that 'continuously ascend from all parts of the body' concentrate.[9] All hygienic practices, even the self-administered ones that are recommended as part of the morning toilette (the removal of the '*caligine*' from eyes, the combing of hair and the cleaning of teeth) are understood to be forms of purging that have a positive effect on the brain: they 'relieve the brain', 'purify the intellect' and sharpen the memory.[10] Some practitioners recommend therefore that the head is not washed too often but rather kept 'neat and dry' by rubbing it with coarse cloth and with combs: 'the feet should be rarely washed, the hands frequently and the head never.'[11]

The barber is also skilled in other evacuative procedures: first, the removal of tartar from the teeth to avoid their 'corruption' and bad breath.[12] 'The filth of the teeth' is to be feared because it also releases 'filthy spirits that ascend to the brain.[13] Second, the cleansing of the ears, 'of that excrement which resembles apple pulp'. This practice is presented in barber tracts as the conclusion to the procedures of hair cutting, and the instrument used, the ear cleaner (*auriscalpium* in Latin), is part of the barber's set of tools.[14]

The scrubbing of the skin to ensure perspiration that took place in public steam baths and, in more exclusive settings, like that of the court, in the steam chamber, was also seen as necessary for maintaining health.[15] Steam baths opened the pores of the skin – which were regarded as a pathway between the inside and outside of the body – and allowed the expulsion of excessive fluids. The idea of the skin's porousness is widespread in early modern notions of the body. In the literature on hygiene, this idea has often been understood primarily in a 'negative' sense: it has been associated mainly with practices of closing up the body to the outside, in order to protect it from any escaping of beneficial humours through dilated pores, or from any penetration of infected air and illnesses.[16] Rather less attention has been paid to the practices aiming to keep the skin open and to purge the body through sweating. It is precisely this 'positive' version of the skin's permeability which seems central to the practices of bodily hygiene performed in the stews. Barbers had a key role in these procedures: public stews were run by barbers and *stufaroli* (who were often part of the same guild);[17] but also at court hygienic practices were often the responsibility of *Aiutanti di Camera* (Chamber attendants) and *baigneurs* who, as we shall see, were often barber-surgeons.

If considered in the light of contemporary understandings of the body the activities of the barber appear therefore less alien to the practice of medicine than they are generally assumed to be; moreover, the fact that treatment becomes increasingly evacuative in the early modern period grants to the barber a central role in healthcare. Blood-letting too had the function of purging the body of excessive humours and was for long time one of the specialisms of barbers. This practice however has been seen as 'impure' and the association of the barber with blood as polluting.[18] But was it really the case? What is the status of blood in early modern views of the body?

Blood and the nobility of the barber's craft

Despite the assumptions about the rough and simple nature of the barber's duties, no proper investigation has been conducted into his skills and how they were seen by contemporaries. Treatises on the barber's craft written in the first half of the seventeenth century by individuals who define themselves as 'barbers' provide some interesting evidence. What does a 'barber' write about? In the first place, as one might expect, about 'clipping hair and beards', an activity presented as an 'art' by Tiberio Malfi, who devotes Part I of his three-part work – *Il Barbiere* – to it.[19] The dignity of the barber's craft derives in the first place from the fact that it has to do with the beard, a component of the body which in itself is particularly valued in the male: indeed not only does facial hair distinguish men from women but it is proof of virility in the adult man, in particular of his capacity to father children, so that it is 'a defect in man not to have it'.[20] But the barber's task also has noble ends when it comes to the hair of the head, one being 'ornament', the other 'cleanliness'. The latter 'is always combined with a paucity of hair' given that hair and beards are seen as a kind of 'excrement': 'the greater it [the amount of hair] becomes, the more it is disagreeable and serious'. Thus the cutting of hair averts sickness and justifies the conclusion that 'this noble craft acts in the service of physic'.[21]

However, the barber does not just concern himself with beards and hair. In these works there is also much discussion of the therapeutic application of living or newly dead animals on the diseased parts, of cauterisation 'with a living flame' ('which is done by means of red-hot instruments') and of 'potential' (which is done with caustic medicaments such as 'quicklime, oil of vitriol, soap, burning sulphur and garlic'), and vescicatories, poultices that 'redden' and, like cauterisation, serve to open up a path for evacuation, to allow 'all the superfluous and intemperate humours' to leave the diseased part.[22] Moreover, a number of sections cover some of the classic areas of surgery: the initial treatment of wounds and contusions, and ligatures. But some chapters are also devoted to functions at intersection of medicine and aesthetics, e.g. cleaning and whitening the teeth, and treatments to prevent the 'slackening' of the gums and the loosening of teeth. Finally, some of the editions of Cintio D'Amato's tract (like the one consulted here) include the section on 'embalming corpses' announced in the title.

These are, therefore, variegated works which confirm the complexity of the figure of the barber. Blood-letting (the *sagnia*), however, has a central role (D'Amato devotes twenty-four chapters to it, and Malfi twenty-two). In studies of the history of medicine, blood-letting is often defined as minor surgery, but it is presented by Malfi and D'Amato as a somewhat demanding procedure which requires not just manual skills on the part of its practitioners, but theoretical knowledge of the functioning of the body and of anatomy. In this respect the barber seems fairly close to the surgeon: he has to know 'the composition of the human body … the distance, difference and location of veins, arteries, muscles, nerves, tendons … '. Phlebotomy is itself defined as 'surgery' by D'Amato, and Malfi also describes its practitioner as a 'Surgeon'.[23] The anatomy of the network of veins is particularly important (D'Amato devotes two chapters to it and Malfi five in all, as well as numerous figures) but it is also necessary to understand the anatomy of the parts to which it connects in order to avoid causing them any injury when the vein is operated on or a cauterisation is done. Moreover, knowledge of anatomy is indispensable in order to identify the precise point in the body on which blood-letting or cauterisation has to be carried out. For example, 'it is a skill to find the lambdoidal suture, as it is called by physicians, and which is not easily found by one who has had no sight of anatomy'[24]. D'Amato insists furthermore on the extreme diversity of types of blood-letting: indeed the area of the body upon which to intervene alters according to the malaise of which the patient complains, as does the technique of blood-letting. There are at least twenty-two points in the body from which blood can be let, from twelve veins (from the saphenous vein, that is from the foot; from the veins in the liver, in the forehead, in the lip, in the head, in the hands, in the nostrils; from the vein under the tongue, from behind the ears, from the buttocks, etc.).[25] Each of these points is associated with the typology of a disease and is discussed in a separate chapter together with the kinds of instruments to be used – whether this be 'the knife' (i.e. the razor, the lancet, or one of a variety of other cutting instruments such as the *zeccarda*, or the *zingardola*), leeches or cupping glasses – and with the method of cutting. Thus blood-letting is portrayed as a complex skill. D'Amato and Malfi also discuss at length the risks associated with it, further emphasising the delicacy of this procedure and the great ability required of its practitioner.[26] The image of the frightened patient in the numerous visual representations of blood-letting included in barbers' tracts is a reminder of the caution and care required in performing such a task. But these pictures also aim to create a reassuring effect: the barber is often represented as a small, slim man, with a slender silhouette, inoffensive and surely gentle in touch. The fact that he comes to the aid of the suffering patient in his or her own house, equipped with simple instruments, underlines the unintrusive character of his tasks. He is helped by a young assistant but often this figure is complemented, or even replaced by, a woman of the household – another element that stresses the integration of the practitioner in the female controlled territory of domestic health-care (see plates 1–2).

The prestige D'Amato assigns to phlebotomy and, indirectly, to the barber's craft, does not surprise us: it should be borne in mind that blood-letting remained the principal evacuative therapy for the whole of the

Plate 1 Barber-surgeon and assistant blood-letting a patient from the tongue, *Il Barbiere*, Naples 1626, p. 127.

early modern period. The usefulness of blood-letting was a cornerstone of medicine: the illnesses to which it was suited, the season when it was best effected, the age of the patient and many other variables were debated by medical writers, both classical and medieval.[27] Interest in it continued through the seventeenth century, and learned practitioners, not just barbers and surgeons, wrote about it: one example, in the Piedmont context, is represented by the Protophysician Bartolomeo Torrino.[28] The

Plate 2 Barber-surgeon blood-letting a female patient in her house assisted by the female members of the household: *Il Barbiere*, Naples 1626.

high regard for phlebotomy did not decline in the following century. One need only recall its centrality in the therapeutic method advocated by Calvo in the early decades of the eighteenth century. Treatises specifically addressing the topic continued to be produced during this period, in Latin too.[29] Quesnay himself wrote two treatises on the effects of blood-letting, in 1730 and 1736.[30] The noble status of phlebotomy could not but reflect positively upon the professional status of those who administered it.

We should also remember the value attributed to blood in the culture of the time. Blood was not merely one of the four fundamental bodily elements but it was seen as the most vital and esteemed of the humours, the one that nourished the body and was responsible moreover for the psychological characteristics of the individual: 'blood is our soul', says Fioravanti.[31] The other humours are only intermediate stages of the process of generating the blood. The superiority of the blood also derives from its association with the heart, which in Aristotelian physiology is the noblest of the organs; it is the blood which transports the vital spirit, born from the heart (*spiritus*). Admittedly, the tripartite Galenic physiology which became predominant in Europe from the late Middle Ages established a distinction and an implicit hierarchy between venous blood – the object of blood-letting – and arterial blood: the latter formed part of what was referred to as the respiratory system, connecting the heart, lungs and arteries, and was regarded as the most elevated because of being associated with the vital faculties; whereas venous blood belonged to the digestive system (the least noble of the three physiological systems), which included the liver, abdomen and veins, and was associated with the functions of nutrition and reproduction.[32] We could see this distinction as confirming the baseness of the blood which was the object of blood-letting, i.e. venous blood. And yet Aristotelian physiology had not been completely superseded, and it enjoyed significant influence in the medical thinking of the early modern period. The discovery of the circulation of the blood itself postulated a unified haemodynamic mechanism and therefore displaced the duality of the vascular systems. And positions such as those of Thomas Willis (1622–1675) and his pupil Richard Lower, which broke with Aristotelian cardio-centrism, far from diminishing the status of the blood, assigned it the central role in supporting life and spirit, thus as the source of vital heat.[33]

It is moreover the heart which is seen by the moralists, theologians and medical men of the early modern period as the seat of emotions – rather than the brain, as conceived by platonically inspired Galenic physiology.[34] This incidentally explains the great importance assumed by the heart in the political symbolism of the period, in the representation of monarchy and then of absolute monarchy.[35] And it is in the early modern period that it becomes the object of collective veneration through the cult of the Sacred Heart of Jesus and Mary.[36] The pierced and bleeding heart of the Redeemer is a central symbol in mystical writings, especially by women, already in the late Middle Ages, but it is only in the seventeenth century that the cult of this organ of the body of Christ acquires a liturgy, a feast and prayers of its own.[37]

As well as being a metaphor for the bonds of affection, the heart is the object of funeral rites. The practice of burying the heart separately from the rest of the body had been the preserve of royalty and medieval princes but became common in the early modern period among the aristocracy.[38] In Turin too there was no lack of such cases: it is in particular pious noble women and princesses who ordered that their hearts be buried in a place to which they were bound by feeling, for example the convent they were connected with, or in the chapel where members of their family also rested.[39]

The link between blood and heart gives us yet another reason to see how blood-letting would be regarded as a delicate skill in its more complex forms, and one with considerable dignity. Moreover, the distinction between venous and arterial blood was probably not so obvious to people at large and does not seem to have impinged upon the deep-rooted belief in the positive role of blood. As a crucial symbol of redemption and salvation in the Crucifixion and the Eucharist, blood was regarded as a depository of revivifying and miraculous powers and was thereby employed in magic formulae, culinary recipes and medical prescriptions.[40] We are not merely in the realm of some presumedly 'popular' medicine: the *maîtres* of the Paris faculty of medicine in the mid-sixteenth century numbered among their recommended remedies whose ingredients included distilled human blood;[41] and in the seventeenth century the official pharmacopoeia of the English and German colleges of physicians included human blood.[42]

Thus the work of the barber is associated with noble and complex tasks. Moreover, there is considerable continuity between the 'barber' who features in the treatises of D'Amato and Malfi and the 'surgeon' who emerges from Calvo's writings in the early 1700s. D'Amato and, in particular, Malfi, frequently cite the authors of antiquity (Avicenna, Galen, al-Ibadi, Albucasis and others) and those 'of our times'. Like Calvo, they display a degree of medical learning. Unlike Calvo, however, they urge respect for the opinion of the physician and acceptance of subordination to his orders, albeit in a contradictory manner. In theory, he, for example, is the one who should indicate which vein should be proceeded upon ('the vein ordered by the physician'), even though in the lengthy chapters on blood-letting these authors are then at pains to demonstrate that they know very well which type of blood-letting is appropriate to the various types of illness. Compared with Calvo, D'Amato and Malfi dwell more on the value of practice: they stress the dexterity required of the barber and therefore the importance of physical qualities such as good eyesight, sensitivity of touch and a steady hand (reasons why the barber should be young). They discuss the differences between the various types of instrument used by the barber – the 'olive branch lancet', the 'sparrow tip' – and boast about the qualities of the ones they themselves have introduced, also supplying visual representations of these tools in the numerous illustrations which supplement their books.[43] Some chapters are straightforward technical instruction: 'How to Hold the Lancet', 'How the Vein Should Be Cut'. What is more, the educational purpose of the two works is made quite explicit: 'To offer enlightenment to beginners and advise them of some common errors committed in our times'. Experience is presented as being of fundamental value in their occupation and this is why the barber ought to practise every day, working in hospitals, convents and other public institutions.[44]

At the same time, however, the barber's thinking about disease, although less elaborated than that of Calvo, seems to be thoroughly imbued with the language of the humours; although D'Amato and Malfi rarely attempt to discuss the causes for the onset of an illness (it appears and that's all there is to it), the reasons why a specific therapy works or else creates complications are explained by them in terms of humoral physiology.[45] Like the surgeon Calvo, moreover, the barber defends his right to administer diets and medicines:

> If the Barber is the Vicar of the physician, he must have knowledge of the same medicines that the Physician knows of [...] therefore I say that since they [the barbers] also give medicines, they must have ample prior education in the medicines, be they simples or compounds.[46]

D'Amato and Malfi confine themselves for the most part to recommending the remedies and diets most appropriate to the patient who has undergone or is about to undergo blood-letting or cautery. They too, however, display their knowledge of the properties of substances which are either simples or extracted from simples (syrups, distillations, poultices) and they occasionally provide recipes for compounds of these ingredients. Compared with Calvo, we can note a greater use of local products as a basis (citrons, oranges, vinegar, hyacinths, apples), and of foodstuffs which are less exotic and in daily use (cheese, oil, honey, pig's gall), apart from the ubiquitous 'musk', as well as less complex compounds, usually blending only two or three simple elements. Yet, as already noted in relation to the surgeon, the separation of the barber from the physician seems more one of scale than of substance: neither diets, medicines, nor ideas about the internal workings of the body seem to be the preserve of physicians, who are simply described as being more learned than the 'barber', knowing about the causes of pathologies as well as their progression, and about highly complex remedies.

As in Calvo, it does not seem possible to reduce the barber's intervention to the surface of the body, because there is no barrier between the inside and the outside, and what is done on the surface has deeper effects. Practices such as 'anointing the heart' with theriac dissolved in white vinegar or orange flower water or with a 'liniment made of a paste of these flowers', recommended in cases of syncope, show the belief in the capacity of external applications to have an internal effect.[47] This is clear also in the application of the still warm open bodies of animals ('cockerels, pigeons, small dogs, frogs and others'), or of the lung of lamb or mutton on the invalid's head, a remedy considered ideal in maladies of the head and in particular in phrenetis or 'inflammation of the brain'.[48] The skin is seen as a conductor through which the warm animals or their organs transfer their powers to the body – 'with the temperate humidity of the aforesaid lung, the pores of the cutis becoming less dense, [heat] becomes drawn into the brain and consequently resolves the malady in question imperceptibly through perspiration'.[49]

It is precisely this two-way permeability of the skin, the fact that it is a vehicle of communication between the outside and the inside of the body, and not a barrier, which makes a sham not only of boundaries demarcating practitioners of the inside and the surface of the body but also of the distinctions we tend to make between health care and what may appear as mere aesthetic treatment. The repertoire of barber's instruments listed by Malfi confirms the continuity between these duties: what begins with the razor, the scissors, the combs and the ear cleaner, the basins and bowls, the boiler for preparing the lye and the bellows for the hot coals, is continued with the fan for keeping insects away from the face, the bowls or fonts for washing the client's hair, the soap, the mirror, and finally the lancets (also called *gladioli*, scalpels or phlebotomisers), the probe or stylet, the curette or curved needle, the tongs or volsella forceps, the cauterising iron and the needles to stitch wounds.[50]

The fluidity of professional labels

If the spheres of activity of barbers and surgeons are to be seen as epistemologically less distinct than it is often assumed, professional hierarchies and divisions also need to be rethought. Let us first consider the legislation. To what extent does it offer confirmation of the allegedly growing distance between the barber and the surgeon in the seventeenth century? A close reading of the provisions regulating the supply of medical services in the duchy reveals that similar measures are often imposed upon the surgeon and the barber as if these involved a single category.[51] They speak for example of barbers, as well as surgeons, who must send their *garzoni* to the university to attend the lectures in surgery.[52] The regulations are eager to demarcate the spheres of competence of surgeons and physicians and of surgeons and apothecaries,[53] but do not make any distinction between the duties of surgeon and those of the barber, nor do they give any emphasis to the supposed hierarchy between the two categories. It is interesting for example that the 1616 ordinance that any suspicious injuries treated should be reported was addressed to the barber, surgeon and physician alike.[54]

If we look at the way in which these professional labels are used in everyday life we find ourselves even more confused. At first sight the two occupations are presented linguistically as separate: the term barber-surgeon, used in other contexts, is not found in Turin and in Piedmont, and only a minority of practitioners speak of practising both 'as a barber and a surgeon', or of having 'a surgeon and barber's shop'. The majority use only one of these terms at a time, defining themselves and being defined as either 'barber' or 'surgeon'.[55] However, the biographical approach enables us to confirm that this is not a matter of rigid labelling: the same individuals are called, and call themselves, 'barber' on some occasions and 'surgeon' on others, quite independently of their official professional status. Certainly, separate patents (i.e. licences to practise) exist for surgeons and barbers: in this sense, the occupational survey drawn up in Turin in September 1695 gives us a picture of clear-cut divisions based on types of patents. A breakdown of the seventy-one practitioners equipped with licences shows forty-five to be 'surgeons', twenty-two to be 'barbers' and four to be 'surgeons and barbers'.[56] Yet this is a representation belied by many other sources. Whether in personal legal documents, or in the various listings of the city population, or yet again in the appointments to professional or municipal offices such as that of *Cantoniere*, what we find is scant adherence to the professional categorisation defined by the type of patent. For example, both Pietro Berrone and Giò Delilla appear as 'barber' in the occupational survey of 1695, but as 'surgeon' in the census of the French carried out five years earlier.[57] Giacomo Francesco Ratti, another 'barber' according to the occupational survey, was categorised as a 'surgeon' in 1688, when he was nominated Cantoniere.[58] The 'barber' Pietro Antonio Camagna was described as a 'surgeon' only five months after the survey, in the wedding contract to which he acted as a witness.[59] Carlo Amedeo Fassina was a 'barber' in 1695, but a 'surgeon' in the deed of purchase of a vineyard which was actually finalised thirty years earlier, and then in all the notarial deeds to which he was a party up until 1696, the year of his death.[60]

Numerous further examples could be given. One might say that, both in self-representation and as perceived by the community and even by the authorities, the distinction between barber and surgeon was of little significance.[61] For example it is striking that, in December 1631, Francesco Emanuelli was described just as 'barber' in the records of the hospital of San Giovanni where he was employed, but eight months later he was appointed by order of the Duke to the prestigious post of Surgeon of the City.[62] In the occupational survey itself some 'barbers' had themselves described at first as 'surgeons', then, probably after they had presented their patents, the term was corrected to 'barber' by the clerk. There is also an inverse case – a practitioner who initially states himself to be a 'barber' but is registered as a 'surgeon' after the checking of his patents – which suggests that it is not merely a mechanism of self-promotion which is being hidden behind these inaccuracies, but a terminological confusion.[63]

There are various explanations for this fluidity of labels. It undoubtedly reflects the scant importance of institutional classifications in the defining of professional identity – and we shall return to this aspect later in the book. It also suggests that there was considerable convergence of the barber's professional practice with that of the surgeon. The work of either one was frequently carried out in the same shop, and even if what seem to us to be the most distinctively aesthetic procedures were perhaps exercised more often towards the start of the surgeon's career, and later by his Garzoni or Giovani, they nonetheless formed part of his expertise, and were tasks which he supervised and was able to teach. Take for example Giò Gallatia, aged 50: in 1689, required to testify to the free marital status of a widow who wishes to remarry, he declares that he knew the deceased husband well 'in his capacity as a surgeon, for he always served him in his illnesses and also served him with regularly shaving him'.[64]

What is more, the gap between the skills and knowledge required of anyone wishing to be accepted as a licensed barber and a licensed surgeon must have been an easy one to overcome. One particularly pleasing piece of evidence in this respect comes from the deposition of Francesco Antonio Doglio, aged thirty-two.[65] To justify the fact that he has opened a barber's shop two months earlier without being equipped with the patents, he argues that he 'had made application four months ago to the Ducal *Protomedico* (Protophysician) for the examination of admission as a Barber, but, the Ducal Protomedico having given him the answer that it was better he should study longer still and would thus secure the patents of surgeon and barber at one and the same time', and since Doglio is on familiar everyday terms with the Protomedico, since 'he shaves his beard', 'he has not made a further application'.[66] One might say that not only was the discrepancy between the two types of patents hardly significant, but that the skills of the barber were part and parcel of the surgeon's stock-in-trade. The fact that the majority of those who are registered as 'barbers' in the professional survey of 1695 reappear on subsequent lists as 'surgeons' may therefore indicate that the progression from barber to surgeon was a fairly commonplace procedure; anyone not yet a surgeon would soon become one.[67]

There is nonetheless one clear trend: in daily usage the term 'barber' is one encountered more often in the first half of the seventeenth century, as if this label were apparently unproblematic and more readily accepted than it was later; then, in the last quarter of the century there is a downgrading of the status of 'barbers', one might say that they all want to be 'surgeons', but without this terminological shift reflecting any significant alteration in professional practice. Quite simply, the term 'surgeon' seems to have assumed a greater dignity and it becomes the term of preference.

That this is more an issue of words than of deeds can be seen in the matter of establishing the College, which was approved by the Duchess in 1676 upon the petition of the University (company) of Surgeons.[68] We can observe in the first place that what in 1660 described itself as the 'University of Surgeons and Barbers', in 1676 had become the 'University of Surgeons'.[69] This body now requested ducal permission to establish a College of Surgeons 'composed of those who are truly Surgeons practising in this city and not those who have the mere capacity of barbering and a little blood-letting (far qualche cavata di sangue)'. The petition seems to aim to distinguish between surgeons and barbers (even though this term is oddly never mentioned). And yet among those who are defined as 'collegiate surgeon' we find in 1697 Emanuele Filiberto Valle, who only two years earlier featured in the occupational survey as a 'barber'. In the census of 1705 he is once again categorised as 'barber'. In 1684, among the sindaci of the College (the Sindaco being the most distinguished office after that of priore), we find Carlo Antonio Bonardo, who is then recorded in the survey of 1695 as 'surgeon and barber'; and in the dowry contract for his daughter Carlo Amedeo Fassina is likewise categorised as 'collegiate surgeon', when only five months earlier he had described himself as a 'barber'.[70] On this point too, numerous further examples could be cited. Clearly the confusion between barbers and surgeons even involves the members of the College.[71]

It seems therefore that the activities of the barber and the surgeon were contiguous and frequently indistinguishable. From mid-seven-teenth century onwards, however, the term 'barber' fell progressively out of fashion and the majority of those exercising this complex occupation increasingly tended to describe themselves as 'surgeons'. The creation of the College, in 1676, sanctioned this kind of general promotion of profes-sional status. Far from separating a more medicalised elite from those who were limited to practising the more basic aspects of the profession, the College authorised the majority of those who had a shop in Turin to describe themselves legitimately as 'collegiate surgeon'. In effect the College would have admitted 'any surgeon at present practising in the city and its territories without further examination, so long as he already has his surgeon's patents issued by the Protomedico'. Admittedly, those who did not yet have these patents were excluded, but for many this meant only temporary exclusion, given that, as we already know from the cases of Doglio, Valle, Fassina and their like, it was not such a great step from the condition of mere barber to that of surgeon, and was one that would soon occur.

Biographical evidence together with the surviving institutional documentation suggest that this new structure did not yet have the elite character that, at least on paper, would be assigned to it fifty years later by the university reforms. In 1721 these provided for the establishment of a College of Surgery, resembling the colleges of law, medicine and theology, composed of only twelve members.[72] We are very far from the numbers which must have characterised the first College, in 1676![73]

We must not therefore let ourselves be misled by the name; whatever the term College might suggest (it is also described in the document as 'Academy'), the new body has all the characteristics of a territorial craft guild which encompasses all local practitioners, and those who will gradually acquire the patents to practise in the city as surgeons. The all-embracing nature of the organisation in fact also covered future eventualities: a supplementary clause made admission into the College a prerequisite for those who in the future wished to 'set up shop and exercise the profession of surgeon in the city and its territory'.[74] Rather than making some conclusive separation between barbers and surgeons and between the learned practitioners and those practically trained, the constitution of the College endowed the occupation with greater dignity by giving its representative body an equivalence in name (but only in name, since it remained de facto an overarching professional body) with the long-established College of Physicians. Even institutional divisions should therefore be taken less literally than has often been the case.

The evidence suggests then that at the close of the seventeenth century the surgeon was heir to the figure who fifty years before had described himself as a 'barber', without however feeling diminished by this legacy. In this transformation of the barber into a surgeon, it is the surgeon who remains the depository of the art of phlebotomy. It is from possible accusation of having performed this procedure that those who still describe themselves as simple 'barbers' defend themselves at the end of the century. In the occupational survey of 1695, for example, Forneri, who has no licence to practise, maintains that he 'only practised as a barber, which is to say cutting hair and beards, and having made some issues of blood, but very few and no more than six a year'. Other barbers, like Senta, Varrone and the Giovane Huysend, who worked with the widow Dalbagna, denied ever having 'let blood, applied cupping glasses, leeches or boxing glasses to anyone'.[75] In the provinces, however, the assumption that blood-letting forms part of the skills of the barber persists for longer: so Antonio Petia, at Chivasso, says that 'in his trade as a barber he only shaves beards, lets blood and applies cupping glasses by order of the physician to patients who need them'. Domenico Bonetti from Druento states that he has 'exercised the profession of barber for a year, blood-letting and cupping, and has not yet any patents'.[76] Although there is no explicit provision in the legislation, it would seem therefore that a transfer of the specialism in blood to the surgeon is taking place, and that the simple barber is now expected to be excluded from this activity.[77]

Barber-surgeons and the expanding demand for beauty care services

In the context of early modern conceptions of the body barbers and surgeons thus appear allied by common wisdom and concerns, their shared outlook encompasses humoral physiology, and hence the need to purge the body of the poisons which are continually produced in it, by means of removing various types of 'excrements', cutting the hair, and letting of blood. A narrative aiming to trace the progressive medicalisation of surgeons and their separation from barbers, has led to an underestimation of the links between their skills. Furthermore, this approach has overlooked the impact upon these occupations of changes in fashion, that is in style of dress, beards and hair lengths, and of phenomena such as the growth of an aristocratic urban culture.

With the appearance of the wide snow-white collars encircling the neck, and the cuffs around the hands, in the late sixteenth and early seventeenth centuries, the face and hair were particularly highlighted. Besides, with the expansion of the Baroque courts, of which the rise of the Turin

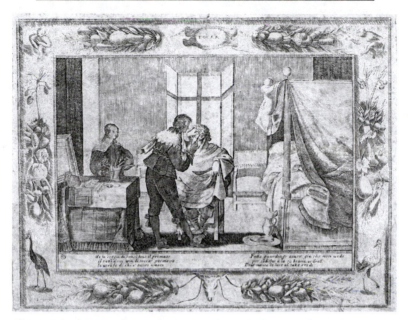

Plate 3 A barber attending to the toilette of a gentleman in his house, Venice c. 1650.

court is one example, and the concentration of the nobility in the capital taking place here, as elsewhere, during the seventeenth century, models of beauty became more refined and the hygienic and cosmetic demands of personal care expanded, making the activities of those who could provide these services much more crucial and also more lucrative. It is unlikely, in this context, that the specialism of the barber might have appeared demeaning, the widening of the demand for more highly developed treatments in personal hygiene and beauty accentuates the role of the barber-surgeon as an 'artisan of the body' rather than reducing it.

After close on a century in which beards and extremely short hair held sway, the tendency for fashionable men to shave and wear their hair long took hold between the third and fourth decades of the seventeenth century, making the services of barbers much more a matter of everyday necessity.[78] Hair attracted greater attention than before: it was curled or crimped, coloured, perfumed and powdered, with eyebrows dyed and plucked. Moreover, make-up for the face became widespread, as did the artificial mole (the patch), for men and women alike.[79] This development of focus on the head led in the second half of the seventeenth century to the introduction of the wig.[80] We must not however imagine that the appearance of the wig cut short the fortunes of the barbers. In the first place, this new fashion was only to increase the services required for the head: the wig had to be combed every day, powdered with either white or blonde powder as appropriate, and perfumed. These operations, along with other cosmetic services, fall to the valet or the lady's maid (of those who have them), but also to barbers and hairdressers who exercise their skills in shops, at court or attended to customers in their houses (see plate 3).[81]

In the second place, the use of the wig became established gradually and it did not involve every class and age group; it was a fashion initially restricted to the court; in any case, as a rule, it left out women and the very young. Around the mid-eighteenth century there were still many sections of society which did not use wigs and went to barber-hairdressers for the styling of their own hair 'as given to them by nature'. Young people, even within the aristocracy, preferred to wear their natural hair, 'dressed impeccably'.[82] In Turin, a document of 1766 lists among them 'soldiers, clerics, ladies, young ladies and girls', and more generally 'the young'.[83] The proliferation of shops offering diverse kinds of service for the hair, and no longer exhibiting the traditional barber's emblem, the three basins, or the fact that the so-called *frizzotini* (literally 'curlers') went to people's homes 'to dress the ladies' locks', provoked local protests halfway through the eighteenth century from the perruquiers, who felt threatened by these dubious figures: 'barbers who are also hair-curlers so that they can at one and the same time shave and dress the hair of those persons who ... love to go about embellished with the hair bestowed upon them by nature'.[84]

The rise of the wig and of the wig-maker did not therefore restrict the barber's territory. Indeed, in the second half of the seventeenth century, when the fashion for the wig was brand new and the city had no wig-makers of its own as yet, we find barber-surgeons as suppliers of wigs: the 'surgeon' Franco Bortolotti, for example, despatching wigs and skull-caps to Prince Maurizio in 1672. In the succeeding decades the production of wigs was also developed locally, and when the wig-makers formed their own company in 1704, there were already more than sixty workshops.[85] Nonetheless, the barbers continued dealing in wigs: in the professional survey of barbers and surgeons in 1695, two practitioners candidly stated that they practised 'the art of the barber and *parrucchiere* [a term that in Italian means both wig-maker and hairdresser]' and one that he 'had applied himself to beards and wigs'. In 1699, the shop equipment that the young surgeon Giò Tomaso Bonardo receives from his father Carlo, also a barber-surgeon provides another piece of evidence suggesting the mingling between the two occupations: this includes twelve different cupping glasses, six tin buckets and 'a wooden head for the wig with a device to hold the candle.[86] Still halfway through the eighteenth century the barbers were accused by the wig-makers of 'underhand' selling to a great many buyers of low-priced wigs of shoddy manufacture (using the curls to cover up the holes left by the weave and making the wig look as if it were made of more hair than was actually there).

The demarcations between barbers and wig-makers are therefore not clearly defined. Just as surgeons and barbers impinge on one another, so do both of them impinge on perruquiers and wig-makers. The history of these occupations has frequently been traced through the perspective of one group's emancipation and specialisation in relation to another, and the taking on of separate identities. Specialisation and modernity, it is often assumed, go hand-in-hand. In the pages that follow I should like to suggest the significance of exploring the connections, rather than the distinctions, between these and other related occupations and what lies behind these connections, within a perspective of cultural history.

Notes

1 For an analysis of past histories of surgery see C. Lawrence, 'Democratic, divine and heroic: the history and historiography of surgery', in C. Lawrence (ed.), *Medical Theory, Surgical Practice* (London, 1992).

2 Gelfand, *Professionalizing*, pp. 24–5.

3 In Paris this occurred legally only in 1743 but the separation between barbers and surgeons had informally taken place already around the turn of the century: *ibid.*, pp. 29, 36.

4 Duden, *The Woman*; Pomata, *Contracting*, chapter five; Wear, *Knowledge*, especially chapters three-four; I. Maclean, *Logic, Signs and Nature in the Renaissance* (Cambridge, 2002), chapter seven.

5 Wear, *Knowledge*, pp. 212, 255–60. In a similar vein, Pomata, *Contracting*, pp. 129–35, who, however, sees evacuative therapies as increasingly associated with popular medicine in the seventeenth century and less common in learned medical practice.

6 Regimens of health, in particular, are a genre in their own right, though a composite one, which still await full investigation. Some helpful considerations are found in H. E. Sigerist, *Landmarks in the History of Hygiene* (London, 1956), chapter one, and M. Mikkeli, *Hygiene in the Early Modern Medical Tradition* (Saarijarvi, 1999), especially chapter three. The production of these medical handbooks spans three centuries, however their contents evolve over time, making them an invaluable source for the study of changing attitudes to health. On the books of secrets, see Eamon, *Science*.

7 *Opera Nova intitolata il Perché* (Venice, 1507), p. 61. This work went through more than twenty editions between 1512 and 1678.

8 *Il Barbiere di Tiberio Malfi da Monte Sarchio Barbiere e Consule dell'Arte* (Naples, 1626), p. 24; for a similar account, *Trattato del Custodir la Sanità de Viviano Viviani Filosofo et Medico Venetiano* (Venice, 1626), pp. 124–5.

9 *Un Breve et Notabile Trattato del Regimento dela Sanità ... di Roberto Gropretiio*

(Venice, 1560), chapter XXI.

10 *Il Breve Compendio di Meravigliosi Secreti … dato in luce dal signor Frate Domenico Auda, Capo Speziale dell'Archiospitale di S. Spirito di Roma e Canonico dello stesso Ordine* (Cuneo, 1666), pp. 235-6 (first published in Rome in 1652 this work had more than ten editions up to 1692). The 'greasy, bilious and bitter' excrement of ears is defined by another author as 'the purging of the brain': *Del Conservar la Sanità del Dottor Roderigo Fonseca Portoghese. Primo Lettor di Medicina nello Studio di Pisa* (Florcene, 1603), p. 102.

11 On whether it is appropriate to wash the head in order to purge it from excrements, see the dispute between B. Trafficchetti and M. M. Bruno: *L'Arte di Conservar la Sanità tutta intiera … per Bartolomeo Trafficchetti da Bertinoro, Medico di Rimini* (Pesaro, 1565), p. 227; *Discorsi di M. Matteo Bruno Medico Riminese* (Venice, 1569), pp. 126-7.

12 On dental hygiene see C. D'Amato, *Prattica Nuova et Utilissima di tutto quello ch'al diligente Barbiere s'appartiene* (Venice, 1669; 1st edn, 1632), chapters XXIV-XXXV, XXXXII.

13 *Scuola Salernitana del Modo di Conservarsi in Sanità* (Perugia, 1587), p. 55; *Il Breve Compendio*, p. 236.

14 *Il Barbiere*, pp. 52, 20.

15 See, among others, *Tratto del Custodir la Sanità*, p. 125; *Svegliarino alli Signori Veneziani per Poter con Sicurezza Viver di Continuo in Sanità sino agli Anni Cento et Dieci* (Venice, 1691), p. 30. On baths and hygiene in fifteenth- and sixteenth-century Italy, see my 'Health, hygiene and beauty', in M. Ajmar-Wollheim and F. Dennis (eds), *At Home in Renaissance Italy* (London 2006), Victoria and Albert Museum publications, London 2006, pp. 65-75, 352-5.

16 I refer in particular to the hugely influential work of Georges Vigarello, for whom fears related to the permeability of the skin were among the principal causes of the disappearance of bathing from early modern hygienic practices: G. Vigarello, *Le Propre et le Sale* (Paris, 1985), pp. 17-20. See also P. Braunstein, 'Dal bagno pubblico alla cura termale privata: tracce per una storia sociale dell'intimo', *Ricerche Storiche*, 16:3 (1986).

17 The documentation on public baths is not available for Turin. On Rome, see A. Esposito, 'Stufe e bagni pubblici a Roma nel Rinascimento', in M. Miglio (ed.), *Taverne, Locande e Stufe a Roma nel Rinascimento* (Rome, 1999), pp. 77-91, and above all A. Pediconi, 'The Art and Culture of Bathing in Renaissance Rome', MA in Renaissance Decorative Arts and Culture, Victoria and Albert Museum and Royal College of Art, 2003. The study demonstrates that, far from being suppressed by religious reformers, public baths in Rome increased hugely in number during the 1500s, so that by the end of the century they existed in every district of the city. The guild of barbers and stufaroli was formed in 1443 and promulgated new statutes in 1559 and 1599, in response to the problems posed by the growing number of practitioners: *ibid.*, p. 141. Barbers and *étuvistes* also appear lumped together in French legislation in the seventeenth century: *Histoire des Perruques où l'on fait voir leur origin … par M. Jean Baptiste Thiers, Docteur en Theologie, Curé de Champrond* (Paris, 1690), p. 28. On Germany see K. Stuart, *Defiled Trades Social Outcasts. Honor and Ritual Pollution in Early Modern Germany* (Cambridge, 1999), pp. 105-11.

18 The work of Mary Douglas has been extremely influential in establishing this negative view of blood and so has a classification of trades drawn along the lines of 'honour-

dishonour'. Pomata, *Contracting*, pp. 66–7. For recent reassessments of the meaning of blood in early modern culture, see G. Pomata, 'Menstruating men: similarity and difference of the sexes in early modern medicine', in V. Finucci and K. Brownlee (eds), *Generation and Degeneration: Tropes of Reproduction in Literature and History from Antiquity to Early Modern Europe* (Durham, NC, 2001); McClive, 'Bleeding Flowers'.

19 In D'Amato's treatise too 'the trimming of hair and beards' is presented as an art; however he decides not to speak of it because 'there are in the works of other barbers most learned and long discussions of it': D'Amato, *Prattica Nuova*, 'A benigni et studiosi lettori'.

20 *Il Barbiere*, chapter IV, especially pp. 21–2. On the beard as a mark not only of sexual but reproductive capacities, see W. Fisher, 'The Renaissance beard. Masculinity in early modern England', *Renaissance Quarterly*, 54 (2001).

21 *Il Barbiere*, p. 34.

22 *Ibid.*, pp. 167–94; D'Amato, *Prattica Nuova*, pp. 61–74.

23 For example: 'And if you wish to know of the difficulties of this *surgery* then place before your eyes the small conduits of blood' (my emphasis): *ibid.*, 'A benigni et studiosi lettori'; cf. *Il Barbiere*, pp. 73, 180.

24 D'Amato, *Prattica Nuova*, p. 65.

25 For Malfi however, the veins which can be opened are nine, *Il Barbiere*, p. 68.

26 D'Amato, *Prattica Nuova*, chapter XI ('On cutting one vein instead of another'), XII ('On the syncope arising from effects of blood issue'); *Il Barbiere*, chapters VII–VIII.

27 For the late medieval treatises on the subject, see Jacquart, *La Médecine*, pp. 197, 202, 259–60, 298–301.

28 B. Torrino, *Consulto se sia Bene Cacciar Sangue a Fanciulli* (Turin, 1659). Among other works by barbers and surgeons in the Italian context, see Horatio Monti, *Trattato della Missione del Sangue contro l'Abuso Moderno ... di Cavar Gran Quantità* (Pisa, 1627).

29 For example G. B. Verna, *Princeps Medicaminum Omnium Phlebotomia* (Padua, 1716); B. Melli, *La Lancetta in Pratica ... opera postuma ... a cui si è aggiunto un breve trattato circa la pratica del ventosare di questo stesso autore* (Venice, 1740). The biographical dictionary of medical practitioners operating in Piedmont erroneously identifies the author of *Princeps Medicaminum* with the much younger Giovan Battista Verna (the cousin of the surgeon Evasio and the nephew of the surgeon Alberto Verna), who will be spoken of below. G. G. Bonino, *Biografia Medica Piemontese*, 2 vols, (Turin, 1824–25), vol. 2, pp. 219–21.

30 Cited by Jacquart, *La Médecine*, p. 29, n. 38.

31 L. Fioravanti, *Capricci Medicinali* (1561), cited in Eamon, *Science*, p. 185.

32 Siraisi, *Medieval and Early Renaissance Medicine*, pp. 80–1, 105–9; J. Pigeaud, 'Cœur organique, cœur métaphorique', *Micrologus*, 11 (2003), pp. 13–16.

33 Cited in F. Hamraoui, 'L'invention de la pathologie cardiaque', *Micrologus*, 11 (2003), n. 25, p. 559: 'le support de la vie est bien moins le cœur que principalement et exclusivement le sang'. For an Italian example of this discussion see *Phlebotomia Damnata a Dominico La Scala Messanensi* (Pavia, 1696), p. 8: 'Sanguis, non cor, est pars corporis princeps'.

34 On the corporeal seat of the passions in medical thinking, see Pigeaud, 'Cœur organique', on the thinking of moralists and theologians on the domain of the heart, M. Flynn, 'Taming anger's daughters: new treatment for emotional problems in Renaissance Spain', *Renaissance Quarterly*, 51 (1998).

35 J. Le Goff, 'Head or heart? The political use of body metaphors in the Middle Ages', in M. Feher, R. Naddaff and N. Tazi (eds), *Zone 3: Fragments for a History of the Human Body* (New York, 1989), Part 3; J. Nagle, *La Civilisation du Coeur. Histoire du Sentiment Politique en France du XIIe au XVIe Siècle* (Paris, 1998); D. Menozzi, *Sacro Cuore. Un Culto tra Devozione Interiore e Restaurazione Cristiana della Società* (Rome, 2001), chapter one.

36 Crucial figures in the transformation of this cult of private devotion into public veneration are the French saints Jean Eudes (1601–80) and Margherita Maria Alacoque (d. 1690). *Dictionnaire de Spiritualité: Ascetique et Mystique. Doctrine et Histoire* (Paris, 1937–95), vol. 2, pt 1, pp. 1030–5.

37 *Ibid.*, pp. 1026–9 for this cult in mystical writings. On its transformation in the seventeenth century, see also *Enciclopedia Cattolica*, 12 vols (Vaticano City, 1948–54), vol. 4, p. 1061, 'Cuore di Gesù'.

38 This practice has been mainly associated with the late Middle Ages and royalty. Gaude-Ferragu briefly notes its revival in the early modern period and its diffusion among the aristocracy but does not remark on its female emphasis. M. Gaude-Ferragu, 'Le coeur 'couronné': tombeaux et funérailles de coeur en France à la fin du Moyen Âge', *Micrologus*, 11 (2003), p. 265.

39 In 1686, for example, the Baroness Margherita Falcombella, the widow of Perachina, set down in her will that her heart should be buried at the convent of the Visitation of Pinerolo, where she had been one of the first boarders and where her daughter was a nun: Ins., 1686, l. 7, 10 July 1686. A few years later, on the death of Princess Ludovica, her heart was removed and laid in the church of Santa Cristina of the Carmelite nuns, close to the body of her mother: Biblioteca Reale, St Patria 726, vol 1 (1690–99), pp. 72–3. Unusually, her entrails were also extracted and buried next to the husband's corpse, a gesture probably aimed at testifying to the link that Ludovica's body had established between the rival parties of the *madamisti* and the *principisti*. The daughter of Duke Vittorio Amedeo and Cristina of France, she had been married to her uncle Maurizio, her father's brother, when she was barely thirteen (he was forty-nine), in order to assuage his aspirations of succession after the end of the civil war, when he had taken up arms against the regency of his sister-in-law Cristina.

40 See for example the recipe 'Quintessenza di sangue umano' in *Il Breve Compendio*, p.147. See also P. Camporesi, *Juice of Life. The Symbolic and Magic Significance of Blood* (New York 1995).

41 Jacquart cites the case of Jacques Despars, and, in the Italian context, of Michele Savonarola, *La Médecine*, p. 479 and n. 168.

42 Stuart, *Defiled Trades*, pp. 160–1.

43 Other examples of treatises on blood-letting with substantial didactic content in this period are: G. M. Castellani, *Filactirion della Flebotolmia et Arteriotomia con aggiunta di un trattato nel qual s'insegna il vero modo d'applicar ventose o coppe* (Viterbo, 1619); *Il Ministro del Medico. Trattato breve di Tarduccio Salvi da Macerata* (Rome, 1608), Part I; T. Lancetta, *De Pestilentia Commune a Bruti ... e un dialogo attinente alla missione di sangue con foglio della vena* (Venice, 1632).

44 'He must tirelessly and studiously practice these skills every day, and the more he does so the greater benefits he will find in employing himself in the hospitals or in the infirmaries of monasteries and convents, or in other public places': D'Amato, *Prattica Nuova*, p. 6. Malfi too mentions his practice in the hospital: *Il Barbiere*, p. 123.

45   For example, the final cause of syncope 'is a fullness of bilious humours which gather in the concave part of the belly, which with agitation and movement, together with the agitation of the blood and of the whole body, rise higher and with their sharp sting adhere to the mouth of the stomach and spread to the heart, infecting the first with diverse symptoms and altering the place of the second, so that it becomes of a languid and deadened nature, whose outcome is syncope': D'Amato, *Prattica Nuova*, p. 17.

46   *Il Barbiere*, p. 56.

47   D'Amato, *Prattica Nuova*, p. 19.

48   *Il Barbiere*, chapters X, XI; D'Amato, *Prattica Nuova*, chapters XXIX, XXX.

49   *Ibid.*, p. 62.

50   *Il Barbiere*, p. 20.

51   'Nor that they [surgeons] and likewise barbers may let blood, apply boxing glasses, cupping glasses, leeches, or make ointments, without an order from the physician except in cases of great necessity' (Duboin, vol. 10, p. 99, 22 February 1709).

52   Borelli, p. 984, 2 November 1634, paragraph 9: 'We order that all the surgeons, barbers who have open shop must send their shop boys to hear the lecture in surgery either at the University or the house of the reader, or pay the penalty'.

53   See chapter one, nn. 10–12.

54   This reaffirmed 'the obligation for physicians, surgeons, barbers and others to notify the judge of any injury or blow that they have dressed or treated, and that this notification give the victim's name, forename, country of origin and place of treatment, likewise at least two of those who have been present at the care of the wounds, and whether these are mortal, dangerous or treatable, whether with disabling of a limb or with a permanent scarring, whether mainly on the face, with what manner of arms, or anything else, all of this upon oath and under penalty of 100 gold scudi' (Borelli, p. 974, 29 July 1616).

55   In Bologna and in the context of criminal proceedings, Pastore equally finds that the terms 'barber' and 'surgeon' are used interchangeably to refer to the same medical experts used by the tribunal to carry out physical examinations: *Il Medico*, pp. 107–8.

56   'Registro delli chirurghi ... di Torino'. All practitioners in the profession must present themselves to show their own patents of authorisation to practise. On the characteristics and enactment of the *Consegna* (referred to here as the survey) see chapter ten below.

57   *Consegna dei Francesi 1690*, depositions of Berrone and Delilla, both of French origin.

58   ACT, vol. 294. For the office of Cantoniere see chapter one, p. 19 and n. 20 and, below, chapter ten.

59   Ins. 1695, l. 6, c. 757.

60   For example, in August 1665 when he acquires a vineyard; in September of the same year, when he borrows the sum of 1500 lire; in the deed of proxy of 1675; in the undertaking of 1683; in the investiture of 1684 and in 1688, the emancipation of his son Sebastiano. On his death in 1696, in the deed of guardianship of his children, he is also described as 'living as a surgeon in this city' (Ins. 1665, l. 10, c. 39; 1665, l. 9, c. 419; 1675, l. 2, c. 563; 1683, l. 4, c. 739; 1684, l. 12 vol. I, c. 163; 1688, l. 11, c. 545; 1696, l. 9, c. 285).

61   We should bear in mind that surveys of the population were drawn up by territorial authorities well aware of the occupations carried out within the district for which they were responsible.

62 AOSG, *Ordinati*, 1 December 1631. The date of the appointment to surgeon to the city is deduced from the successive appointment as surgeon to His Highness: PCF, R. 9, 1644–45, fo. 422.

63 This is the case of Carlo Giuseppe Alberico. Another instance of apparent lowering of professional status is that of Amedeo Astesano, who appears as a 'surgeon' in the 1695 survey, but states himself to be a 'barber and surgeon' in the 1705 census.

64 AAT, 18.4.8, 2 August 1689.

65 In 'Registro delli chirurghi … di Torino'.

66 The year before, however, Doglio was already defined as 'surgeon' in a notarial document he had witnessed: Ins. 1694, l. 10, c. 505.

67 Of the fourteen recorded as 'barbers' in 1695, we find in the census of 1705 or in the appointments to Cantonieri in that year that eleven have become 'surgeons': these are Detat, De Tomatis, Furno, Gianolio, Isnardi, Mitton and Forneri, along with Berrone, Delilla, Ratto and Doglio who have already been mentioned (Art. 530; ACT, vols 294 and 295; AST, s. I, *Provincia*, m. 1, fasc. 1, 1714).

68 PCF, 1676, l. 1, fo. 231 ff., also published in Duboin, vol. 14, pp. 470 ff.

69 The existence of a University of Surgeons and Barbers is proved by the deed of franchise from the archbishop, in response to a petition by this body for an altar in the cathedral (Ins., 1660, l. 8, c .589, 593 for the ratification of the University). The building of the chapel does not appear to have taken place. This document and the one mentioned in the previous note appear to be the only surviving documents relating to professional associations of barbers and surgeons.

70 Valle is described as a 'collegiate surgeon' when he acts as a witness to a deed of receipt for Paolo Bernardo Calvo: Ins. 1697, l. 7, c. 1481. Fassina appears as a 'collegiate surgeon' in the deed for his daughter Anna Camilla's dowry: *ibid.*, 1695, l. 6, c. 757. Carlo Antonio Bonardo describes himself as a 'collegiate surgeon and currently Sindaco of the College of surgeons' in his petition to be appointed Surgeon to the poor. ACT, vol. 294.

71 The constitutive document does not in itself explain what the duties of a surgeon might be, except by default; its wording seems to suggest that it is someone who does not 'merely' shave and 'occasionally' let blood but regularly carries out this latter activity.

72 Duboin, vol. 14, pp. 474, 655. This provision however remained at the planning stage given that there seems to have been no approval of the statutes. The College probably became reality only in 1729 when the number of members was increased to twenty-four by the Constitutions; in the professional census of 1742 it appears to have been reduced again to thirteen (the same number as in the College of Physicians). 'Stato dei negozianti e artisti … 1742'.

73 Unfortunately we have no list of the signatories to the petition. Sixteen years earlier, the University of Surgeons and Barbers already had a membership of at least fifty-two (this figure is reached by adding up the names of the members participating in the two deeds referred to in note 69).

74 Only the court surgeons, appointed directly by the Duke to the service of the Ducal Household, were exceptions to this; the College could impose no conditions upon them (PCF, 1676, l. 1, fo. 231, clause III).

75 'Registro delli chirurghi … di Torino'.

76 'Registro degli … cirugici e barbieri … della Provincia di Torino'. Other examples include Rigillino, a 'barber' at Chivasso, Ballengo in Orbassano, Garrone in Borgaro, Polla at Rivara.

77 It seems significant of the semantic shift described here that an instruction issued by the College of Physicians in 1670, relating to the method to be observed in a particular kind of blood-letting (the so called 'revulsive method', which is to say with 'opposing points between the remedy and the sickness'), is addressed only to *cerugici* (chirurgeons). Duboin, vol. 14, p. 656, 1 January 1670.

78 R. Levi Pisetzky, *Storia del Costume in Italia* (Milan, 1964–69), vol. 3, pp 331ff.

79 *Ibid.*, p. 339. See also M. A. Laughran, 'Oltre la pelle. I cosmetici e il loro uso', in Belfanti and Giusberti, *La Moda*, p. 69; C. Pancino, 'Soffrire per ben comparire. Corpo e bellezza, natura e cura', in *ibid.*, p. 39.

80 Its spread in Italy was slower than in France where the complete wig was introduced to the court in the 1630s, becoming widespread only in the second half of the century. Levi Pisetzky cites for example the prohibitions in Venice and Florence in 1668 and 1692. *Storia del Costume*, vol. 3, pp. 336–7; *Histoire des Perruques*, chap. I. At the Turin court this French fashion first came in with the regency of Cristina, the sister of the King of France, in the 1640s, even though the supplying of wigs appears in accounts only from the 1650s.

81 On the success of this figure in Venice see Malamani, *La Moda a Venezia*, P.III, p. 236, citato in Levi Pisetzky, *Storia del Costume*, vol. IV, p. 155.

82 Levi Pisetzky, *Storia del Costume*, vol. 4, p. 150.

83 AST, I, *Commercio*, Categoria IV, m. 5, fasc. 8, 'Parere del magistrato del Consolato sul ricorso dell'Università dei Parrucchieri', 3 April 1766.

84 *Ibid.*, The term Frizzotini, designating those who curl or frizz or backcomb hair, is found in the 'Sentimento del Magistrato del Consolato,: *ibid.*, fasc. 7, 24 July 1760.

85 There are sixty-six in the census, albeit this is incomplete, given that the inspections of fifteen out of 126 *Cantoni* are missing: Rondolino, 'Vita Torinese'.

86 Ins., 1699, l. 4, c. 563.

3

Barber-Surgeons and artisans of the body

Duties in the Chamber

In the context of the court we find fresh evidence of the wide-ranging duties that fall to the barber-surgeon, and in particular of the closeness between medical care and the care applied to hygiene and appearance. From the second half of the seventeenth century, the court becomes a career opportunity for many practitioners in the city who, alongside their everyday work, take quarterly turns serving in one of the numerous households into which the ducal family is broken up.[1] Here in fact we often find them numbered among the household staff in the role of 'barber', 'baigneur', 'baigneur and perruquier' or stover (*stufatore*); moreover the position of personal attendant (*Aiutante di Camera* or his subordinate *Garzone di Camera*), which is to say the role of the person who assists the master in all the most intimate functions that occur in the Chamber, was frequently undertaken by 'surgeons' or 'barbers'. Examples of this type include the barber Marc'Antonio Giacomelli, the attendant of Prince Maurizio in the 1630s; the surgeon Bernardino Bruco, the latter's attendant from 1654 and the surgeon Antonio Cavagnetto, whom we find in this role in the 1660s; the barber Pietro Antonio Gorgia, who attended on Princess Ludovica between 1650 and 1671; the surgeon Giò Francesco Meda, her attendant in the 1680s; as well as the barbers Enrico Prodomo, Pietro Choisy and Michele Moriceau, personal attendants to the Duke in the 1650s, 1670s and 1690s respectively.[2] Sometimes the title of personal attendant was subsequently added to that of the personal surgeon; this was what happened to Sebastiano Fassina, His Majesty's Surgeon in 1716. His brother, Carlo Giuseppe, also became Aiutante di Camera in 1722, after having already been employed on the Duke's household staff for some years as 'baigneur' (the person responsible for attending to the hygiene of the master).[3] The personal medical staff (the physician, surgeon and apothecary) are also part of the Chamber's personnell who come under the purview of the Great Chamberlain. And yet, though we occasionally find an apothecary among the personal attendants (Tifner and Aventura are examples), we never find physicians involved in these services, which require a direct and tactile relationship with the body of the master.[4] Barber-surgeons are on the contrary prominent in these roles. Other occupations frequently represented among the *Aiutanti* are those of tailor and jeweller, and upholsterers are by far the most numerous. There is nothing surprising about this: as we shall see, the figure of the personal attendant encroaches on those whose primary function is the upkeep of clothes, jewellery and the furnishings of the Chamber, roles that are often fulfilled by a tailor, a jeweller or an upholsterer.

At the Savoy court the personal attendant is a figure who takes shape in the course of the seventeenth century. He is the descendant of the sixteenth-century *valet de Chambre*, a kind of man of all work: in 1577 the terms Garzone di Camera and valet de Chambre are used interchangeably.[5] By the end of the sixteenth century the functions of the Aiutante di Camera are already associated with personal ministrations, whereas the term 'valet' remains linked to the business of dress, in other words looking after clothes and their movement from wardrobe to Chamber.[6] In our period this figure comes to be defined as *Aiutante di Guardaroba*.[7] And yet the two posts are still closely connected and are frequently consecutive in a single career, or else they converge in the same person. A typical example is Eustachio Pastor; in the course of a forty–year long career at court he moved from the position of groom (attached to the Stable) to that of *Garzone di Guardaroba*, and then in addition obtained the title of Garzone di Camera, in a typical progression from outside to inside, towards the heart of power.[8]

Let us take a closer look at these figures.[9] In the seventeenth century, the personal attendant (Aiutante di Camera), or rather attendants (as there were always at least two or three contemporaneously, serving in quarterly rotations), formed part of that vast stratum of court servants subordinate to the gentlemen-of-the-bedchamber which has been little examined until now. In court studies attention has focused so far on higher posts and noble personnel, and yet these servants of lower rank had a vital role, not just assisting the noblemen in their functions but often performing these functions directly, so that the gentlemen were left with a predominantly ritual role in those activities of the Chamber which were codified by protocol.[10] But at all other times the attendants are the sole stable presence in the Chamber, which they must never leave, not even when the master is absent.[11] And even at those rare public rituals taking place in the Chamber (dressing, undressing and the serving of a meal there), the attendant occupies a privileged position. Admittedly he participates in the serving of the meal and the ritual of dressing in a subordinate manner: the attendant presents the food, or the linen and clothes to be worn, to the gentleman, who then hands these to the master. And yet, along with the Aiutante di Guardaroba (who brings the linen and the clothes and then puts on the master's stockings and shoes, laces all the ties on the clothes, and ties the master's neck cloth), the Aiutante di Camera is the only servant of low rank to be present at the point when the master rises or goes to bed, which is a privilege even for noble courtiers.[12] When they are not on duty, the gentlemen themselves can enter only when the Duke has put on his shirt and stockings, and the rest of the court only when he 'begins to comb his hair'.[13]

The Aiutante di Camera and the Aiutante di Guardaroba are thus involved in a special intimacy with the person of the master. And it is possible that their role was an even more direct one in the households of other members of the ducal family. The principal rules of protocol available to us (drawn up in 1679) concern the house of the reigning duke, but we should bear in mind that, along with the duchess, any brothers of the duke or their widows, and any sons and daughters of the reigning duke were all provided with their own personal manservants or lady's maids and with gentlemen or ladies-in-waiting. These parallel royal households have attracted scant attention, partly because of the paucity of sources which would illustrate their workings. We in fact do not know to what extent formalised rituals of the kind described above mattered in their case. It seems significant however that the regulations surviving for one of these minor ducal households should allude to the closer involvement of the Aiutanti in dressing: 'if there should be no gentlemen present when we are dressing, in this case they [the Aiutanti] may be permitted to give us our clothes'.[14]

The gentlemen-of-the-bedchamber are again present, along with the Aiutanti di Camera and di Guardaroba, when the master goes to bed, in order to help him undress, to light and extinguish the candle by his bed and draw his curtains. But then they vanish, only reappearing in the morning, since they have no night duties.[15] Only the Aiutante remains within reach when the master takes his rest, sleeping in the antechamber, 'and even in the very Chamber of His Royal Highness, should it be so ordered'.[16] His subordinate, the Garzone di Camera, or *Barandiere*, actually sleeps fully clothed in the antechamber and will always keep a candle lit 'so as to avail himself of light as needed'.[17] According to the protocols of the period 1640–50, it is only when the master is indisposed that the gentleman is required to sleep in his personal apartments.[18]

Outside the times codified by the rules of etiquette, personal distances are therefore diminished. During the night the Aiutante responds directly to the master's every need: he must have ready 'bread, wine, water and broth ... a silver salver, napkins and glasses', should the master wish for refreshment; he has the Garzone bring the commode if required, which he washes after His Highness has availed himself of it.[19] More generally, the Aiutante assists the master when he retires to his personal apartments, whenever for example he amuses himself with 'gambling', as the first rules of etiquette makes the provision that 'whenever there is gambling in our Chamber the gratuities shall be shared between them [the Aiutanti]'.[20]

The literature on the courts has made much of the political role of the Chamber, which has been studied primarily as a place of government where the most confidential state business is carried out and the most crucial decisions are made.[21] Important though it is, this perspective has led to an underestimation of the fact that the Chamber is also a place of solitude and private entertainment; the master is not completely deprived of moments of privacy and the Aiutante is in fact the guardian of this personal dimension, together with other important figures such as the Chamber Doorkeepers. For instance, it seems significant that it is his duty to make the bed in the morning and to keep intruders away from this intimate place – 'and until it is made he should allow no one to enter'.[22] Moreover, we already know that he must never leave the room; even during the absence of the master he is therefore responsible for the seclusion of his most personal domain.

Because of the closeness that is established through services performed in the Chamber, the Aiutanti often win the special confidence of the master and appear to be trusted figures, often carrying out secret tasks for the master. We shall see this more clearly in chapter four. In earlier years this special relationship was sometimes even rewarded with letters of nobility (the Aiutante Giò Nicot, for example, received this privilege for himself and his children in 1584).[23] In the course of the seventeenth century, however, the expansion of court staff and the growing complexities of protocol meant that a greater number of people surrounded the master, the stratification between courtiers of low and high rank was accentuated, and thus that between nobles and non-nobles. As a consequence, the Aiutante di Camera became less likely to experience a degree of social mobility or a career advancement within the court that would carry him far away from the artisanal world of his origins. He normally remained part of the middling ranks of the city, where he or other members of his family might have had a shop, but enjoyed considerable material and symbolic benefits from his service at court.

Despite the paucity of explicit references to practises of hygiene and cleanliness, this is another area of activity which was taking place in the Chamber. This silence in the Savoy protocols contrasts with the abundance of detail dwelling on this aspect in the protocols relating to a minor court, that of Urbino, in the late fifteenth century.[24] In Urbino, the list of duties of the *Cameriere* (who corresponds to the Aiutante at the Turin court) includes preserving the 'cleanness' of the master by frequent washing of his legs 'with appropriate and sweet-smelling washes'; 'and every morning his hands and face are washed, and every evening his feet are to be well cleaned'. It is suggested that keeping 'a bath or small steam bath for washing the person of the master would be most useful', and that 'the nails should often be cut and the cuticles tended with tools suitable for the purpose'. The Cameriere must moreover attend to the cleanliness 'of the bed linen', and ensure 'that shirts, handkerchiefs and headcloths are frequently changed' and perfumed, 'smelling of some appropriate but not excessive fragrance', that 'undershirts and hose be kept dry from sweat and changed very often', that clothes be 'mended' and everything kept clean, 'and most importantly from sweat'.[25] It is likely that similar functions were also assigned to lower-ranking staff of the Chamber at the Turin court in the next two centuries. In Turin too the duties of the Aiutante seem strictly connected with the master's bodily needs; we have learned, albeit in much more reserved terms, that he is expected to attend the master when he is taking food and in his bodily functions, to look after his bed and therefore the cleanliness of the bed linen, and more generally see to his comfort whenever he is in the Chamber. The absence of greater details about care of the body, in contrast with the much more explicit Urbino instructions, is partly explained by the increase in protocol which came about in the course of the seventeenth century, leading to the exclusion from the rules of all those activities which were not defined by a precise code of behaviour and which do not set problems of precedence.[26] In part this silence is likely to be the sign of a raised threshold of embarrassment and an increasing reticence in language relating to care of the body during the seventeenth century.[27]

It is likely that the brief mention of the barber's duties in the undated Protocols refers in fact to the functions of cleanliness: 'he will be there at our awakening to carry out what is required of him, as in the evening upon our going to bed'.[28] In the rules of 1679, however, the services of bodily hygiene are no longer mentioned, not even in this cryptic form, nor is 'the barber' now named among the staff of the Chamber included in the protocol. And yet we know that places and structures assigned to bodily hygiene, especially steaming, were annexed to the Chamber. For example, in 1655 money was being 'spent on the building of the alcove, the bath, the stew (*caldara*) and the privy of her ladyship the Princess'.[29] It is likely that these functions, also increasingly linked to the care of appearance, were absorbed by one of the Aiutanti di Camera, and, in the case of the female courts, by the *Fame di Camera*.[30] This would explain the fact that the Aiutante is often a barber or a surgeon, in other words someone who has the knowledge and the professionalism to take care of these aspects. Moreover, we can see from the payments that the 'barber' continues to feature among the stipendiaries, and, from the late seventeenth century we see the figure of the '*baigneur*' appear, sometimes described as 'barber and *baigneur*' or '*baigneur* and perruquier' or 'barber and stufatore', that is stover.[31] These terms suggest that in the care of the body steam baths have not ceased to play an important role. This variably defined figure was expected to be present at the morning 'toilette' of the master; we see this from the type of equipment used for example by Carlo Giuseppe Fassina, '*baigneur* and perruquier' to His Highness, reimbursed in 1705 for having provided 'combs, essences, powder for the hair, and other items for the toilette of His Highness'.[32] Aiutanti di Camera, barbers and *baigneurs* (figures which are sometimes found combined in a single person) therefore share between them in various ways the responsibilities for the cleanliness and appearance of the master's body, these varying with time and being subject to the fashion of the day.

Other aspects of the master's appearance are also within the scope of the Aiutante: in the mid-seventeenth century, despite the advent of the Guardaroba, it is the Aiutante who takes delivery of the new clothes from the tailor and gives him others to be mended or altered.[33] The Aiutanti di Guardaroba are instead charged with picking up clothes and linen which had been taken off at night to 'be cleaned and mended'.[34] Moreover the tailor 'will receive his orders from the wardrobe or the Aiutante di Camera in respect of work to be done on the clothes of His Royal Highness'.[35] Interestingly, the division between the functions of care for the person and for apparel remains blurred despite the official differentiation of responsibilities. Moreover, there is considerable overlap between the roles of looking after the body of the master, and what covers and ornaments it, and the maintenance of the setting in which the master spends his time in private. The duties of the Aiutante do in fact extend to the care of the immediate surroundings, he is responsible for the cleanliness and decorum of the Chamber. The Garzoni who are his subordinates have to carry out 'all the menial functions pertaining to the Chamber', namely 'keeping the apartments of the master clean by sweeping up every day and every time they might be dirtied'. Assisted by the Garzoni, the Aiutante must then see to the creation of an environment which is not only clean but comfortable and 'fitting' for the needs of the master. It is he who has to light the candles and have the fireplaces lit in the Chamber, regulating light and heat not merely in accordance with the season and time of day, but also with circumstances.[36] The Urbino protocols also make much of these skills for the Cameriere, but since they are as ever more explicit, they give us a greater appreciation of the delicacy of these functions.

> Let there be fires at all times in the Chamber when it is the season, greater and lesser according to the weather. And thus lights atop the candlesticks in fitty manner the Chamber until my lord should rest, and let these lights be increased or diminished *according to company or solitude and whether there are strangers or not, and all with discretion'* (my italics).[37]

The explicit advice about the diverse situations and kinds of encounters that can occur in the Chamber reminds us that this apparently mechanical task in reality requires a notable degree of perspicacity. We can also see from these words how much the lower-ranking staff in the Chamber are witness to the most personal and confidential meetings that come about in this place which is inaccessible to the majority, and therefore how appropriate is the reminder of the 'discretion' which is required in their duties. In the Chamber the master receives messages, private or semi-public visits, he confers with advisers and has amatory encounters. The Aiutante comes to know not only who is visiting, but for what purpose. He is used to announce the visitors or act as a filter for the visits: 'moreover, anyone wishing to speak with him [His Highness] or to have something written delivered' will be sent by the doorkeeper to the gentleman on duty in the Chamber or other gentlemen 'to let us know what he wishes', and should these be absent he will tell the Aiutante di Camera who will inform the master directly.[38]

Now this variegated figure whose work entails sweat, perfumes, personal and bed linen, bodily hygiene and propriety of dress, the lighting and heating of the apartments and access to them, is frequently a barber or a surgeon. Service in the Chamber in other words makes explicit that continuity between purging, cleaning, corporeal well-being and appearance which is a key to understanding the figure of the surgeon in this period. This perspective of continuity is confirmed by the fact that the same barbers and surgeons whom we find numbered among the staff of the Chamber occupy posts which appear to us as fully 'medical' in the society outside the court: namely they can be the chief surgeon in a hospital, a military surgeon or a municipal Surgeon to the Poor. The professional biography of Giò Francesco Meda offers an example. In the 1680s he was employed at court as surgeon to the household staff of Princess Ludovica, a post earlier held by his uncle Giulio Cesare, though with the title of 'barber'. In 1686 he was promoted to the dual role of Aiutante di Camera and surgeon to the Princess Ludovica, a function he held until 1692, when he took his leave of the court to join the army as a military surgeon. In parallel with the court posts however, from 1680 he was also senior surgeon at the Carità hospital (another post which he gave up when he left on the military campaign). Bernardino Brucho is an analogous case, even though when he arrived at court he was already an established surgeon: he had been the surgeon at the hospital of San Giovanni since the 1630s and municipal Surgeon to the Poor by the time he became the Aiutante di Camera to Prince Maurizio in 1654. In 1660 we encounter him as a member of the 'University of Surgeons and Barbers'.[39] Pietro Anto Gorgia was Aiutante to the Princess Ludovica between 1650 and 1671, after having been an *Infermiere* (a term designating any 'young surgeon' employed in the hospital) at the San Giovanni. These biographical features show how care for health and for appearances, even in the work experience of an individual, turn out to be more connected than it is generally assumed.

Kinship between occupations

The convergence of aesthetic, hygienic and surgical functions concerns not only individual biographies but family biographies, it is replicated in the occupations of various members of a kinship group. We have already observed that in the Chamber the barber-surgeons worked back-to-back with craftsmen who specialised in the adornment of the body and the creation of an environment conducive to well-being. These were upholsterers, jewellers and tailors who featured as part of the Chamber personnel in the official roles of Upholsterer, Keeper of Jewels and Keeper of the Wardrobe. In the course of their careers, each of these figures, the court upholsterers in particular, were also extremely likely to occupy the post of either Aiutante di Camera or *Usciere di Camera* (Doorkeeper of the Chamber). What is interesting is that these occupations were frequently to be found clustered within the same family. If we look at recurring occupations within the kinship network of a barber-surgeon we can see that he may very well have been related to other surgeons and barbers, but also frequently to perruquiers, upholsterers, jewellers and, although less so, to tailors. In other words we shall find that his brothers and his sons work in

Figure 3.1 Giò Francesco Meda and his kin

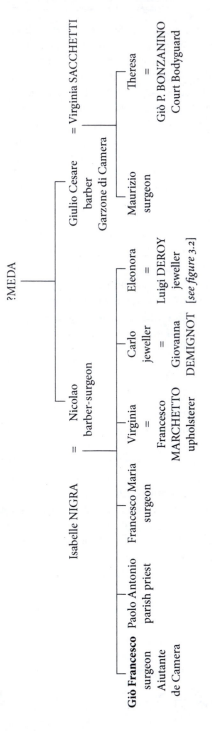

these occupations, likewise the brothers of his wife, and the husbands of his daughters and sisters.

Let us take the case of Giò Francesco Meda, whom we have already encountered in his dual role as senior surgeon in one of the city hospitals and as Aiutante di Camera at court (see figure 3.1). He followed in the professional footsteps of his father, the surgeon Nicolao, as did his younger brother, Francesco Maria, who later inherited their father's shop. The third brother, Carlo, became a jeweller and married Giovanna Demignot the daughter of an upholsterer, while the fourth brother entered the Church and became a parish priest in a small town outside Turin. There were also two sisters, Virginia and Eleonora, who respectively married an upholsterer, Francesco Marchetto, and a jeweller, Luigi Deroy.

Let us turn now to the occupations of the generation before them: the brother of Nicolao, father of the Meda siblings, was Giulio Cesare, barber to the royal pages and subsequently Garzone di Camera to Prince Maurizio. His son was the surgeon Maurizio, while his daughter, Teresa Margherita, married Giò Pietro Bonzanino, a bodyguard to Madama Reale (the duchess). With few exceptions therefore, the same professions crop up repeatedly in the kinship network.

If we then consider the kinship network of the Meda siblings' spouses, we find the same pattern. Let us look at the occupations and marital connections of the siblings of jeweller Luigi Deroy, Eleanora Meda's husband (see figure 3.2). His brother, Giuseppe, was a surgeon and his sister Teresa married a jeweller, Enrico Vautier. If we go back a generation we see that the Deroys were the children of a surgeon, Domenico Deroy, and that he married the daughter of a Garzone di Camera, Eustachio Pastor. Eustachio's two other daughters respectively married a barber, Margheri, and an Usciere di Camera, Gambino, while the only sister of Domenico Deroy, Lucia, married an upholsterer, Giacomo Verna. If we consider the kinship network of the latter (see figure 3.3) we see that the Verna sisters (Deroy's cousins), Caterina and Paula, respectively married a perruquier and a surgeon, the Fassina brothers, and that the third Fassina brother was a *baigneur* at court and the husband of an upholsterer's daughter (Anna Franca Marchetta), while their sister, Camilla, was the wife of the perruquier Bert. The father of the Fassina siblings, Carlo Amedeo, was a barber-surgeon. Giuseppe, the Vernas' third son, was, however, a merchant. A similar pattern appears in the kinship networks of two other Meda spouses, Francesco Marchetto and Giovanna Demignot; they come from families where there is a predominance of upholsterers (and they are already mutually related through the marriage between Leonora Marchetto and Michel Antonio Demignot) and where there are

Figure 3.2 Luigi Deroy and his kin

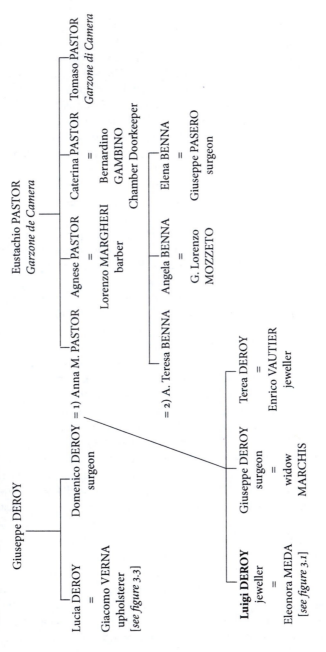

marital connections not only with other upholsterers (Sigismondo Cigna) but with jewellers (Meschiatis) and physicians (Capellis).

Further examples could be given, though at the risk of tedium, if we were to linger and consider the same range of professions within any of these kinship networks. The sister of the barber Lorenzo Margheri (mentioned above; see figure 3.2) married the goldsmith Mareni, and although we do not know their father's occupation, we know that their stepfather, the second husband of their widowed mother Lucretia, was the surgeon Ludovico Paysio. Margheri's son would in turn become a barber and would marry the sister of a tailor, Gerolamo Troja. The point is that if we consider the bilateral kinship network we can see an extraordinary recurrence of professions: as well as jewellers and goldsmiths (the distinction between these two occupations seems tenuous), upholsterers, perruquiers, perfumers and tailors. We also encounter instances of the medical professions (physicians, apothecaries, as well as *droghisti*: grocers who supplied both apothecaries and lay clients with the raw materials for medical remedies), even though there are fewer of these than we might expect. Finally, we find individuals engaged as Bodyguards and Doorkeepers to the Chamber at court, along with *Credenzieri* and Sommeliers. As we shall see from other examples in this and later chapters, the tendency to form kinship relations within a restricted range of occupations was not restricted to the court environment but a constant even among individuals who were not employed at court. Moreover, many members of the kinship networks I have studied here have no personal connections with the court.

If we consider that the 'Registry of Traders and Artists' compiled in 1742 lists around 100 occupations carried out in the city of Turin, while the more detailed census of 1705 shows as many as 290, we can see what restricted choices our artisans made in terms of marriage and career.[40] There seems to have been a 'kinship' between trades, such that men engaged in a limited range of occupations come to share both blood ties and marriage ties. Thus the first question that arises is: why were these individuals apt to enter into alliances? What is it that binds together occupations so seemingly remote to us as those of the upholsterer and the surgeon? What do they have in common? These questions are all the more significant since, as we shall see below, there is a substantial overlap between the kinship and social networks of the barber-surgeons. The answers depend upon us jettisoning the way in which we think of these occupations today and exploring the precise reality of an upholsterer, a jeweller or a tailor's activities in the early modern period, and what these craftsmen's expertise might consist of. This investigation into the

Figure 3.3 Giacomo Verna and his kin

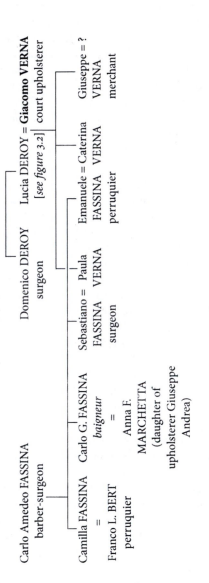

professional culture of some early modern occupations will demonstrate, I hope, that their binding connections cannot simply be explained in terms of similar economic status or rank, nor shared technical know-how. Rather, I will suggest that in their everyday practice these occupations had a common field of values and concerns. So let us return to court in order to investigate the sphere of activity of these servants of the household, and attempt to map their cultural profile.

Jewellers, tailors, upholsterers

Even in the work of the jeweller, the tailor and the upholsterer we find that the care of personal appearance and environment is greatly allied with concerns relating to the client's physical and mental health. We need to bear in mind that at this time precious stones functioned not just to ornament the body but to protect and care for it. They were not viewed as inanimate objects but as active forces; they had the magical value of amulets against the evil eye, against accidents and misfortunes, and they served as a shield against epidemics and infections. They were also endowed with specific therapeutic powers in relation to particular diseases. Moreover, they had an effect on temperament; different stones were seen as conveying specific emotions and were used to reinforce desirable character traits perhaps lacking in the personality of an individual: courage, resolve, purity, etc. According to the precepts of classical medicine body and mind were closely connected; each somatic type corresponded to a specific psychological type. Any imbalance in the bodily humours would also be translated into an alteration in psychic equilibrium and, conversely, the emotions had a somatic impact. The mental health of the patient therefore fell fully within the domain of the carer, and the remedies prescribed by the latter aimed to influence the individual's emotional balance as well as physical equilibrium.[41]

Precious stones were in every respect regarded as medicinal remedies, and as such they appeared in the pharmacopoeia, and among the items sold by the apothecary.[42] Once brought into contact with the body, they irradiated their special qualities to the diseased organ – in yet another confirmation that the skin was perceived as a permeable element. Ground up, jewels were common ingredients of potions to be taken by mouth as remedies for specific diseases or states of mind. The books of receipts, which circulated among healers of different kinds and even reached a lay readership, fostering the practice of domestic medicine, also carried medicinal remedies based on precious stones. The *Ricettario Fiorentino*, first published in 1499 but still in print and in use during the second half of the seventeenth century, prescribed elixirs made from fragments of emeralds, garnets, sapphires, rubies and the gem known as hyacinth.[43] Thus the seventeenth-century receipt book by the apothecary Domenico Auda, which went into several editions in the course of the century, carries among its 'chemical secrets' prescriptions for confecting essence, salts and oil of pearls or corals, as well as a 'magistery' of gems and other precious stones.[44]

The treatises on the 'virtues' of gems (the word itself is meaningful), had roots deep within the works of natural philosophy by the ancients (Dioscorides, Aristotle, Pliny, Avicenna, etc.), yet they continued to circulate in printed and manuscript form during the early modern period. These make clear the particular powers of each stone.[45] For instance, the *Tesoro delle gioie* printed in Venice in 1670, tells us that the hyacinth 'gives freedom from the danger of plague, fortifies the heart, fosters cheerfulness, banishes sadness, invigorates the limbs and promotes sleep'; a topaz 'placed upon a wound staunches the blood, secondly works against haemorrhoids, thirdly against delirium, fourthly against rage, fifthly against fitful passions, sixthly and finally against melancholy'.[46] It is therefore conceivable that when jewellers obtained gems for their clients they did so not solely on the basis of aesthetic judgment but also in terms of the client's 'complexion', which is to say his or her humoral balance as revealed in physical characteristics, not to say psychological type.[47] Which virtues of mind and body did this individual need at that particular time? For example, if a woman were close to confinement it was thought that the symbol of the Lamb of God or the pelican would protect her from related hazards; corals were used in particular to safeguard the health of children; the sapphire exalted chastity and humility, the pearl purity; emeralds quickened hope, rubies charity; topazes were a treatment for sadness. The figures on the jewels likewise had significant values: the snake and the dragon for example gave protection from poisons (one of the great fears of the early modern period).[48] Despite the attack launched on superstitious practices by the Counter-Reformation Church, this magical value that jewels possessed did not decline in the period in question; indeed, the late sixteenth and the seventeenth centuries saw the development of the religious gemstone, in particular the reliquary in the form of a medal worn around the neck, or of a ring, and prayers carved on gems, further augmented their power. Thus the gemstone continued to exercise its protective and miraculous power through its contact with the body, although now this power no longer derived just from the precious stone but also from the sacred materials incorporated into the gem: the fragments of the body of the saint enclosed in it, substances from sacred places such as the earth from Jerusalem or the Lamb of God made out of Paschal wax from the Roman basilicas, or else prayers written inside it.[49]

In this light, the know-how employed by the jeweller and the kind of service he offered to the client may seem less remote from the skills and competence of the barber-surgeon than might have appeared at first sight. A concern for the health and well-being of the client as well as for his or her ornament and physical appearance were central to his professional practice. An analogous argument can be made regarding the tailor who provides the body with its covering, balancing ornament and protection according to the rules dictated by humoral theory. The colours of the fabrics, like those of the gemstones, were linked with aspects of the personality, promoting spiritual endowments and thereby impacting on the mental and physical health of the wearer.[50] Moreover, each 'complexion', that is specific cocktail of humours, was to be matched by particular colours.[51] Significantly, barbers and surgeons' treatises sometimes specified the colour of the cloths that should be used in treatments, for example in dressing wounds.

However strange this may appear, the upholsterer's sphere of expertise was quite close to that of the barber-surgeon. Both at court and among the nobility, during this period the upholsterer was not so much someone who made wall hangings and coverings for furniture as someone who supplied, cleaned, fitted and repaired them. The local manufacture of wall hangings developed late in Turin and yet for a long time the number of shops was restricted.[52] The most luxurious tapestries and wall-hangings were therefore picked out and purchased by the upholsterer on trips to France or Flanders; in addition he would see to the upholstering of furniture and, more generally, take care of every aspect of room furnishings, even the most trivial -- for instance, he would see to making up the waxed fabrics for windows, provide nails and cords for hangings and upholstery, and he would pay porters.[53] The upholsterer also took care of the great variety of textiles found in the Chamber (wall and bed-coverings, bed-curtains, carpets, cushions) and of furniture, keeping them clean and in good order, and protecting them from humidity and insects. The upholsterer:

> upon our awakening shall enter our Chamber wearing neither hat, cloak nor sword, to draw back the bed curtains and open those at the windows; when we go to mass he shall enter to clean the bedding, tablecloths, chairs and upholstery. And he shall take particular care of all the upholstery, beds, furniture and other things of which he has been made custodian. And he shall take particular pains that said furniture is placed in a good dry room, upon tables, avoiding any damage from

rats, or moths, or rain from the roof. And in the case of anything being broken or spoiled, he shall repair it or see to its repair. And he shall keep a general inventory of everything under his care.[54]

In this sense the functions of the court upholsterer are in alignment with those of the Aiutante di Camera: it is he who sets up a decorous and healthy domestic environment for his master or mistress, and is responsible for the comfort of the spaces in which he or she moves.[55]

We should bear in mind that during this period the room resembles a kind of stage-set which is continually rearranged; like clothing, domestic furnishings are subject to alteration and are adapted to whatever events or meetings are to take place in the room. Thus the upholsterer completely alters the furnishings as circumstances dictate, as well as the tapestries and wall hangings, the tablecloths and floor rugs, the chairs, cushions and bed draperies which match the upholsteries. Like the Aiutante di Camera, the upholsterer has the task of interpreting the moods and requirements of the master in his arrangement of an appropriate environment. He too calibrates the colours and patterns of the upholstery, conscious of their emotional impact, and chooses the right furniture for ensuring the comfort of any guests in the room as appropriate to the circumstances. Furniture was also changed seasonally, another feature of the strong analogy that contemporaries established between the body, which required different cures in different periods of the year, and the domestic environment.[56] Finally, the upholsterer was responsible for the ventilation of the premises, a delicate task when one considers the threats that are deemed to lurk in the air, then regarded as the chief carrier of infections.[57]

Historians have drawn attention to the role that medical theory at the time attributed to the quality of the environment in the preservation of health and the prevention of disease. Thus far, however, research has focused on the external surrounding, on the world outside the home.[58] In reality the domestic environment too was viewed as having a powerful effect on the mental conditions and the balance of humours, and indirectly on health: in addition to colours, which could be pleasant and restful or, by contrast, could unleash negative passions, importance was given to the degree of light and the ambient temperature (excessive heat or cold were seen as emphasising certain humours or depressing others). Comfort mattered too: the gentleman's well-being could be harmed by too much softness, but equally by over-Spartan surroundings. All of these environmental states were regulated by the court Upholsterer or the Aiutante di Camera. In a period when a crucial advice for maintaining health is the need to rest and refresh the body, never overdoing physical exertions (which lead to loss of weight, which 'hinder sleep and sap strength, which also give rise to fevers and are the root of many infirmities, and make the individual melancholy'), the roles of these artisans of the body become equally central.[59]

Artisans of the body: a culturally defined milieu

Perhaps now we can return to the questions we raised to start with: why is it that occupations so disparate as those of the barber-surgeon, the jeweller and upholsterer are so often conjoined in the family and individual network, why do marriage partners choose one another from such a limited range of trades, and why do these same occupations appear foremost in their choice of careers? I would like to argue that the occupations in question form a common culture of the body. What holds them together is their involvement in different aspects of the care and protection of the master's body, its appearance, health, comfort, rest, nourishment, privacy and security. In their relationship with their clients, these 'artisans of the body' speak a common language; they have a similar field of expertise, knowledge and concern.

In studies of artisans, occupations tend to be classified in modern terms which fail to ask what these might have involved in the period in question. This has frequently prevented us from appreciating any alignment between trades which in our own time appear remote from one another. Recurring alliances between particular trades have often been observed; sometimes these form joint corporations whose reasons for association remain obscure to us. Referring specifically to the barber-surgeons of the sixteenth and early seventeenth centuries, Pelling tells us about the English city guilds in which they were allied with the wax-chandlers, hardwaremen, hatters, cappers, skinners, 'wyedrawers' and cardmakers. Pelling also shows us that they were frequently associated with the making of nets and of musical instruments, as well as the malting, brewing and selling of alcoholic drinks.[60] In terms of matrimonial choices, Claire Dolan has observed in her study of the artisans of Aix-en-Provence that 'people of certain trades or families intermarried tightly among one another, while among other trades or families networks of marriage extended over a wider area but nonetheless remained intelligible.'[61]

The reasons given to explain these regular but often unexpected combinations between trades relate partly to poverty and the barber-surgeon's need to undertake supplementary occupations which could be carried out in his shop when work was scarce – such as the making of bowstrings, lace, silk fringes and purses. These also relate to the services offered at the barber's shop, which included musical performances and the serving of drinks.[62] Another classic set of explanations postulates a resemblance of techniques and technologies between some trades, for example between barbering and wigmaking, which both work with the hair and employ similar tools, such as scissors and curling implements.[63] There are additional references to these craftsmen's participation in different stages of the same productive process, or to the circulation of raw materials between the trades in question; if we stick with the same example, the barber cuts hair and supplies the wigmaker with the material necessary to make wigs. Claire Dolan, for example, has suggested that the frequency of marriages between carders and leatherworkers in sixteenth-century Aix-en-Provence can be explained by the fact that both of these occupations are based on the transformation of the wool and hides of sheep and goats.[64] In many instances these explanations are well-founded and valid, but other aspects of the matrimonial patterns encountered by Dolan remain largely unaccounted for. Moreover, none of these explanations accounts for the inter-trade ties found in the kinship networks of the Turin surgeons (for example the association between surgeons and jewellers or upholsterers).

While the interpretations offered so far are mainly concerned with experience of the trade at a practical and economic level, I would like to suggest a link between these apparently unconnected occupations at a discursive level: the concerns for the health and well-being of the client, patient or master that are shared by the wig-maker, barber, surgeon, tailor, jeweller and upholsterer. I would argue that these 'artisans of the body' constitute a culturally homogeneous occupational milieu. In the services they provide they strive to make the body healthy, attractive and comfortable by their care and treatment of the figure, the hair, the complexion, and any physical scars. They also act on the surrounding domestic environment. To these ends they use medical remedies, beauty products, clothing, jewels and pleasant interior decor. Their common professional ethos explains why they are so frequently found in association, often establishing kinship ties with one another.

I believe that this principle also serves to explain the presence within the barber-surgeons' kinship networks of figures such as the Bodyguard or the Doorkeeper, whom we have encountered in the kinship networks examined above (I am referring to Giò Pietro Bonzanino and Bernardino Gambino in figures 3.1 and 3.2), as well as those office-holders assigned to the table of a prince or princess, such as the Sommelier and the Credenziere. If we add yet another component to our kinship networks (see figure 3.1), and look at the composition of Nicolao Meda's network, we see that the latter's brother, the barber Giulio Cesare, was married to Virginia

Sacchetti, the daughter of the Sommelier and Credenziere Giacomo, and that Virginia's two brothers inherited their father's two roles. Like the occupations considered above, these are also services that share a single ethos of protecting the master's body and his privacy. The Doorkeepers control access to the apartments of members of the court, identifying those who may enter and those who may not, and they make sure that those loitering in the antechamber are kept away from the doors 'so that they cannot hear what is being talked about'.

The Bodyguard is in charge of the safety of the master, especially outside the palace, and he guarantees protection from threatening external agents. Within the Chamber and dining hall this same task is performed by the Aiutante and the Doorkeeper, together with the Sommelier and Credenziere.[65] The Sommelier provides the drinks, especially the wine, purchasing it and serving it. He is responsible therefore for the quality of this substance which is regarded as an essential component of the diet for its nourishing and therapeutic powers. He is directly involved in the prince's safety, since it is his job to taste any drinks before they are served to him – a task which, significantly, is performed by the Aiutante di Camera whenever a meal is served in his private apartments.

The Credenziere takes care of the table linen, its cleanliness and the appearance of the table.[66] Special effort is deployed to make sure that this is always snow-white, and to this end tablecloths, serviettes and other linen are changed every day, even at the table of minor officers. The value placed on the neatness of the table is analogous to the care applied in this period to personal underwear and bed linen (the domain of the Aiutante di Camera), which must be spotless and tidy, and discreetly on display to prove the virtue of the person; here, by extension, the linen displays the virtue of the house. Like the Sommelier, the Credenziere also performs protective functions for the sake of the prince's safety, for he is the one who tastes the water in which the prince or princess will wash their hands before and after the meal.

Bear in mind that the attraction between those I have described as 'artisans of the body' does not merely derive from the fact that they happen to work in the same physical environment, namely the Chamber of a member of the ducal family. Not only are many members of the same kinship networks outsiders to the court, but those who do work as servants in such roles are often employed in different households, in the service of different individuals. They are therefore 'work fellows' in only a remote sense. Moreover, to a certain degree their kinship networks also extend beyond the Chamber, to other areas of the court: Credenzieri and Bodyguards are for example part of the House and are answerable to the

Master of the House.[67] It is noteworthy, however, that out of so many occupations carried on within the court, those most intertwined in terms of family and social connections are the ones that present similarities through their functions in relation to the master's body.

Even if we stay within the court, setting out to understand the logic of alliance between court employees, we should think in terms of cultural proximity rather than physical or social proximity. For one thing, the idea that individuals come together according to their common level of status, a notion frequently used to explain the patterns of matrimonial choice, does not really hold water, for as we shall soon see, defining the status of an occupational group is somewhat problematic. The kinship between trades we have identified can better be explained as the expression of a culturally defined occupational milieu with the same shared language of skills and with similar professional values. The concept of occupational milieu is crucial for many reasons: on the one hand, as we shall see later, it forms the context in which the reproduction of the trade and its apprenticeship take place. On the other it raises questions concerning the place that barber-surgeons occupied in society.

Notes

1 The Savoy court worked on the model of the court of Burgundy which also adopted the rotation of courtiers and court employees. On the social effects of this system, which multiplied the number of those involved at court and therefore the links between court and society, see W. Paravicini, 'Structure et fonctionnement de la cour bourguignonne au XVe siècle', in J. M. Cauchies and G. Chittolini (eds), *Milano e Borgogna, Due Stati Principeschi tra Medioevo e Rinascimento* (Rome, 1990), pp. 78–9.

2 Some sixteenth-century examples are mentioned in P. Merlin, *Tra Guerre e Tornei. La Corte Sabauda nell'Età di Carlo Emanuele I* (Turin, 1991), pp. 150–3.

3 The information on careers of court employees is derived from the patents of appointment (PCF) and the orders for stipends, gifts and reimbursements for goods supplied found in the accounts of the various households that make up the court between 1650 and 1712. These are the households of Prince Maurizio (brother of the Duke), of his widow, Princess Ludovica, of the dukes and of the duchesses (AST, s.r., Art. 221, 402, 404, 405, 217 and 219, par.1).

4 The personal apothecary is also the one who tastes the medicines administered to the master when he is sick. 'Memorie per il regolamento' of 1679, paragraph thirty-two (see note 9 and 14).

5 See for example the papers regarding Giò Nicot, defined as Garzone or valet to Carlo Emanuele I in AST, s. I, *Cerimoniale*, m.1.

6 See for example the patents, dated 1592, for Giò Novello, *ibid*.

7 As with many other court functions a differentiation comes about of the duties carried out in the Chamber, prompted also by the emergence of a newly created section, the Wardrobe (placed under the purview of the Maestro di Guardaroba, who is in turn

subordinate to the Great Chamberlain). This complicates the original division of the ducal households into three sections: the Chamber (*Camera*), the Stable (*Scuderia*), and the House (*Casa*), which are managed respectively by the *Gran Ciambellano* (the Chamberlain), the *Gran Scudiere* (the Equerry) and the *Gran Maestro di Casa* (the Master of the Household). The process of specialisation of court roles from the late sixteenth century is common to other European courts. See for example J. F. Solnon, *La Cour de France* (Paris, 1987), pp. 44–5. For a helpful overview, see M. A.Visceglia, 'Corti italiane e storiografia europea', *Dimensioni e Problemi della Ricerca Storica*, 2 (2004).

8 PCF 1631–2, fo. 170; 1654 fo. 213.

9 As well as from the sources cited in n. 2, what follows is based on the analysis of two court regulations, one undated but likely to have been issued in the 1640s or 50s (see below, n. 14), the other drawn up in 1679: 'Ticheta'; 'Memorie per il regolamento'.

10 For interesting remarks on the low-ranking staff, albeit not specifically on the Aiutanti, see M. Fantoni, *La Corte del Granduca. Forma e Simboli del Potere Mediceo fra Cinque e Seicento* (Rome, 1999), chapters two, three and four; P. Peruzzi, 'Lavorare a corte: 'Ordine et Officij'. Domestici, familiari, cortigiani e funzionari al servizio del Duca d' Urbino', in G. Carboni Baiardi, G. Chittolini and P. Floriani (eds), *Federico di Montefeltro*, vol. 1, *Lo Stato* (Rome, 1986); G. Castelnuovo, '"À la court et au service de nostre prince': l'hôtel de Savoie et ses métiers à la fin du Moyen Âge', in L. C. Gentile and P. Bianchi (eds), *L'Affirmazione della Corte Sabauda: Dinastie Poteri ed Elites fra Savoia e Piemonte dal Basso Medioevo alla Prima Età Moderna* (Turin, 2006).

11 'Ticheta', p. 7; 'Memorie per il regolamento', paragraph twenty-one.

12 'Memorie per il regolamento', paragraphs twenty-two, three, eight, fifteen and twenty-one; 'Ticheta', p.7.

13 'Memorie per il regolamento', paragraph eighteen.

14 'Ticheta', p. 8. This is the household of Prince Tommaso, the brother of the Duke. The document appears without a date but it can be dated to the 1640s or 1650s. The fact that it refers to a period following the death of Tommaso's father, Vittorio Amedeo, in 1637, can be deduced from the section on the ushers of the Chamber, which reads 'they will permit entry to all the noble gentlemen and others as higher servants either of the *late* Duke our Lord father or of [...] Prince Maurizio my brother'. Given that Tommaso was engaged in active warfare until the peace of 1645, living at Ivrea until 1648, it is likely that the document refers to the period subsequent to his return to the court in Turin, namely between 1648 and 1656, the year of his death.

15 'Memorie per il regolamento', paragraph eighteen. Whenever the master ate in his personal apartments, it likewise fell to the gentlemen-in-waiting to lay the table, with the help of the Aiutanti, but only when the master was present; if the master was not in the Chamber during the laying of the table, this task was carried out by the Aiutanti. (*ibid.*, paragraph fifteen).

16 *Ibid.*, paragraph twenty-one.

17 *Ibid.*, paragraph twenty-four.

18 'Ticheta', p. 3.

19 'Memorie per il regolamento', paragraph twenty-one.

20 'Ticheta', p. 8.

21 D. Starkey, 'Intimacy and innovation: the rise of the Privy Chamber 1485–1547', in D. Starkey et al., *The English Court from the War of the Roses to the Civil War* (London,

1987).

22 'Memorie per il regolamento', paragraph twenty-one.

23 AST, s. I, *Cerimoniale*, m.1. This is usually the elevation to 'noble of the Holy Roman Empire' which entailed neither titles nor feudal incomes. Even in this earlier period it was exceptional that an Aiutante obtained feudal possessions. Examples include the barber Courtet and the surgeon Aurelio Malpenga. Merlin: *Tra Guerre*, pp. 152–3.

24 There is some controversy about the precise date of these regulations. See Peruzzi, 'Lavorare a corte', p. 241 n. 51; p. 244 n. 56.

25 S. Eiche (ed.), *Ordine et Officij de Casa de lo Illustrissimo Signor Duca d'Urbino* (Urbino, 1999), pp. 98–102.

26 By contrast, the ceremonial aspect is almost absent from the Urbino ordinances, which tend to be practical instructions.

27 N. Elias, *La Civiltà delle Buone Maniere* (Bologna, 1982), pp. 257–310.

28 'Ticheta', p. 10.

29 AST, s. I, Art. 405, 1655, p. 38. As in other establishments of this kind, the term *caldara* does not refer to a cauldron for the boiling of water but rather to a stew that produced the heat necessary to create a sauna-like environment: Pediconi, 'The art and culture of bathing', pp. 148–50.

30 This is the term designating the *Femme de Chambre*, on whom see below, chapter seven.

31 For example, Giuseppe Stura was appointed Barber to the young Duke in 1676. PCF, 1676, reg. 1, fo. 182. In 1682 Luigi Moriceau was named 'barber and *baigneur*' of Duke Vittorio Amedeo II. In a patent dated 1682 he is described as 'barber and stover' that is *baigneur*': *Ibid.*, 1682, fo. 44.

32 AST, s. r., Art. 217 reg.169, 1705.

33 'Ticheta', p. 12.

34 *Ibid.*, p. 9.

35 *Ibid.*, p. 12.

36 *Ibid.*, p. 15; 'Memoria di regolamento', paragraph twenty-four.

37 Eiche, *Ordini*, p. 99.

38 'Ticheta', p. 8.

39 For the court functions of the Medas and the Brucos, see AST, s. r., Art. 402, 1652; Art. 405, 1655, 1689–90; Art. 221, m. 4, 1692.

40 'Stato dei negozianti e artisti ... 1742'; Rondolino, *Vita Torinese*, pp. 47 ff.

41 Examples of this link in diagnoses and in the complaints of patients are given in Duden, *The Woman*, pp. 140–8.

42 E. Merlo, 'Gli speziali milanesi nel Settecento. Storie di antidoti e affari di droghe', in A. Guenzi, P. Massa and F. Piola Caselli (eds), *Corporazioni e Gruppi Professionali* (Milan, 1999), p. 683.

43 *Ricettario Fiorentino di nuovo illustrato* (Florence: Vangelisti, Vincenzo & Matini Piero, 1670), book XII.

44 *Il Breve Compendio*, pp. 159–61.

45 Among the most popular sixteenth-century treatises are C. Leonardi, *Speculum Lapidum* (Venice, 1516), still reprinted in 1717, and *Libri Tre di M. Ludovico Dolce nei quali si tratta delle diverse sorti di pietre che produce la natura* (Venice, 1565). See also the manuscript by Agostino Del Riccio (d. 1598), *Istoria delle Pietre*, ed. R. Gnoli and A. Sironi, Turin 1979. For the seventeenth century see C. Arnobio, *Tesoro delle gioie*,

trattato curioso, nel quale si dichiara breuemente la virtu, qualita e proprieta delle gioie ... Raccolto dall'Academico Ardente Etereo (Venice, 1670; 1st edn, 1602).

46 *Ibid.*, pp. 16–18, 10–11.

47 On the concept of 'complexion', see Siraisi, *Medieval ... Medicine*, pp. 101–4, 131.

48 P. Venturelli, *Gioielli e Gioiellieri Milanesi. Storia, Arte, Moda (1450–1630)* (Cinisello Balsamo, 1996), p. 134; J. Musacchio, 'Weasels and pregnancy in Renaissance Italy', *Renaissance Studies*, 15:2 (2001), and 'Lambs, Coral, Teeth, and the Intimate Intersection of Religion and Magic in Renaissance Italy', in S. J. Cornelison and S. B. Montgomery (eds), *Images, Relics, and Devotional Practices in Medieval and Renaissance Italy*, Medieval and Renaissance Texts and Studies, V. 296 (Tempe, 2005).

49 Venturelli, *Gioielli*, pp. 128–40. Jewels had been receptacles of protective and miraculous substances in earlier period. In the fifteenth century there had been a fashion for perfumed jewels, which combined precious metals with amber or musk paste, substances which were meant to purify the air of contagious vapours. These took the form of pendants worn around the neck or on belts, or else in a pomander, a small sphere pierced with holes around the size of a nut – through these apertures it exhaled the health-giving perfumes of the herbs or other substances contained in it. On scapulars and Lambs of God worn inside the clothing, see L. Borello, 'Reliquie a Torino. Memorie sconosciute da scoprire', in *BSBS*, C:2 (2002), pp. 561–2; Cavallo, 'Health'.

50 On the sixteenth-century treatises on colours, which continued to be reprinted in the following century, see M. Brusatin, *Storia dei Colori* (Turin, 1983), pp. 52–5. An example is G. P. Lomazzo, *Trattato dell'Arte della Pittura, Scoltura e Architettura* (Milan, 1585), in particular book 2, chapter XI.

51 *Ibid.*, book 2, chapter XIX.

52 When a request was eventually made to form a company in 1738, there were only twenty-one master upholsterers. (AST, Cat. IV, m. 1, fasc. 1, 'Parere del Consiglio di Commercio'.)

53 See for example the payments to the Marchettos (members of the kinship network discussed above), for decorating the church of San Giovanni; for providing waxed blinds for six large windows; for setting up the funeral of Carlo Emanuele II; for seeing that 'tables, stools and door curtains' were made 'to complete the furnishings of the green pavilion'; for the items of furniture supplied for the new Academy of Fine Arts (PCF 1669–70, fo. 189; 1675–76, fo. 198; 1676, fos 14, 205; 1678, fo. 1). For the Demignots, whom we have also encountered earlier, see the payments for the 'repair and maintenance' of all the Flemish tapestries and Turkish rugs (*ibid.*, 1635–6, fo. 19 and 1676, 1°, fo. 227).

54 'Ticheta', pp. 10–11; see also 'Memorie per il regolamento', paragraph 26, 'Funzioni de' tappezzieri di SA'.

55 For example, 'He will see that the *tradi* [sic] and cushions are brought to the place where, each day, the master hears mass ... wherever it is said by the chaplain'. ('Ticheta', p. 11.)

56 'Since our furniture must change with the altering seasons, he shall have the porters help and serve him in this': *ibid.*

57 R. Palmer, 'In bad odour: smell and its significance in medicine from antiquity to the seventeenth century', in W. F. Bynum and R. Porter (eds), *Medicine and the Five Senses* (Cambridge, 1993); M. Jenner, 'Civilisation and deodorisation? Smell in early modern English culture', in P. Burke, B. Harrison and P. Slack (eds), *Civil Histories* (Oxford,

2000).

58 Wear, *Knowledge*, pp. 184–209; A. Wear 'Making sense of health and the environment in early modern England', in A. Wear, *Medicine in Society. Historical Essays* (Cambridge, 1992); Pelling, *Common Lot*, chapter two.

59 'Trattato bellissimo per conservarsi in sanità', in *Il Breve Compendio*, pp. 231, 234; Cavallo, 'Health'.

60 Pelling, *Common Lot*, pp. 222–5. This phenomenon has also been observed in relation to medieval Italian cities. See for example L. Gai, 'Artigiani e artisti nella società pistoiese del basso medioevo', in *Artigiani e Salariati. Il Mondo del Lavoro nell'Italia dei Secoli XII–XV* (Pistoia, 1984), pp. 237–8.

61 C. Dolan, 'The artisans of Aix-en-Provence in the sixteenth century: a micro-analysis of social relationships', in P. Benedict (ed.), *Cities and Social Change in Early Modern France* (London, 1992), p. 181.

62 Pelling, *Common Lot*, pp. 224–5.

63 A. Grandi, 'Il monopolio delle forbici. Il conflitto tra barbieri e parrucchieri a Bologna nel XVIII secolo', in Guenzi, Massa and Piola Caselli, *Corporazioni*, p. 669.

64 Dolan, 'The artisans', p. 182.

65 In the smaller households, the Doorkeeper has complex tasks that go well beyond that of guarding access and overlap with those of the Chamber attendants. In the household of the Prince of Soysson, for example, Giacomo Fegola (known as Giulicoeur) shared with the Garzone di Camera Domenico Nigra the duty of seeing to the bleaching of table linen for the Prince and his staff, and kept up stocks of salt, vinegar, crystals and glass for their table, all in all acting as a kind of housekeeper (AST, s.r., Art. 217, reg. 169, paragraphs twelve and twenty-seven.

66 'Memorie per il regolamento', paragraphs twenty, twenty-two. More precise details of the work carried out by these officials can be deduced from the accounts of the household to which they are attached. In the case of the Sommelier and Credenziere Giacomo Sacchetti, a member of the Meda kinship network, and subsequently of his sons, Pietro Antonio and Giuseppe, who inherited his two posts, see Art. 221, m. 1, reg. 36–43; Art. 404, reg. 1657–70, where we find reimbursement of payments made by him for the 'upkeep of table linen and table ware' and for the provision of wines.

67 For the sections into which the Court is divided see above note seven.

4

The place in society
of artisans of the body

How can artisan status be studied?

E ven though there are no in-depth studies on this question, and there has been an almost exclusive concentration on the social profile of the physician within the medical profession, the generally held view is that the surgeon occupied a social position greatly inferior to that of the physician.[1] While the latter had a university education and has been described as a gentleman and a scholar moving in elite circles, well bred and with a vast range of intellectual interests, it is usually assumed that the surgeon, with his practical training and largely manual occupation, was someone with coarse manners and negligible cultural ambitions who exercised his occupation mainly among 'people of middling and humble means'.[2] And yet, if we address this question more closely, we will become aware of a much more contradictory and even problematic picture.

The first difficulty we encounter is in identifying variables that might help us to pinpoint the social position of our surgeons. It has been widely observed that status is an elusive concept; because it is not defined by any single criterion, we derive differing impressions according to whichever factors we take into account. It is perhaps because of this complexity that historians have often tended to privilege indicators of wealth or income – seemingly straightforward enough to identify – when assessing a person's social worth. In reality, a purely economic definition of status presents many methodological problems. In the first place, economic power is somewhat difficult to define, not just because it often comes about through a range of sources of income, but also because in a society dominated by credit, which is granted on the basis of a person's trustworthiness, spending power might well have little to do with income.[3] In the second place, we must remember that we are dealing with economies which are largely non-monetary: the numerous barbers and surgeons employed in the ducal (and, from 1713, royal) Chamber, in the business of ensuring health or hygiene, were steeped in a gift economy, since the salaries they received (which incidentally were far from pre-established and can therefore be seen as a form of gift) were only one of the advantages bestowed on them by their presence at court.

One possible corrective to a merely economic view of status consists in shifting attention to the ways in which economic power was used, and thus to the style of living, the particular choices made about using income or savings, and what they were spent on. The assumption in this approach is that the manner in which money is spent can differ widely even among people with similar incomes. Living standards are not a mechanical expression of economic possibilities nor are they simply predefined by rank but reflect aspirations of social belonging. It is possible, therefore, to conceive of a form of social stratification based on consumer patterns. If seen from this perspective, where would our barber-surgeons be situated? With whom do they share their consumer aspirations? In what follows I shall begin to investigate some evidence about the patterns of consumption adopted by barber-surgeons and allied occupations, hoping that they may provide new insights into the social position of these categories. I shall consider such things as the use of domestic services expressed in the presence and number of household servants, expenditure on domestic space and on practices that can be regarded as 'holidays', and the kind of possessions that brides brought into their new home.

A long scholarly tradition has already insisted on the limitations of using exclusively economic criteria in defining personal status and suggested that in the early modern period personal value was determined by a hierarchy of honour which only partly corresponds to levels of income and wealth. Privileges ranging from tax exemption to immunity from prosecution, from symbolic rights to the right to bear arms or wear the most sumptuous clothes and jewels were determined by rank (noble rank for example) rather than by mere economic power.[4] This view has been applied also to the lower orders. It appears that in the world of the artisans too occupations were sometimes ranked according to their more or less honourable status. In some German cities, for instance, the business of being a barber-surgeon or a bathmaster would often be associated in symbolic terms with the work of the skinner and the executioner, which were regarded as impure and dishonourable occupations, and this also had certain legal implications. These groups formed in fact a kind of caste of 'untouchables' who were not permitted to mix with other artisans, either socially or through marriage.[5]

Such ideas of purity-impurity, and the resulting stigma borne by

the barber-surgeons, were however not universal; they have no equivalent in the Italian states, perhaps because of the more positive meaning
attributed there to blood and other bodily excretions (as we have seen in
chapter two) and to practises of dissecting the human body.[6] Moreover,
there are serious drawbacks in the procedure of attributing a particular
degree of status to an entire occupation as well as in seeing status as an
immutable, ascribed quality. As it will become apparent in the following
pages, a range of social conditions is to be found within a professional
group and these depend on a variety of factors, other than income and
rank, which we are still in the process of mapping out. In the case of barber-
surgeons, for example, an important principle of internal stratification is
given by the geographical identity of the practitioner: the primacy of the
surgeons active in the capital city by comparison with those operating in
other parts of the state even prompted specific strategies for constructing
identity among those who were originally immigrants but were fashioning
themselves as 'citizens'; it encouraged, for example, property investments
within the city and brought a converse move away from property rights in
native towns and villages. The distinctions between a 'surgeon in Turin', a
surgeon in a provincial town and a surgeon in the villages would eventually be incorporated into the legislation reforming Turin University in
the 1720s and establishing different grades of competence for these three
categories, along with greatly varying tariffs in relation to the payment of
licences.[7]

The social value of a person was therefore changeable and could to
some extent be reinvented. An element often overlooked is that even at
individual level status appears fluid and bound to change at different
points in life (depending on factors such as the personal and family life
cycles, the size of the family, or simply good or bad luck).[8] I shall argue,
moreover, that status depends upon the circles into which someone is
accepted and on degrees of closeness to the wealthy and powerful.
Belonging to the court entourage, and more specifically to the staff of the
Chamber – a very special privilege allowing direct, unmediated access to
a member of the royal family – creates another significant stratification
between surgeons. In addition, it aligns them with other artisans of the
body at the same time as it distances them both from physicians – who
according to the professional hierarchy had precedence over them – and
from the more prosperous apothecaries.

What follows is a far from conclusive account. It aims to sketch out
an initial view of the social position of barber-surgeons from a variety
of often competing perspectives – in terms of property, income, living
standards, material culture and social connections. My analysis will also

indicate some of the problems to be found in this undertaking: the limitations or the ambiguousness of the sources and the poor reliability of many apparent indicators of status.

Property and lifestyle

Undoubtedly, some of the variables relating to the surgeon's lifestyle show this to be of a lower standard than that of the physician and even the apothecary. For example, if we consider how many of the medical practitioners recorded in the census of 1705 have servants living in the home we see that servants are almost the norm in the physician's household, yet this is rarely the case in that of the surgeon. While 79 per cent of the forty-seven physicians and 42 per cent of the thirty-one apothecaries number at least one servant in their own domestic nucleus, only 26 per cent of the ninety-one surgeons have servants, and these are almost exclusively either households in which the head is elderly or unmarried, or else extremely large households (sometimes with relatives from the extended family also living with them). Moreover, with only two exceptions, the surgeons' domestic staff consists of only a single female servant, most probably making up for the scant presence of female labour in these 'elderly', male households.[9] In the homes of those who describe themselves as 'barbers' there are no servants at all. It would seem therefore that, as a rule, the management of the household among the barber-surgeons was the responsibility of the women of the family, while in the physicians' families it was often entrusted to household servants, at least in part.

At first sight, the contrast between lifestyles is also marked if we compare information relating to home ownership: in the same census we find that owner-occupiers account for 14.9 per cent of the physicians, 9.7 per cent of the apothecaries and 7.6 per cent of the surgeons. But this kind of evidence underestimates ownership of the home because it refers to ownership of the entire building or a large part of it (city buildings were in fact called after the majority owner: Casa Meschiatis, Casa Villa, etc.). We know however that the surgeons frequently purchased outright portions of a building, these being apartments that usually extended over several floors. A typical case is that of Domenico Deroy, who in 1672 purchased three rooms with a workshop, two cellars and two mews in the house of the widow Vaccarina, consisting in all of fifteen rooms. The cost was 8,500 lire.[10] Somewhat similar was the apartment (one of the three that made up Casa Marra) that Deroy's brother-in-law, the surgeon Pasero, bought in 1681 for 5,500 lire; it consisted of three rooms and two *gabinetti* (very small rooms) situated over three floors – one of the rooms was a kitchen located on the top floor, with a flat roof over it and one cellar. This property also had a loggia overlooking the communal courtyard and it carried the right to use the common well in it.[11] Fairly similar in its dimensions and its value was the apartment purchased in 1694 by the surgeon Giò Pietro Busano from the widow of a tailor, for 5,555 lire. Here too there were five rooms, one above the other, with three loggias over three floors, two cellars and one smaller cellar, besides of course the workshop and the back of the shop.[12] These and other examples suggest that, at least for well-established surgeons, it was relatively common to be in the position of owning the home in which they lived. They also give us a sense of the domestic and work space to which a surgeon would aspire once he had opened his own shop, started his own family and achieved his first professional successes. In all three examples these are surgeons aged around thirty who have been in business for themselves for some ten years, have been married for seven to eight years and have young children; two of them have only recently gained appointments, respectively as hospital surgeon and municipal Surgeon to the Poor.[13] Ownership of an apartment with a workshop was desirable not only for the sake of the saving in rent it would entail, but also for it secured continuity of fixed premises. Rent contracts for apartments usually had a term of only two or three years.[14] This was probably designed to protect the landlord from tenants defaulting on payments, while for those without any arrears the majority of tenancies were renewed. Whatever the case, the desire for a stable location, which, as we shall see was a feature of the independent surgeons, meant that buying an apartment with a workshop, or at least the workshop itself, was a common aspiration. It was worth buying even a single room with a small cellar, perhaps in partnership, as happened with the surgeons Pietro Calvo and Matteo Stura in 1681.[15] This room would have been Matteo's dwelling, and was probably also used as a shop.

However, the dividing up of buildings in the early modern city makes it somewhat difficult to ascertain the ownership of individual dwellings by the artisans of the body. The extent of property tends to be hard to pin down as we have very few post-mortem inventories available for our surgeons (with even these for the most part relating to the second half of the eighteenth century). We can however form at least an impressionistic notion of their expenditure, by putting together the information drawn from wills, deeds of purchase and other financial transactions which, if concluded in the city, were usually registered in notarial records. It is clear that the majority of the surgeons did not own substantial properties, but very few of them lived only by their work; many sought to purchase at least one form of investment income. This might consist of a *censo*, from a bond of public debt issued by the city or by some other secure source of income.[16] In the case of the surgeon Carlo Antonio Reyneri, this is a cobbler's 'business' (effectively a licence) and workplace, purchased by him half in 1679 and half five years later.[17] He would probably have had no difficulty in renting it out, given its location under the arcades of the royal square.

As his career and his earnings progressed, it was not unusual for a surgeon to invest in buying a 'vigna' on the hills around the city. The term vigna referred to a farmhouse, usually surrounded by vineyards, which, for the better-off inhabitants of Turin, would function as a second home during the summer period.[18] All the aristocratic families had one, and there was even 'Madama Reale's vigna', which is to say the one belonging to the Duchess. This practice, however, was by no means unknown among the middling groups of which the surgeons formed part. For example, in 1707, at the age of thirty-nine, Paolo Bernardo Calvo bought a vigna with two giornate of 'vines and woodland' for 5,000 lire, from the fondighiere (grocer of drugs) Ranghis, who, being of an advanced age, wanted to get rid of it.[19] This was a modest residence (the furniture consisted of six chairs, two tables, two chests and a credenza, six wooden benches and a number of pictures) and it was used not just to provide a place outside the city for passing the summer months, but also as a means of producing wine, a central component of the diet, and perhaps also other foodstuffs.[20] For all that, the existence of the vigna as a property owned by some of the surgeons, marked out their prosperity and high living standards, and probably demonstrated aspirations to a gentility that distanced them from other artisans. It appears that such purchases were usually beyond the immediate means of the surgeons and took them some years to pay off.[21] But it was clearly worthwhile to take on debts in order to acquire this status symbol.

Building up substantial land assets was less common. It emerges that Domenico Deroy had bought a farmhouse at Venaria that his sons later sold, but this is an unusual case. Of the surgeons I have studied in some depth, only Alberto Verna stands out as an investor in land – a venture which would later be continued by his nephew, the surgeon Evasio Andrea, then by the latter's son-in-law, the surgeon Giuseppe Reyneri.[22] In general, property owned by the surgeons appears to have urban roots, and even those with a rural background who at some point inherited farms and pieces of land in the countryside from which they had emigrated, very quickly get rid of these in order to invest the capital thereby released within or around the city.[23] This is one factor that seems to indicate the strong desire of the incomer surgeons to assume a fully urban identity.

Although clear patterns of investment can be seen, there is nonetheless an extreme range of situations in terms of personal assets. There is an enormous gap between the financial circumstances of the surgeon Alberico, who on his death left his wife only 'a few pieces of furniture, insufficient to repay her dowry [amounting to 2,000 lire] and its increase (*aumento*)' and the estate of Alberto Verna, who, in 1737, in legacies alone left annuities from a capital of 9,000 lire, as well as 60 giornate of land from his native countryside and an entire city house in Turin.[24]

The broad range of financial situations is also confirmed by looking at the sums paid or received by the surgeons as dowries. Wedding contracts, which record the amount of the dowry supplied by the bride's family, have often been regarded as one of the most exact tools for establishing the prosperity and status of different families or social groups.[25] Yet in the case of the surgeons we can see an extreme variation in the sums paid; these ranged from the 400 lire paid in 1691 for the marriage of Caterina Coppa to the surgeon Ratti, to the 16,000 pledged in 1721 for the nuptials of Vittoria Chiarmet and the surgeon Evasio Andrea Verna.[26] Admittedly the latter is an exceptional case, in which the bride happened to be the sole heir to the substantial estates of her father, mother, uncle and aunt.[27] Yet even aside from these two extremes there was still a substantial range of variation, giving us a considerably uneven picture of the status of this professional group. Out of forty dowries paid or received by the Turin surgeons between 1651 and 1727, eight (20 per cent) were less than 1,000 lire, nineteen (48.6 per cent) can be placed between 1,000 and 2,000 lire, nine (21 per cent) between 2,001 and 4,000 lire, and only four (9 per cent) reached higher levels: two at 5,000 lire, one at 7,000, while only the aforementioned dowry of the multiple heiress Vittoria Chiarmet rose well above 10,000, a sum commonly found for the dowries of the nobility. This distribution is similar to that of the dowries brought in or handed out by other artisans of the body, even though in this case there is a higher preponderance of dowries in the range between 2,001 and 4,000 lire. Of the twenty dowries pledged between 1667 and 1716, three were below 1,000 lire (15 per cent), seven ranged between 1,000 and 2,000 lire (35 per cent), and nine (41 per cent) between 2,001 and 4,000 lire. Nonetheless a good number were between 2,000 and 4,000 lire, the range for many dowries paid or received by physicians, another group within which dowries offered quite a broad span of values (although the lowest dowry values among physicians were higher than those among barber-surgeons).

The most significant piece of information to emerge from an analysis of the amounts of dowries is therefore that they indicate a high degree of stratification within the profession. But there is something more. This variation in circumstances also offers evidence that, as far as range and aspirations went, status was fairly mobile in the course of an individual's life, a factor rarely considered in discussions of the status of different social groups. Let us observe, for instance, the dowries paid for the marriage of women connected with the surgeon Domenico Deroy. While in 1665 he received 4000 lire as a dowry from his wife Anna Margherita Pastor (without taking into account the bride's *fardello* – the regional term for the trousseau – valued at more than 500 lire), ten years earlier, when Domenico was still a boy and his family was supported only by his widowed mother's work as housekeeper to the Countess of Verrua, his sister Lucia brought only 600 lire to the upholsterer Giacomo Verna.[28] In 1695, at the peak of his career, Domenico was to pay as much as 7,000 lire (and more than 500 for the fardello) at the marriage of his daughter Teresa to the goldsmith Enrico Vautier. But, after his death, his two sons Luigi and Giuseppe, after having had to split their father's estate with their half-brothers from the latter's second marriage, would receive respectively 3,000 and 5,000 lire from their brides Eleonora Meda and the widow Marchis.[29] The dowries paid and received for the sisters, wives, daughters-in-law and daughters of a single individual therefore present substantial variations (between 600 and 7,000 lire!) and they suggest that status cannot be seen as a rigidly ascribed value.

There are, moreover, many other criteria besides economic means that enter into play in deciding the amount of a dowry. This is significantly influenced by the number of children in a family, and in particular the number of daughters requiring dowries. But the state of health of bride and groom and any gap in age between them may also be significant factors. For example, does the physical weakness of a bride who dies after only six months of marriage and a long illness have a bearing on the dowry settlement?[30] And there was perhaps an implicit promise and expectation of being cared for in the marriage between the surgeon Reyneri's twenty-year-old daughter and the wealthy apothecary Bruno, who was more than thirty years her senior, making Ludovica's modest dowry of 1,800 lire in all acceptable to him.[31] Indeed, Bruno died only three years after the wedding and Margherita got married again almost immediately, this time to the son of a notary, and with the much more considerable dowry of 3,700 lire.[32] Thus it is crucial to distinguish between wedding transactions for a first and later marriages, because the existence or otherwise of children, how many and how old they are, the bride and groom's capacity for work and earnings, have a notable impact on the value of the dowry. The dowries of widows remarrying, for example, are often much higher than those for the first marriage, and they also differ in their make-up.

These considerations raise doubts about seeing the dowry as an infallible signal of status. Perhaps a subtler indicator of the social aspirations of the surgeons can be found in the fardello, the dowry's material component.

The bride's trousseau

Until now the very few studies which have looked at the fardello have limited themselves to discuss its legal status, its composition has received no attention.[33] What is the fardello? In addition to the cash dowry, the majority of marriage contracts included a component of material assets that the bride was bringing into the marriage. These objects were usually described and often also valued at the foot of the dowry contract. From a quantitative point of view, the fardello could amount to quite a significant proportion of the dowry: in the majority of the contracts involving surgeons and artisans of the body it fluctuates between 12 and 27 per cent of the overall sum, though in some cases it reaches more than 30 per cent of the total dowry. In poorer dowries there is a clear tendency to compensate with the fardello for the low monetary component; thus dowries of below 1,000 lire have fardelli equivalent to between 26 and 27 per cent of the overall dowry (in two cases the fardello actually amounts to 40 per cent and 50 per cent of the total sum!). At the other extreme, dowries of above 4,000 lire have fardelli equivalent to 11–15 per cent of the overall sum. When it comes to the wealthiest dowries, the fardelli amount to only 7 per cent or as little as 1.6 per cent of the total.[34] Clearly, in these cases, the bride's rank is established by the monetary component. But in other cases it is through objects that the bride's distinction is declared. It is therefore worth turning to the composition of the fardelli: which elements, in these, would function as indicators of status?

The first observation is that, unlike the fardelli of the lower classes, those of the women with whom the surgeons are or become related seldom include furniture and household goods for setting up the new home.[35] Whenever an item of furniture is included it is detailed as a special piece of furniture, included in the fardello not for its functionality but for its aesthetic interest. It is clear, for example, that the 'castellated walnut writing-desk with stucco-work and other ornamentations' that the surgeon Pietro Calvo assigned to his daughter Caterina for her wedding in the codicil to his will, was regarded as a special object.[36] Otherwise, the only other item of furniture regularly given within this social milieu was the walnut chest containing the fardello, often made to order for the occasion.[37] The fardello was customarily kept in it, stored there throughout the couple's married life, marking out those possessions that were the exclusive property of the bride, so that these would not be confused with all the other domestic possessions, which were normally considered the property of the husband and his descendants. Occasionally we also come across a warming-pan or other objects for heating or light; in one case we find a barrel for wine, in another a tin table service, and in a third a wool press, but in general furniture and household objects do not feature in the fardello.[38] In two cases only, among those I have considered, there is a longer list of furniture and objects for the household.[39] Clearly it was expected that furnishings would be provided by the husband and that the wife would bring only decorative objects (such as the writing desk mentioned above or 'a ribbon trimming for around the bed') in addition to those for her personal use. In fact we know that furniture was customarily provided by the bridegroom, and we occasionally find it mentioned in the legal deeds of emancipation through which men whose fathers were still alive were freed from their *patria potestas* (see below, chapter nine). From this evidence it appears that household goods were sometimes handed on from father to son when the latter left the home. Often, however, it was the young men themselves who had achieved some independence and, by means of their 'virtue and industry', bought the furniture needed for their home. For instance, the document emancipating the surgeon Giacomo Antonio Reyneri from the authority of his father records the list of furniture in the rooms already lived in by the son, and that he will shortly be sharing with Delibera (the daughter of the upholsterer Dematteis), whom he is about to marry. These consist of bedding and bed coverings, and six chairs covered in the same material as the latter, a *burò* (bureau) with a mirror, a small table and matching small chest, two mattresses and one palliasse and four small benches to support it, four paintings representing the seasons, two other paintings with gilded frames and one of Saint Francis, two fire grills and one small walnut table with various books.[40] This evidently represents the essential furnishings required for the start of married life – only kitchen utensils are missing. The potential for setting up one's own home with one's own earnings from the first few years of independent work is actually presented in the deeds of emancipation with a certain amount of pride and appears to be seen as a sign of masculinity in this social group. The women contribute objects for purely personal use: those for the bride's toilette, for example, such as 'two new combs, of different sizes, made of ivory', 'a mirror with a black frame and an oak shelf', various 'boxes' or 'caskets' for jewellery and cosmetics, covered or trimmed with leather and studs or lined with cloth, as well as objects emphasising those female virtues which will be expected of the bride: boxes for needles, lidded wooden cups filled with cloth which she will sew on to the linen to come in the future, and lengths of linen or hemp which she will use to make sheets, napkins or other household linen.[41]

The bulk of the fardello is however made up of clothing and personal linen in considerable quantities. Clothing regularly amounts to some 40 to 50 per cent of the overall value. It includes various types of garments and head coverings, as well as gloves, handbags, fans, shoes and silk stockings, and sometimes a mask – indicating a refined wardrobe to suit public and festive occasions, and not merely for everyday domestic use. We can see this in the 'shoes trimmed with silver decoration' that feature in the fardello of Anna Margherita Busano, who married the surgeon Tomaso Formento in 1723, or the ones 'with silk ribbons' belonging to Anna Catta Cizaletta, who married the surgeon Matteo Stura in 1669.[42] Sometimes we find lengths of expensive fabric (damask, muslin, Persian silk) for making clothes.

Linen is the other substantial component of the fardello, usually accounting for some 35 to 40 per cent of the overall value. It unfailingly consists of personal linen, which is to say a number of women's shifts varying between twelve and thirty-six, sometimes embellished with lace, along with nightcaps, little capes, pinafores and handkerchiefs, as well as numerous aprons that indicate the active involvement of women in the work carried out in the homes of artisans of the body. Items of household linen, that is sheets, napkins, tablecloths, pillowcases and towels for the use of the family feature much less frequently; they are few and far between in many of the fardelli, and indeed not there at all in a fifth of the cases studied.[43] In the fardello of Francesca Margherita, the youngest of the surgeon Asinelli's five daughters, who was married to the merchant Borbonese in 1703, the linen only included twelve women's shirts, twelve handkerchiefs, twelve nightcaps and bonnets, a little cape and then a long list of different types of 'lace to trim nightcaps and shifts'.[44] Although the dowry as a whole was the same as that paid for the weddings of her four sisters, the impression is that the discrepancy in the composition of Francesca Margherita's fardello, the only one to include nothing but items for the bride, was an expression of higher social aspirations. Indeed the fardello provided by a noble family presents these same features: the total absence of household goods or goods that can be shared with others.[45] The bride's standing seems therefore to be expressed through the composition of the fardello and not just its overall value: the greater the proportion of objects for purely personal use and ornamental value, the higher the social standing of the family.

Jewellery and precious objects also hold an important symbolic place in the fardello and the marriage transaction as a whole: when these are included in the fardello their value ranges between 7 per cent and 18 per cent of its total value. Among them are rings, earrings and necklaces, as well as items of clothing embellished with silver or precious stones, such as the 'belt of double silver' in the fardello of Francesca Margherita Asinelli. In fact the boundary between clothing and jewellery and indeed between these and devotional objects was very imprecise in that period.[46] For this reason the fardello often included rosaries, holy emblems or reliquaries decorated with lace, ribbons and precious metals that could be worn as ornaments. Examples are provided by 'the two crowns and emblems with silver medals' or the 'fastenings with reliquaries' that Caterina, the daughter of the surgeon Pietro Calvo, brings in her fardello to her marriage with Carlo Antonio Giove (merchant) in 1685, or the 'papal Agnus Dei embroidered with various flowers' found in the fardello of Anna Catta Cizaletta.[47]

Sometimes these pieces of jewellery were given not as part of the dowry and the fardello, but separately as wedding gifts to the bride. In this way they would not be entrusted to the husband, nor would they be subject to the regulations governing the handing down of dowry possessions; instead, they would be free from any ties and would fully be the property of the bride. Although they were not technically part of the dowry, such gifts are often listed, and sometimes even valued, at the bottom of the dowry deed, and we can therefore have some idea of their nature and what they were worth. We can see, for example, the wedding gifts received in 1686 by Maria Christina Asinelli, the daughter of the surgeon Giuseppe and the bride of the surgeon Busano: a silver salt cellar (30 lire), a crown with a medal and one emblem with silver plate (12 lire), two rings (34 lire), a casket with lace trimming (20 lire).[48] Other common gifts are pictures with fine frames, like the painting 'with the Annunciation in a gilded frame' received on her marriage by Francesca Margherita Asinelli, the sister of Maria Christina, and mirrors, likewise often in frames worthy of description. The existence of gifts of this kind, of a value amounting to substantial sums (Maria Christina's add up to 105 lire, while her cash dowry comes to 1,500 lire and her fardello to 500 lire) confirms the pattern among the surgeons and other artisans of the body of endowing brides with luxury and ornamental goods devoid of any practical function, along the lines of marriage transactions among the elite. They also confirm the existence in the homes of these artisans of objects made of precious materials and with a purely decorative function.

If we turn our attention to consumption we therefore find a different image of the barber-surgeon from the one expected. Even though their ownership of immovable property and credits is normally modest, purchases relating to appearances are considerable. This should not surprise us. Although the surgeon is often described as rough and unsophisticated, and his occupation as a bloody and messy one, we know from the previous chapter that in reality he was not just associated with blood and the battlefield, but with court life. We can speculate on the influence that his frequent contacts with the ducal court may have had on the surgeon's tastes and lifestyle. He was, after all, expected to spend many hours of his day in close contact with members of the ruling family and their courtiers. This would certainly have affected his tastes, manners and appearance.

Stipends, gifts, privileges and proximity to power

It should be made clear that the connection with the court does not appear to have been limited to a handful of surgeons, but that it more or less directly involved the majority of surgeons active in the city. It is unusual to find any surgeon who, even though not personally employed at court, would have no close relatives connected to court servants, especially in the Chamber. We see this in the Deroy kinship network (see figure 3.2): Deroy has no court post but his brother-in-law is an upholsterer at court, his father-in-law is a Garzone di Camera, his mother is housekeeper to the Countess of Verrua, one of the ladies attending the Duchess. Another example is provided by the connections that the brothers Enrico and Matteo Stura have with the court through the third brother, Giuseppe, who was a ducal barber, and their sister, who was married to Benedicti, assistant to the surgeon of the ducal household, while Enrico's second wife was the sister of Madama Reale's confectioner, Revigliotto. Through family ties, a very large number came into contact with this world of the elite, along with its manners and tastes. This happens far less in the case of physicians whose relations tend to be found among merchants, lawyers and state functionaries rather than other court employees.

It is precisely proximity to the powerful that has been seen as one of the factors creating a separation between physicians and surgeons. Among the various types of medical practitioner, it was the academically trained and cultured physician who was supposed to enjoy a privileged relationship with the aristocratic classes and be the main beneficiary of their patronage.[49] We have already seen that, despite his practical education, the barber-surgeon played a part in the same discourse on the body as the physician, and employed the language of the humours as well as references to the classics of medicine. But the relationship that the surgeon frequently maintained with the court environment also leads us to modify the commonly expressed opinion about his connections and the social and cultural capital that these offered him. In a city with a court setting, serving in the royal Chamber gave the barber-surgeon and the other artisans of the body many more opportunities for proximity to members of the aristocracy and the ducal family, to their tastes and values and the possibility of gaining their trust, than were available to the physician. We have already seen this in our analysis of the tasks carried out in the Chamber and a study of the accounts of the Household Treasurers provides further proof of it.

Along with the upholsterer, whether in his role as surgeon or as barber and *baigneur* to the royal person or household, or else as Aiutante or Garzone di Camera, it is the surgeon whom we encounter most frequently as beneficiary of gifts and reimbursements for duties carried out by order of the Prince with whom he serves. Often we are not told about the precise nature of his duties: the surgeon Borrello, for example, received reimbursements in 1663 and 1674 for journeys made to Aosta in the service of His Highness and, together with a midwife, to Bavaria; then, in 1668, he travelled to Vaudier with the Aiutante di Camera Villanis, 'bringing with him an upholsterer'.[50] But whenever the precise duties carried out by these artisans of the body are specified we can see that these also include tasks seemingly remote from their sphere of professional competence. One thing they do for sure is procure objects – such as wigs, 'plasters' and 'supplies from Paris' – which might be connected with personal adornment;[51] but also other kinds of goods that are less to be expected: jewellery for example. The personal surgeon Tevenot was reimbursed for the sale to His Highness of a cross with diamonds that the latter made as a gift to the painter Mielli, and the Aiutante di Camera Platea received 810 lire for a ring with a large diamond, also sold to the Duke.[52] These transactions indicate an affinity of taste with members of the reigning family that is surprising. Moreover, the servants most constantly close to the master are upholsterers, Aiutanti di Camera and barbers. They accompany the prince on his travels, and the first two groups often precede him so as to make everything ready in those dwellings where he will be staying.[53] Or else they are sent by him to accompany and serve respected guests, which further confirms the trust bestowed on these figures, trust in their discretion and ability to find out and interpret the needs and tastes of different high-ranking guests[5.4] They even assist the master in resolving contingent financial problems. In fact, surgeons and other Aiutanti sometimes make loans to the master: in 1676, for example, Tevenot lent the Duke the grand sum of 10,000 lire at a 7 per cent rate of interest.[55]

These findings provide further evidence of the complexity and flexibility of the Chamber personnel's income. Court employees are also directly responsible for supplying the means and the labour necessary for keeping the master's private rooms and wardrobe clean and in good order: we find regular reimbursements to the Garzoni di Camera and the *Aiutanti di Guardaroba* for 'provision of small items for the Chamber' or for outlay of monies 'relating to the Wardrobe' of the various princes they served. They are often given the task of seeing to the little indulgences (*minuti piaceri*) of their master or mistress, as indicated by reimbursements 'for quantities of drinking chocolate and coffee supplied in the service of Madama Reale'.[56] The distinction we are inclined to make between service work and trade becomes anachronistic in the setting of the court, where the majority of the servants were suppliers of both labour and goods. It was they who provided the materials and the products necessary to their work, which we have already seen in the case of the Sommelier, who also supplied wine for the table as well as serving it. The same principle applied for all the other servants: the Garzone di Camera provided 'brooms and buckets' and 'other small supplies for sweeping the salone and the other rooms in which His Highness lives'; the Aiutante di Guardaroba made sure that the Prince's personal linen was bleached; the perruquier/*baigneur* obtained items relating to the toilette.[57] In 1720, for example, the *baigneur* Carlo Giuseppe Fassina received an annual stipend of 250 lire 'for the upkeep of the toilette', in addition to his salary of 1,300 lire.[58] The constant contacts that these court employees clearly had to maintain with suppliers and artisans outside the court, turning them into working entrepreneurs, indicates not just the complexity of their respective professional identities but, yet again, the close ties kept up between the court and the city. What is more, these examples demonstrate the degree to which the artisans of the body were in touch with the everyday needs and whims of the master they served.

Perhaps by virtue of this special intimacy, the salaries of the surgeons and other artisans of the body were surprisingly high. For example, in the middle of the seventeenth century Enrico Prodomo, Aiutante di Camera and Barber to His Highness, received an annual salary of 1,375 lire, whereas the Physician to the Camera and to the Household, Reynaudi, was paid only 400 lire and the other four physicians to the Camera, the protophysician included, were paid only 200. The salaries of the two chief surgeons, Pietro Tevenot and Giacomo Borrelli, were also quite high: they received, respectively, 1,300 and 1,000 lire annually, while the salary of only the lowest-ranking surgeon, Chiarnace, was, at 140 lire, lower than that of the physicians.[59] The same discrepancy between physicians, surgeons and barbers (a hierarchy reversed by comparison with one's expectations) can be found in the 1670s. In the 1680s, however, it was a physician, Fansago, who enjoyed the highest salary, an annual 3,025 lire, while the surgeon Tevenot received 1,955 and the surgeon Borrello 1,400. The two chief barbers (who by now probably shared the same post), Choisy and Moriceau, were each paid 750 lire, more than the Protophysician Torrino, who received 717 lire. Only the third surgeon, Chiarnace, and the third barber, Stura, both of them juniors, had lower salaries, at 540 and 500 lire respectively.[60] In 1697 the annual salary of the *baigneur* and perruquier Carlo Giuseppe Fassina (1,000 lire) was still higher than that of the Protophysician Torrino, which remained at 717 lire; it was equal to that of the Household Physician, Ricca, but lower than that of the personal Surgeon Sebastiano Fassina.[61] Comparisons between what the medical staff were paid lead therefore to surprising outcomes that call into question the gap between the status of the surgeon and that of the physician. In fact, the criterion of financial reward is often used as proof of the latter's superiority; he is supposed to be better paid, partly as a reflection of his academic status and partly because of his orientation towards a better-off clientele.

The variations in pay between employees of the Camera and between the same people over different periods also show the complexity of how salaries were determined, and how far removed this was from the rigidity of modern parameters. Both initial salary and future increases were to a very great extent defined according to the individual (*ad personam*) and presented as a gracious concession by the master. The boundary between salary and gift appears therefore much more blurred than we would expect. Salaries only partly reflected an implicit scale of status and this mirrored the standing of the personages being served rather than a predefined hierarchy of professional functions. This meant that the personal surgeon tended to have a higher salary than that of the household surgeon, who treated courtiers and staff, and there was also a hierarchy between the various members of the ducal family (and hence between their servants). Seniority in age was another element that was frequently rewarded, but at the same time a man's reputation outside the court also mattered, this sometimes leading to a young man being paid considerably more than an older employee. In addition, salary was affected by the sharing of a post with someone else or by being its sole holder – a privilege that was not automatically granted, but reflected a subjective rise to favour; and again there was the fact of already being effectively appointed to a post or, instead, only holding the role of 'supernumerary' (*sovranumerario*) and therefore being in a situation of waiting for the death or resignation of the post's current holder in order to become 'effective'.[62] Both salary and the nature of the post itself were thus extremely sensitive to grading, to merits accumulated before and during service, and it was a measure of proximity to the master and of the trust that could thereby be achieved; in this sense the notion of salary is not easily distinguishable from that of gift, against which it is usually set.[63]

Salary seems, moreover, a crude indicator of status in the court setting, where payment often takes the form of a gift in kind or in privileges.[64] Gifts in kind traditionally match some of the services rendered: for example, when the surgeon bleeds a member of the ducal family he receives a bed sheet.[65] Moreover, gifts mark the life cycle of our court servants: gifts of considerable sums of money are frequent on the marriage of the employee, and later when daughters marry.[66] Positions for relatives, or the right of sons, nephews or grandsons to inherit a post can be other types of gift.[67] For example, besides being prompted by the talent he had already demonstrated 'in the service of the household servants', the appointment of Giò Francesco Meda to the post of Surgeon and Aiutante di Camera to Princess Ludovica was motivated by the 'merit and affection inherited from various of his relatives who have faithfully served us [the Princess and her deceased consort] well'.[68] In old age, moreover, when the capacity for service is diminished, a post is held more or less on an honorary basis. Widowhood is another event that prompts the intervention of the master, providing help for the widow and the orphans.[69] But the gifts are also frequently responses to the need for unusual expenditure – for instance, covering the cost of an outfit or a horse – and thereby revealing the master's familiarity with the circumstances of the servant.[70]

The advantages of being in some way connected with life at court are therefore quite extensive. Moreover, we can presume that contact with the court and its tastes had an impact on the purchasing aspirations and the lifestyle of many artisans of the body who, as we know, were often connected with services to the Chamber, either directly or indirectly. Immersion in an economy of gift-giving meant moreover that their purchasing power was not bound by the financial scope defined merely by monetary income. Some of the privileges they enjoyed also have a direct connection with the culture of appearances. For much of the seventeenth century, court personnel, including those at the level of Aiutante di Camera, were exempt from the restrictions imposed by the sumptuary laws, and could therefore wear fabrics and jewellery forbidden to the ordinary citizen.[71] What is more, those who received an item of apparel from the ruling house were exempt from any sumptuary restrictions. Displays of luxury were allowed even at the funerals of court servants, given that the restrictions imposed on the number of torches did not apply to those usually sent from the ducal household to honour their own officials.[72] The new regulations of 1679 theoretically eliminated all these privileges, with exceptions made for gentlemen and any *Guardia di Corazza* (armoured bodyguard) but it is interesting to note that positions as Guardia di Corazza were in fact made as ducal gifts and that many of our Garzoni and Aiutanti owned one of these. The owner was then often exempted from any obligation to fill the position directly and this was rented out to others while the privileges it bestowed remained his. We can argue that part of the allure of such a post derived precisely from the advantages to which it gave access – including exemption from the ruling of the sumptuary laws.[73]

Even though certain features of the surgeon's lifestyle make him seem inferior to the physician (ownership of a house, the presence of servants, dowries), others such as vigne, fardelli, court stipends and material possessions seem to indicate his participation in fairly high levels of consumption and above all in similar types of comsumption. Although we have no systematic evidence of what their houses looked like, sporadic evidence of the goods in their homes in some cases show a level of refinement that we would not expect. Examples are offered by the existence of silver and paintings in substantial quantities in the home of the surgeon Asinelli – who was not even employed at court – or by the jewels and silverware of the surgeon Nicolao Meda's widow. Patterns of consumption, as revealed by the composition of the bride's trousseau, certainly offer a more varied picture of the social position of barber-surgeons than traditional indicators such as property and land. Moreover, as we have seen in the case of stipends, economic indicators are themselves rather unstable when subject to close scrutiny, nor we can identify a fixed hierarchy of honour associated with specific court functions. And yet, even though physicians and surgeons were often not so far apart in terms of earnings, lifestyle and patterns of consumption, they tended to belong to separate social worlds. We shall see this in the next chapter. It is not their relationships with the powerful which set them apart; the barber-surgeons were used to dealing with the cream of society. It was rather the world of their social peers that was different.

Notes

1 For a discussion of the principles on which this assumption is based, with relevance to the English context, see Pelling, *Common Lot*, chapter ten, especially pp. 231–2, 236.

2 On the profile of the physician, see the hugely influential N. D. Jewson, 'Medical knowledge and the patronage system in 18th-century England', *Sociology*, 8 (1974), and, for a more complex picture, H. Cook, *The Decline of the Old Medical Regime in Stuart London* (Ithaca, 1986), pp. 22, 56–60. For a recent reassessment, see Pelling, *Medical Conflicts* pp.

14–17. On Italy, and more precisely on the Roman case, S. De Renzi, 'Medical competence, anatomy and the polity on seventeenth-century Rome', in S. Cavallo and D. Gentilcore (eds), *Spaces, Objects and Identities in Early Modern Italian Medicine*, *Renaissance Studies* 21:4 (2007). On the barber-surgeon's clientele, see R. Jutte, 'A seventeenth-century German barber-surgeon and his patients', *Medical History*, 33 (1989).

3 C. Muldrew, *The Economy of Obligation: the Culture of Credit and Social Relations in Early Modern England* (Basingstoke, 1998), chapter six.

4 This tradition, initiated by Roland Mousnier, has flourished particularly within French historiography. For applications to the artisan groups, see J. F. Farr, *Hands of Honor. Artisans and their World in Dijon, 1550–1650* (Ithaca, 1988), chapter three; L. Allegra, 'Un modello di mobilità sociale preindustriale. Torino in età Napoleonica', *BSBS*, CII:1 (2004).

5 Stuart, *Defiled Trades*, 'Introduction'. A similar approach is to be found in F. Egmond, 'Execution, dissection pain, and infamy. A morphological investigation', in F. Egmond and R. Zwijnenberg (eds), *Bodily Extremities. Preoccupations with the Human Body in Early Modern European Culture* (Aldershot, 2003), p. 126.

6 On the early emergence of practices of autopsy and dissection in Italy, in contrast with trends in Central and Northern Europe, see K. Park, 'The life of the corpse: division and dissection in late medieval Europe', *Journal of the History of Medicine and the Allied Sciences*, 50 (1995).

7 The first provision in this sense dates from 1721: Duboin, vol. 14, p. 731, Royal Edict of 29 October 1721. We will return to this subject in chapter eight.

8 Craig Muldrew has recently drawn attention to the instability of status among the middling and lower social groups in England. See his 'Class and credit: social identity, wealth and the life course in early modern England', in J. Barry and H. French (eds), *Identity and Agency in England 1500–1800* (Basingstoke, 2004).

9 Only two of the surgeons have more than one servant: Bellotto and Oseglia. It is in these two households that we find the only male servants (Art. 530).

10 Ins. 1672, l. 12, c. 419.

11 *Ibid.*, 1685, l. 6, vol. IV, par. 1, c. 3391.

12 *Ibid.*, 1694, l. 10, vol. II, c. 1857. The intended purpose of the five bedrooms is not further clarified; probably one of these was destined to be the kitchen.

13 When he bought the house Pasero was twenty-nine, had been married for seven years, and a year before had become a surgeon at the Carità hospital. Busano was thirty-two, had been married for eight years, licensed as a surgeon for thirteen years, and a year before had become Surgeon to the Poor. We don't know Deroy's age but we know that he had been married for seven years and for fourteen years had held the post of hospital surgeon.

14 Only in special cases, for example when the tenant committed himself to have building works done in the apartement, in view of a future purchase, a contract was granted for a longer period. For this reason, for instance, Ravizza rented the floor of his house to Busano for six years (private handwritten note dated 17 November 1694 inserted at the bottom of his will and sale of 10 April 1697: Ins. 1697, l. 4, c. 319).

15 Ins. 1681, l. 4, c. 835. The price was 750 lire of which Calvo put up 450 and Stura 300.

16 The censo was a mortgage on a property that brought in income, for example a house or a levy on a community. Whoever acquired the censo would have the right to the corresponding income every year.

17 Ins. 1683, l. 2, c. 135. The purchase of the first half, which took place on 13 September 1679, is also mentioned in this deed.

18 A *maison des champs*, equivalent to the vigna discussed here, was also a common feature in the assets of the Parisian physicians studied by Lehoux. Unlike Turin's surgeons, however, many of them built large landed estates: Lehoux, *Cadre*, p. 349.

19 Ins. 1707, l. 7, c. 359; 1709, l. 11, c. 177. A giornata was equivalent to 3,810 square metres. Other examples are those of the barber Lorenzo Margheri who, in 1684, bought a vigna with more than six giornate of land at Moncalieri for 5,000 lire (Ins. 1685, l. 1, vol. I, c. 101), and of Domenico Deroy who, in 1686, bought a vigna and land for 9,000 lire from the lawyer Violetta (Ins. 1686, l. 7, c. 87). It is worth noting that the cost of these rural properties was equivalent to that of the apartments which, as seen above, many surgeons acquired in town.

20 The inventory of furniture included in the deed of 1707 also mentions equipment for making and storing wine, namely a wine-press, bottles and barrels, among other things. Moreover, Calvo also inherited the contract between the vendor and the *vignolante* who worked on the vineyards, and the one with the *massaro*, whose duties covered the corn, hay and grass produced on the property, as well as looking after two cows.

21 For example, Domenico Deroy took six years and four instalments to pay off the vigna he purchased in 1686 (Ins. 1692, l. 5, c. 993). Calvo paid off the price of 5,000 lire in two years, but in order to do this he had to borrow 2,000 lire from a third party and since he was unable to pay off this debt he was compelled to sell the vigna in 1710 (Ins. 1710, l. 11, c. 231).

22 In addition to individual deeds, this is documented by the inventory of what was owned by Evasio Andrea (Ins. 1759, l. 4, vol. II, c. 901).

23 Out of the rural goods inherited, for example, the surgeon Busano keeps only the use of four rooms in the house at Mortigliengo (division between the Busano siblings, Ins., 1688, l. 1, c. 819, and donation of goods to their brother, a parish priest, Ins. 1693, l. 6, c. 339). Other examples of this type include the alienations of rural property held in Balangero by surgeons Carlo Antonio Reyneri and then by his son Giò Domenico (Ins. 1685, l. 4, c. 629; 1698, l. 1, c. 411); and the sale of good inherited from his father in Mondovì by surgeon Pasero (Ins. 1681, l. 9 c. 163).

24 See Ortensia Alberica's testament (Ins. 1726, l. 11, c. 521). The dowry contract does not specify the amount of the increase to be made by the husband (Ins. 1685, l. 8, c. 791). However, according to local custom, this would have been a third or a quarter. For Verna's testament (Ins. 1737, l. 2, vol. I, c. 369).

25 See, among others, G. Delille, *Famille et Propriété dans le Royaume de Naples (XVe–XIXe siècle)* (Rome, 1985); S. K. Cohn Jr, *The Laboring Classes in Renaissance Florence* (New York, 1980), pp. 72–3; S. Cerutti, *Mestieri e Privilegi. Nascita delle Corporazioni a Torino secoli XVII–XVIII* (Turin, 1992), p. 203; Hardwick, *Practice of Patriarchy*, pp. 58–9 (and works cited in note fifteen); Farr, *Hands of honour*, pp. 96–7.

26 Ins. 1691, l. 7, c. 755; 1721, l. 9, c. 205.

27 Left fatherless shortly after her birth, Vittoria had been brought up by an aunt and uncle on her father's side, a childless couple from whom she had inherited their huge estate. And since all her siblings had taken religious vows in the years following her father's death, she had also been left sole heir to her parents' estate. In chapter six, I shall return to the situation of Vittoria, and her mother Caterina.

28 Ins. 1665, l. 2, vol. II, c. 423; 1657, l. 5, c. 251.

29 *Ibid.*, 1695, l. 3, vol. I, c. 455; 1706, l. 4, c. 127; 1708, l. 1, c. 353.

30 This is the case, for example, of Camilla Fassina. After her death a transaction was made whereby the dowry, which according to custom had to be returned untouched to the family of origin whenever there were no descendants, was split into more or less equal parts between her mother and her husband, actually allowing for her long illness during the early months of married life and the costs thereby incurred by the latter (*ibid.*, 1697, l. 7, c. 1798).

31 For the estate of Giò Domenico Bruno see the inventory drawn up in 1725 (*ibid.*, 1741, l. 6, cc. 587–622). The value of the two shops and back shops alone comes to more than 11,000 lire.

32 *Ibid.*, 1727, l. 5, vol. II, c. 705.

33 J. Kirshner, 'Material for a gilded cage: non-dotal assets in Florence, 1300–1500', in D. Kertzer and R. P. Saller (eds), *The Family in Italy from Antiquity to the Present* (New Haven, 1991). I began to analyse the composition of the fardelli in 'Proprietà o possesso? Controllo e composizione dei beni delle donne a Torino 1650–1710', in G. Calvi and I. Chabot (eds), *Le Ricchezze delle Donne. Diritti Patrimoniali e Poteri Familiari in Italia (XIII-XIX secc.)* (Turin, 1998); and in 'What did women transmit? Ownership and control of household goods and personal effects in early modern Italy', in M. Donald and L. Hurcombe (eds), *Gender and Material Culture: Historical Perspectives* (Basingstoke, 2000).

34 These observations are based on the analysis of thirty-one dowries paid or received by surgeons and artisans of the body for which the value of the fardello is stated in precise terms. Among those cases in which the values of the dowry and the fardello are exceptionally closely split is that of Caterina Pastor, the daughter of the *Garzone di Camera*, Eustachio. She married the *Usciere di Camera*, Gambino (her fardello amounted to 405 lire and her cash dowry to 600 lire). Among those in which the two values are very far apart, are the marriage transactions between Teresa, the daughter of surgeon Demenico Deroy, and the goldsmith Enrico Vautier (7,000 lire in cash and only 523 lire in material goods), and the one already instanced a number of times, that of Vittoria Chiarmet, the wife of surgeon Evasio Verna (16,000 lire in cash, whereas the fardello was worth only 250 lire!). Ins. 1695, l. 3, vol. I, c. 455; 1721, l. 9, c. 205.

35 On commoners' dowries in Venice and Verona, see M. Chojnacka, *Working Women of Early Modern Venice* (Baltimore, 2001), p. 5; E. Eisenach, *Husbands, Wives and Concubines. Marriage, Family and Social Order in Sixteenth-Century Verona* (Kirksville, 2004), pp. 47, 68–9; cf. R. Sarti, *Europe at Home. Family and Material Culture 1500–1800* (New Haven, 2002), pp. 45–8.

36 Ins. 1681, l. 7, c. 397.

37 There is a vast literature on the Renaissance marriage chest. For a synthesis of the debate see C. Klapisch-Zuber, 'Les coffres de mariage et les plateaux d'accouchée à Florence: archive, ethnologie, iconographie', in S. Deswarte-Rosa (ed.), *À Travers l'Image. Lecture Iconographique et Sens de l'Oeuvre* (Paris, 1994). However, in relation to the period immediately following, the marriage chest has received rather less attention.

38 Ins. 1687, l. 2, vol. II, c. 735; 1665, l. 11, vol. II, c. 421; 1694, l. 3, vol. II, c. 831.

39 This is the case with Anna Catta Cizaletta, who, in addition to the usual goods, brought the surgeon Matteo Stura 'a Pont chair in different colours, one cradle (not new) in walnut with a cloth for covering, one middle-sized table in walnut, one warming-pan, fireside shovel and lamp'; likewise Leonora Marchetto, who married the upholsterer

Demignot, brought with her 'a small black table, a desk with drawers and bed fittings (not new)' (*ibid.*, 1670, l. 8, c. 91; 1685, l. 2, vol. II, c. 645).

40 *Ibid.*, 1725, l. 2, c. 261. However, in the case of the apothecary Giacobi Brena, who was emancipating his son Giò Michele in 1676, furnishings, including personal linen, household linen (sheets, napkins, bath towels and hand towels), table ware and kitchen utensils, along with some furniture and paintings, were all provided by the father, together with a sum of money (*ibid.*, 1676, l. 8, c. 529).

41 On the domestic production of household linen, see R. Ago, 'Il linguaggio del corpo', in Belfanti and Giusberti, *La Moda*, pp. 132–5.

42 Ins. 1723, l. 10, vol. IV, c. 2467; 1670, l. 8, c. 91.

43 Instead of the finished product, some of the *fardelli* include lengths of linen or hemp from which the necessary items would later be made.

44 Ins. 1703, l. 9, c. 243.

45 Cavallo, 'What did women', p. 45.

46 Venturelli, 'Gioielli', pp. 94–6.

47 Ins. 1685, l. 6, c. 1955; 1670, l. 8, c. 91.

48 F. Arro, *Del Diritto Dotale secondo i Principi del Gius Romano* (Asti, 1834), pp. 447 ff.

49 Jewson, 'Medical knowledge'.

50 PCF 1663, fo. 179; 1674–75, fo. 251; 1668–69, fo. 168.

51 See for example the numerous reimbursements to Moriceau (*ibid.*, 1682–83, fo. 71; 1684–85, fos 49, 207; 1696–97, fo. 180).

52 *Ibid.*, 1663, fo. 72; 1668–69, fo. 109. Another example is the reimbursement to Aiutante Giò Herlanouix for providing a silver sword that His Highness then donated to a French officer made captive during the lifting of the siege of Turin (Art. 217, 1705–7, entry 388).

53 See for example the reimbursements to the upholsterer Pietro Marchetto 'for monies spent on food in the train of HRH on his journeys to Alba, Verrua, Trino and Vercelli' (*ibid.*, 1667) and Sigismondo Cigna 'for monies to be spent on food on the journey back and forth to Nice where he has been sent at the command of Madama Reale to measure the rooms that must be draped for HRH's stay there on his way to Portugal' (*ibid.*, 1682), and to 'barber and stover' Moriceau who accompanied the Duke to Portugal (PCF 1682, fo. 44).

54 Art. 217, 1667, for reimbursements to the Aiutante di Camera Antonio Passerat and the aforementioned Marchetti 'sent by HH to serve the Abbot Rossigliotti' to Ferrara and to Bramant, Chivasso, Susa and Crescentino; *ibid.*, 1673, for reimbursements to the upholsterer Giò Michele Matthei for monies spent on food at the Castle of Rivoli where he had travelled 'to furnish and make ready the rooms … on the occasion of the visit of the Duchesses of Imola and Modena'.

55 PCF 1676, fo. 69.

56 See for example the annual reimbursements of 35 and 17.10 lire to Cesare Negrino, Garzone di Camera to the Princess Margherita, and to Eustachio Pastor, Garzone di Camera to HH (Art. 217, 1660), or those to Giò Vermetto, Garzone di Camera in the same household, of 70 lire (*ibid.*, 1687), and to the Usciere di Guardaroba, Paolo Antonio Deleani (Art. 219, par. 1, 1697).

57 See for example the reimbursements, of 292 lire to Giaco Verney, Garzone di Camera (Art. 217, 1667); of 496 lire to Nicolao Chiavarino, Aiutante di Guardaroba (*ibid.*, 1673). For further examples referring to the female personnel, see chapter seven.

58 PCF 1720, reg. 2, fo. 128.

59 Art. 217, 1657, 1660 and 1667. In the 1670s, the barber and Aiutante di Camera Pietro Choisy received 1,485 lire annually, and the barber Giuseppe Stura received 500 (*ibid.*, 1673, 1677).

60 *Ibid.*, 1682.

61 *Ibid.*, 1697.

62 The role of 'supernumerary' is relevant to the majority of posts held, including those of surgeons, and will be discussed in depth in chapter five. Being in such a position usually involved a substantial workload and did not always guarantee a salary.

63 Hence the salaries of the surgeons have discrepant increases: Tevenot's went up from 1,300 lire in the 1650s as high as 2,180 lire in 1687, whereas Borrello's rose by only 400 lire over nearly thirty years (from 1,000 to 1,400): Art. 217, 1660, 1687.

64 M. Fantoni, *La Corte del Granduca. Forma e Simboli del Potere Mediceo fra Cinque e Seicecento* (Rome, 1994), especially chapter 3.

65 This custom is mentioned in PCF 1664–65, fo. 53.

66 In 1651, for example, the barber and Aiutante di Camera Antonio Gorgia received 2,000 lire for his wedding (Art. 402, 1651, fos 7–8). Among the gifts towards the dowries of daughters of Aiutanti di Camera and court Upholsterers were 500 lire to Ludovica Parisot in 1679, 400 lire to Franca Maria Gambina, and as much as 4,000 lire to Franca Maria Bonauda, in four annual instalments (PCF 1679–80, fo. 74; Art. 221, 1696; Art. 405, 1685).

67 See for example the concessions of succession (*sopravvivenza*) to their fathers granted to the Garzone di Camera Pietro Tomaso Pastor and the upholsterer Michele Demignot; and the right to suceed to his uncle bestowed on upholsterer Marc'Antonio Marchetto (PCF 1654, fo. 212, and reg. 1°, fo. 227; 1679, vol. 2, fo. 33).

68 Art. 405, 1686, fo. 37.

69 One example is the payment arranged over four years to the widow of Luigi Parisot, Aiutante di Camera to Madama Reale, 'for the upkeep of her children': PCF 1667–68, fo. 105.

70 Likewise the gifts to the Garzone di Camera, Eustachio Pastor: *ibid.*, 1635–36, fo. 70; 1626, reg. 1, fo. 156. See also the granting of plots of grounds in the City Council's square to the surgeon Tevenot so that he could invest the money he had just inherited in building a house for himself and his family at short distance from the ducal palace where he served (*ibid.*, 1667–68, fo. 19).

71 This is a custom already sanctioned by an order of 1565: 'The secretaries and officials of ourselves, the Duchess and the Prince, may wear garments of silk according to the standing of their office' (Borelli, pp. 685–7). Until 1679, 'the wearing and use of pearls and other true jewels' was also granted to court officials, their wives and their children, 'so long as these do not exceed the value of 300 gold ecus, and it is granted to the ladies to wear necklaces or strings of pearls provided that these do not exceed the value of 1000 gold ecus' (*ibid.*, p. 691, edict of 1635, clauses eight and ten; p. 693, edict of 1679, clauses two and three).

72 *Ibid.*, p.689.

73 Examples of Aiutanti or Garzoni di Camera who were the beneficiaries of positions as guardia di corazza include Carlo Emanuele Platea and Francesco Masson (PCF 1676, vol. 2, fo. 117; 1674, fo. 140), Andrea Pellerino and Giuseppe Marchetto (Art. 217, 1682 and 1687).

5

Social and kinship ties

Social networks: siblings, in-laws and neighbours

Let us now turn to the social world of the surgeon. Marriage partnerships allow us an initial insight into his social horizons. The spouses of surgeons and their daughters come largely from the occupational milieu that I have described as 'artisans of the body', and sometimes from the ranks of merchants involved in the sale of goods related to personal appearance and health such as luxury fabrics, perfumes and medicinal groceries. Moreover, physicians and apothecaries are sometimes to be found among these spouses, whereas artisans and merchants engaged in other sectors (say leather, metals, wood, etc.), albeit of considerable financial status, are markedly absent. Physicians, by contrast, chose their brides and married off their daughters within the circles of lawyers and state officials, who are almost entirely absent from the surgeons' network.

If we examine the way in which new families were formed in the surgeon's milieu, it will become clear that in most cases marriage did not 'create' a relationship but consolidated pre-existing links between members of the two families involved. Let us take for example the kinship network of surgeon Domenico Deroy, already discussed in chapter 3 (see figure 3.2). The marriage of Domenico with Anna Margherita Pastor probably came about within the court environment where Deroy's mother was housekeeper to the Countess of Verrua, one of the Duchess's ladies-in-waiting, and Pastor was *Garzone di Camera* of His Royal Highness in those same years; likewise the marriage of Domenico's sister, Lucia, to the son of Verna, Captain of the Hunt and court Upholsterer. The marriages of Deroy's children also reflect professional relationships: in 1694 his daughter Teresa married her brother's business partner, the jeweller Enrico Vautier, while in 1706 his son Luigi married the sister of the Meda surgeons, who had both trained under Domenico Deroy at the

San Giovanni hospital and subsequently remained very close to him. This closeness was more than professional; Giò Francesco Meda, in particular, appears as a witness to a number of Deroy's legal deeds and indeed was a witness at his wedding.[1] Professional relationships are thus a significant factor in matrimonial choices, but frequently there are also local ties between husband and wife: Vautier, for example, lived two blocks away from the Deroys. Likewise Domenico Deroy's second marriage, to Anna Teresa Benna, seems to have had its roots in neighbourhood connections: his future bride lived with her family in the same block as his daughter and son-in-laws Vautier (see plate 4, Cantone 53).[2]

Professional and local ties also seem to be intertwined in the marriages of Domenico Deroy's nieces, Paula and Caterina, the daughters of his sister Lucia and Giacomo Verna (see figure 3.3). They married, respectively, Sebastiano Fassina, one of Deroy's *Giovani,* and his brother Emanuele, a perruquier. Sebastiano Fassina's connection with Deroy, through his marriage to the latter's niece, would consolidate the special relationship already existing between the two surgeons. Indeed Fassina was involved in witnessing important legal documents for his master, such as his will, long before becoming related to Deroy.[3] Their relationship was to continue over the years, so that Fassina later succeeded Deroy as anatomical dissector at the University, a post which he perhaps had shared with him from an earlier date, as was often the case with designated successors. It is hard to say how much the double marriage of the Fassina brothers with the Verna sisters, Deroy's nieces, was a strategic consolidation of a desirable relationship with a powerful surgeon who had in his gift a number of professional posts in the city's hospitals and the University, and how much it arose out of attraction for the young girls who lived across the road from where their uncle kept his shop and Sebastiano Fassina practised (see plate 4, Cantone 134). The local aspect of these marriage partnerships suggests that the decision to marry was to some degree a reflection of the everyday contact between the young people living and working in the neighbourhood, and therefore of a certain freedom of choice on the part of the future spouses. At the same time these matrimonial choices also reflect the density of interchange that was an aspect of neighbourhood life and, within it, the connections among individuals engaged in allied occupations. The marriage ties which I have described were formed between families who (except for the Medas) lived in three neighbouring blocks and who, moreover, were occupied in trades concerned with the care of health and physical appearance, a factor which probably multiplied the opportunities for everyday contact.[4]

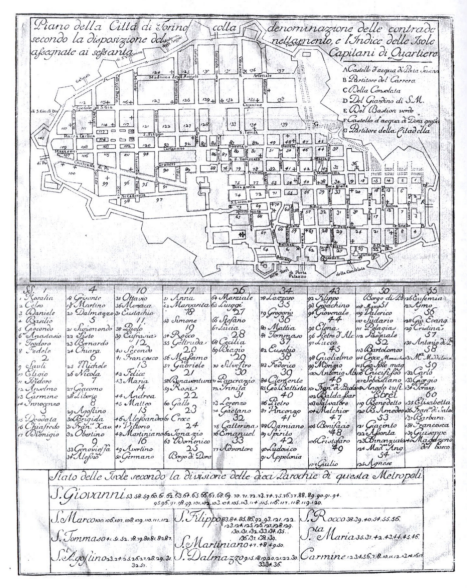

Plate 4 Plan of the city of Turin showing the division into *Cantoni*, 1724.

Not only does marriage arise out of the local fabric of relationships, but the fact that the new couples settle in the same neighbourhood gives the kinship network a local dimension which favours exchanges between in-laws. Indeed, those in-laws resident in the same area play a crucial role in the life of the individual. We can see this from their repeated participation as witnesses and guarantors in legal deeds and economic transactions carried out in the presence of a notary (loans and sales, division of assets between heirs, dowries and wills); from their involvement (as witnesses and godparents) in rituals of marriage and the christening of children, whereby ties of spiritual kinship were established that would often fulfil an important function in the life of the child; and lastly, from their role as guardians of orphan children and their property. This kind of evidence has been seen as one of the few indicators available to historians for reconstructing patterns of social relationship between early modern people.[5] In the case of Turin the analysis of witnesses, sureties and procurators in legal acts, as well as of godparents and guardians of wards, points to a very high level of contact between neighbourhood kin, especially in-laws, and their constant involvement in each other's affairs (some of them clearly charged with considerable emotional value).

We can take as an example the kinship network of the surgeon Giuseppe Asinelli, for which we have particularly detailed documentation concerning the places of residence of the different households, along with the names of godparents and marriage witnesses (see figure 5.1).[6] At least three of the five daughters of Giuseppe Asinelli married men already living in the neighbourhood and four married men who were engaged in trades allied to that of their father. In 1686 Maria Christina married the surgeon Giò Pietro Busano (a migrant from a village in the provinces), who was already active in the area, and kept shop near the church of San Francesco d'Assisi. Then, in 1700, came the wedding of Adelaide to the surgeon Pietro Ruiz, who, like Asinelli, was from the Milanese state (Como), and who, in 1693, was already living in the same house as the Asinelli family.[7] Lastly, in 1703 Francesca Margherita married the merchant Spirito Borbonese, a widower whose parents lived in the same house as the Asinellis. It is possible that the husbands of the two other daughters, the goldsmith Giò Stoper and the merchant Sebastiano Giacinto Mariano, both natives of Milan, were also already resident in the area, though not in the same parish, since this seems to have been a district settled by Milanese incomers (these marriages took place in 1679 and 1693).

In any case, all five new couples settled in the neighbourhood (see plate 4). The Mariano, the Ruiz and the Borbonese couples took up residence in

Figure 5.1 The Asinelli family

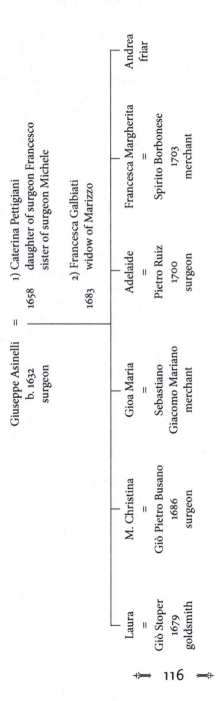

Giuseppe Asinelli = 1) Caterina Pettigiani
b. 1632   1658 daughter of surgeon Francesco
surgeon   sister of surgeon Michele

              2) Francesca Galbiati
         1683 widow of Marizzo

Laura
=
Giò Stoper
1679
goldsmith

M. Christina
=
Giò Pietro Busano
1686
surgeon

Gioa Maria
=
Sebastiano
Giacomo Mariano
merchant

Adelaide
=
Pietro Ruiz
1700
surgeon

Francesca Margherita
=
Spirito Borbonese
1703
merchant

Andrea
friar

the same Cantone of San Simone (53), opposite the Cantone of San Rocco (54), where the Asinellis had lived before they too moved to San Simone in 1680. The Busanos lived a little further down the road, in San Felice (42). The Stopers then moved two blocks further away towards Piazza Castello (75), while the Busanos left the area for good in the 1720s (23). However, for many years the Asinelli sisters and their husbands continued to live quite close to one another, and near their father and stepmother. They provided mutual support, entrusting important matters to one another, including the interests of each other's children. For example, Asinelli named his sons-in-law, first Stoper, then, in his second will, Busano, as guardians of his young son, who was still a minor, in case of his own death. As a father-in-law Asinelli acted as a witness to the various agreements whereby Busano legalised the purchase of a house in the Cantone of San Felice, and was depository of the sum paid by the buyer as guarantee to the creditors of the vendor. It was his brother-in-law Mariano who acted as proxy for the young Asinelli, who had become a friar, and cashed a credit due to him, while his fellow brother-in-law Borbonese acted as witness. It was again the brothers-in-law who acted as witnesses in church at the weddings of Ruiz to Adelaide and Borbonese to Franca Margherita Asinelli, and witnessed their dowry contract. Later on they would once again be witnesses to the wedding contracts of the children of their brothers-in-law.[8]

Thus we can see considerable cohesion in the kinship network created through marriage and residence in the same neighbourhood. As is clear from the examples given so far, a particularly active role operates across horizontal kinship, especially the group of siblings and brothers- and sisters-in-law. As Hardwick has observed in relation to the social world of notaries in Nantes, 'kin of the same generation formed a primary cohort in these kinds of networks'.[9] It is this group, for example, that most frequently stands as godparents at the baptism of children: six of the fourteen godfathers and godmothers of the Ruiz couple's children and nine of the twenty-two godfathers and godmothers of the Borbonese children are made up of aunts, uncles or cousins of the child, all living in the same neighbourhood. Even though connections of support and trust also exist with the previous generation (in this case the parents of the wives), marriage and place created the framework for especially intense exchanges between siblings and in-laws. Unlike the Nantes case, however, in Turin the connection between cousins appears to have less significance; admittedly the young female cousins regularly stand as godmothers, at the behest of their parents, when they are scarcely fifteen years old, but cousins are not necessarily a regular presence in the individual's life, unlike the brothers-in-law and, frequently, the uncles and nephews too – as we shall see below.[10]

The importance of the in-laws' role is also evident in the other kinship networks: for example, the guardianship of young orphans is often entrusted to a brother-in-law or a son-in-law in Deroy's network. In his first will, made in 1678, Domenico Deroy entrusts this responsibility to his wife Anna Margherita Pastor, but in the case of her death she is to be replaced by Deroy's brother-in-law, Gambino, Doorkeeper of the Chamber and husband of Anna Margherita's sister Caterina. In his next will, made in 1694, Deroy again nominates his wife, by then Anna Teresa Benna, as guardian of the younger children from both marriages, but with the proviso that 'she should not enter into contracts without the approval of her brother-in-law, Giò Lorenzo Mozzetto', the latter being her sister's husband.[11] Some years later, the tutorship of Deroy's young children from his first marriage was passed on to Vautier, Deroy's son-in-law.[12] When the widow wished to remarry, in 1699, it was Mozzetto again, together with another brother-in-law, the surgeon Giuseppe Pasero, who examined the accounts she presented of her own administration of the children's property. More than a decade later Pasero again became involved, this time in the settlement of the quarrel that had arisen between the widow of Deroy and her step-children (Deroy's offspring from his first marriage).[13]

Pasero epitomises the variety of key roles performed by brothers-in-law and uncles in horizontal kinship relations and the overlap between kinship, professional and neighbourly ties. As well as being related to him, Pasero was a neighbour (Cantone 52) and a colleague of Deroy, the two of them having shared the post of surgeon at the Carità Hospital since 1688. For thirty years he acted as a trustworthy figure for his brother-in-law and his children. From 1703 he came in fact to play an active role also in overseeing the interests of Deroy's nephews, the children of his daughter and the deceased jeweller Vautier.[14] Vautier himself had in fact appointed as joint guardians to his own children, in addition to his wife Teresa, his brother-in-law, the jeweller Giò Enrico Lacroix (his first wife's brother and himself resident in the neighbourhood), and Giuseppe Pasero, his wife's step-uncle.[15] Apart from this complex affinal tie, Pasero was also close in age to Vautier, as was Lacroix. The links between the three men were therefore multifaceted, being based on closeness in age and residential proximity as well as on a history of professional association. In the case of Lacroix this went back to his youth for, when still unmarried, and presumably working as journeymen in their occupation as goldsmiths, Vautier and Lacroix had shared an apartment, together with four other young men, in the same parish in which they then settled as adults.[16]

The first feature emerging from this evidence is therefore the importance of 'horizontal' kinship in the life of an individual, and more precisely
of affinal ties. The family connections acquired through the wife, sister
or daughter seem to enjoy the full confidence of the testators and their
heirs. There seem to be no distinctions of value between blood relationships and those created by marriage. It is worth pausing to consider this
bilateral character of kinship, which is in contrast with the strongly patrilinear notion of kinship ties that has usually been associated with the
early modern period.[17] Studies on Italy in particular have set great store
by the prevalence of a patrilinear pattern in the transmission of assets, as
well as name, and have often implicitly assumed that the agnatic principle
governed every aspect of family life. In reality, the family as defined by
rules of succession is very different from the one which plays an often
crucial role in economic transactions and other types of exchange in
everyday life, including the professional experience of individuals. We
should not therefore give excessive weight to the principles regulating
the circulation of the patrimony, even more so when we deal with social
classes for whom the inheritance often had scarce economic significance.
Their understanding and practice of family relationships might have been
rather different from that of patricians. The vocabulary used by the latter
to define kinship ties may well appear to suggest that these were ordered
hierarchically according to their nature and degree.[18] However, if we turn
our attention to exchanges between kin there is ample evidence of the
vitality of ties between in-laws, at least in relation to urban groups of
middling sort.[19]

Property itself did not simply follow patrilineal routes. Certainly,
large components of the patrimony did, and when the owner died intes-
tate the law favoured the agnatic line. However, if we do not restrict our
definition of property to real property, but take into account moveables
and consumer goods, or even immaterial goods such as professional
resources, we see that the devolution of patrimony followed lines which
were much more complex.[20] Morever, the study of surgeons' networks
reveals relationships with in-laws as having a key role even in matters
of property, for example, in taking care of the patrimonial interests of
orphans.

It could be that, in the surgeon's milieu, the wife's relatives were
actively preferred as administrators of the children's property because
for the most part they had nothing at stake and were 'disinterested' by
comparison with members of the same line, the latter having the right
of succession were the heirs of the deceased to die. For the same reason,
as Giulia Calvi has suggested, it was usually mothers who were granted

guardianship of the fatherless children, because they could not advance any rights of succession.[21] Admittedly, the testators in question are often from outside the city and their families of origin mostly live elsewhere. Hence there are frequently no members of the bloodline to take care of the interests of orphaned minors concerning inheritance. This reinforces the tendency to nominate as guardians of young children a brother-in-law or a son-in-law (together with the wife of the deceased). The father may simply have no brothers (Deroy's case) or the brothers may live elsewhere (the Asinelli situation); migration, which as we shall see is a feature of a great many barbers-surgeons' experience, has a marked influence on the configuration of their kinship ties.

These observations concerning the demography and geographical mobility characteristic of artisan groups may lead us to conclude that the importance of in-laws was a distinctive feature of the middling urban classes.[22] And yet it may also be that the part played by affines in the social networks of the individual has been underestimated even in studies of the aristocratic and patrician classes, given that such studies have generally drawn upon surnames to reconstruct family ties, a method which inevitably leads to an emphasis on agnatic connections. In fact the recurrent involvement of brothers-in-law in mercantile partnerships has been noted by many authors, even though the reasons behind this preference for establishing business associations with relatives by marriage have been scarcely explored.[23]

It can be argued that in the case of the barber-surgeons, marriage brings about such a profound penetration into the wife's kinship group because, as we have seen, it merely consolidates pre-existing bonds that are professional, friendship-based, grounded in the shared locality, and often founded on common interests and a common language, relating to the care of physical appearance and the health of the body. The marriage tie therefore transforms existing and already significant relationships by raising their quotient of trust. These social bonds are made more lasting and secure by participation in the rituals and the language of solidarity that mark out family ties, and by inclusion in a web of family relations characterised by a high degree of interchange and hence cohesion.[24] It is unlikely that this pattern is exclusive to artisans of the body; the need to create mechanisms that increase the trustworthiness of relationships and dealings between kin characterises early modern society as a whole, even though trust is perhaps a particularly scarce resource in a population as mobile as that of the middling classes.[25]

The search for trust also explains the significant presence of neighbours among the witnesses and godparents used by the surgeons. When these roles are not covered by kin it is mostly neighbours who are represented. Those involved however, are not 'just' neighbours but are drawn from a defined network of neighbours, many of whom are often other artisans of the body: among the godfathers and godmothers of the surgeon Asinelli's grandchildren, we find for instance the goldsmiths Romero and Bogetti, and the tailors Lasagna and Costamagna. Although not predominant, members of the nobility also put in an appearance among the godparents. But in this case too it is neighbours who are involved, indicating that neighbourhood life in a city not yet marked by a politics of social segregation offered yet another opportunity for establishing inter-class relationships. Unlike the situation of the Dijon artisans studied by Farr, in Turin the ties of ritual kinship with socially superior godparents appear to be an expression of relationships between good neighbours rather than simply of ties of patronage.[26]

Credit networks

There are however significant differences between what takes place between relatives (who are also neighbours) and what takes place between unrelated neighbours. For example, choosing a neighbour as guardian for orphaned children is a rare occurrence, although there are instances of it. When Paolo Bernardo Calvo, whom we have already met, was left an orphan at the age of eleven along with his sister Caterina, the guardians named in his father's will were the boy's godfather, Paolino Verdello, and the surgeon Enrico Stura, who lived in the same house as the Calvo family and was the elder brother of Matteo Stura with whom the testator practised his profession.[27] It is primarily when the neighbourly relationship is linked with a professional one that neighbours may, on rare occasions, assume some prominent and delicate role in those family matters we normally find connected with in-laws.

More usually, neighbours were participants in financial transactions involving the surgeons. It was they who would be relied upon more frequently to obtain loans, and to sell or buy a property in the city. Territorial stability was a professional aspiration and hence ownership of one's dwelling was highly desirable; good relationships with neighbours favoured these strategies of permanent settlement in a specific area of the city. The small number of legal documents (aside from those concerning dowries) which took surgeon Asinelli and his son-in-law, surgeon Giò Pietro Busano, to the notary's office, involved transactions with neighbours in almost every case. These were people of diverse social extraction and those who were artisans were predominantly artisans of the body. In 1676 Asinelli made a two-year loan of 2000 lire, in the form of a charge against property income (*censo*), to the surgeon Bruco, who lived two blocks away from his own (Cantone 40). In 1690 he lent 10,000 lire to Count Fontanella, the owner of the house in which he rented his own apartment.[28] In 1694 Busano bought at auction a house in the block adjoining the one where he lived, purchasing it from the widow of the tailor Perinetto, now remarried to another tailor, Gilardi; he then rented an apartment in the house next door to this one, from a Captain Ravizza.[29] The room purchased by the surgeons Calvo and Stura in 1681 was in a house belonging to the surgeon Rustichelli which had been repaired and extended by two floors by means of a loan from a wealthy neighbour, Count Patavino, the owner of the house next door.[30] The court, moreover, constituted a 'neighbourhood' in itself, given that many of those employed there lived in the area around the ducal palace. The transactions, for example, of Giò Francesco Meda, court surgeon, also involved court employees often living in the San Luigi cantone.[31]

It should be made clear that the expression 'neighbourhood' is used here to refer to individuals who live in the same Cantone (also defined as *isola*, that is 'island', at the time), or in contiguous Cantoni.[32] They may have been parishioners in the same parish or adjacent parishes, but belonging to a particular parish does not seem to have provided any territorial identity within the city. In contrast with what is suggested by Hardwick for Nantes, parishes in Turin do not appear to be 'powerful parameters of urban space', all the more so given that they were rarely the principal centre of an individual's devotional activity.[33] Instead, this might take place in the church or chapel of the confraternity to which he or she belonged, which might well be located in a different parish. For example, even though their homes came under the parish of San Giovanni, both Asinelli and his son-in-law Mariano were brothers of the confraternity of San Rocco, which was based in the parish of Santi Stefano e Gregorio, whose parish priest (a member of the same fraternity) was the brother of another of Asinelli's sons-in-law, Busano.[34] Patterns of devotional practices, which it has not been possible to study systematically here, add another dimension to relationships between in-laws.

Many surgeons seem therefore to have operated in a somewhat narrow social space where neighbourhood, professional and ritual connections are repeatedly overlaid, thus making transactions more trustworthy. This microcosm of relationships provides in fact the fabric within which financial exchanges take place. The reckoning of debts and credits which frequently drag on over years and are more often than not moved around or transferred to others, is thus known and kept track of within a wider community which shares in the lender's risks.[35]

Kin, in contrast, are seldom used for borrowing large sums of money (those which are unfailingly registered in a notarised deed). The greater the risk, the less relatives are exposed. Clearly there is no wish to endanger those relationships that matter most. Moreover, not just the patrilineal family but also collateral relatives and in-laws see themselves, however tenuously, as forming a unity of inheritance, since there is always a remote possibility that the sisters will inherit from the brothers, or the sisters from the sisters should there be no male children or living agnates. This makes the moving of large sums from one family nucleus to another undesirable; all the members of the kinship network would suffer, feeling that their rights of inheritance were put at risk. Large amounts of money were sought outside the group of kin, with relatives acting as witnesses if called upon, or as intermediaries between the parties, thus making the transaction more secure and simultaneously overseeing the family members' investments, in which they themselves always felt in some way involved.

Yet this does not rule out the circulation of credit even between bilateral relatives. Loans were granted, particularly between siblings and in-laws, but they consisted of modest sums, albeit important in the life of the individual, and they were often made informally, without any written document resulting. For instance, the widow of the surgeon Maurizio Meda made numerous loans to her brother-in-law between 1690 and 1692, a period when he was 'overwhelmed by lengthy and costly infirmities'. Moreover, Antonio Domenico never paid her the legacy of 100 lire left to her by her husband, his brother, in 1687. Yet it is not until 1693 that a notarised deed is made whereby Antonio acknowledges his total debts to Maria in respect of 440 lire, and commits himself meanwhile to pay her interest at the rate of 5 per cent.[36] Besides money, loans take the form of objects and services (maintenance, keeping an individual under the same roof or looking after that person). Maurizio Meda's will tells us that he loaned his cousin Giò Francesco, also a surgeon, 'five razors, three of silver and two of unornamented copper with a hammer mark, fairly new, and three iron scrapers', and that these must be returned after his death and sold.[37] Sometimes these credits are cancelled out by dowries or other rights of inheritance, even though what is owed is seldom counted with arithmetical precision; these are more a matter of lump-sum repayments. Enrico Stura made good to his brother Giuseppe the 250 lire which he was still owed for the board and lodging provided to him at home for six years and four months, and for similar provision made to him during his stay in Paris, 'as confirmed in letters' hereby remitted to Giuseppe in exchange for surrender of his portion of inheritance from the father.[38]

In other cases, although the debt is discounted, it appears important to make mention of it, thus emphasising that a credit has been acquired, and keeping open a flow of obligations. So in the dowry contract of Anna Catta Cizaletta, the wife of the surgeon Matteo Stura, the bride's parents make a point of noting that besides having paid the dowry and the cost of the trousseau, as they had done for their other daughter, they had also fed and maintained the young newlyweds 'from 8 June 1669 up until the present (February 1670)' and that 'they are happy' to go on housing them until the following Easter.[39]

Even though one is often surprised by the exactness with which contemporaries indicate debts owed by their family members, this is not a reflection of any meanness in family relationships, nor of it being unusual to help out kin. This language of accountancy rather reflects the concern for equity that, at least in the shared rhetoric, is uppermost in parents' relationships with their children and, more generally, in relationships with eventual heirs.[40] The demographic instability of the period meant that a great many people were potentially in this position of potential heir. It should be borne in mind that a family inheritance was not perceived as an individual asset during this period but as a collective possession to be preserved for successors.[41] There was therefore considerable fear of giving rise to suspicions of unfairness towards all those who had a stake in the inheritance, and references to money spent on a descendant had the function of silencing the discontent of others and keeping open the flow of exchanged favours which was nonetheless a feature of many family relationships. Giulio Cesare Meda gave his stepdaughter bed and board for eleven years without having deducted this cost from her inheritance; in his will he acknowledged the rights of his three children to be reimbursed for this, 'if they so please'. We can find no indication of this being done, but the acknowledgement of a credit established by their father perhaps enabled the young Medas not to feel deprived by the fact that a part of the family property had been diverted to their step-sister.[42]

The 'horizontal family'

Our surgeons and artisans of the body moved within two concentric and partly overlapping circles of relationships. The neighbourhood formed the wider of the circles, and its members, particularly individuals with a contiguous professional identity, were a source of significant solidarities. Moreover, it was often here that new families were formed and neighbours turned into kin. With those relatives acquired through marriage, who were frequently also neighbours, relationships were even more intense and variegated, and this constituted the second sphere of the social contacts of artisans of the body.

We have begun, therefore, to see how the importance of family ties can be fully grasped only if we go beyond the nucleus of those living under the same roof and analyse the relationships between kin who belonged to different domestic groups. In fact, the tendency to make the 'family' synonymous with the household has greatly inhibited our understanding of its functions.[43] Although the view of the family as co-residential unit has been criticised in various quarters, the study of kinship relations has attracted considerably less interest, among early modernists, than that of relationships within the nuclear family.[44]

If we set out to extend this analysis to the wider kinship group we must however meet two important conditions: in the first place, as already noted, we must pinpoint the 'active' kinship network, in other words identify those with whom there are frequent exchanges of a varied kind, rather than limiting ourselves to consider ties which may exist only on paper.[45] In the second place, we have observed how crucial it is to consider the role of kin relations created through marriage, not only blood and patrilineal relationships, and how therefore the study of inter-actions between kin cannot be limited to individuals who have the same surname. Even those studies that have placed greater emphasis on the role of kinship have usually interpreted the kinship group as meaning mainly the agnates. The extent to which this restrictive view of kinship can be misleading is clear: in the case of the artisans of the body in Turin, ties with in-laws, besides those with siblings, have emerged as most vital.

These findings are of particular interest if we consider that among artisan groups, who unlike patricians have weak patrimonial interests and even weaker political ambitions, kinship ties have been seen to carry little significance. This view, established in the 1970s by Diane Owen Hughes in a hugely influential article on late medieval Genoa, has subsequently been repeated in many studies of the low and middling urban groups in the Renaissance and early modern age.[46] According to this thesis: 'It was the household, rather than any ties of kinship that might extend beyond it, that was essential to the artisan's concept of life'.[47] My findings contra-dict the notion of an opposition between conjugal family and the broader kinship group underlying this argument. In the horizontal family strong conjugal ties coexist with strong horizontal kinship ties; far from being incompatible they reinforce one other. If one considers that a brother or sister-in-law is also the sibling of one's wife or husband it becomes evident how the two types of tie, matrimonial and affinal, are interconnected and reciprocally supportive. Put in another way, the relevance of the marital bond in this milieu depends precisely on its ability to ensure loyal relationships between a husband and his wife's kin. The role of women is therefore enhanced in this kinship system, for they play a crucial part in maintaining these horizontal relationships of professional partnership and alliance. If anything, it is relationships between generations that often appear rife with tension within this family configuration, as we will see in chapter eight.

Professional networks: the peer group

Thus far we have explained the mutual attraction between the specific occupations we find in the surgeons' kinship networks in terms of a shared discourse, which is to say a common culture of the body that links these occupations. And yet there were also important practical consequences of this tendency to group together. The matrimonial strategies of surgeons and the horizontal configuration of their families had implications for their careers and professional lives; the ramifications of these were numerous, concerning not just professional alliances but the transmission of knowledge as well as of posts and shops. I shall begin with the first of these aspects and the relationships between individuals close in age that could be consolidated through marriage. It is true that often surgeons of different generations who were already working together became related as a consequence of marital union. One instance already discussed is that of Sebastiano Fassina and Domenico Deroy, the former being a pupil of the latter and their cooperation becoming even closer after Fassina's marriage to Deroy's niece. And yet a glance at Deroy's kinship network tells us that marriage ties also created family relationships between barber-surgeons of the same generation (see figure 3.2): for example, Giuseppe Deroy and Giò Francesco and Francesco Maria Meda, who became brothers-in-law through the marriage of Giuseppe's brother, Luigi, to Eleonora, the sister of the Meda surgeons; or in the generation before them, the marriages of Domenico Deroy and Lorenzo Margheri to two of the Pastor sisters. If we consider that after their respective marriages Deroy and Margheri – the one a surgeon, the other a barber – lived and worked in the same house, the house their wives had inherited from their father, it will strike us that their marriages will have strengthened a professional relationship between brothers-in-law more than any between these men and their father-in-law, the Garzone di Camera Eustachio Pastor (who was, moreover, already dead within a year of Margheri's wedding to his daughter).[48] Indeed it is fairly likely that Domenico Deroy and Lorenzo Margheri were also in professional partnership; engaged in allied and, one might say, complementary occupations, and working in the same house, they could offer clients a range of services, from basic to complicated treatments of the aesthetic/surgical kind (we will see in the next chapter that these complementary partnerships were common). We may wonder therefore whether Deroy had married Pastor's daughter or Margheri's sister-in law. Marriage was certainly an 'alliance', as historians of the family have accustomed us to think, but an alliance between which parties? Often what is significant is not a comparison between the occupation of the bride's father and that of her bridegroom; at least when there is a considerable age gap between son-in-law and father-in-law – as between Pastor and Deroy or between Pastor and Margheri – what matters rather more is the relationship the marriage consolidates between the bridegroom and the bride's brother or between brothers-in-law. These are in fact individuals who happen to be in a similar phase of their careers and who therefore experience the same kind of problems in selling their services in a competitive market. In short, to grasp the real implications of inter-occupational marriage, we should once more redirect attention from genealogical observation to 'horizontal' kinship ties. In particular, the effects of matrimonial strategies on work opportunities can be better evaluated if we focus on the kinship group of peers, that cohort of men and women belonging more or less to the same generation and related to one other by marriage and blood.

But how are we to identify peers and horizontal kinship when this is frequently masked? We cannot simply rely on the degree of kinship (by confining ourselves, for example, to taking brothers-in-law or cousins into the reckoning), because the demography of the early modern family (the broad distribution of age among siblings and the frequent disparity in age between husband and wife, especially in the case of second or third marriages) often brings about a narrowing of the age gap, even between father-in-law and son-in-law or uncle and nephew, making more equal a relationship that we would expect to be hierarchical. If we return to Domenico Deroy and Sebastiano Fassina we find that this is in fact the case: although the kinship relation acquired was that of uncle and nephew, the difference in their ages amounts to much less than that between generations. This closeness in age, coupled with the already observed residential patterns adopted by artisans of the body, made their tie extremely valuable and enabled the forging of professional alliances. In chapter eight we shall look further into the importance of these diagonal or 'half-generational' ties at the professional level. It is nonetheless clear that in order to understand the impact of marriage and the ties created by it on professional experience we must pay attention to the respective ages of the members of the group of kin rather than exclusively to the kinship relation between them.

Typical examples are the wedding between the surgeon Francesco Domenico Reyneri and Angelica Cappa (the sister of the surgeon Ottavio and the physician Guglielmo) and the marriage of Ludovica, the daughter of Francesco and Angelica, to the apothecary Bruno (see figure 5.2). The role of these marriages in the professional life of Giò Domenico lies not so much in the consolidation of the bond with the much older brother-in-law Ottavio, also a surgeon, living and practising in a different area of the city (Cantone 130), but in the strengthening of a relationship between neighbourhood colleagues: namely, with the other brother of Angelica, Guglielmo, a physician, and with the apothecary Bruno, who became his son-in-law. The former resided in the same Cantone as Giò Domenico (82) and the latter in the block opposite his (134) (see plate 4). It should be noted, moreover, that not only were the two brothers-in-law Giò Domenico and Guglielmo the same age, having been born respectively in 1668 and 1669, but the apothecary Bruno was a widower two years younger than his wife's father. It was likely that the two weddings consolidated a connection between colleagues – a surgeon, a physician and an apothecary – who provided complementary medical services and who, given their closeness in age, happened to be at a similar stage in their careers and coping with the same problems of securing and maintaining a loyal clientele. We know from other sources and other situations that these informal partnerships between different branches of medical practice existed unofficially and could be prosecuted by the law: in 1709, for example, we find an ordinance prohibiting 'any physician from making any pact or agreement with the surgeon or apothecary, whereby there might be any sharing of financial gain either to a greater or lesser degree'.[49] These unofficial coalitions were a way of establishing some control over local areas and sections of the market; ties between their members through marriage promoted their consolidation.

The same logic was to be found in more complex forms of building kinship networks, and between professions that were not strictly medical but could, as we have seen, be regarded as allied. Let us look, for example, at the string of cousins, brothers-in-law and siblings created by the marriages in the Deroy kinship network (see figure 5.3). The dates of birth of four of these men show that they were close in age, and the year of the first marriage of some of the others also offers some indication of their age group: these are individuals separated by an age difference of no more than ten to fifteen years, who are all active at the same time in the market for services relating to the body. Clearly, these men and women are peers

Figure 5.2 Giò Domenico Reyneri and his in-laws

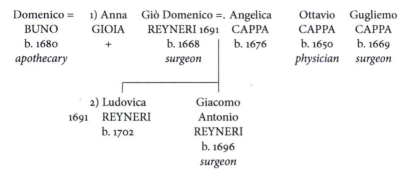

=: marriage bond

who will pursue their careers over a similar timespan; the fact that they are all engaged in the restricted range of occupations we are already familiar with appears to have some significance. In fact their working activity revolves around only three occupations, those of the surgeon, the perruquier and the jeweller: eight men and three occupations. What repercussions did this have on their professional lives?

On the one hand, the kinship ties established between them promoted the formation of partnerships within the profession: we already know that the marriage of Teresa Deroy to the jeweller Enrico Vautier, the partner of her brother, Luigi, transformed what was a working relationship between the two men into a more involving family relationship. This was Vautier's third marriage and the preceding unions had had the same function of reinforcing professional cooperation: Vautier's first wife, whom he married in 1685, was the sister of goldsmith Enrico Lacroix, already a partner of Vautier. Two years later, the widowed Vautier remarried Lacroix's cousin, Maddalena Buré, daughter of the *piumacciere* of Madama Reale, Enrico, thus re-confirming his bond with his brother-in-law.[50]

It is very likely that the tailors, perruquiers, jewellers, apothecaries, barbers and surgeons whom we find repeatedly linked in the kinship networks and who, as we know, tended to occupy precise areas of the city, were also in a position to create market monopolies by offering their clients a set of services that at the time were perceived as connected. Just as a surgeon's client would be sent to the trusted apothecary who was also the surgeon's relative, or medicines would be procured from him for the surgeon's patients, it is likely that these networks of artisans of the body made a concerted group effort to satisfy the greatest number of needs relating to the health and bodily enhancement of a clientele which has

Figure 5.3 Horizontal kinship between artisans of the body

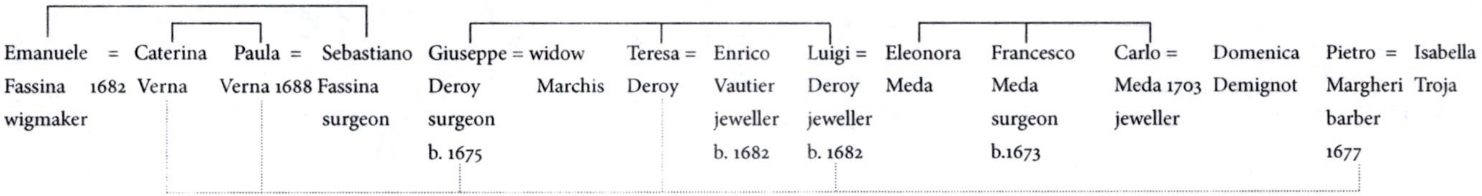

Emanuele = Caterina Paula = Sebastiano Giuseppe = widow Teresa = Enrico Luigi = Eleonora Francesco Carlo = Domenica Pietro = Isabella
Fassina 1682 Verna Verna 1688 Fassina Deroy Marchis Deroy Vautier Deroy Meda Meda Meda 1703 Demignot Margheri Troja
wigmaker surgeon surgeon jeweller jeweller surgeon jeweller barber
  b. 1675 b. 1682 b. 1682 b.1673 1677

=: marriage bond
b.: born
other dates refer to date of marriage
subling tie ————
cousins ⋯⋯⋯

aptly been described as capricious and choosy. It seems worth noting, for example, that surgeons like Giuseppe Deroy also invested his financial capital in the shop of his brother and his brother-in-law, jewellers.[51]

The key to understanding the associative strategies of the artisans of the body is therefore the complementarity of their occupations as perceived by their contemporaries. Scholars who have observed the tendency of some occupations to cluster in social life and in the same locality have tended to explain this in terms of their similarity (in skills, tools, techniques or materials employed).[52] In the instance that I have analysed, instead, the driving force in social groupings seems to be the tendency for complementary occupations to combine: companion of functions and services and the cultural identity created by a common discourse could generate informal occupational coalitions which, for those involved, secured a degree of control over areas of consumption.

Many studies over recent years have insisted that the provision of medical services was dominated by market mechanisms. One aspect of the expansion of consumption which took place in the seventeenth and eighteenth centuries was that expenditure on health also increased, medical services became fashionable and this led to a proliferation of healers on the market, along with intense competition between them. The result was that practitioners were forced to specialise in one service or operation or another, or offer miraculous cures and specially concocted potions in their attempts to win over a demanding and faddish clientele that was prone to shop around.[53] This picture presents us with a scenario of open rivalry, created by the fickle attitude of clients who see individual practitioners at odds with one another. In fact, precisely because these were highly competitive circumstances, various expedients were adopted to limit this competition, and these strategies were pursued by practitioners clustering together rather than by single individuals on their own. The patterns of kinship formation and local settlement that I have described so far offer one example; they made it possible to exercise considerable network pressure on the clientele and likewise conspired to increase control over customer choices. The market for medical services was far from deregulated nor as fragmented in rivalries between single individuals as is often assumed. While historians have normally looked for evidence of institutional regulation, via the rules issued by state authorities and professional bodies for example, our analysis highlights various practices through which competition was limited 'from below' and forms of monopoly of sections of the market were achieved. We shall see in the next chapter how access to the occupation was also far from being open, another element that undermines the image of a 'free' medical marketplace.

Notes

1 AAT, 18.1.16, 24 April 1688; Ins. 1678, l. 12, c. 441. For the Meda brothers' training in the hospital, see OSG, *Ordinati*, 20 September 1676 and 8 February 1689.

2 For those living in the parish of Santi Simone e Giuda details of residence are drawn from the Registry of Souls available for the period 1648–1728 (AAT, 18.1.1/6). For those who lived in other parishes information on family settlement can be obtained from notarised deeds, which often record the *Cantone* of residence.

3 Ins. 1678, l. 12, vol. II, c. 745.

4 In Italy, the tendency to residential endogamy among the lower and middling urban classes is also a feature of the earlier period. See Cohn, *The Laboring Classes*, pp. 74–82, 117–23; D. Kent and F. W. Kent, *Neighbors and Neighborhood in Renaissance Florence* (New York, 1982), pp. 48–66; Grubb, *Provincial Families*, p. 7; for examples from other European countries, see J. F. Farr, *Artisans in Europe 1300–1914* (Cambridge, 2000), p. 247. The strength of local ties, especially between members of the adjacent occupations of tailor, silk merchant and fabric retailer, also emerges in Simona Cerutti's work on the rise of guilds in Turin. The author however sees them as evidence of ethnic ties and of political strategies in relation to the control of guilds, rather than of neighbourhood and territorial professional ties: Cerutti, *Mestieri e Privilegi*, pp. 34–40, 64–5, 196–8.

5 Examples of this kind of study include Dolan, *Le Notaire*; D. O'Hara, 'Ruled by my friends: aspects of marriage in the diocese of Canterbury c.1540–1570', *Continuity and Change*, 6 (1991); Cerutti, *Mestieri e Privilegi*, chapters two and four; Hardwick, *Practice of Patriarchy*. The evidence from Turin will be compared primarily with studies concerned with 'middling sort' urban groups and above all with Hardwick's study of Nantes, which is close in approach to the one adopted here.

6 AAT, 18.1.1/6 (see note two). Moreover, the registers of baptism and marriage give the names of godparents and witnesses (*ibid.*, 18.1.7/13).

7 His presence there is discontinuous, but this may be due to the wars of the 1690s.

8 Ins. 1684, l. 10, c. 540; 1688, l. 2, c. 627; 1694, l. 10, c. 1861; 1697, l. 4, c. 319; 1704, l. 3, c. 101; AAT, 18.1.16, 24 January 1700 and 21 July 1703; Ins. 1703, l. 9, c. 243; 1723, l. 10, vol. 4, c. 2467.

9 Hardwick, *Practice of Patriarchy*, p. 175 and, more generally, chapter five.

10 *Ibid.*, pp. 176–7.

11 Ins. 1678, l. 12, vol. II, c. 745; 1694, l. 10, c. 343.

12 In fact this responsibility passed on to the eldest of Deroy's children, who had reached his majority, but since he was outside state territory, he appointed his brother-in-law Vautier as his proxy. Ins. 1699, l. 2, c. 575. Responsibility for the children of the second marriage remained however with their mother, Anna Teresa Benna, widow of Deroy.

13 *Ibid.*, 1700, l. 3, c. 381; 1713, l. 5, vol. I, c. 73.

14 Moreover, he acted as a witness to Deroy's weddings and to the marriage and dowry contract of their brother-in-law Mozzetto. AAT, 18.1.16, 24 April 1688 and 11 January 1693; Ins. 1693, l. 2, c. 167.

15 *Ibid.*, 1702, l. 1, c. 779.

16 AAT, 18.1.3, 1685.

17 For examples of correctives to this model see the Introduction to *Quaderni Storici*, 86 (1994), and the articles therein.

18 According to Klapisch-Zuber, separate terms for defining blood relatives and affines

were used in Renaissance Florence. Even more precisely, the close and paternal blood relatives (*congiunti*) were distinguished from the non-blood relatives and the maternal kin, who were grouped together under the label *parenti*. Moreover, a separate term, *consorti*, was used to define distant blood relatives such as paternal cousins. See C. Klapisch-Zuber, 'Kin, friends and neighbors: the urban territory of a merchant family in 1400', in her *Women, Family, and Ritual in Renaissance Italy*, (Chicago, 1985) pp. 74, 76, 81.

19 This statement also seem to apply to earlier and later periods of Italian history. For the bilateral character of the artisan family in the Renaissance see C. Klapisch-Zuber, 'La vie domestique et ses conflits chez un maçon bolonais du XVe siècle', in P. Boglioni, R. Delort, C. Gauvard (eds), *Le Petit Peuple dans l'Occident Médiéval. Terminologies, Perceptions, Réalités* (Paris, 2002). On its horizontal character, see my 'L'importanza della 'famiglia orizzontale' nella storia della famiglia Italiana', in I. Fazio and D. Lombardi (eds), *Generazioni. Legami di Parentela tra Passato e Presente* (Rome, 2006).

20 See my 'What did women transmit?'

21 G. Calvi, 'Widows, the state and the guardianship of children in early modern Tuscany', in S. Cavallo and L. Warner (eds), *Widowhood in Medieval and Early Modern Europe* (Harlow, 1999), p. 212. Obviously a mother could inherit if her child nominated her his/her heir. And this is what happened to Deroy's widow, Anna Teresa Benna, mentioned above, who inherited a large part of the share that would have gone to her two sons from their father's inheritance: her son Francesco, a cleric who had already inherited the share of his brother Domenico, who died in childhood, died in turn, having made his will in favour of his mother (Ins. 1713, l. 5, vol. I, c. 73).

22 Hardwick seems to incline to this explanation: 'kinship among these middling urban families clearly emphasised kin ties from the families of both spouses rather than favouring patrilineal kin' (*Practice of Patriarchy*, p. 166).

23 For example E. Grendi, 'Associazioni familiari e associazioni d'affari. I Balbi a Genova tra Cinquecento e Seicento', *Quaderni Storici*, 91 (1996), and works cited in I. Ben-Amos, 'Gifts and favors: informal support in early modern England', *Journal of Modern History*, 72 (2000), nn. 43–45. See also n. 49 below. Klapisch-Zuber notes the role of affines in settling family disputes and more generally as peacemakers rather than in commercial affairs: 'Kin', pp. 85–7.

24 This does not mean to say that there were no conflicts: Deroy's widow's remarriage, for example, probably did not go down well with the children of her first marriage, and likewise with their relatives on their father's side, Giuseppe Verna and Enrico Vautier, who refused repeatedly to attend the reckoning of accounts of guardianship required in these cases by the law (Ins. 1700, l. 3, c. 381).

25 On the high level of migration in Italian cities in this period, see A. Arru and F. Ramella (eds), *L'Italia delle Migrazioni Interne. Donne, Uomini, Mobilità in Età Moderna e Contemporanea* (Rome 2003); for Turin, G. Levi, 'Mobilità della popolazione a Torino nella prima metà del Settecento', *Quaderni Storici*, 17 (1971).

26 Farr, *Hands of Honor*, pp. 127–9.

27 Ins. 1679, l. 3, vol. II, c. 625 (Calvo's will); *ibid.*, 1683, l. 3, c. 531 for evidence of Enrico Stura's residence.

28 *Ibid.*, 1679, l. 6, vol. II, c. 547; 1690, l. 5, vol. II, c. 559. Two other loans in the form of censi, for lire 3000 and 4000, were made in 1679 and 1681 to a colleague, the surgeon

Noè la Viviera: *ibid.*, 1681, l. 2, c. 434.

29 *Ibid.*, 1694, l. 10, vol. II, cc. 1857, 1861; 1697, l. 4, c. 319.

30 *Ibid.*, 1681, l. 4, c. 835.

31 *Ibid.*, 1688, l. 5, c. 503; 1691, vol. II, c. 677; 1692, l. 3, c. 245; 1692, l. 5, c. 1007; 1692, l. 7, c. 416.

32 As we already know, the Cantone consisted of the agglomeration of houses bounded by three or four streets containing a number of inhabitants varying between 150 and 300.

33 Hardwick, *Practice of Patriarchy*, pp. 192, 174, 177–8.

34 See Asinelli's wills (Ins. 1684, l. 10, c. 540; 1688, l. 2, c. 627; 1704, l. 5, c. 513); Mariano's will (*ibid.*, 1695, l. 11, parte II, c. 37); and the will of the parish priest Busano (*ibid.*, 1711, l. 4, vol. I, c. 151). Even baptisms and burials often took place in churches others than the parish's, although they were recorded in the parish registers.

35 On payment delays and the circulation of credits see Ben-Amos, 'Informal support', p. 329 and, more generally, pp. 307–8 for the hazard of economic transactions and the need for guarantors and intermediaries in 'a society with no banks'; also Muldrew, *The Economy*, chapters 3–4.

36 Ins. 1693, l. 2, c. 669.

37 *Ibid.*, 1686, l. 12, c. 47.

38 *Ibid.*, 1683, l. 3, c. 531.

39 *Ibid.*, 1670, l.8, c. 91.

40 Of course this is a rhetoric that explicitly acknowledges the superior rights of sons over daughters. But at least within the sexes and in terms of what is openly avowed, equity is still aimed for. In practice there are substantial inequalities, particularly between the sons, and we shall see some examples of these below (chapter eight). This has also been confirmed by an analysis of testamentary practices in Turin during this period: Cavallo, 'Proprietà o possesso?', pp. 190–1. On inequalities in expenditures for different children, see G. Levi, 'Comportements, ressources, procès: avant la 'révolution' de la consommation', in J. Revel (ed.), *Jeux d'Echelles. La Micro-Analyse à l'Expérience* (Paris, 1996), pp. 202–7.

41 D. Frigo, *Il Padre di Famiglia: Governo della Casa e Governo Civile nella Tradizione della 'Economica' tra Cinque e Seicento* (Rome, 1985), chapter five.

42 Ins. 1681, l. 3, parte I, c. 279.

43 As noted by J. Goody, 'The evolution of the family', in P. Laslett and R. Wall (eds), *Household and Family in Past Time* (Cambridge, 1972), p. 119; M. Chaytor, 'Household and kinship in Ryton in the late sixteenth and early seventeenth centuries', *History Workshop Journal*, 10 (1980); G. Levi, 'Household and kinship: a few thoughts', *Journal of Family History*, 15 (1990). For a helpful overview of recent approaches to the study of family ties see P.-A. Rosenthal, 'Les liens familiaux, forme historique?', *Annales de Démographie Historique* (2000), pp. 49–81.

44 Valuable exceptions are Cressy, 'Kinship and kin'; N. Tadmor, *Family and Friends in Eighteenth-Century England: Household, Kinship, and Patronage* (Cambridge, 2000), especially chapters three and four. See also D. W. Sabean, *Property, Production, and the Family in Neckerhausen, 1700–1870* (Cambridge, 1990); Delille, *Famille et Propriété*.

45 Following Bourdieu, Hardwick distinguishes between 'practical' kin relationships and 'official' kin relationships, 'which were of limited importance in daily life'. Hardwick, *Practice of Patriarchy*, p. 161 and chapter five; P. Bourdieu, *Outline of a Theory of*

Practice (Cambridge, 1977), pp. 33–43.

46 D. O. Hughes, 'Domestic ideals and social behavior: evidence from medieval Genoa', in C. E. Rosenberg (ed.), *The Family in History* (Philadelphia, 1975; repr. 1984); D. Romano, *Patricians and Popolani: The Social Foundations of the Venetian Renaissance State* (Baltimore, 1987), pp. 56–64. For a dissenting voice, see M. Chojnacka, *Working Women of Early Modern Venice* (Baltimore, 2001), pp. 7–11, 25.

47 Hughes, 'Domestic ideals', p. 126.

48 Ins. 1666, l. 11, c. 449.

49 The ordinance of 22 February 1709 recalls the one already issued on 20 October 1568: this was therefore a fairly deep-rooted practice: Duboin, vol. 10, p. 100; Borelli, p. 966. For similar informal partnerships in the Venetian mainland, se D. Bartolini, *Medici et Comunità. Esempi della Terraferma Veneta dei secoli XVI e XVII* (Venice, 2006).

50 On the relationship between Lacroix and his cousin see Ins. 1700, l. 3, c. 429 and l. 8 c. 175. It would seem that the duties of the '*piumacciere*' consisted of taking care of the feathers and down which filled mattresses, pillows and cushions in the Chamber as well as of the feathers used in the head-dressed and attire of the duchess, all features which qualify him as 'artisan of the body'.

51 Carlo Giuseppe turns out to be a 'partner and participant' in the goldsmith's shop kept 'jointly' by his brother Luigi Deroy and his brother-in-law Enrico Lacroix: *ibid.*, 1703, l. 10, c. 25.

52 See works cited in chapter three, nn. 60–64.

53 The introduction of this paradigm is normally attributed to Cook's study of the London College of Physician: Cook, *Decline*. This model has recently been criticised by Pelling in her *Medical Conflicts*, especially pp. 342–3. For a thorough reassessment of this concept, see the forthcoming M. Jenner and P. Wallis (eds), *Medicine and the Market in England and its Colonies, c. 1450–1850* (Basingstoke, forthcoming).

6

Age, working relationships
and the marketplace

Apprenticeship

We have seen that marriage and horizontal kinship structured the professional life of the surgeon, his relationships with colleagues and with clients. However, they also played a key role in the transmission of occupational knowledge and the handing down of the shop. Those who have tried to measure the transmission of occupational knowledge from one generation to the next have come up with relatively low figures. Whether in Venice or York, Bruges, Vienna, Lyons, Paris or Dijon, it was far from being automatic that a son would follow his father's profession.[1] Nonetheless, it should be noted that the studies in question have normally inquired into the rate of reproduction of the same occupation; moreover, they have confined themselves to looking at occupational transmission solely from father to son. If we adopt these same criteria, the handing down of the trade within the family appears to be scarce even among the barber-surgeons of Turin. For example, of the eighty-six surgeons and barbers listed on the professional survey of 1695 (we are excluding the two widows and the 'medicone' – an unqualified healer) only nine state the father's occupation as surgeon or barber.[2] The rate of occupational transmission turns out to be much higher, however, if we take into consideration the wider kinship group and the set of trades to which a particular occupation was related. In our case, this is a question of redirecting attention from barber-surgeons to those I have described as 'artisans of the body'.

Where were the basics of the trade learned? In my research I have found very little material on the apprenticeship of barber-surgeons, the apprentices in this occupation appear to be almost non-existent. Let us take for example the 1705 census of the population in Turin. Only four apprentices are to be found as part of a surgeon's household, whereas we find twenty-four *Giovani* (young surgeons).[3] This seems to suggest that apprenticeship did not as a rule involve moving into the master's household, while this was often the case for the young surgeon, or else that 'the apprentice' was actually not a common figure in this occupation. Indeed, in my examination of notarial records I have found no contract of apprenticeship relating to barber-surgeons. All the same, references to the existence of 'apprentices' in this occupation are occasionally to be found in other sources. In a deed of agreement between the surgeon Giuseppe Reyneri and his father, Giacomo Antonio, also a surgeon, laying down the division of earnings between father and son, one of the clauses states: 'It will be open to either to accept within the household Giovani or *imprendizzi* [apprentices], requiring from these a sum of money due to

Table 6.1 Age of *Giovani* and *imprendizzi* in barber-surgeon's shops

Age	Giovani	Imprendizzi
15	–	2
16	–	–
17	2	1
18	5	–
19	4	–
20	–	1
21	1	–
22	5	–
23	1	–
24	1	–
25	2	–
26	–	–
27	–	–
28	1	–
29	–	–
30	1	–
31	–	–
32	–	–
33	1	–
Total	24	4

Source: Art. 530.

whoever shall accept and maintain them'.[4] But here the term Imprendizzo seems to be used interchangeably with that of Giovane, and this hypothesis is also backed up by other clues. In his testament for example, the surgeon Giuseppe Deroy bequeathed the three Giovani in his workshop the sum that they owed him 'for their apprenticeship (*imprendissaggio*)'.[5] It would seem that the terms Imprendizzo and Giovane were to some degree interchangeable, but that the second term was more commonly used to refer to the variety of subordinate roles in the shop. Even the age of the members of the two categories suggests that there was not always a clear distinction between the two figures (Table 6.1). Two of the four Apprendisti recorded (aged seventeen and twenty) are in fact quite grown-up and fall within the age band covered by the term Giovane, which includes men who are seventeen to thirty-three years old.

We shall return later to this broad age range. For now we still have to explain the fact that only two of the 28 Giovani and Apprendisti found in the shops of the barber-surgeons were less than seventeen years old, in other words that there is an absence of adolescents around thirteen to fifteen years old bound to a master. How then were the rudiments of the trade learned? Did training begin only around the age of seventeen? It is plausible that many young boys acquired the fundamentals within the family environment, and for this reason we find few instances of their moving into the household of a master; likewise, apprenticeship did not involve the drawing up of formal contracts, but came about in a much more informal manner. The family environment should however be understood in a broad sense, as both biological and acquired kinship; moreover, this environment frequently overlapped with sections of the neighbourhood, as we already know.

There are many indicators which suggest that initiation into work was often entrusted to members of the family or the kinship network. The agreement drawn up between the surgeon Giuseppe Reyneri and his father Giacomo Antonio, stipulating the division of responsibilities and earnings between father and son, notes, for example, that Giuseppe, a successful surgeon who had been living independently for years, and as head of his own family for the past four, 'will be responsible for teaching his brother'; this was Bartolomeo, who was younger and living and working with their father.[6] This clause supplies us with an example of what was normally expected of members of the same family or kinship network: that acquired knowledge and professional achievements were shared among siblings – just as earnings were, in theory, shared, at least until the father's death. Indeed we find this pattern repeated a number of times, particularly among surgeons who experience early success: they become responsible for the training of at least one of the younger brothers and his introduction into the world of work. This is the case with three of the Stura brothers, who originally came from Buttigliera d'Asti: Enrico established himself as a surgeon in Turin and set his younger brother Matteo on the same career path: he then had another younger brother, Giuseppe, trained as a barber, keeping him at home with him in Turin for more than six years and paying the cost of a trip to Paris for him to polish his skills. After the death of their father, Enrico also sent for his sister Caterina. Presumably she became acquainted with the surgeon's occupation in her brother's house and, perhaps with the benefit of this experience, she later married the surgeon and neighbour Angelo Benedicti.[7]

The point is therefore that the family had a key role in the transmission of skills, but this frequently happened between an older brother and a younger, or between an uncle and a nephew or between an older cousin or brother-in-law and a younger one. Particularly when there were a large number of children in a family we can see that in the formative period of adolescence some of the children may be entrusted to prosperous and successful relatives. A case in point is represented by Alberto Verna's nephews.[8] He was the only member of the family to have moved to Turin from the village where he was born, and there within a short time he became a prominent practitioner and chief surgeon at the hospital of San Giovanni. At this point he sent for a number of his brothers' adolescent sons to come from the family's village of origin and live with him in Turin. He trained two of these in his chosen profession, while the third was launched on a career as a physician. Although they lived and worked with him, the Verna boys were not however described in the population census of 1705 as Apprendisti, nor as Giovani, but merely as 'nephews', and there do not appear to be formal contracts between Alberto and the boys' parents.[9] I have found traces of written agreements only in the more delicate case of young boys whose father is dead, and these are, however, private documents, not drawn up by a notary. An example is that of the fifteen–year-old Ludovico Deroy, the son of the late surgeon Domenico by his second marriage. In 1697 he was apprenticed to his brother-in-law (the husband of his stepsister) Enrico Vautier, a jeweller, who was clearly much older than him.[10] The agreement between Ludovico's brother-in-law and the young orphan's guardian allows for an apprenticeship lasting four years. We do not know whether this involves moving into the brother-in-law's household, but it is possible that this was unnecessary, given that the Deroys and the Vautiers lived in the same neighbourhood, an extremely short distance apart. A similar case is that of Cesare Antonio Senta, orphan, and brother of the surgeon Matteo, he was apprenticed to his sister's husband, the apothecary Horto.[11]

In cases when it does not occur at home or within the kinship network, the apprenticeship takes place with a neighbour, in situations where the families have known one another for a long time. Only exceptionally do we come to know about these informal agreements. We learn, for example, that in 1712 the goldsmith Stoper had five years earlier taken in and given board to the son of the deceased jeweller Vautier, his neighbour of twenty years, to train him in the profession. The young Vautier was an orphan and his inheritance was therefore subject to guardianship. The delicacy of this case probably explains why, when the young man resolved to leave Stoper, the guardian decided that the settling up of what he owed and the conclusion of any obligations towards Stoper should be set down by a notary. Thus we discover the terms of an agreement which, under normal circumstances, we would not have known about.[12]

It is this general responsibility for the training of the young which has the effect of making apprenticeships invisible. It is not that there was no learning at home during childhood and adolescence, but in the case of large families, embarking on a specific trade (and later the transmission of professional positions and ties) was something that frequently took place within the web of relationships created by kinship and residential proximity, and not just within the nuclear family. This suggests that the transmission of professional knowledge within the family cannot be measured merely by comparing the occupations of father and son, as has often been done. Such a form of occupational continuity certainly existed but this procedure overlooks a simple but crucial fact: that there was usually more than one son (at least at the point of taking up an occupation), and that these sons could not all inherit the father's shop and his limited resources.[13] The trade they pursued was unlikely however to be totally unfamiliar and extraneous to those practised within the family in the broad sense. It will be an occupation that is already present within the kinship network – that of the older brother, the uncle, the cousin or the brother-in-law – and which at any rate has at least cultural affinities with the one practised in the family of origin. This suggests that the knowledge acquired at home seeing the family at work had a certain versatility and could be transferred to related occupations. Only a limited number of crafts are actually to be found within the kinship network, as we have repeatedly observed. The concepts of 'occupational milieu' and 'kinship between occupations' are therefore crucial whenever we are addressing the issue of the transmission of trades.

Surgeons' *Giovani*

For many males a basic grounding would have been acquired either in the home or with a kin or neighbour, and this would have been followed by a period of several years when the aspiring surgeon worked as a Giovane with one or more masters who already had an acknowledged professional identity. This meant that the young man gradually gained training in every aspect of the profession, and at the same time became known as he established relationships in a locality and with a clientele. He was also forming ties with certain masters who would assume a significant role in his future career, helping him to set up his own shop and possibly to secure important positions such as professional posts within institutions. The early years were therefore a crucial period when potential was explored and new bonds were created, often beyond those of the family. Of course there were plenty who did not leave the family but worked with their fathers. Among the surgeons we have already encountered for example, Giò Pietro Brucho describes having trained his son Giò Domenico in the profession; Carlo Antonio Bonardo undertook his post as municipal Surgeon to the Poor along with his son Michele, only seventeen at the time, who would go on to be his successor in this post.[14] For every son who remained there were however others who left; we have already seen that scant family resources at this level in society were not enough to give every child a future – parents often had little more to their name than the earnings from their work.

For many Giovani there was therefore a separation from the family and a period of living by their own efforts before marriage. In terms of domestic arrangements these years as subordinate workers took various forms: on the face of things there were not many who lived with a master (as noted, the 1705 census recorded only twenty-four living-in Giovani) and yet, for those from Turin, there were sometimes mixed living arrangements combining the family home and that of the master that puzzled the takers of the population census and perhaps led to an underestimation of the numbers of Giovani attached to a shop. We find this suggested by the case of Ignazio Morin, aged seventeen, and a Giovane with the perruquier Maurizio Brochiard. According to the census, he 'sleeps at his master's house but takes his meals at his father's'. And we must not limit ourselves to considering only those living-in. It would seem that Giovani sometimes set up households of their own; this was the case with the jeweller Vautier, who, in 1685, we find living with six other young men, most of them likewise of French origin and at least some of them also jewellers. Or else they would rent individual rooms, like the young surgeon Pietro Ruiz. In 1693 we find him living on his own in the same building as the surgeon Asinelli, for whom he probably worked (he was to marry the latter's daughter seven years later).[15]

The domestic arrangements of the young surgeons were as varied as their working relationships. From the age of seventeen or eighteen they would enter into various kinds of working partnership entailing a broad spectrum of relationships that were subordinate to some degree or another.

This period of training and building of professional relationships often went hand-in-hand with geographical mobility. There was a huge movement of young men from the provinces towards the capital of the region. With its ninety surgeons' shops and its hospitals, Turin clearly exerted a strong attraction for those young men drawn to the prospects surgery seemed to offer. Of the twenty-eight Giovani and apprentices found in the 1705 census, as many as fourteen were recorded as coming from outside Turin, and this gives us a sense of the huge extent of ad hoc migration to the city for the sake of further training in the profession. This impression is confirmed by the data relating to the young surgeons who rotated as trainees (*Infermieri*) at the city's main hospital, the San Giovanni. Of the fifty-two whose place of origin we know, only six are from Turin, while forty-six are incomers. The data available about the ages of young surgeons suggests that their move to the capital normally took place when they were young men rather than adolescents: with only one exception the ten Infermieri whose age is known are all over twenty.[16]

Various indicators suggest that, at this same stage in the life cycle, there was also a more modest flow in the other direction, a movement away from the capital. To start with, the training of young men who showed very early promise in their profession often involved a period of practice in France, at the Paris hospitals, which at the time were regarded as the Mecca of surgery. The twenty-five–year-old Giuseppe Reyneri, for example, 'one of the best young men associated with this profession in Turin', had been in Paris for some years 'for his education'.[17] What is more, the French capital exerted a powerful attraction over future perruquiers, barbers, *garzoni* and *baigneurs di Camera*, who underwent specialist training in hygiene and aesthetic enhancement. Among typical examples we encounter the young surgeon Giovan Battista Verna, the future *baigneur* to His Majesty. In 1741 he borrowed 2,000 lire from his cousin Evasio, an already established surgeon, 'to cover the travelling and living expenses' he would incur in Paris, where he was going for further training in his profession.[18] Many were strongly tempted to remain there. At the age of nineteen, in 1678, Emanuele Fassina, the future court perruquier,

Plate 5 Five surgical operations taking place in a surgery, 16th century.

was thinking of staying on in Paris, where he had gone to learn his trade, but was then 'persuaded by friends and relatives to settle in Turin'.[19]

Besides this movement to and from the city, or from one place to another, there was also movement within the city, from one shop to another, from one neighbourhood and social network to another. Even for those who were natives of Turin or long since resident in the city and sons of surgeons or barbers, it was common to move away from the family to train with other masters, to 'look around' and fashion relationships that might well supply opportunities of employment other than succeeding to the father's shop.

The supply of barber-surgeons' Giovani was therefore surprisingly high. To what extent was the labour market able to absorb it? To address this question we have to consider the organisation of labour in this occupation. Although the literature on the medical marketplace has tended to describe the medical practitioner as someone who offers his abilities individually on the market for medical services, regardless of the type of service performed, and in clear competition with equally individual rivals, barber-surgeons did not as a rule work alone. Visual representations of the barber-surgeon's shop typically depict his work place as populated by several figures, of different ages, intent on providing

Plate 6 Surgeons and assistant operating on the battlefield: J. Browne, *A complete discourse of wounds*, London, 1678.

a range of services to different clients (plate 5). Likewise, images of barber surgeons at work outside the shop, on the battlefield or in the patient's domestic environment, classically show him working with his Giovani

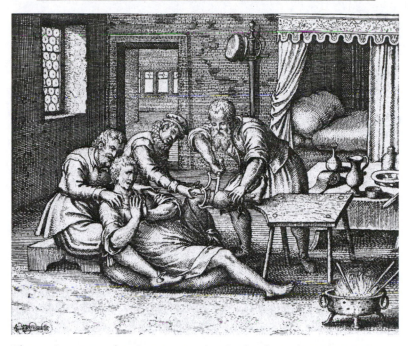

Plate 7 Surgeon and assistants operating in the domestic environment: Fabricius, *De Gangraena et Sphacelo*, c.1620.

(plates 6–9). Theirs was a business where assistants were required: in the first place to keep the patient still during the various surgical operations carried out, including blood-letting (Plate 1), but also to provide help with medication and ligatures.[20] It is also the Giovani who are left in charge of the shop whenever the surgeon has to go out around the city on emergencies, or when he has to serve as a surgeon on a military campaign. For example, the surgeon Giovan Battista Garrone was represented by one of his Giovani at the occupational survey that took place in Turin in 1695. The latter was left to manage the shop while his master was senior surgeon and director of the field hospitals at Frassinetto Po and Valenza.[21] The Giovani were needed also because they were usually sent to give medication to the patients under the surgeon's care after these had been seen by the surgeon himself. Lastly, as we already know, the shop would offer a variety of services, some of them cosmetic, and these were often carried out by the Giovani. Presumably barber's services were also performed in Giuseppe Deroy's shop (and Deroy was chief surgeon at one of the three city hospitals), given that in his will he left the shop's three Giovani 'the razors, a shaving basin to each one, and every other instrument of surgery owned by himself the testator'.[22]

The young surgeon, a figure neglected so far in accounts of the occupation, was therefore crucial to the working of the trade. There is also a substantial presence of Giovani to be found in the various institutions where surgeons were employed. The military hospitals were practically run by the senior surgeon (who sometimes, like Garrone, was also the director of the hospital) and a large number of his assistants; at the Vercelli military hospital in 1696, there were five, then six young surgeons, and eleven, then twelve Infermieri, for a number of patients ranging between 200 and 300. Alongside this slew of surgeons there was only ever one physician.[23] It should be explained that while in the city hospitals the terms 'Giovane Chirurgo' (young surgeon) and Infermiere (nurse) were used as synonyms, in the military hospitals a more complex stratification of the personnel assisting the senior surgeon was adopted. Thus the Infermiere occupied a grade lower than that of the Giovane chirurgo, possibly reflecting more or less demanding duties and responsibilities, but these were in fact related duties, given that the Infermiere could later be promoted to Giovane Chirurgo.[24] Moreover, the pay differential between the two categories was negligible or non-existent: during the period in question the Giovani Chirurghi received 15 lire a month, while the Infermieri were paid between 12 and 18 lire a month (board was always included).[25] The huge gap between these remunerations and what was paid to the senior surgeon in a military hospital, who at that time earned around 240 lire a month, does however give us a measure of the distance the Giovane had to travel in order to become independent. And yet the wages paid to the surgeon's staff were anything but paltry if we consider that during this period municipal surgeons in the capital received only 45 lire a year to serve the poor in their neighbourhood.[26] However hazardous, war was clearly a money-spinner for these groups of workers. The accounts, however, show that the demand for Infermieri in the military hospitals was fairly flexible (clearly depending on the fortunes of war and the number of wounded that ensued) so that some would serve perhaps for a number of short terms lasting only a few days.[27]

In the city hospitals too the senior surgeon could count on the help of a number of Giovani to assist him in his ever-growing duties. From the middle of the seventeenth century the hospitals had expanded considerably in terms of beds and patients, and, as they acquired staff in greater numbers, they began to make regular use of young surgeons, described as Infermieri.[28] At first they were kept on for an indefinite period of some years, but subsequently the number of applicants just to be put on the waiting list for these training posts increased to such a point that in the 1680s the hospital of San Giovanni reduced the training period to two years. In 1699 this phase was further cut to only one year.[29] Unlike the senior surgeon, the Infermieri lived in at the hospital and therefore played a key part in its management, presiding as they did over the acceptance of patients and their registration.[30]

Another arena for subordinate work came about through the activity of the so-called *chirurghi dei poveri* (Surgeons to the Poor), who were employed by the municipality to provide the less well off with treatment and prescriptions that gave the right to medicines free of charge. Their role within the city had expanded considerably. By 1680 the number of shops run by Surgeons to the Poor had risen from one to four, one for each of the four districts into which the city was divided (the population at the time standing between 30,000 and 40,000 inhabitants), and a large number of patients had to be dealt with.[31] Surgeons to the Poor could also regularly count on the assistance of young surgeons for the performance of their duties. Indeed, in 1684 this system of subordinate work was institutionalised with the creation of the post of 'supernumerary' (*sovra-numerario*) Surgeon to the Poor, in other words on a waiting list. This title effectively gave access to the group from which the future Surgeon to the Poor would be chosen whenever the post fell free through the death or resignation of the incumbent, and it was therefore extremely sought after. In the meantime it gave to those of its holders who already had their own shop the right to display the sign 'Surgeon to the Poor' with the arms of the city upon it; they could also prescribe free medicines.[32] In other words they could have a part share in the appointed surgeon's field of influence. Below those few who managed to secure the title of 'supernumerary', there were still many young surgeons without their own shop who also gave their services to assist the office-holder surgeons, in the hope of becoming supernumeraries and eventually Surgeons to the Poor.

The system of supernumeraries highlights how crucial was the period spent as a young surgeon dependent on a master. Of course, succession to the shop and a professional post sometimes took place within the family, but it was often the outcome of the relationship between master and pupil. This system was deployed on a massive scale: the post of supernumerary is also to be found in association with court surgeons and surgeons to various bodies and military garrisons,[33] and unofficially around the senior surgeon in the hospitals and the post of anatomist at the University. It is no accident, for example, that, as we shall see below, all the hospital and university posts held by Domenico Deroy were distributed among three of his pupils, as well as his son Giuseppe.

Those surgeons who held posts had a considerable influence on their assistants' longer-term establishment in the world of work. Only those who had worked for years under one of these surgeons had enough credibility to make an application to the authorities to act as a substitute whenever the post fell free. And, although formally the appointments were conferred by the administrative authorities (that of Surgeon to the Poor by the municipality, that of court surgeon or surgeon to a military garrison by the duke), the incumbent himself exerted a considerable degree of control over a public post. The choice of successor depended on the pleasure of the surgeon in post and sometimes his consent was even mentioned in the deed of appointment: for example in 1684 Antonio Dalbagna was elected to the 'continuance' (*sopravvivenza*) of the post of Surgeon to the Company of Archers of the Duke's Bodyguard (in other words, to occupy it in the future), then 'owned' (*posseduto*) by the surgeon Chiarnace, 'having obtained the consent of [Chiarnace] himself.'[34] The terminology is clearly significant: even if such a post had not techni-cally been 'bought', as was customary only for more remunerative offices, nevertheless it was regarded as somehow in the gift of the incumbent. On the other hand, the same logic of private ownership can be found also in the transmission of other court posts, not just that of surgeon: for instance, in 1683, Giò Antonio Marchetto, who was already acting as the Duke's Aiutante di Camera, but with supernumerary status, was appointed to the continuance of the post of regular Aiutante di Camera, 'given the consent of the First Aiutante, Servilla'.[35] The right to hand down the post, any post, even the lowest, was seen as a natural prerogative: it was often to the benefit of a man's own son or nephew, but also of one of his assistants.[36]

This power over the career of his own assistants allowed the surgeon in post to place a good number of young surgeons in a position of depend-ency and to use their labour in exchange for very little remuneration or even without any payment at all. The prospect of eventually succeeding to the position, or at any rate participating in the advantages entailed in being assistant to a well-established master, in terms of reputation and access to a share of his clientele, was clearly a considerable attraction. We have only incidental information about the monetary payment of these helpers, which suggests that in general their wages were not subject to regulation by the authorities, but that instead it was entirely up to the surgeon in post to determine their remuneration. We know that the supernumerary of the Surgeon to the Poor did not get any payment from the municipality but incumbent surgeons were encouraged 'to give them something or part of their stipend'.[37] Sometimes, however, young surgeons appointed to the 'continuance' of a surgeon to a military garrison actually received one third or even two thirds of the official stipend.[38] Yet there were times too when an appointment to the position of assistant came with the 'obligation to fulfil it at one's own expense'; indeed, the subsequent promotion to a stable post was often legitimised by the fact that the chosen candidate had for a long time been treating the soldiers of that garrison 'without enjoying any recompense'.[39] Of course, there must have been agreements between the surgeon in post and his assistant, but we have no record of these. It is likely that over these years of insecurity the Giovane also treated patients on his own account and thereby survived financially, in some cases he would even have ran a shop: the borderline between licensed and unlicensed practice was, as we shall discover in chapter ten, often trespassed upon.

Lavorare in compagnia: working in partnership

We have seen how the organisation of work within the surgeon's trade made the position of the Giovani somewhat precarious not only financially but also in terms of career prospects, and how important it was in this phase to establish a good and enduring relationship with a master. Much evidence suggests also that the vulnerability of the Giovane's position was often at odds with his actual knowledge and skills. The working situation in which Giovani found themselves could vary greatly and the duties they performed were in their nature rather diverse. The depositions of those caught practising without a licence in 1695 and other scattered evidence suggest that the category of Giovani included both those skilled in the trade (*periti*) and those who were still training and carried out minor procedures such as shaving, medicating the wounds of patients already under the master's care, and preparing the compresses to be applied to wounds, or else letting blood with cups or leeches, which is to say without cutting into the vein. Some were also capable of carrying out 'a great many treatments worthy of consideration which have been applauded by the esteemed Physicians and by other Surgeons', as affirmed by Carlo Meyner, from Pianezza, who for four years was a Giovane in Turin, at the shop of Ghidella, Surgeon to the Household of Madama Reale.[40] Giovani such as Meyner, employed in the shops of the Surgeons to the Poor or surgeons to the ducal households, serving a vast clientele, had to know how to perform a majority of the surgical duties provided, not only the most commonplace. A Giovane was essentially someone who was not yet independent, neither having his own shop nor any professional position, but not necessarily someone who had not yet mastered the profession.

What is more, the Giovane was not necessarily young in years. The period of dependent work was in fact extremely variable in length. It began, as we have seen, around the age of seventeen or eighteen, and for many it lasted for four to six years, after which they would set up on their own. During these years the Giovane trained with either one or two masters, and periods of service in the shop would be alternated with time spent in a city hospital or one of the military hospitals.[41] For others the status of Giovane went on for much longer, for ten or fifteen years or more, and it could involve either a long spell in a single shop or practising with a long series of masters. There are certainly instances of early independence, which is to say surgeons who find themselves running their own shops at ages as young as nineteen, but these are often cases of young surgeons who took over from a father, a brother or an uncle who had died prematurely and who, as we shall see in the next chapter, could also draw upon the work of mothers and sisters who were presumably well grounded in aspects of the profession.

The relationship between Giovane and master involved various levels of asymmetry and a whole range of working relationships. There are examples of Giovani who worked for established masters in positions of considerable responsibility. In the survey of barber-surgeons carried out in the provinces we even find some Giovani who ran separate shops, in the hamlets, for masters living and practising in the main village or town. Typical examples are those of Caulet and Roscio, who 'kept' two shops at Ozegna for their master Tapperi at Agliè, and that of Rosso, who ran a shop at Oglianico for his master Nitia from Favria.[42] And among the military surgeons we find post-holders who do not even live in at the garrison, despite this being required, and who are entirely substituted by their assistants.[43] Even the range of remunerative situations must have been fairly varied. In its more advanced stages, the role of Giovane could also involve reasonable earnings, on a scale making it possible to embark on family life. Notwithstanding the common practice whereby marriage coincided with setting up in business for oneself, we find examples of Giovani who were married and had children. Michel Angelo Benedicti, for example, practised for 14 years in the shop of Ghidella, Surgeon to the household of Their Highnesses, before opening his own shop in 1689. Yet in 1684 he was already into his fourth marriage and the father of a son. In 1695, Giò Colombatto, who had worked for all of eighteen years 'alongside' other surgeons (*in compagnia*) before taking over his uncle's shop, turns out to have been married, clearly for a number of years given the size of his family (his eldest daughter was ten years old).[44]

Moreover, we encounter examples of Giovani who collaborated

with colleagues close to them in age, and also without their own shop, or with young masters who had only recently opened one. These appear as relatively equal partnerships rather than relationships of clear-cut subordination. Take for example the case of Giuseppe Pasero, who obtained a licence and opened an independent shop in his early twenties, but from the beginning ran it with his stepbrother, Andrea, and then a Giovane who was nearly his peer: it seems likely that such workshops were in reality joint ventures between a licensed surgeon at the beginning of his career and one or more surgeons fairly close in age but still unlicensed.[45] As the barber Forneri stated in his deposition, these arrangements made it possible to share the expenses of the shop, while each practitioner kept his earnings for himself. Moreover, agreements like this meant that, for the time being, one of the two partners could spare himself the expense involved in buying a licence.[46]

A comparison between the ages of employers and employees confirms the impression that the Giovane frequently occupied a position midway between a partner and a subordinate (see table 6.2). In over a quarter of the cases (eight out of twenty-nine) there is a gap of no more than ten years between the master and his Giovane; sometimes they are the same age, and there is even a case in which the Giovane was three years older than the master with whom he worked. The language used by many Giovani to describe their working relationships is also significant: some

Table 6.2 Age gap between masters and *Giovani*

Years	Number of Cases
−3	1
0− +5	4
+ 6−10	3
+11−15	4
+16−20	8
+21−24	1
+25−29	–
+30−34	6
+41−56	2
Total	29

Source: 'Registro delli chirurghi ... di Torino'; Art. 530, and biographical research on parish registers.

speak of working 'for' or 'under the orders of' a master, but others state that they work 'with' or 'alongside' (*in compagnia di*) another surgeon. Giò Tommaso Surdis worked for five years 'alongside' the surgeon Giuseppe Gloria, in the shop kept by the latter in the city's new district (Contrada Nuova). Likewise Paolo Bernardo Calvo, already familiar to us, stated at the age of twenty-six that he worked 'alongside' a surgeon of the same age, Bellino, who had opened his own shop only two years earlier; contemporaneously, he was treating the poor, 'under the orders of Stura, Surgeon to the Poor'.[47] Calvo's experience seems to have been a common one: often a Giovane pursued different strategies simultaneously, working under the patronage of well-established older masters and at the same time working in partnership with surgeons closer to him in terms of status, professional reputation and age.

We can see therefore how the supply of medical, cosmetic and aesthetic services which concerns us here found expression in the decades at the turn of the seventeenth and eighteenth centuries across a spectrum of work coalitions, ranging from the most hierarchical to those of relative equality. These did not however assume the individualist forms that have been posited by representations of the medical marketplace as a battleground between rival practitioners. Moreover, although representations of artisanal work frequently tend to project a structured and hierarchical image of the organisation of labour, the way in which the surgeon's shop functioned has little to do with the theoretical division of the labour force into three tiers (apprentices, journeymen and masters) clearly separated by age, skills and status.[48] There were no career standards, nor any precise, well circumscribed age bands that we can associate with the condition of being apprentice, Giovane or master. It was possible to be a master at twenty and a Giovane at thirty-three. Long periods of service with the same master, sometimes for much more than a decade, offer another indication of the fact that the progression from one condition to the other was far from regular. In some cases, the condition of Giovane was a permanent one: an exemplary case is offered by surgeon Mitton who, in his will of 1729, left to his Giovane, Antonio Bosio, 'the victuals, clothing and habitation of his house for the rest of his natural life', together with an annual stipend of 350 lire. Moroever, if we consider the age at which a licence was acquired for setting up practice independently, we come up with a fairly broad distribution (see table 6.3). As far as barber-surgeons are concerned, shops were frequently set up between the ages of twenty-five and twenty-seven– in ten cases out of twenty-four – but the remaining fourteen show a wide range of ages with some rather low incidences (ages eighteen to nineteen) as well as rather high ones (thirty-

Table 6.3 Age at which a licence was acquired

Age	Surgeons	Barbers
18	1	–
19	3	–
20	–	–
21	3	1
22	1	–
23	–	–
24	–	1
25	2	–
26	5	1
27	3	–
28	1	–
29	1	1
30	–	–
31	1	–
32	–	–
33	1	3
34	2	2
Total	24	7

Source: Dates at which a licence was acquired are drawn from 'Registro delli chirurghi. di Torino' and from 'Stato de' Cerusici e flebotimisti'. Ages are drawn from Art. 530 and from ACT, vols 294–96.

three to thirty-four). The opening of a barber's shop, which on its own had less potential to survive, makes its appearance even later in the male life cycle (in one case only this occurs below the age of twenty-two). A barber would preferably work for a while as a partner in a barber-surgeon's shop, where a variety of services would be offered.

The career inequalities indicated by these data are confirmed if we look at the ages at which hospital posts were obtained: there are cases of appointment as chief surgeon at the age of nineteen or twenty. At the opposite extreme we find Giovani who cannot even recall how many or which surgeons they have worked with, 'given the great number' (*la gran moltitudine*), or else surgeons who have worked for as long as sixteen years in the war hospitals before settling in one place and opening their own shop.[49] Some never found their way out of the relationship of subordination to a master. This is the case with Giuseppe Coppa, from Costigliole d'Asti. He arrived in Turin at the age of nineteen, in 1701; we find him at twenty-three as the Giovane of Giò Pietro Busano, Surgeon to the Poor. Twenty years later he seems still to be operating entirely within Busano's sphere of influence, and it is only in 1722, when he is forty-one years old, that Coppa is appointed his 'supernumerary' with the obligation to provide free services to the poor. At this point, after more than twenty years of working in his trade and living in Turin, his total possessions amounted to only 500 lire, extremely modest assets when we consider that in the same years Busano's son, aged thirty-two, declared his as standing at 8,000.[50] As far as we know, Coppa was never to become a post-holding Surgeon to the Poor, and I have found no appointments relating to him. Presumably, he remained Busano's subordinate for most of his life.

From young surgeon to master

These examples give us a measure of the difficulties and uncertainties involved in moving from work as a subordinate to working independently. Although there were no serious institutional barriers and securing a licence was a fairly simple matter, invisible obstacles hindered many from fully taking their place among the city's independent surgeons. If we ask how many of the numerous would-be surgeons who populated the shops and hospitals as Giovani actually managed to achieve a position as head of a shop, the answer seems to be very few. A look at the professional register of 1695 and the 1705 census tells us that no more than 20 to 25 per cent of the Infermieri trained at the hospital of San Giovanni in the preceding decades were working in the city with their own shops. This is a low proportion even if we allow for the fact that many of them could have died between the two dates, while others may well have eluded these surveys, both of which were carried out during wartime, when some surgeons were absent from the city, serving in the military hospitals. It is also true that a certain number of those who had moved to the capital for training later left it to take up work in the town or region they had come from, in the provinces or even much further away (we shall see this in chapter ten). Yet it is clear that many never managed in the end to become independent masters. Obviously there were informal mechanisms that regulated and limited access to the profession, as we have already seen in the way that posts were handed down: only one of the numerous Giovani working for the various Surgeons to the Poor or the surgeons to military garrisons would later take over his post. But even as far as ordinary shops are concerned, one has a strong sense of an artificial 'ceiling' on access to the occupation, given that the number of these establishments remained static between 1695 and 1742 despite the considerable growth in population over these decades, and the increase in consumption that, among other things, probably involved medical services, and despite the large supply of surgeons. In 1695 there were eighty-nine shops recorded in the occupational survey, including those with proper licences and those without; in 1742 there were eight-eight, made up of barbers (twenty-five), phlebotomists (nine), non-collegiate surgeons (forty-one), and collegiate surgeons (thirteen).[51] It is likely that the stable number of shops was artificially maintained; in reality the number of surgeons operating in Turin had substantially increased but many of them did not succeed in setting up an independent practice, and instead worked in subordinate positions for more established masters, or else in partnership with others.

This cannot be explained by dynastic control over the occupation; the number of father-son successions was limited, as we have already said. There is also an extremely high turnover of surnames. Although the handing down of the craft was artificially contained, it did not take place merely within a patrilinear and blood descent.[52] This meant that, for many young men, even incomers to the city, their chance of entering the system was a feasible option. In chapter eight we shall see in greater detail the variety of forms that might be assumed by the transmission of the shop and other professional resources. The more common route seems to have been by winning the favours of an established master without male children, or one with sons who chose either more prestigious occupations or a religious vocation, or else a master with a number of positions to pass on, and therefore potentially more than one successor. The majority of public positions and of shops were handed down through interpersonal relationships of this kind. In this respect there is no difference between the strategies pursued by natives and incomers, by surgeons' sons and those of other artisans. Even for those with a surgeon as a father, finding a place in the professional fabric of the city was not automatic. For them too, the relationships formed in their youth, in the key years of training with other surgeons and working as subordinates, were crucial for opening up the potential for permanent working status.

In this chapter and the one before we have looked at some of the expedients deployed by barber-surgeons and more generally by artisans of the body, to hold back the competition and maintain control over sections of their clientele. We have talked about the limiting of competition through horizontal kinship and more generally through kinship and geographical ties between artisans of the body. But well before reaching the point of selling one's own services in one's own shop there were other expedients set in motion to limit access to the occupation. The mechanisms of containment of the trade were powerful, but informal and not institutional. They had to do with the existence of ties of dependency and kinship networks that allowed some shops or groups of shops to exert control over pools of potential clients in specific areas of the city. Those masters with thriving shops also managed to keep a check on potential competitors through careful and judicious management of how they reassigned the professional resources (including the reputation of a shop) they had managed to build up in certain parts of the city. At this point we find it hard to reconcile these observations with the paradigm of the medical marketplace that has been so influential in studies of the medical profession in recent years. Such a paradigm appears anachronistic, particularly if contrasted with the principle we have seen to be deep-rooted during this period that official posts belong to those who occupy them; and if set against those practices of transmission within the family or between master and pupil that we have begun to take note of.

Notes

1 For a synthesis of these studies see Farr, *Artisans*, pp. 248–9; also Romano, *Patricians*, p. 83; for tailors in Turin, Cerutti, *Mestieri e Privilegi*, p. 194; for nineteenth-century Turin, Allegra, 'Un modello di mobilità', p. 67.

2 Although mention of the occupation of the father was not a requirement, comparison with other documents suggests that when the latter exercised the same trade this was normally signalled.

3 Art. 530.

4 Ins. 1755, l. 6, vol. I, c. 525.

5 *Ibid.*, 1730, l. 2, vol. I, c. 449.

6 *Ibid.*, 1755, l. 6, vol. I, c. 525.

7 *Ibid.*, 1683, l. 3, cc. 531–5. Giuseppe was to become the barber of the Prince of Piedmont. The other two Stura brothers and three sisters settled in their native village.

8 For Alberto Verna's biography see below: chapter eight, notes twenty-eight and twenty-nine.

9 Art. 530.

10 This private agreement has come to our knowledge accidentally through a notarial record in which the orphan appoints a guardian to contract the terms of apprenticeship on his behalf: Ins. 1697, l. 3, c. 153.

11 *Ibid.*, 1682, l. 8, c. 85.

12 The agreement provided for a payment of 400 lire at the end of the fifth year should the boy decide to leave on this date; there would be no payment to be made should he agree to remain for two more years as a worker drawing no salary but his board. At the end of the five years Vautier chose to leave Stoper and to pay the 400 lire due. The notarial act ratifies the payment made of what was due on the part of the aunt and

uncle with whom the widow Vautier had invested her son's inheritance: *ibid.*, 1712, l. 12, c. 439.

13 Analogous considerations are to be found in G. Levi, 'Carrières d'artisans et marché du travail à Turin (XVIII-XIXe siècles)', *Annales: Economies, Sociétés, Civilisations*, 45 (1990), pp. 1353–5.

14 ACT, vol. 294, c. 54.

15 AAT, 18.1.3.

16 The records of their appointment and departure are registered in the minutes of the Board of Governors of the hospital (AOSG, *Ordinati*), compiled from 1607 onwards. Infermieri were present also at the hospital of Santi Maurizio e Lazzaro, but in this case the sources are much less complete.

17 AST, s. I, *Regie Università*, m. 4, fasc. 9, 'Stato della regia Università: Della Chirurgia', fasc. 10, 'Lettera del Conte di S. Laurens', 1750.

18 Ins. 1743, l. 4, c. 392.

19 *Ibid.*, 1679, l. 7, c. 15. See also the previously mentioned case of Giuseppe Stura (note seven), who also went to Paris for further training; his expenses were covered by his brother as well as the court.

20 The role of the assistants is mentioned for example by Calvo, when he discusses amputations, ligatures and trepanations. *Delle Ferite*, pp. 91, 97, 164. An assistant's desirable features are listed in *Il Chirurgo. Trattato Breve di Tarduccio Salvi da Macerata* (Rome, 1613), p. 4.

21 'Registro delli chirurghi … di Torino', deposition of M. Vittone; AST, s.r., Art. 330 m. 5, 1695–96, m. 2 n. 78, 1694.

22 Ins. 1730, l. 2, vol. 1, cc. 449–50.

23 AST, s.r., Art. 330, m. 5, n. 122, 1696.

24 *Ibid.*, n. 121, 1695. Thirty years later, there is an even greater stratification to be found: at the military hospital in Cremona, for example, alongside a physician and a senior surgeon we find an assistant surgeon, as well as a 'first young surgeon' and ten young surgeons, for 119 patients. The Infermieri were in turn subdivided into three chief Infermieri and twenty-eight ordinary Infermieri: *ibid.*, Art. 331, m.1, n.3, 1730.

25 *Ibid.*, Art. 330, m.5, n.122, m.2, n.78.

26 The stipend was 45 lire (three *doppie* and 1/3) in 1684 and 1696, 82 lire in 1701 and 200 lire in 1727: ACT, vols 294, fos 52, 255; 296, fo. 71. Hospital salaries were somehow higher: at the hospital of Santi Maurizio e Lazzaro the surgeon received 150 lire per month in 1669 (the same stipend as the hospital physician) and 200 in 1683. OSML, m. 1, c. 17, 'Registro delli mandati spediti alli officiali … 1659–1679'.

27 See the payments for two to nine days made to individual Infermieri at the Vigna hospital for soldiers in AST, s.r., Art. 330, m. 4, n. 118. It is, however, possible that this high turnover of Infermieri was also a sign of an unstable labour supply produced by young surgeons moving from one hospital to another.

28 The San Giovanni hospital, the largest in the city, grew from some thirty-six beds, around 1650, to 220 beds in 1730. Cavallo, *Charity and Power*, p. 144.

29 AOSG, *Ordinati*, 13 January 1699. Many applications were accompanied with recommendations from influential figures, asking that the applicant be appointed at least to future posts falling vacant.

30 From 1672 the Infermieri were given the task of keeping daily records of the patients 'who present themselves at the hospital'; the confessor kept another register with

names, surnames, patients' place of origin and date of death (*ibid.*, 4 December 1672).

31 Medical outdoor relief had grown immeasurably, partly as a result of the expansion of the city and its population, partly because there were abuses of the system and it was not only the poor who were treated. Cavallo, *Charity and Power*, pp. 75–80, and chapter ten below.

32 See the applications and appointments in ACT, vols 294, 295, 296. The prerogatives of this post and the reasons why it was desirable will be discussed in chapter ten.

33 See the appointments to military surgeon in *Contadoria Generale* and in *Regie Patenti e Commissioni*.

34 *Contadoria Generale*, vol. 22, 1683, c. 299. Also the appointment of Melle came with the consent of the incumbent surgeon Battezzati, see n. 40 below.

35 PCF 1682–3, fo. 111.

36 For examples of this handing down to nephews see chapter eight. The right to transmit medical posts held at court is also found among Parisian physicians. Lehoux, *Le Cadre*, pp. 334–6.

37 ACT, *Ordinati*, 1688 (24 April), fo. 104.

38 This is the case with Campana and Bruno, designated successors to the post of senior surgeon to His Highness's Bodyguard in 1704: Bruno then became official surgeon in 1707 (*Guardie del Corpo di S.M.*, 1704).

39 See for example, in the 1670s, the appointment of Fabiano Melle to the post of Aiutante to the ducal cavalry surgeon, Battezzati, with assigned right to succeed him after his death (*Contadoria Generale*, vol. 16, 1673–74, c. 252), and that of Ameri to surgeon to the Asti garrison after the death of Cocito (*ibid.*, vol. 15, 1671–2, c. 34).

40 'Registro delli … cirugici e barbieri … della Provincia di Torino'.

41 See for example the testimonies of Pietro Berrone, Francesco Bellino, Carlo Francesco Turco in the occupational survey of 1695: 'Registro delli chirurghi … di Torino'.

42 'Registro delli … cirugici e barbieri … della Provincia di Torino'.

43 *Contadoria Generale*, vol. 19, 1679–80, c. 107.

44 'Registro delli chirurghi … di Torino', statements of Benedicti and Colombatto; for the composition of Colombatto's household, Art. 530. For Benedicti's marriages and the births and deaths of his children see chapter nine, n. 66.

45 AAT, 18.1.3, 1675–84.

46 'Registro delli chirurghi. di Torino', Forneri's statement. See chapter ten for the cost of licences.

47 *Ibid.*, statements of Surdis and Calvo.

48 The variety of forms that working relationships between master and journeyman or between journeymen themselves could assume (from direct alliance to subcontracting agreements and confederations between workers in the opening of unofficial shops), is documented by G. Rosser, 'Crafts, guilds and the negotiation of work in the medieval town', *Past and Present*, 154 (1997), especially pp. 16–18. A more cautious picture, reaffirming the distance between master and journeyman. is proposed by Farr, *Artisans*, in particular pp. 191–2.

49 This is the case with Giò Colombatto from Turin and Claudio Rustagno, a barber-surgeon from Rivoli, who practised his profession for twenty years, being 'in His Highness' troops' for sixteen of them. See their respective statements in 'Registro delli chirurghi … di Torino' and 'Registro delli … cirugici e barbieri … della Provincia di

Torino'.

50 We learn this from the testimony given by Coppa in 1723 of the unmarried status of Busano's daughter, and that given by Maurizio Busano in 1727: AAT, 18.4.12.

51 'Stato dei negozianti e artisti ... 1742'.

52 For examples of this classic argument in the literature on early modern artisans see Farr, *Artisans*, pp. 247–8.

7

Women in the body crafts

Daughters and wives of artisans of the body

What about women? Much of what has been said so far about male workers applies also to girls. It was even more unusual for them than for their brothers to leave home at an early age to take up an apprenticeship. Yet they too absorbed valuable skills within the family or kinship milieu, though with one difference: while a considerable number of the males would later have left this setting to be engaged as Giovani with one or more masters, until, all going well, they opened a shop of their own, the young women would have kept on working with their fathers or brothers until they married. At that point, as we already know, they would have married a man who in many cases worked in a craft or trade relatively close to the one practised in the shop they had grown up in, these being occupations allied with those already familiar to the young brides. Indeed, in Turin there was a very high level of intermarriage between tailors, perruquiers, jewellers, upholsterers and barber-surgeons. We have already noted this phenomenon in the case of the kinship networks analysed so far, but further evidence, drawn from a study of two samples of marriages that took place between 1658 and 1725, confirms this pattern. The first sample consists of forty marriages of daughters and sisters of surgeons: the spouses of these young women are in two-thirds of cases goldsmiths, perruquiers, upholsterers, apothecaries and tailors; only one wed a physician, three married merchants (in at least one case dealing in products connected with the care of the body), and one a ducal bodyguard. The same cluster of crafts is found in the second sample, consisting of thirty marriages involving daughters and sisters of other artisans of the body: five of the brides married men who practised the same craft as their father or brothers, while the rest married other artisans of the body. The only exceptions to this pattern are three marriages concluded with a physician, a notary and a pastry-cook respectively.

What were the consequences of this pattern of marriage for women's work? What were the occupations of wives, daughters and sisters of barber-surgeons and other artisans of the body? Did they also play a part in the transmission of the body crafts? The high level of intermarriage between specific crafts suggests that the skills and knowledge these women had absorbed at home, as they watched and assisted their fathers or other members of the family in their work, would later have borne fruit in the husband's shop. Although the evidence relating to the transferability of skills is largely indirect, the cultural connections we have discerned between artisans of the body suggest that these young women arrived at their weddings fully equipped with skills that could be turned to account in occupations allied to the one carried out within the family of origin, not just in the trade of the father. Although the crafts that concern us here are usually represented as male, it is quite possible that women's contribution to these was not negligible.

These considerations cast new light on the question of the transmission of the trade. Data relating to occupational endogamy have surprised and confused scholars of artisans. Similarly to what we have observed in relation to the handing down of a craft from father to son, the rate of transmission through a daughter of skills, tools and other resources linked to an occupation tends to be much lower than one might expect.[1] In his study on Venice, Dennis Romano comes to the conclusion that 'profession was not a crucial consideration when artisans went about the task of selecting spouses'. Similarly, James Farr finds an 'astonishingly low rate' of matrimonial endogamy among Dijon artisans in the seventeenth century.[2] One cannot easily discern an explanation for these findings: Romano asserts that 'The advantages to be gained from exogamous marriages are harder to see'; others have suggested that these were deliberately avoided in an effort to establish connections within the wider world of artisans and therefore extend individual relationships beyond the restricted confines of the occupation.[3] Such explanations seem over-generalised, however, and fail to address the question of what patterns craft transmission, which nonetheless must have taken place, assumed. Professional endogamy turns out to be much higher if we shift our attention from the individual craft to the much wider occupational milieu, and, in the case that concerns us, from barber-surgeons to those I have described as artisans of the body.

There has been frequent mention of the fact that wives collaborated with their husbands in the running of the workshop, so that when they were widowed they were often capable of keeping on the business.[4] It should however be emphasised that informal apprenticeship in the trade took place much earlier and participation in a family shop began at an early age.[5] One eloquent example comes to us in the records relating to the family of a perruquier who died prematurely. In 1701, Lorenzo Chiarmet died leaving his wife Anna Caterina, who was pregnant, and three young children: two boys aged eight and one, and Anna, aged nine.[6] The guardianship of the children was taken on by Lorenzo's brother, Claudio, a tailor, who, on behalf of his wards, brought about a partnership between the widow and Giò Francesco Marentier, who had worked 'in the said shop for a long time'. The latter, we learn from another source, was in fact only twelve years old.[7] Given that the heirs, 'in consideration of their young age remained quite unfit to maintain the perruquier's shop and workshop left to them by their father', their guardian agreed with the widow and Marentier, 'as experts and qualified persons', that they should maintain 'the same shop and workshop in partnership together, to keep this shop in business and with it earn an income to support the said children'. The partnership was set up for five years and in the deed of enactment a reckoning was made of the labour-force on which the shop could rely: this included not only the contribution of the widow and the young worker but also that of little Anna. In fact the agreement made provision so that where it was decided that Anna be placed 'elsewhere and to some better purpose [...], as a participant in said partnership, she will have to be replaced by another young girl *of similar stature* to [...] Anna, this young girl being kept to work in the service of the shop, without claim to any payment other than her board' (my italics).[8] The male children, in contrast, were declared 'unfit to work since being of an age to be wards' and in their place a young man had to be taken on who was trained in the profession of perruquier and would be paid and given board at least until the eldest male child, Giò Matteo, should begin working in the shop.

The story shows at what an early age daughters were brought into the domestic productive unit and also gives us some appreciation of the contribution that they might make. Anna did not marry but, in 1710, at the age of eighteen, she became a nun, presumably after having worked in the shop for some years.[9] Had she married she would probably have brought some of the skills she had acquired in the family shop to a marriage with either a perruquier or an artisan of the body. This was to be the direction taken by Anna's little sister, Vittoria. Having grown up in the house of her uncle Claudio, the tailor, she then married Evasio Verna. These were circumstances similar to those of her widowed mother, Anna Caterina Chiarmet, the daughter of a tailor and the sister of a tailor. When marrying a perruquier, she had probably been in a position to transfer some of her skills to her husband's business as a wig maker. Perhaps this was also why, when she lost her husband, ten years after her wedding and at the age of only twenty-six, the young widow could be regarded as an 'expert and qualified person' in the perruquier's trade. And she must have been the effective head of the shop, considering the young age of her 'partner', who was only twelve years old! In her case too, the terms of the partnership contract are a clear recognition of her capacities, as made explicit by a further clause in the agreement whereby: 'if the widow were to enter into a marriage with a perruquier she shall declare herself discharged from the partnership, this being of serious prejudice to it'.[10] Clearly, the transfer of labour and expertise to a rival shop that remarriage would entail was perceived as a threat.

Even if it was not through the formal channels of a bound apprenticeship (which, as we have seen, was unusual even for male children in this occupational milieu), the training of girls in specific skills did therefore take place within the family, and this was the case also in those occupations where women would seem to be well-nigh absent, like that of the perruquier. For example, the Turin population census carried out in 1705 lists only four women as perruquiers, all of them widows (among them the widow Chiarmet). Surprisingly, there is no occupation listed for any of the women recorded as the wives, sisters, daughters and mothers of the sixty-three master perruquiers, even though the case of the young Anna Chiarmet, who worked in the family shop from a very early age, cannot have been an exception.[11] How reliable is this picture? I would see the silence surrounding women's participation in the family business as a prejudice structuring the sources rather than as indicative of their absence. We find in fact a consistent pattern: in the census female work (as frequently for male minors if they are living with their parents) is practically never recorded when the women are living within the family and the father and husband are still alive. Their work identity is mentioned on a more regular basis if, still unmarried, they live and work under an employer, that is if they are waged workers; frequently, moreover, their status as working women is recorded if they are part of a household where there is no male head, for example where a widow is in charge of the family unit.[12]

This under-representation of women's contribution to family enterprises should be taken into account when we outline any general trend in female work. For example, the strong female presence in textile work to be found in Turin, as elsewhere, in this period has often been viewed as an indication of the 'feminisation' undergone by these occupations during the early modern age, and of the growing separation between occupations that are regarded as masculine and feminine.[13] However, this perception of an increasingly male artisanal world and of a specialisation of skills along gender lines has been inflated by the tendency of sources to record female dependent and waged work – which happens to be concentrated in the textile sector – by comparison with the work done by women within family-based workshops.

In the case of Turin, the fact that this is indeed a distorted picture is made clear by a comparison between the 1705 census and the evidence from a source that is by its nature relatively free of gender conventions: the list of French residents in Turin compiled, just fifteen years earlier, at a time of war against France. Tending as it does to a precise identification of the foreign population and the kinds of work in which it is engaged, this source provides a rather more reliable and quite different picture of female work: in 1690 as many as ninety-four of the 104 French women resident in Turin turn out to have an occupation. The range of work they did extended even to trades with predominantly masculine connotations: we find a female cobbler, two pastry-cooks, a confectioner, two upholsterers, a jeweller, two haberdashers, two cloth merchants.[14] There are five female perruquiers and, most significant of all, four of them actually have husbands and children, while only one is single. This less prejudiced source does in fact reveal the substantial economic role performed by married women within family workshops, which is usually so elusive. Of the ninety-three women recorded as having occupations, forty-six in all are married at the time, often with children; the rest are widows or unmarried.

In a recent synthesis Geoffrey Crossick maintained that however much the sources tend to underestimate the role of women in artisanal production, 'it would be wrong to see the masculine nature of artisanship as a function of representation alone'. The vast distance between the evidence provided by the two population listings examined above urges us however to emphasise the effects of the under-estimation of married women's work in the historical record and to question the idea that during the early modern period 'the role of women in craft enterprise remained restricted and came to be increasingly so'.[15]

Mothers, sisters and servants

Research into the work undertaken by women 'in the service of the shop' should not however stop at the contribution of the daughters and wives of artisans, but should also consider the crucial role often played by the mothers and sisters of young masters. Particularly in cases of early succession, when an adult but still young son was compelled by the death of the father to take control of the shop, the role of these figures seems to have been vital. In such cases, when both family and shop unexpectedly have a new head, we frequently find the forming of a kind of sodality between mother and son or brother and sister that will last for years.

In many cases marriage took place within the life cycle of the barber-surgeon at the same point when he became master and head of his own shop. But there are also cases of established masters who ran a shop without ever marrying or who, at any rate, delayed marrying for a considerable time. Even though professional independence and the means to marry and become the head of one's own family have been seen as an indispensable combination for acquiring the status of an adult man, it is clear that the routes to achieving masculine identity were more complex, as we shall see in greater detail further on.[16] These cases of permanent or temporary bachelor status allow us to identify another aspect of the female contribution to the shop of the artisan of the body that has so far been neglected. If we look at the composition of the household nucleus of the bachelor masters we see in fact that they almost always live with a mother who is fairly young, and sometimes also with one or more sisters.

Giò Domenico Bruco presents one case in which the role often performed by the wife seems to have been absorbed by the mother, herself the widow of a surgeon, and by the sisters. Domenico inherited his father's prosperous shop at the age of twenty-six, and five years later we find him as the head of a family consisting of his mother, aged forty-six, and three unmarried sisters, aged twenty, nineteen and eleven. In 1705 there were additional family members: a female servant and a young male assistant. Giò Domenico remained a bachelor and in charge of the family until 1711 when, on his mother's death, he formed a family of his own.[17] Francesco Maria Meda is a similar case. The sudden death of his father, followed two years later by that of his elder brother, also a surgeon (Giò Francesco, already referred to), compelled him to acquire a licence and to take control of the family shop when he was only twenty years old. This also put him in charge of a large family whose youngest member was only five years old. As the years went by, his two brothers took up different occupations and left the household; likewise his two sisters married.[18] Francesco, however, remained a bachelor and went on living with his mother, Isabella, for another twenty years after the last of his sisters left the house.[19] Even without any direct documentation, one might easily surmise that his mother played a significant part in the running of the shop: if we look at her history we can see that she had lived in close contact with a barber-surgeon's environment from early childhood, when her widowed mother married the barber and *Garzone di Camera*, Giulio Cesare Meda. Isabella then married within the same occupational milieu (as well as family), becoming the wife of her stepfather's youngest brother, a barber-surgeon. For some then, these domestic arrangements not based on marriage became permanent. For others, like Bruco, marriage came late, when they were over thirty, and even well over that age. Giuseppe Deroy is another example: he succeeded his deceased father in the running of his shop and in his post as senior surgeon at the hospital of Santi Maurizio e Lazzaro in 1695, when he was only twenty years old. At the same time he became formally responsible for a household consisting of his stepmother, two little stepbrothers aged four and two, and a fourteen-year-old brother. Later, the stepmother remarried and moved out of the household, but she was shortly replaced by Giuseppe's sister, the widow of a jeweller, and her children. Only in 1708, aged thirty-three, did Giuseppe get married and set up his own family.[20] Besides demonstrating that marriage was not the only means by which men could achieve the status of head of household, cohabitations of this kind suggest how important was the part played by one or more women in the domestic nucleus of the bachelor. Giuseppe, for example, was able to absent himself for months from Turin to specialise in his trade in Paris, evidently leaving the headship of the household (and shop?) to his stepmother.[21]

These cases help us to understand the value that marriage had for these artisans. It was not so much the need to achieve full male status that impelled many surgeons to marry at a point in life coinciding with the acquisition of a license and the opening of their own shop. Those surgeons who had become professionally independent needed a wife, for she provided services that were indispensable for the working of the household and the shop more than as proof of their masculinity.[22] Then there was women's involvement in the work carried out in the shop, this being essential even though barely apparent in the sources.[23] And yet in the case of single men, the place of the wife was taken by other women who also contributed essential work for the efficient maintenance of the shop and the household. These were usually close relatives, typically a widowed mother or stepmother or one or more sisters, as in the cases discussed above.[24] There is only one case where we find no female presence in a single man's household: that of a seventy-five-year-old widower, the surgeon Doglio, who lived with his two unmarried sons aged forty-two and twenty-eight, both of them also surgeons. In some circumstances female servants could also be involved. Interestingly, however, their presence in the household of single men was limited to the older surgeons:

of the nineteen surgeons without a wife in the 1705 census, only four lived not in a family nucleus but with a female servant. With the exception of the military surgeon Cuoca Castello, aged forty-five, who had a living-in female servant aged forty, the other three (aged fifty-three, fifty-four and sixty-one respectively) could all be regarded as 'old' by the standards of the period. For reasons of decency and respectability there was probably a certain reluctance to set up cohabitation between young or adult men and female servants. Servants were however to be found in male households where groups of single men of different generations lived together, a situation that perhaps guaranteed more propriety in behaviour. This was the case in the household of the thirty-seven-year-old surgeon Alberto Verna, whom we have already encountered; he lived with three nephews aged eighteen, fourteen and eleven, another young boy of nine who was a lodger, a forty-year-old cleric and teacher (probably the nephews' tutor), and two female servants aged twenty-eight and thirty.

As far as the hospital surgeons are concerned, the domestic labour usually provided by the wives or other female relatives could be performed by the hospital staff. It appears that some of these practitioners took up residence in the hospital, even though this was not required.[25] And yet it is likely they were able to make use of the services it provided, from laundry to the preparation of food and the maintenance of clothing, even if they resided elsewhere. These services could also extend beyond the walls of the institution for those who were regarded as members of the so-called 'hospital family'. Let us return for example to the case of Alberto Verna, a renowned surgeon who remained a lifelong bachelor, and whose household I have described above. His two female servants were former foundlings brought up at the hospital of San Giovanni where Verna was chief surgeon, and were clearly given into his care as a person who could be trusted.[26] For more than thirty years his household benefited from the services of the two women without any payment of wages, as if they were wives, mothers or sisters. We learn this from his wills, in which, exactly as was done with widows or elderly mothers, Alberto left them an annuity and some furniture to furnish a small dwelling for them to move into in case they were unable to continue living in what would become the house of his heirs after his death.[27]

There were, therefore, other women whose work could replace tasks that were normally the duty of a wife. For many young men, as we have seen in the case of Deroy and of Meda, this coincided with taking on premature responsibilities for which they were perhaps not yet prepared, and being placed under substantial pressure, especially when there was a shop or a family business to keep going. The part played by an experienced mother who had worked for years by her husband's side, and by older sisters, could well have been crucial in this sudden transition from dependency to independence. But the solidarity between mothers and fatherless sons also entailed a degree of inertia in the domestic structure, either delaying or ruling out marriage. Far from being an obligatory rite of passage, for these men marriage remained a remote option, at least for many years to come. Women's contribution to the shop of the artisan of the body related to the entire arc of their lives and to various family roles: mothers and sisters, daughters and wives could be crucial working partners in these apparently male occupations.

Women serving in the Chamber

The precise nature of women's involvement in the practical work of the barber-surgeon remains difficult to ascertain. The depiction of surgical practice in iconography presents the barber-surgeon's craft as exclusively male. It is always men who are seen carrying out either the most risky or the most delicate operations within the setting of the shop. And yet in paintings with medical subjects, numerous especially among the Dutch masters, there is frequently a mature woman present, carefully observing and apparently assessing the actions of a barber-surgeon (see plate 8). This seems to suggest that the procedures carried out by the barber-surgeon have connotations that are not exclusively male, and that there is some overlap between men's and women's knowledge in these matters and between the services they offer. The figure of the female observer in paintings depicting surgical operations, to which Margaret Pelling has drawn attention, seems to have various layers of meaning, as percipiently noted in her study.[28] It seems relevant, however, that the presence of a woman surveying the practitioner's competence is a commonplace to be found only in images of the surgeon in action, alone among visual representations of occupations. Moreover, scattered evidence does exist at both visual and written level to suggest that women did practise the occupation in some form, or else aspects of it, in relatively public environments. Two women figure, for example, among the personnel (represented as monkeys in the image) of a busy barber shop which is the subject of a 1601 Italian print (plate 9).[29] Although the small size of the print, originally part of the illustration for a fan, makes it difficult to identify all the details, one of the women seems to be occupied in shaving a client and the other in warming up water on the fire. As for the male figures, one is trimming the hair or beard of another client, another is tending to a wounded or fractured arm and a third is mixing ingredients (perhaps for a poultice

Plate 8 Interior of a barber-surgeon's shop with surgeon, assistant and apprentice, and female viewers. Follower of David Teniers, 17th century.

for the wounded). Depictions of the 'surgeoness' at work, albeit satirical, also exist (Plate 10).

Indeed, it would seem that the duties of a barber were sometimes continued by his widow. Why otherwise would we find in the paltry inventory of Ortensia Alberica, for many years previously the widow of the surgeon Carlo Giuseppe, '4 razors for the beard, 2 iron brushes for the hair, two basins and a bowl of thin steel, together with one walnut chair with a balustrade [*a balustra*]'.[30] Why had these items not been sold if unused? Moreover, the 1695 occupational survey of surgeons and barbers records among the unlicensed practitioners subject to fines the names of the widows Dalbagna and Ferraris, aged fifty and thirty-five respectively. Both of them had continued to keep their husbands' shop open after their death (these being surgeons with licences fully in order) – and in the case of Ferraris, the death had occurred not less than four years earlier. Both of them had taken on a young surgeon who, at the time of starting work in the shop, was only sixteen years old.[31] As in the case of the female perruquier Chiarmet (whose 'partner' was barely twelve years old), attention to the age of these workers sheds fresh light on their collaboration with the widows, an issue that has been given considerable emphasis in the literature on artisans: their young age suggests that their presence in the shop

Plate 9 The barber-shop. Siena c. 1600.

of a widow, often required by the guilds, was in actual practice a formality
and that, rather than giving necessary guidance to the widows, it was the
latter who performed the function of providing the boys with education

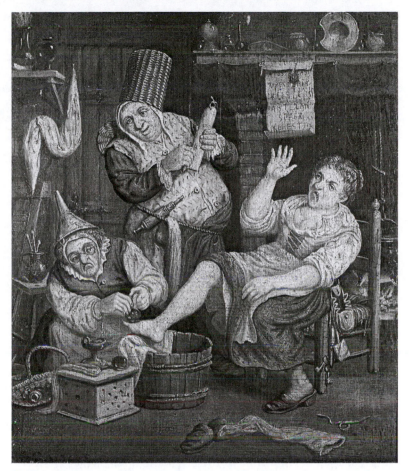

Plate 10 Caricature of woman barber-surgeon blood-letting from a patient's foot. Cornelius Dusart, 1695.

and training. Ten years later we find that the widow Dalbagna has not remarried but is living with her son, also a surgeon, his wife and their two young children, perhaps continuing to play a part in the shop. As for the younger widow, Ferraris, she has married her assistant Vercellis, who is a good fifteen years younger than her.

Yet in the population census of 1705 no female barbers or surgeons appear. This is no surprise to us by now, and there is an almost total absence of medical professionals among the (few) women recorded; even midwives account for only two. There is however a woman 'tooth puller',

Rosa Sachetti, a twenty-year-old who features as the head of an entirely female family consisting of her sixteen-year-old sister and seventy-eight-year-old grandmother.[32] And among the French women we find a married woman of forty who 'looks after the sick'.[33] These are accidental clues to a phenomenon that we can surmise was much wider, and that emerge against the odds from extremely reticent sources. And yet one source that is perhaps less ideologically loaded, the accounts of the military hospitals during the military invasion of parts of the state in the 1690s, produces a quite different picture. It shows a consistent female presence in this exclusively male environment. These women are to some extent employed in occupations typically reserved for them: the bleacher of linen is a woman, likewise the seller of 'hot water' (this probably referred to infusions or broths regarded as particularly good for invalids) and the repairers of mattress casings. But it seems that quite a few were also employed in health care: in fact a number of women are included among the *Infermieri* (literally nurses), a term usually associated with male service in Piedmont and used as a synonym for a 'young surgeon', referring therefore to future professionals who practised the most basic duties – for example, the dressing of wounds – under the supervision of a master surgeon. In the years to come many of the Infermieri encountered serving in these field hospitals will indeed be found working as independent surgeons. In the military hospital known as della Vigna, ten of the forty-three individuals listed under the heading 'Infermieri' are women; like their male counterparts they are paid a daily rate.[34] In the cavalry hospital at Chieri, as many as twenty-four of the *'stipendiati e Infermieri'* (stipendiaries and young surgeons) are women, while in another hospital for the cavalry two widows feature among the ten Infermieri.[35] So it is interesting that in periods of emergency and the scarcity of medical staff women too were employed in duties akin to those normally undertaken by young surgeons.

The setting in which we find perhaps even clearer examples of a female involvement in the performance of services related to the body, is that of the court, where there were numerous women employed as *Femmes de Chambre*. This position seems to be none other than the counterpart of the *Aiutante* and *Garzone di Camera* with regard to the female members of the ducal family. We do not know exactly what a Femme de Chambre did, because, as usual, the professional standing of this work is denied by the sources: the handbooks of rules which, over various periods between the late 1500s and 1680, establish the tasks of court personnel, have not a word to say about those performed by women, as if they did not exist.[36] Certainly, as Susan Broomhall's study of chamberwomen at the French and Spanish courts has showed, they performed the roles of child-carers and controlled the domain of female reproductive health in the house-holds of the young princes and royal women.[37] But it is likely that, like male artisans of the body, they were also responsible for the hygiene, comfort and appearance of their mistresses.

The presence of a multitude of Femmes de Chambre is revealed to us by a drier, but nonetheless valuable source: the financial accounts of the various court households. From these we learn that every female individual in the ducal family had in her service a number of *Fame di Camera*, or sometimes *Figlie di Camera* in the case of the unmarried princesses, varying between two and eight, and who, like their male counterparts, served by quarterly turns.[38] Alongside these Fame we find other women among the staff of the Camera, and not only in the service of the women at court: every Camera has a bleacher of personal linen, lace and other embellishments of clothing; in the Camere of the minor princes there are wet nurses who remain in service for much longer than the period of breast-feeding.[39] We find moreover the role of the *potagera* (soup-maker), a figure whose job it is to 'maintain supplies of vegetables, salt, vinegar and other small provisions for making broth', a restorative dish that was typically taken in the chamber, and even called for at night, and which was particularly recommended at times of illness or physical debility, such as the period following a woman's confinement.[40] These court appointments were positions of importance in the lives of these women, lasting for decades, sometimes lifelong, and they also involve moving from one role to another and between different ducal households: Gioanna Vermetta, for example, was wet nurse to the Prince of Piedmont, the future ruler Vittorio Amedeo II, in the 1660s and 1670s; then she was a Fama di Camera and *rameusa* to his daughter, the Princess Maria Adelaide, in the 1680s, and a *Fama serviente* to the Duke's other children in the early 1700s. Finally, in the following decade, she became a Fama to Madama Reale, the Duke's mother.[41] She was married to His Highness's pastry-cook, Bartolomeo, and gave birth to at least seven children between the date of her marriage and the death of her husband in 1684.[42] For these women, a life in service therefore coincided with married and home life, and, as in the earlier examples relating to female artisans of the body active in the family shop, working responsibilities continued well beyond the death of the husband.

Like the male servants, the Fame derived many advantages from the intimacy they established with members of the ruling family. Occasion-ally, albeit more rarely than in male cases, women employed in the Camera were fortunate enough to be pensioned off when they stopped serving at court.[43] In some cases the pension would go on being paid to her family even after her death, for instance to the husband.[44] When alive, they did receive quite respectable stipends, fairly close to what male servants were paid. For example, in 1712, Madama Reale had eight Fame taking turns in her service and being paid annual stipends of between 600 and 1,500 lire. These stipends were roughly equivalent to those of Madama Reale's own Aiutanti di Camera, which varied between 800 and 1,500 lire, and actually no lower than those of the seven Aiutanti di Camera of her son the King (which fluctuated between 700 and 1,200 lire).[45] The Fame and other female servants of the Camera were then in a position to receive gifts, tax exemptions and favours, but unlike the male employees of the Camera, they were seldom the direct beneficiaries of these gratuities. At least when these took the official form of a letter patent, the concession was more often bestowed on sons, husbands, sons-in-law and other male relatives of the woman. For instance, between 1684 and 1715, Gioanna Vermetta, whom we have already encountered, became a widow and obtained for her son the post of Garzone di Camera, some financial assistance for marrying off her three daughters, and for her niece an apothecary's shop to be brought to her future husband as a dowry.[46] Gifts received directly by the Fama from the hands of her employer must however have been frequent, even substantial, although we rarely have any record of them. One example is provided by the case of the most fortunate of Gioanna Vermetta's daughters, Teresa, Fama to the Princess of Savoy Maria Luigia, who was married to Philip V and therefore became Queen of Spain. By Teresa's own account, the trousseau she brought to her husband, the richest of all those we have looked at in this social group, contained many 'clothes, linen, silverware and precious things' given to her by the Queen, including a pearl necklace which alone was worth as much as 700 lire.[47]

A study of women employed in the Camera confirms then that the services carried out there were a 'family' occupation: indeed what strikes us in perusing the registers of payments to Chamber personnel is the recurrence of the same surnames among male and female staff. Unsurprisingly, the women are often related by blood or marriage to men employed at court as surgeons, Aiutanti di Camera, Aiutanti di Guardaroba, keepers of the jewels and upholsterers. In contrast, the names of wives or daughters of physicians are almost entirely absent. Let us take one year at random: 1657. A good number of the surnames found in the lists of Aiutanti di Camera and Guardaroba (Simonetta, Fontana, Antiborg, Moro) and of ducal surgeons (Borello), are also to be found among the Fame or the wet nurses.[48] Although there are five physicians among the stipendiaries of the ducal Chambers that year, the only surname that crops up among the female staff is Destefanis.[49] Moreover, this is an almost unique case: in my scrutiny sample of the registers of payment, I have found no other wives or daughters of physicians employed among the staff of the Camera.[50] It is conceivable that ideals of decorum prevented these women from performing services which involved direct contact with the body and this tallies with the therapeutic roles expected of their husbands or fathers, who were not supposed to 'cure the body with the body'.[51] Moreover, we have already seen that servants were very much in evidence in the homes of the physicians, suggesting the wish to spare the women of the family the manual aspects of household management. The fact that physicians were present at court on an individual basis only while artisans of the body were there in family groups confirms our earlier impressions that the latter were much more rooted within the court environment than the former, and more exposed to its influence in terms of taste and consumption as well as opportunities. Indeed, the involvement of women of the family has the effect of heightening the tendency of artisans of the body to create real dynasties of court employees: for example, the Marchetto family are present at court through Francesco, upholsterer, Aiutante di Camera and keeper of furniture to the Duchess and then to the Duke from the 1630s to the 1670s, and subsequently his sons, Cesare and Pietro, both upholsterers, and Giuseppe and Giò Antonio, respectively Aiutante di Guardaroba to the Prince of Piedmont and Aiutante di Camera to the Duke. Cesare was to die a bachelor, but the wives of the other three brothers also performed services in the Camera. Isabella (the widow Manfredi) was a wet nurse and later a Fama to the Prince of Piedmont; Francesca Margherita was a Fama to the Princess Adelaide; Francesca Bonauda was a Fama to the Princess Ludovica. This means that, thanks to its women, the Marchetto kin managed to achieve a presence in as many as four different Camere, that is in several court households, thereby increasing the influence, access to information and relational capital of the group.[52] We should also note the 'horizontal' character of the presence of this family at court: it is a string of brothers and sisters-in-law which occupies a number of adjacent positions in the households of different members of the ruling family.[53]

The existence of kinship ties between employees of the Camera is to be found also among the more lowly occupations: between the bleacher of linen and the Garzone di Camera Coatto, for example, and between the *potagera* and the household surgeon Ghidella.[54] As in the artisan's shop therefore, women at court worked in a kind of family enterprise, but their presence among court servants did not simply depend on their husband's or another male figure's position. In fact, the women employed there often remained in their post after being widowed.[55] The presence of members of the kinship network among the servants of the Camera would feed, moreover, into the productive and commercial enterprises of other relatives: we can only speculate, for example, on the importance that the employment in different Chambers of at least four members of the Masson kinship group in the second half of the seventeenth century and early decades of the following one had for the fortunes of jewellers Giacomo and Giovan Battista Masson and their wives, and then of Giovan Battista's son, Michele, suppliers of a great many jewels and precious objects to the Dukes in this same period.[56]

By studying the occupations of the women we therefore find new evidence that they played a crucial part in the same sphere of activities as the men of the family and that they used this expertise in ways that were economically significant. Affinities existed between specific occupations in such a way that the knowledge acquired at home had a degree of versatility and could be applied, even by married women, within a set of interlinked duties. In recent years scholarship has paid much more attention to the working experience of single women – be they unmarried or widows – than to that of women who worked in a family setting. The opacity of the sources is one of the reasons for this trend: any attempt to analyse the contribution made by mothers, wives and daughters to artisan enterprises runs up against a decided reticence in the documentation, concerned as it is to represent the women of the family as dependents – we have seen this in repeated instances. Hence, many of the recent generalisations concerning women's work are based on the more easily documented situation of women working as employees: for example, the idea that the female workforce in the early modern period was relegated to unskilled and poorly paid work, and that the barrier between 'male' and 'female' occupations increased. This chapter has attempted to identify ways of penetrating a little further into those areas of work carried out by women within the family enterprise. Although the evidence is scattered, consistent indicators emerge from this investigation to show women engaged in a range of occupations that is much broader than expected, urging us to resist the temptation to see their contribution as being limited to 'female' sectors. They show moreover how women were economically active throughout their whole lives, not just when unmarried or widows. In this sense, the Femmes de Chambre are a particularly eloquent example: most of them were in fact married women whom we see, as we seldom do, producing an income that was far from insignificant.

There are many analogies between the patterns of female and male work at court: like the Aiutanti and Garzoni, the Fame worked at court only for part of the year (for spells of three months at a time), and presumably they also had outside occupations that we can surmise were akin to their court employments. Moreover, like the men, the women employed in the Camera performed complex roles, handing out commissions for outside services and provisions, rather than just being engaged in service work. For example, in cases of emergency, the Fama would find and pay a wet-nurse; the laundress of linen would obtain all the materials necessary for doing the washing; and the bleacher would be concerned with getting lace items mended whenever the need arose.[57] In addition, they often enjoyed the trust and affection of their master or mistress, as demonstrated by the length of their careers, by their moves from one Camera to another when the first ceased to exist because a prince or princess had grown up, and by the gifts and favours they managed to obtain. This makes them key figures in opening up career opportunities for members of their family both outside and within the court. Yet there are also differences between male and female court employees, and these are similar to the ones we find in the shop. Although women performed a key role in transmitting skills and relationships, they did not have 'pupils' outside the family and they could not create extended lines of descent such as those the men developed through the Giovani and the supernumeraries. The way in which they reproduce their craft takes place more exclusively within the family than it does in the case of males. We will see this more clearly in the next chapter.

Notes

1 Farr, *Artisans*, p. 245.
2 Romano, *Patricians*, p. 78; Farr, *Hands of Honor*, p. 136.
3 Romano, *Patricians*, p. 78; Farr, *Hands of Honor*, pp. 138, 149; Cerutti, *Mestieri e Privilegi*, pp. 18, 67, 170.
4 The literature on women's work in the early modern period is huge. Helpful syntheses are M. Wiesner, *Women and Gender in Early Modern Europe* (Cambridge, 1993), chapter three; O. Hufton, *The Prospect Before Her* (London, 1995), pp. 92–4, 163, 238–45; on England, M. Keniston McIntosh, *Working Women in English Society 1300–1620* (Cambridge, 2005); on Italy, A. Groppi (ed.), *Il Lavoro delle Donne* (Rome, 1996) and the references therein. On women in medical occupations, see Pelling, *The Common Lot*, chapters seven to eight, and *Medical Conflicts*, chapter six; S. Broomhall, *Women's Medical Work in Early Modern France* (Manchester, 2004).
5 On the rarity of formal apprenticeships for girls see A. Groppi, 'Lavoro e proprietà delle donne in età moderna', pp. 133–4, and S. Laudani, 'Mestieri di donne, mestieri di uomini', p. 189, both in Groppi, *Il Lavoro*.
6 Anna's age is missing from the documents drawn up immediately after her father's death, but it can be calculated from the 1705 census.
7 Marentier's age is given as sixteen in the 1705 census.

8   Ins. 1701, l. 2, c. 575, guardianship and care of the Chiarmet children; *ibid.*, l. 3, c. 217 ff., partnership between Claudio Chiarmet and the widowed Anna Caterina Chiarmet.

9   *Ibid.*, 1718, l. 3, c. 894. We do not know how long the partnership lasted; it was certainly still active four years after its formation: Art. 530, m. 2, vol. 3.

10   Ins. 1701, l. 3, c. 217 ff.

11   Art. 530.

12   Even in the case of widows, however, their occupation is still not always mentioned, and very often such a woman is described merely as a 'widow'.

13   On this process see Laudani, 'Mestieri di donne', pp. 192–3.

14   AST, s. I, Provincia di Torino, m. 4, fasc. 20.

15   J. Crossick, 'Past masters: the artisan in European history', in J. Crossick (ed.), *The Artisan and the European Town 1500–1900* (Aldershot, 1997), p. 13.

16   See below, chapter nine and works cited in notes twenty-four and twenty-five.

17   ACT, vol. 295, c. 46, 1701; Art. 530; Ins. 1708, l. 2, vol. I, c. 415, and 1711, l. 9, c. 699.

18   *Ibid.*, 1692, l. 7, c. 416; 1698, l. 8, c. 341; 1706, l. 4, c. 127; 1712, l. 12, c. 507.

19   *Ibid.*, 1725, l. 4, c. 476.

20   Art. 530; Ins. 1700, l. 3, c. 381, 1708, vol. I, c. 353.

21   *Ibid.*, 1696, l. 10, c. 164.

22   On the complex tasks required to manage a house, even a poor one, that fell to the women of the household, see H. Wunder, *He is the Sun, She is the Moon. Women in Early Modern Germany* (Cambridge, Massachusetts, 1998), pp. 94–7.

23   *Ibid.*, pp. 86–9.

24   Other examples of cohabitation of this kind are to be found in the households of the barber-surgeons Furno, Clemente Pasero, Tohesca, Ailardo, and Rocho: Art. 530.

25   This seems to have been customary at the hospital of Santi Maurizio e Lazzaro, at least in the middle decades of the eighteenth century. See the cases of surgeons Peretti and Benini in OSML, *Inventario Regolamenti e Istruzioni*, m. 27, fasc. 208, 1733, and m. 6 n. 210, 1734, 1739, 1744, 1757.

26   As well as being the main hospital for the sick, the hospital of San Giovanni also took in foundlings who were raised there for a number of years. The males were then discharged while the females were either married off or set to work as servants in the hospital itself or with well-known families.

27   Margherita is remembered in the will of 1710 (Ins. 1710, l. 3, vol. 3, c. 771) and, together with Agnese, also in the subsequent wills of 1731 and 1737 (*ibid.*, 1731, l. 6, c. 8; 1737, l. 3, vol. 1, c. 369). Both Margherita and Agnese were already present in the Verna household in 1705, so they had been kept on for at least thirty-two years.

28   M. Pelling, 'The body's extremities: feet, gender, and the iconography of healing in seventeenth-century sources', in Marland and Pelling, *The Task of Healing*, especially 224–32, 240–3.

29   My thanks to Flora Dennis for drawing this picture to my attention. For women practising as barbers and surgeons in England, see D. E. Evenden, 'Gender differences in the licensing and practice of female and male surgeons in early modern England', *Medical History*, 42 (1998).

30   Ins., 1726, l. 11, c. 521–22. The razor, the basin, the bowl and the mirror appear among the items making up the barber's equipment in Tiberio Malfi's *Il Barbiere*, p. 20.

31   'Registro delli chirurghi … di Torino'.

32   Art. 530, m. 2, vol. 3.

33 *Consegna dei Francesi 1690.*

34 AST, s.r., Art. 330, m. 4, n. 118, 1691.

35 *Ibid.*, m. 1, n. 75, 1694; m. 5, n. 121, 1695.

36 See the rules cited in notes thirteen and fifteen and for the 1587 rule: (*ibid.*, Art. 259 par. 2, m. 1, n. 29).

37 Broomhall, *Women's medical work*, pp. 188–202, 214–21.

38 One of the Fame is usually described as '*fama e* [and] *rameuse*'. The latter may refer to the woman who rocks and cradles infants.

39 This is in contrast with the situation at the French court, where, in the sixteenth century, wet-nurses held 'a purely functional position' and were appointed just for the period in which their role as feeders was required: Broomhall, *Women's Medical Work*, p. 194.

40 AST, s.r., Art. 219, 1677; Art. 217, 1712.

41 PCF 1673–4, fo. 31; *Ibid.* 1713–17, fo. 112; AST, s.r., Art. 217, 1687, 1705–7, 1712.

42 There were seven children alive at the time of her husband's will, Ins. 1685, l. 6, c. 3973.

43 See for example the pensions of 300 lire awarded to the female servants of the Prince of Piedmont when he reached the age of seven (AST, s.r., Art. 217, 1673), or the case of Anna Giulia Crova, Fama to the Duke's sister, the Duchess of Bavaria, who in 1661 was awarded a pension of 800 lire for ten years instead of expenses only for her food, which she already received (*ibid.*, 1660–61, fo. 74).

44 For example, the Aiutante di Camera Osasco drew the annual maintenance award made to his deceased wife, who had been a Fama di Camera (*ibid*, Art. 217, 1682).

45 *Ibid.*, 1712. This equivalence of stipends is in contrast with the disparity between male and female wages to be found in the non-military hospitals, where the female nurses were paid around two-thirds of what their male counterparts earned: for example, at the hospital of Santi Maurizio e Lazzaro in the second half of the seventeenth century, female nurses received fifty-four lire while a male 'servant' in the male wards received eighty-one. OSML m.1 c. 17, Registro delli mandati spediti alli officiali … 1659–1679, and c. 54, Bilancio delli Officiali 1683. Information relating to wages within the hospital setting is however somewhat scant, given that, as already noted, the majority of staff came from the ranks of 'young surgeons' who were unpaid.

46 PCF, 1684–85, fo. 227, 1694–95, fo. 137, 1702–4, fo. 11, 1713–17, fo. 112. The extra payment ordered directly for Gioanna was fairly modest: a present of 100 lire in 1673: *ibid.*, 1673–74, fo. 31. See also the wedding contracts of her daughters, Ins. 1685, l. 6, c. 3973; 1704, l. 12, c. 1219.

47 *Ibid.*, 1704, l. 12, c. 1219. It is interesting that these goods (perhaps regarded as too precious to be worn by the Fama?) were sold and converted into cash so as to increase the dowry from the 1,500 lire that could be given by the mother to the fair sum of 6,750 lire.

48 These are the wet nurse Allasina Mora and the Fame of the Princess Margarita: Caterina Borrello, Caterina Simonetta, Gioanna Fontana, Margarita Antibor: Art. 217, 1657.

49 This is Lucia Maria Destefanis, the wife of Giò Destefanis, the physician who was Medico di Camera to His Highness.

50 I have analysed the registers of accounts of the various households on the basis of one year in every seven from 1657 to 1712.

51 G. Pomata, 'Practising between earth and heaven: women healers in seventeenth-century Bologna', *Dynamis*, 19 (1999), p. 123.

52 Like his sister-in-law, Isabella, the widow of Manfredi, Giuseppe served for a long time in the Camera of the Prince of Piedmont. He subsequently moved on to serve in the Camera of the Prince's son. PCF, 1702–4, fo. 82.

53 There are also instances, however, in which married couples served in the same Camera, as in the case of Giovan Battista Fontana and his wife Gioanna, who were respectively Aiutante di Camera and wet-nurse (later fama) to the Princess Margherita in the 1650s, or that of Carlo Emanuel Platea and Margherita Platea, both employed in the Camera of Madama Reale in the 1690s: PCF, 1641–42, fo. 159; Art 217, 1657 and 1660; Art. 219, 1697.

54 For the Coattos, *ibid.*, Art. 217, 1677, 1687, 1697; for the Ghidellas, *ibid.*, 1687, 1697, 1705–7, 1712.

55 Among numerous cases, we can mention that of Anna Maria Tevenot, for some decades Fama to Madama Reale, and later her First Fama. She was married to Pietro, surgeon to this same Madama Reale. Anna Maria was widowed in 1697 but still occupied her own post ten years after her husband's death.

56 Between 1664 and 1680 alone some thirty payments made to the Masson jewellers can be found in the letters patent (PCF). It is interesting that these were not always made out to Giacomo or Giovan Battista, but also to the former's wife, Caterina, and, after Giovan Battista's death in 1676, to his widow, Francesca. The Massons employed at court are the couple Francesco and Lucretia, respectively Garzone di Camera and then Garzone di Guardaroba, and Fama to Princess Adelaide (Art. 217, 1667, 1671, 1682, 1687; PCF 1670–71 fo. 47, 1674 fo. 140, 1678–79 fo. 155, 1680 l. 2 fo. 195, 1680–81 fo. 225, 1682–83 fo. 32, 1699 fo. 146); another Lucretia, the wife of Michele, jeweller, Fama to the little Princes (Art. 217, 1705–7, 1712); and, briefly, Anna Margherita, bleacher of the personal linen and lace (Art. 217, 1687).

57 See for example the reimbursements made to the Fama Martin for her payment to a wet-nurse for three days, for 69 lire, and to Anna Margarita Masson for the mending of lace items (Art. 217, 1687); to Isabella Prochietto, laundress of the personal and table linen of His Royal Highness, for having provided 'a new barrel ringed with iron, a large cauldron, a copper box and other things ... to be used for laundering linen in Portugal' (Art 217, 1682).

8

The weak father

Youth: neither dependency nor rebellion

Studies on masculine identity tend to delineate a polarised picture of the male condition in the early modern period, one that seems substantially split between the experience of the so-called *figlio di famiglia* ('son within the family', an expression that underlines his dependent status) and that of the father: while the attitude of the former is seen as characterised by restlessness and unruliness, that of the father is instead informed by ideals of sobriety, restraint and responsibility. Research on youth has in fact privileged the study of practices whereby tensions were expressed towards authority and social conventions, ranging from the more moderate, such as the rituals performed by youth associations and the multifarious and itinerant life of *compagnonnage*, to more openly subversive episodes of transgression.[1] The more responsible, constructive and strategic aspects of young men's experience have instead been little acknowledged or researched. Within this perspective youth appears as a marginal period, a 'dark age' supposedly characterised either by passive obedience to the pressures of superiors or by rebellion.[2] In contrast, analysis of male adult experience has been dominated by the figure of the *pater familias*, imposing decorum and control over his own life and that of his subordinates (wives, children, servants, apprentices). Entry into the state of matrimony would seem therefore to have decisive repercussions for male ways of living, marking an end to excess as well as the dependency that had characterised the period of youth. Albeit in a different manner than for women, for men too marriage is seen as establishing the fundamental break in the course of a life: men freed themselves from the yoke of the *patria potestas* and gained legal rights and autonomy in managing and disposing of their own earnings, in addition to the political personhood of full citizenship. Indeed, in some European countries the potential to join corporative or representative bodies such as guilds or community assemblies were the preserve solely of heads of households.[3] The only public role exercised by bachelors, besides the military and religious, would have been the ritual one of upholders of community standards in the matter of moral and social conventions within youth associations.[4]

This picture supports therefore Mitterauer's contention that marriage, rather than age, was what gave a man adult status in the early modern period.[5] However, the biographies of barber-surgeons active in Turin display features that are somewhat different from those usually associated with the phases of male life cycle in this period. As we have observed in chapter six, the young surgeon leaves the home, supports himself with his own work and takes charge of his own life at a time when, legally, he should still be subject to the father's authority. Financial independence from the family of origin and autonomy from paternal authority arrive not with marriage, as often suggested, but well before, when the young man is in his late teens and is taking the first steps in his professional career. Marriage then occurs after years of independent life: although for some it takes place below the age of twenty-one, it is more likely to happen around the age of twenty-six or twenty-seven and in not a few cases even at thirty or older (Table 8.1).[6]

What is more, in the period of youth significant relationships are built outside the family and its networks, and these will later have a considerable bearing on the young man's career. The second expectation to be discredited is that the father played a crucial role in the building of his son's professional success, and that the positions the latter acquired had

Table 8.1 Age at first marriage

Bridegroom's age	Number of Marriages
17–20	5
21–24	12
25–28	16
30–36	6
Total	39

Source: The bridegrooms' ages are obtained from the population census of 1705 (Art. 530). The dates of their marriages are drawn from their wedding contracts or from the parish registers.

been handed on or secured thanks to strategies and investments orchestrated by the parent. In some cases, as in that of Busano and Pasero, the young men in question had actually been fatherless for many years by the time they opened their own shop or attained their first professional achievements; the young Domenico Deroy had been fatherless for at least sixteen years when he secured the prestigious post of chief surgeon at the hospital of San Giovanni.[7] Despite still being overlooked in estimations of the weight of paternal authority in the early modern period, the absence of a father from the young man's life was in fact a frequent phenomenon. Studies on the late sixteenth century make this plain: in Aix-en-Provence, at least 65 per cent of the fathers of bridegrooms were deceased at the time of their marriage; in Venice, the figure within the stratum of 'citizens' alone was 50 per cent.[8]

But even when the father was alive, it was often thanks to their own initiative that the sons rose to prestigious professional positions. For many migrants, like Alberto Verna, Enrico Stura, Giò Pietro Busano, Giuseppe Asinelli, to name only figures we have already met, the move to the city was an individual experience, at most pursued along with a brother, marking a move away from the authority and influence of the father and the family of origin. These young men arrived in Turin in their late teens, from small provincial towns, or from neighbouring states, leaving the rest of the family behind them. From that moment on their professional rise seems to have been due entirely to their capacity to make themselves valued by the masters with whom they came into contact, and from whom the most fortunate would eventually inherit professional positions or a clientele.

But for the Turinese too and even for those who were the sons of surgeons, like Fassina, Meda and Reyneri, professional success was often connected with relationships forged on their own account, during the period of training and subordinate work, with influential surgeons or with members of their kinship networks. They may well have been given a start in the craft in the father's shop (we have no information about their apprenticeships), but it is thanks to these bonds that they rose well above the status of their family of origin. For Giuseppe Reyneri it was his relationship with the master Evasio Verna, from whom he learned the lucrative skills of *accoucheur* (male midwife) and from whom he would inherit the post of chief surgeon at the Carità hospital. For Meda and Fassina it was their being employed as *Giovani* by Domenico Deroy, one of the most prominent surgeons in Turin in the closing decades of the seventeenth century. The appointment to chief surgeon at the Carità hospital that was conferred on Meda in 1680 seems to have been within

Deroy's sphere of influence; he already occupied the same post in the city's two other hospitals, the San Giovanni and the Santi Maurizio e Lazzaro. Fassina, who in 1679 had already secured an appointment as one of the city's four Surgeons to the Poor, would later succeed Deroy in the post of university anatomist. As for Meda's professional success, what also counted was the influence of his paternal uncle, Giulio Cesare, who was a barber at court. Together with the protection of another court family, the Nigras, who were related to his mother, this secured him the post of Household, then Personal, Surgeon to Princess Ludovica.[9] As in many other cases, here the fact that father and son were surgeons proves only the inheritance of a professional vocation, it does not signify, as is often assumed, that the son succeeded to the father's business, which is to say his shop, clientele, status and professional connections.[10]

A picture of youth as a very dynamic period emerges from these stories, its impetus not only geographic but within the social space of the city, as the cases of Fassina, Meda and Reyneri demonstrate. Early youth does not therefore appear as a period of absolute dependency on paternal authority or on surrogate father figures such as the master. Neither is this a phase of ritual disorder but one of fairly deliberate individual investment in an occupation where there was at the time ample scope for failure, but also for considerable advancement in the case of able and enterprising young men. Indeed, the career of surgeon offered exceptional possibilities. In chapter six we discussed the case of the many who did not succeed in becoming independent practitioners, but there are also numerous instances of young men from modest backgrounds, whether or not the sons of surgeons, who within a few years attained prominent posts among the city's surgeons, and subsequently sanctioned their new status with the acquisition of a lifestyle greatly superior to that of the family they had come from.

It is possible that these meteoric careers were in part linked to the particularity of the craft of barber-surgeon, which could be said to reward youth. We tend to think of early modern society as highly hierarchical and to suppose that age differences constituted one of the chief principles of authority. In reality, the validity of criteria of seniority needs to be subjected to further scrutiny and may well vary according to different occupations. For surgeons, opportunities to attain posts of authority did not increase with age; rather, the most prestigious appointments open to them (in the hospitals, at court or at the University) often arose when they were young, in a phase when many were opening their first independent shop, or even earlier (table 6.3). Giò Francesco Meda became a surgeon at the Carità hospital when he was barely twenty; Alberto Verna became surgeon at the same hospital at the age of twenty-five and chief surgeon at the hospital of San Giovanni when he was twenty-seven; Giuseppe Reyneri was appointed professor of surgical institutions in 1750, at the age of only twenty-five. Conversely, surgery seems to have been an occupation that, after a certain age, could not be pursued alone, and we can see that by the age of roughly fifty, the surgeon who performed any public role was bringing in a son, a nephew or an assistant alongside him. In 1715, at fifty-three, the municipal Surgeon to the Poor, Giò Pietro Busano, began drawing on the assistance of his son Pietro Francesco Maurizio, likewise a surgeon, in the fulfillment of his professional duties. Other Surgeons to the Poor (Brucho, Bonardo, Bellino) took the same route, and quite early on in his career, the surgeon Alberto Verna is unfailingly mentioned in tandem with his nephew in the documents of the hospital where he worked. Of course, these sodalities between father and son or uncle and nephew had the function of legitimating the designated successor to the post, but perhaps they also indicate a widespread perception of a certain fragility associated with age.

How exceptional is the case of surgeons and this occupation's faith in the merits of youth? It may be that there are specific requirements linked to the manual aspect of its craft: occupational tracts do in fact mention youth as a requisite of both the surgeon and the barber. The surgeon must be 'young, or else close to youth, his hands skilful'; the barber 'should be deft, his hands steady as well as capable, never wavering [...]. His eyesight must be sharp and clear; likewise the other senses unimpaired, and perfect; and it is singularly youth that will provide this; which is in keeping with the common view of the world, and is thus necessarily required.'[11] Moreover, the pace at which the career develops is here accelerated when compared with other occupations. This peculiarity of the craft is highlighted in a study comparing patterns of property creation in a series of occupations practised precisely in Turin in the period 1683–1727: surgeons are the group with the greatest increase in assets between the two age cohorts, twenty to twenty-nine and thirty to thirty-nine.[12] This is in particular contrast with the trend identified for the classic liberal professions (the notary, the lawyer), which instead reward maturity. And yet it is possible that the opportunities open to young surgeons were not so exceptional, and that this is merely a still under-researched aspect of generational identity. There is no doubt that some public appointments seem to have favoured the young: for example the post of *Cantoniere*, the municipal official whose task it was to oversee public order in individual districts of the city, keeping himself informed about arrivals and departures, disorders, brawls and even domestic quarrels. This was often awarded to men around the age of thirty, and was a role that required not just a considerable degree of rootedness in the fabric of the neighbourhood, but social esteem and experience, qualities we find hard to associate with men of such a young age.[13]

Thus our stories reward us with a somewhat unconventional picture of generations and relationships between them, a far cry from the hierarchical and vertically orientated image often emphasised by the literature. For our young men youth is a creative period during which many worked out their own strategies for making their mark and getting ahead.

Ruptures: the negotiable family

The biographical itineraries of these young men also highlight the redefinition of the family and social network that is a frequent feature of this phase of their lives. The new connections formed or consolidated in youth often involve a detachment from the father and parts, at least, of the family of origin that is not only physical but, it could be said, emotional. A special rapport was often forged with the master. At the time when Sebastiano Fassina and Giò Francesco Meda were Deroy's Giovani, their involvement in the master's property and family affairs evince the signs of some degree of closeness: both were present at the bedridden Deroy's dictation of his will in 1678, during an illness from which he would later recover, and likewise at the division of inheritance between Deroy and his two brothers-in-law after the death of the father-in-law.[14] Three years later this bond would be strengthened by the marriage of Sebastiano's eldest brother, the already established perruquier Emanuele, to Caterina, Deroy's niece through his sister. This union underlined the familiarity with the master's household and neighbourhood that had now been achieved by the two Fassina brothers (Caterina lived with her family in the block opposite the one occupied by Deroy himself); these were some distance from the area where the brothers' father lived.[15] The wedding took place shortly after the legal deed of emancipation whereby Emanuele was freed from all financial obligations towards his father, Amedeo, and towards his numerous siblings, in exchange for giving up the share of inheritance due to him, as well as paying his father the not inconsiderable sum of 600 lire.[16]

These events already point to the formation of an alternative professional and kinship network to the one centred on the father, Amedeo Fassina. The distance between the Fassina brothers and their original family and background was made all the plainer in 1688, when Sebastiano married Paula, Deroy's other niece and Caterina's sister. At this time, as the legal documents show, Sebastiano also freed himself from the *patria potestas* of Amedeo, having lived apart from his father and by his own earnings for a good number of years.[17] Thereafter, the circumstances and destinies of the Fassina family members would be quite decisively split. The two brothers, Emanuele and Sebastiano, now an integral part of the Deroy kinship network, which extended to the four children of the master's first marriage along with their spouses and in-laws, maintained these connections without interruption for the rest of their lives. However, the ties with their parents and their other siblings became weaker. The only exception is their relationship with their young brother Giuseppe, who was also attracted to court in the footsteps of his successful brothers (since 1695, Sebastiano had been Ducal Surgeon and General Surgeon to the Armed Forces and Emanuele was a court perruquier), first as a *baigneur,* then as *Aiutante di Camera.* The two groups of siblings were separated by a wide gap in wealth and lifestyles. One immediate measure of comparison is supplied by the contrast between the dowries paid within the two groups. In 1695, Amedeo Fassina paid out 900 lire to marry off his daughter Anna Camilla to the perruquier Bert, and he provided her with a trousseau of around 200 lire; in 1708, Amedeo's young son Giuseppe, *baigneur* to His Highness, received in the presence of his brother Sebastiano the sum of 5,000 lire, in addition to a *fardello* reckoned at 551 lire, from the father of his young bride, Anna Francesca Marchetta, the daughter of the Aiutante di Camera Giuseppe Marchetto.[18]

It was in large families most of all, like those of the Meda and Fassina brothers (where there were respectively six and eight siblings), that the reorganisation of family ties tended to split the siblings into two groups. There were nearly always some siblings who stayed on, one inheriting the father's business, the others nonetheless making their way within the same social milieu and remaining faithful to inherited loyalties. This continuity with origins is what has gained the greatest attention. We have repeatedly seen how historians have been attracted to a model of father-son transmission and been surprised to find it so rarely. Other siblings, however, impelled perhaps by the paucity of family resources, opted decisively and at a fairly young age to make their own way by gaining a foothold in other environments; if successful, this would lead them to a clear-cut reconfiguration of identity and relationships and would inevitably estrange them from a set of original family ties.

The split within the group of siblings also occurred in the case of incomers. Frequently, the move to the city would be made by one or more siblings among whom lasting connections would be maintained, while they would tend to lose touch with those who stayed on in the town of origin. This is what happened to Giuseppe Busano, whom we find in Turin with his brother, the parish priest Francesco, and for a time with a younger brother, Pietro, who was also training as a surgeon.[19] Busano had a third brother and three sisters, but these stayed on at Mortigliengo and there is no evidence of further contacts with them.[20] Enrico Stura also came from a large family consisting of eight siblings besides himself. Of these, only two of his brothers and one of his sisters moved to Turin, living with him for a while. As we already know, he saw to the expenses of his brothers' training in a craft and also arranged his sister's marriage to a neighbour, another surgeon.[21] Maybe the fact that Enrico was married to a widow considerably older than himself and, perhaps for this reason, had no children of his own, was what made it possible for him to show such generosity to some of his siblings.[22] Judging by the mutual participation in landmark events (weddings, baptisms) or financial transactions and contracts, we can see that it was only with some of their siblings that artisans of the body maintained an intense relational life. As we have noted earlier, there was a shared inclination among migrants to be rid of all property in the place of origin, and it is as if by cutting off their property ties they also cut off emotional ties to the part of the family still left there.

This separation of siblings and their dispersal to different households of kin should not surprise us; it seems to have been common practice among the middling groups. It is even foreseen in many arrangements of care and guardianship made for orphans. For example, when the children of the perruquier Chiarmet lost their father, their uncle Claudio assumed guardianship of them, but while the elder siblings stayed on in the shop run by their mother and a journeyman, the newborn Vittoria was brought up in the home of Claudio and his wife Prudenza. It was Claudio who administered her property and then arranged her marriage to the surgeon Evasio Verna in 1721, whereas her relationship with her mother, who remarried in 1716, seems to have been weakened and soured by the long legal suit that ensued over the mother's contribution to Vittoria's dowry.[23] There are even cases where orphans do not all have the same guardian. The care and guardianship of the Senta orphans, for instance, was entrusted to three different individuals: the eldest brother, the barber-surgeon Matteo, assumed the care of Cesare, aged seventeen; that of Carlo and Margherita, aged sixteen and fifteen, was taken on by their maternal aunt, while a brother-in-law took on the guardianship of the youngest child, Claudio.[24]

But there were also cases of informal 'adoptions' of one or more siblings by members of the kinship network while the parents were still alive. To understand this family model we have to take into account the span of a man's reproductive life, which was made continuous through the repeated recourse to remarriage in the wake of a wife's death. If a father had married around the age of twenty-five, as was common in this milieu, by the time he was forty he would have offspring old enough to support themselves while also having others who were still young children. In this situation what we consistently see is that the older ones moved out of the family home at an early stage, followed, at intervals, by some of their younger siblings: for them the older brother takes the place of a father figure, while the father concerns himself with the youngest children. In short, these large families have more than one father figure, meaning that the role of providing for dependants, signing legal documents on their behalf and having an authoritative say in the decisions that affect them is not just fulfilled by the biological father but often by an older sibling. The same mechanism is found among siblings who are already adults: those who are unmarried or without children relieve a married brother or sister of responsibility for one or more of their offspring, taking these nieces or nephews into their homes and seeing to their education and marriage arrangements. Giò Colombatto, the nephew of surgeon Marentier, known as La Ramea, left the joint household of his father and his paternal uncle in his early teens to go to his maternal uncle, from whom he learned the craft of barber-surgeon and with whom he worked for several years.[25] Although this uncle had a son, it was Giò who inherited the shop, together with Marentier's surname, becoming Giò Colombatto 'known as La Ramea'.[26]

One particularly well-documented case of informal adoption was that of the Vernas, an uncle and his nephews. We have already looked at the unusual composition of their household, which consisted of teenage nephews, female servants and tutors.[27] These nephews were the sons of Alberto's three brothers who, along with his two sisters and his parents, had stayed on in the home village. Alberto had been the only member of the family to move to the city, where he met with considerable success, securing appointments as a hospital surgeon, at court and at the University as anatomical demonstrator. As soon as he had established himself as a surgeon he sent for his teenage nephews.[28] From then on he acted effectively as a father to them, giving them a home, paying for their education and training and going so far as to arrange their marriage contracts. A few years later, four more nephews moved from Rosingo to Turin to be entrusted to their uncle, who once again played a crucial part in their transition to adult life.[29] The surprising thing is that the young Vernas, like their uncle, never returned to the village. They pursued a career in Turin or else moved further away still, to Savona (in Liguria), even as far as Spain, and like their uncle, rose well above their origins, both socially and economically.[30] The ties between the young Vernas and their families seem to have been cut off: their natural fathers, although still alive, appeared at none of the landmark events in their lives, and it was their uncle who stood as a witness at their marriages and the baptisms of their children, and at their economic transactions.[31]

This move away from the family of origin and adoption by other members of the kinship network or the master's family is a structural occurrence rather than being something exceptional in this section of society, at any rate in families with several offspring and scant resources. We should note that these arrangements involve kin in both the maternal and paternal line, affines as well as blood relatives, confirming the highly bilateral characterisation of the kinship group, which we have already observed in previous chapters. These cases simultaneously give us confirmation of the fragility of certain family relationships and the strength of others. The enduring nature of family ties in the life of the adult individual, or their dissolution, have often been presented as antithetical patterns of relationships by historical demographers; these supposedly opposite tendencies have moreover been laid down as corresponding to different areas and cultural environments in Europe.[32] According to this thesis the nuclear family was a prevalent model in the countries of northern Europe, where young people can be seen leaving home at an early age, then independently forming their own families and cutting off ties with the family of origin. In these areas, kinship ties outside the nuclear family are seen as lacking both intensity and relevance. In southern Europe the stem family is said to have been prevalent, with several generations living together. Young people in this context leave home later and ties with the family of origin are never broken; kinship retains a fundamental significance in the life of the individual.

In reality, these generalisations about the quality of family ties, and whether they are 'weak' or 'strong' as a rule, melt away when we look at the life trajectories of flesh and blood individuals. While some family ties get forgotten, others acquire a central importance. And it is not the degree of kinship that determines the significance of the relationship: the biographies of the surgeons do confirm the importance of bonds between siblings, but not of those between all siblings; similarly, we can see that some of the offspring would maintain strong ties with their father while others became independent of him early on. Nor are there any laws that determine the age for leaving home: some sons stayed on in the family until their marriage, while many left in their teens. This coexistence of models and variety of attitudes and behaviour completely eludes the generalisations that have been made about the meaning of the family in southern Europe. The proposed pattern of southern European family formation takes for granted that family ties are universally important in these regions. In other words, the 'family' is presented as something fixed and definitive, which, while it does expand with marriage, is never anywhere reduced, no piece of it being lost. In reality, although family ties remained crucial within the professional strategies of the artisans of the body, the family spoken of during youth or in adult life is frequently very different from the initial one. It is a family reshaped to fit personal needs, strengthening the relationships with some members of the kinship network or with some in-laws; it is in other words a family that is chosen and created and not, as is frequently assumed, one that is simply allotted.

Non-patrilinear forms of transmission

Giving all the children the chance of a future did not simply rely upon succession to the father; rather, professional and material resources were also transferred within the larger kinship group, to the benefit of young men who were not necessarily one's sons – as in the examples we have looked at. Often, it was the tangible and intangible assets of kin who were unmarried or childless that were diverted to the nephews or younger brothers, but the transmission of resources, especially of posts, skills and social capital, also took more complex routes, as we shall see below, and often occurred to the benefit of a pupil who then became a member of the master's kinship group. In order to understand the significance of these transferrals we have to adopt a wider idea of property, one that encompasses not just the assets in land, buildings and money, on which attention normally focuses, but also professional and other intangible assets which often represented the real wealth of these groups: reputation, clientele, knowledge, instruments, local visibility and appointments (these bringing with them prestige, influence, a secure stipend and the hope of an annuity in old age). It should be borne in mind that among these groups what we are traditionally accustomed to define as 'property', that is family assets, would frequently amount to no more than the furniture that was in the house and the shop, along with credits or goods for a few thousand lire. Once divided among the many children these assets provided them with a very meagre share.

Of course, father-to-son transmission was practised and for one or more of the sons could also amount to a significant prospect. For example, the surgeon Giacomo Antonio Reyneri, father of two sons, both surgeons, favoured the younger, Antonio Bartolomeo, by leaving him the shop and a few other possessions, while at first leaving only the legal minimum of his estate to the elder Giuseppe.[33] Antonio Bartolomeo was to tread in his father's footsteps, remaining a modest local surgeon, while his 'disinherited' brother Giuseppe was to become not only a university professor, the Surgeon to the Royal Person and General Surgeon to the Royal Armies, but also a specialist in the new 'art' of obstetrics. As often happened, therefore, the family patrimony certainly did not allow for all the children to be settled on and inheritance concentrated on one son. Many young men had to look around and see whether they might place themselves in a position of benefiting from other potential channels of succession. We have already considered those within the kinship group, but there were also possibilities outside the family. In the first instance there were masters without any offspring, either because they had never married or because they had no surviving children. The sixty-five-year-old surgeon Lorenzo Mitton was one of these. In his 1729 will he left to his Giovane Francesco Delbò, who was thirty-five years old, all the furniture in his shop except for the mirror and the pictures, which were to stay with his widow. After Mitton's death Delbò kept his business going, clearly also inheriting the clientele. From his master he also inherited the municipal post of Cantoniere, this being the guardian of public order in the *cantone* where the shop was located.[34] In other cases, it is through marriage that the Giovane might join the kinship network of a master without any sons: for instance, Ghidella, surgeon to the household of Madama Reale, while not depriving his only daughter, at the time a widow, of her inheritance, left the use of the house and the shop he owned to a young couple: Alessandro Moran, who had been his Giovane, and his wife Angela, Ghidella's niece or daughter-in-law (*nipote*).[35] The couple also received outright possession of the shop furniture, 'the tools and other devices and the waters, drugs and anything else belonging to the surgeon's profession', as well as plates, towels, sheets and 'all the cloths in the shop'.[36] A few years later we find that, clearly in recognition of the inheritance they had received, the Moran couple have also adopted their benefactor's surname, and are now called 'Moran Ghidella'.[37]

Even when there was male offspring, inheritance was often handed down along non-biological routes. This happened, for example, where the father had risen considerably in professional and economic terms, as in the case of the surgeon Evasio Verna, whose three sons rose above artisan level by turning to more prestigious legal and ecclesiastical careers. While property assets (quite considerable in this case) went to surgeon Evasio's biological sons, especially to the lawyer Giacomo Giuseppe, his professional assets, namely the posts he held in the hospitals, at the University and at court were passed down in part to his young cousin, Giovan Battista, and in part to his promising pupil and son-in-law to be, Giuseppe Reyneri. In Evasio's will, the choice of Giovan Battista and Giuseppe as his professional heirs also took the form of bequests in material items: to the former, Evasio left 'the green surgeon's case with all his surgical instruments', while the latter received all the other instruments and the books of surgery 'except for half of the surgeon's cases, lancets and flasks for urine' which were bequeathed to another son-in-law, the surgeon Roccavilla, who lived outside Turin.[38]

Thus while material property followed the expected patrilinear routes of inheritance, professional capital was distributed more widely, not just to sons, but to affines, lateral kin and former pupils. It was not necessarily the son who continued the father's business. Besides those who were drawn to other crafts 'of the body' or, in the case of the more fortunate, towards the legal profession – which meant a liberation from manual work – it was not unusual for a son to choose a religious career in a monastic order, even when he was the only male heir. For instance, the only son of the surgeon Giuseppe Asinelli became a monk and the father's professional assets were passed on through his five daughters, all of whom married surgeons or other artisans of the body.[39] Thus, although laws and practices concerning inheritance favoured male over female heirs, there were still women who inherited and hence transmitted professional resources through marriage.[40] And it was often the religious vocation of brothers (clearly not always to be seen as an imposed decision) that lay behind such instances of female succession.[41] Among the most striking cases is that of Vittoria Chiarmet, the future wife of the surgeon Evasio Verna: all three of her siblings (two brothers and one sister) pursued a religious career, with the result that the patrimonies of her late father, her mother and the childless aunt and uncle who had brought her up all fell to her.[42]

Masters and pupils: 'diagonal' relationships between men

These unconventional forms of transmission in relation to the patrilinear model are not always to be explained by the absence of sons continuing with the father's business or by the lack of male children. The most established masters, who had numerous professional resources to transmit, did not concentrate these only in the hands of a son. One of the sons of Domenico Deroy, for example, would also be a surgeon but not the sole beneficiary of his father's appointments (which included concurrent posts as chief surgeon in the city's three hospitals, as well as that of anatomical demonstrator at the University). These would be split up between Deroy the younger and Domenico's three pupils: Giò Francesco Meda, Sebastiano Fassina and Alberto Verna. To understand these decisions we need to stop considering the pupils as mere successors and beneficiaries of influential masters and think of them instead as allies who allowed the latter to increase their own power and create professional lobbies. In the relationship between master and pupil, the former is of course the patron of the latter but he also gained what might be termed 'political' advantages from the pupil's work and success that helped him to preserve his influence and extend it to new areas. There is, therefore, an element of reciprocity in these ties, rather than just one party's dependency on the protection and favour of the other.

Relationships between these men were not always an extension of the father-son tie, creating a pseudo-fatherhood, and there was another reason for this: that of age. The age gap between master and pupil was often much smaller than that normally existing between father and son. Deroy's eldest son, Giuseppe, was a child in the 1670s, when Fassina, Meda and Verna were already working as young surgeons with his father. When Giuseppe became a surgeon at the hospital of Santi Maurizio e Lazzaro, inheriting his father's appointment, his father's pupils (who were by now his kin) had been holding surgical posts for over ten years. Long before any biological successor is guaranteed, a successful surgeon like Deroy has an urgent need to establish ties with professional allies and possible successors. This leads him to form close cooperative relationships with individuals only a little younger than himself who are initially subordinate but may however shortly become partners in the enterprise of establishing a monopoly over certain surgical posts and surgical practice in particular areas of the city.

It is precisely age gaps of around ten to fifteen years between these men that allow scope for such alliances. These are likely to be more mobile relationships than those where the gap is generational: while at the start there is an element of asymmetry of skills and status between the parties, before long, once the pupil becomes a colleague and an ally, these differences are bound to be rebalanced. These are in a certain sense, therefore, more professionally useful relationships than the one between a father and son sharing the same craft, since they lead not to an overnight replacement but the opening up of channels of reciprocity that will continue to bring advantages for professional life over a long time span. The professional relationships between uncles and nephews, and between older and younger brothers and cousins that I analysed in the preceding section were often characterised by this reduced age gap. Between Alberto Verna and his nephew Evasio, who became his long-time professional partner, there was for example a gap of seventeen years.

To understand more fully the role of these relationships we must again consider professional advancement not as the outcome of an individual strategy, but as something achieved through the formation of a network of allies. In chapter five we have already observed the tendency to create horizontal alliances between equals, that is between brothers-in-law, cousins and brothers engaged in different but connected occupations; we can now also see, within the same profession, the tendency to create partnerships and alliances that could be termed 'diagonal', which is to say between men with an age difference less than that of a generation. Relationships of this kind between men seem to have been central to the practice of surgery at the time. We already know that there is not always a marked age difference between master and Giovane (see table 6.2). Often the gap is between ten and sixteen years, at times it is even as little as five, three or two years, and in one case the Giovane is three years older than the master. On the other hand, although the surgeons who have Giovani are quite wide-ranging in age (from twenty-three to seventy-four years old), we can observe that extremely young masters are also represented (table 8.2). Ten surgeons between the ages of twenty-three and thirty-three have Giovani (and some, like Calcan and Pasero, aged twenty-nine and twenty-seven respectively, have two), and likewise ten between the ages of thirty-five and thirty-nine. As many as twenty out of the thirty-three masters who have Giovani in their shop turn out to be

Table 8.2 Age of masters with *Giovani*

Age	Number of masters
>25	2
25–29	3
30–39	15
40–43	4
44–52	–
53–74	9
Total	33

Source: Art. 530; AAT, 18.1.3; wills of Giacomo Ghidella, Giuseppe Deroy and Lorenzo Mitton. Ins. 1710, l. 3, vol. I, c. 741; 1730, l. 2, vol. I, c. 449; 1731, l. 2, c. 101.

Figure 8.1 Ties between holders of surgical posts, 1660–1750

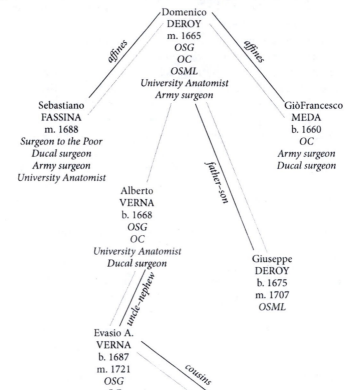

OC: surgeon at the Carità Hospital; OSG: chief surgeon at the hospital of San Giovanni; OSML: chief surgeon at the hospital of Santi Maurizio e Lazzaro.
b.: date of birth; m.: date of first marriage

········· master and pupil tie; ——— kinship tie (affinal or biological)

below the age of forty. If we consider that the birth of a first child took place in the majority of cases when the father was between twenty-three and twenty-seven years old (see table 8.1) it is clear that, up until the age of forty, the need for assistants and partners had to be met from outside the family. Later on, masters could obviously use their own children – it is not accidental, therefore, that we can record a fall in the number of masters with Giovani after the age of forty. The age range between forty-four and fifty-two in particular shows no masters with Giovani in their shop, whereas the number of Giovani rises among older masters, whose sons have become independent.

These observations lead us to modify the idea of authority that we associate with the relationship between master and journeyman, one usually seen as bearing the hallmark of subalternity. The ties binding some Giovani to the head of the shop and his family also appear in a more intimate and egalitarian light than we might expect from a master–pupil relationship. We have already mentioned that we find Giovani required to act as witnesses to the master's private legal documents, such as his will or the division of assets between his co-heirs, or to testify to the unmarried status of members of his family; we can also see the forging of ties of spiritual kinship between the master's family and his Giovane.[43] Clearly, during these years of working side by side, interpersonal connections are formed that will endure into the young surgeon's independent professional life, when they are often turned into ties of kinship through marriage into the master's family, and thereby into potentially permanent professional alliances.

Perhaps the sense of my argument can be rendered visually in a single image (see figure 8.1). The leading Turin surgeons in the years between 1660 and 1780 were almost all connected by kinship ties that by and large were not biological but acquired. There was only one professional tie that was not also a bond of kinship: that between Deroy and his pupil Alberto Verna. Yet even though it largely consists of a group of kin, the network represented in the figure did not have a patrilinear physiognomy: there was only one father-son connection; the rest were ties between uncle and nephew, cousin and cousin, father-in-law and son-in-law, or else relationships between in-laws at a second or third remove. Kinship did indeed function as a channel for handing on appointments from the eldest to the youngest, but this was largely through lateral or affinal ties. This means that, unlike what takes place within a patrilinear system of succession, here the members of the network often stood on an age scale where there was seldom an entire generation between one rank and the next.

We can therefore see the importance of taking age into account in our thinking about male relationships, as well as the need for exploring further the variety of ties between men that are all too often reduced to the father-son bond and to those that echo these roles. If we look closely at the roles that men held within the family as brother, uncle, father-in-law or cousin, and also at the relationships they maintained with other men outside the family, in the work environment for instance, we discover an entire universe of 'diagonal' male relationships, which are not always markedly hierarchical in kind; we find relations of authority more nuanced than that between father and son.[44] Biographical reconstruction brings to light the significance of a pattern of relationships between men who are separated by an age gap less than that of a generation; this seems to bear a crucial weight in the structure of the artisan's working life. In a fast-changing professional situation like that of surgery during this period, individual mobility relies upon relationships of this kind, frequently outside the close family group, and therefore it is liable to result in a turning away from paternal authority and filial dependency, thus leading to male entry into adult life at a fairly early age. The majority of generalisations about the roles of fathers and sons, the principles of authority within the family and male succession, are based on studies relating to the propertied classes. Shifting the focus of inquiry to urban groups that earned a living primarily from their work leads to quite different conclusions. It emerges, for example, that patrilineality was only one of various forms taken by the transmission of social and professional capital, and sometimes even by the handing down of a man's name.

Notes

1 There is a vast literature on the experience of young males. On the artisan groups see M. Wiesner, 'Wandervogels and women: journeymen's concepts of masculinity in early modern Germany', *Journal of Social History*, 24 (1991); L. Roper, 'Blood and codpieces', in her *Oedipus and the Devil* (London, 1994); C. M. Truant, *The Rites of Labour. Brotherhoods of Compagnonnage in Old and New Regime France* (Ithaca; London, 1994), pp. 175–8, 187–9; A. Shepard, *Meanings of Manhood in Early Modern England* (Oxford, 2003); R. Karras, *From Boys to Men. Formations of Masculinities in late Medieval Europe* (Philadelphia, 2003), chapters 3–4; two case-studies are R. Darnton, 'The great cat massacre of Rue Saint Séverin', in his *The Great Cat Massacre and Other Episodes in French Cultural History* (London, 1984), and D. Roche (ed.), *Journal de ma Vie. Jacques-Louis Menetra Compagnon Vitrier au 18e Siècle* (Paris, 1982). On youth 'abbeys' see note four. For the Italian case, see E. Crouzet-Pavan, 'A flower of evil: young men in medieval Italy', in G. Levi and J. Schmitt (eds), *A History of Young People in the West* (Cambridge, Massachusetts, 1997), volume one; R. Weinstein, "Thus will *giovani* do'. Jewish sub-culture in early modern Italy', and O. Niccoli, 'Rituals of youth: love, play and violence in tridentine Bologna', in K. Eisenbichler (ed.), *The Premodern Teenager.*

Youth in Society 1150–1650 (Toronto, 2002).

2 See P. Griffith's reflections in his 'Masterless young people in Norwich, 1560–1645', in A. Fox, P. Griffith and S. Hindle (eds), *The Experience of Authority in Early Modern England* (Basingstoke, 1996), pp. 146–50.

3 For access to the guilds see J. Ehmer, "Servi di donne". Matrimonio e costituzione di una propria famiglia da parte dei garzoni come campo di conflitto nel mondo artigiano mitteleuropeo', *Quaderni Storici*, 80 (1992), particulaly pp. 475–6; for the political rights of married men, see L. Roper, *The Holy Household: Women and Morals in Reformation Augsburg* (Oxford, 1989), p. 31.

4 This phenomenon has been widely studied. See, among the many contributions, N. Z. Davis, 'The reasons of misrule', in her *Society and Culture in Early Modern France* (Stanford, 1975); N. Schindler, 'Guardians of disorder: rituals of youthful culture at the dawn of the modern age', in Levi and Schmitt (eds), *History of Young People*, volume one.

5 M. Mitterauer, *I Giovani in Europa dal Medioevo ad Oggi* (Rome, 1991), p. 77. See also R. Ago, 'La costruzione dell'identità maschile: una competizione tra uomini', in A. Arru (ed.), *La Costruzione dell'Identità Maschile nell'Età Moderna e Contemporanea* (Rome, 2001), pp. 25–6. In fact the concept of majority in age is a fluid one in the early modern period and it is marked decisively only for orphans, for whom it signals the end of legal guardianship.

6 Although we know the precise age at first marriage for only eighteen barber-surgeons, for another twenty (for whom the first parish of residence is known) we can work out the birth date of their first child and thereby have at least an approximate indication of the date of marriage. The sample is small because parish registers have been preserved only for some parishes; moreover, since a wedding would take place in the bride's parish, the record of marriage is harder to locate than the baptismal records.

7 In fact, Deroy's mother appears as already widowed in the record of a loan made in 1645. Ins. 1654, l. 2 c. 137.

8 Dolan, *Le Notaire*, p. 77; A. Bellavitis, *Identité, Mariage, Mobilité Sociale. Citoyennes et Citoyens à Venise au XVIe siècle* (Rome, 2001), p. 171.

9 There is explicit mention of the merits of his kin in the patent of appointment. See chapter four, n. 68.

10 For example J. Dambruyne, 'Guilds, social mobility and status in sixteenth-century Ghent', *International Review of Social History*, 43 (1998), pp. 31–78.

11 Salvi, *Il Chirurgo*, p. 3; *Il Barbiere*, p. 45; see also D'Amato, *Prattica Nuova*, p. 7.

12 Levi, 'Carrières d'artisans', Table 1, p. 1356.

13 Among the surgeons who held this office, Emanuele Filiberto Valle obtained it at the age of thirty-three, Guglielmo Cerrutto at thirty-one, Giacomo Francesco Ratti at twenty-eight; Tommaso Bonardo came to share the office with his father at only nineteen (ACT, vols 294 and 295). Carlo Tommaso Carone was a Cantoniere at the age of thirty-one, though we do not know when he had been appointed (Art. 530).

14 Ins., 1678, l. 12, c. 745 and 441.

15 *Ibid.*, 1683, l. 5, c. 319 (but November 1682). He lived and worked in the canton of San Secondo (40), under the parish of Santi Stefano e Gregorio, while Deroy and the Verna nephews lived in the cantons of San Eusebio (82) and Santa Teresa (134), under the parish of San Filippo (see plate 4).

16 *Ibid.*, 1679, l. 7, c. 15.

17 *Ibid.*, 1688, l. 5, c. 503; 1689, l. 1, c. 827.

18 *Ibid.*, 1695, l. 6, c. 757; 1708, l. 9, c. 347.

19 Pietro then moved back to their town of origin after contracting an advantageous marriage, in Turin, with a neighbour, Domenica Chiolera, who, jointly with her sister, had inherited from her deceased parents: Ins. 1700, l. 1, c. 233; 1706, l. 2, c. 581.

20 *Ibid.*, 1688, l. 1, c. 819.

21 See chapter six, note seven.

22 In 1664 Enrico had married the widow of surgeon Ferrini, who died twelve years later. In 1678 Enrico remarried but no children were born from this marriage either, which lasted four years. AAT, 18.2.10, June 1664; 18.2.11, 26 September 1678; 18.2.14, 17 February 1676 and October 1682. For the wives' dowries and wills, see Ins. 1670, l. 3, c. 99; 1676, l. 2, c. 455; 1682, l. 9, c. 89.

23 Ins. 1721, l. 4, c. 205; 1722, l. 6, c. 991. The details of the quarrel are summarised in *ibid.*, 1724, l. 10, c. 255.

24 *Ibid.*, 1682, l. 8, c. 81. This was because of the paltry financial resources of the guardian, who had to demonstrate assets equivalent to those he had to administer.

25 Ins. 1697, l. 5, c. 1051; 1694, l. 1, c. 15.

26 'Registro delli chirurghi ... di Torino', statement of Giò Colombatto known as La Ramea. Marantier's son, Filippo, was eighteen years old when his father died and was still learning a trade: Ins., 1694, l. 1, c. 15. For another example of informal adoption by an uncle see the Ghidella case discussed in the next section.

27 Chapter seven, p. 167.

28 These are Evasio Andrea, Giuseppe Maria and Giò Alberto, all of them sons of Giovan Battista Verna. We find them cohabiting with their uncle when they are aged eighteen, fourteen and eleven respectively (Art. 530).

29 These are Michel Angelo and Giovan Battista, sons of Stefano Verna; Pietro Francesco, son of Antonio Francesco Verna; and Francesco Antonio, son of Giovan Battista Verna (Ins., 1731, l. 6, c. 8; 1737, l. 2, vol. I, c. 369).

30 Michel Angelo, a physician, died young; Evasio Andrea and Giovan Battista would both be surgeons in Turin, and Francesco Antonio a lawyer, also in Turin; Giò Alberto, the youngest, became a physician and moved to Savona, where he lived until a few months before his death (*ibid.*, 1753, l. 5, c. 36). Pietro Francesco became an administrator of the Royal salt mines for the Spanish crown (1756, l. 6, vol. II, c. 710).

31 *Ibid.*, 1721, l. 9, c. 205; 1725, l. 5, cc. 77, 386; 1717, l. 7, c. 131.

32 The first formulation of this thesis is found in J. Hajnal, 'European marriage patterns in perspective', in D. V. Glass and D. E. C. Eversley (eds), *Population in History* (London, 1965), and in J. Hajnal, 'Two kinds of preindustrial household formation systems', *Population and Development Review*, 8 (1982). This model has recently been proposed again by David Reher in his 'Family ties in Western Europe: persistent contrasts', *Population and Development Review*, 24 (1998). See also P. Laslett, 'Family, kinship and collectivity as systems of support in pre-industrial Europe: a consideration of the "nuclear hardship" hypothesis', *Continuity and Change*, 3 (1988).

33 Ins. 1754, l. 12, c. 731. In a later will Antonio also left Giuseppe a farmhouse, for which he had however only made an initial payment; more than two-thirds of the total price was still outstanding: *ibid.*, 1763, l. 4, c. 214. We will return to the ambiguous financial relationship between Reyneri father and his elder son in chapter nine.

34 *Ibid.*, 1731, l. 2, c. 101, 1 July 1729; ACT, Coll. XII, *Rolli della popolazione*, 1730.

35 AAT, 18.2.11, 7 November 1708. It has not been possible to confirm the degree of
    kinship between Ghidella and Angela. The latter has a different surname and is not the
    daughter of Ghidella's surviving daughter. The spouses had met in Ghidella's house:
    they were both part of his household well before they got married (Art. 530).

36 Ins. 1710, l. 3, vol. I, c. 741.

37 *Ibid.*, 1725, l. 4, c. 621.

38 *Ibid.*, 1759, l. 1, vol. II, c. 875. The books and surgical instruments are listed in Evasio's
    post-mortem inventory: *ibid.*, l. 4, vol. II, c. 901.

39 *Ibid.*, 1704, l. 5, c. 513. On the sister Asinellis' spouses see above, chapter five.

40 On the rules and customs of inheritance in the Duchy of Savoy, see L. Mongiano,
    Ricerche sulla Successione Intestata nei Secoli XVI-XVIII. Il Caso degli Stati Sabaudi
    (Turin, 1990); on discrimination between sons and daughters, Cavallo, 'Proprietà', pp.
    190–1.

41 On spontaneous vocations see B. Diefendorf, 'Give us back our children: patriarchal
    authority and parental consent to religious vocations in early Counter-Reformation
    France', *Journal of Modern History*, 68 (1996).

42 Ins. 1721, l. 9, c. 205. Another example is supplied by the Chiolera orphans: here too,
    the only son became a monk and the two sisters (one of whom was to marry the
    surgeon Pietro Busano) inherited all of their parents' property: *ibid.*, 1704, l. 5, c. 555.

43 Some further examples, in addition to the ones given in note fourteen and in chapter
    five note one: in 1723 Giuseppe Coppa, Giovane of surgeon Busano, was witness to the
    unmarried state of his master's daughter; in 1691 Giuseppe Forneri was a witness at
    the marriage of barber Ratti, in whose shop he worked (AAT, 18.4.12 and 18.4.8). In
    1684 the wife of surgeon Ghidella was godmother at the baptisms of the son of her
    husband's Giovane: AAT, 18.2.6.

44 Significant observations on the role of these figures can be found in L. Davidoff,
    'Where the stranger begins: the question of siblings in historical analysis', in her *Worlds
    Between. Historical Perspectives on Gender and Class* (Cambridge, 1995).

9

Respectable men

The emancipated son

We have already seen that the surgeon Sebastiano Fassina and his brother, Emanuele, a perruquier, were formally 'emancipated' from their father's authority. What does this mean? Emancipation consisted of a notarial deed whereby the son was freed from the sovereign power of the father, therefore from the state of legal dependency on him. The procedure was adopted on a fairly regular basis: in seventeenth-century Turin fifteen or so deeds of emancipation were drawn up every year, and, although numbers fell, the practice still continued well into the eighteenth century. Emancipations are documents of considerable interest for the study of relations between generations, yet they have received very little attention.[1] Alongside its ritual formulations, the deed does often give us an indication of the son's and father's ages and of their occupations; sometimes it mentions the size of the family, whether the son was living apart from the father and for how long, whether he was married and he himself was a father. The information is supplied in an unsystematic way, in order to prove that there were well-founded reasons for the attainment of emancipation, and does not easily lend itself to statistical treatment; but even such sparse detail does throw light on the bond between an adult son and his father and family of origin within various social groups – a subject about which we still know so little.

One frequently overlooked aspect is that the father-son relationship had specific features in different parts of Europe, and that paternal authority was of variable duration according to different legislative systems. In Piedmont, and, I believe, in other Italian states too (although this needs confirmation), just as in those regions of southern France regulated by written law, a rigid application of Roman law prevailed: paternal power was perpetual, lasting therefore until the death of the father, and the son could free himself from this only through a legal deed of emancipation agreed to by the father. So long as the latter was alive the son remained subject to his *patria potestas,* and was not truly in charge of his own earnings, because the father could make a claim on them for use in favour of his other children. Moreover, the son could not be a party to any contracts or transactions without his father's involvement; nor could he make a will, given that he was not the free and sovereign owner of his goods. This is in contrast with the situation in the rest of France: in the *pays de coutume,* 'the power of the father ends with the marriage of the son, or his emancipation, or his accession to certain appointments, and above all in his achieving his majority, fixed at the age of 25'.[2] It is likely that similar regulations applied also in German lands, given that there marriage entailed the male's acquisition of political and citizenship rights; moreover, the transfer of assets usually took place *inter vivos,* and therefore the son's release from paternal authority also occurred while the father was still alive.[3]

People of the middling sort seem to have resorted to emancipation more frequently than any other social group, and we shall try to understand why this was so. They include shoemakers, velvet weavers, smiths, small traders (button merchants for example); the artisans of the body – tailors, druggists, perruquiers, barber-surgeons – were strongly represented, besides low-ranking court personnel, especially bodyguards or ducal soldiers, often the sons of artisans. Professionals, particularly lawyers, physicians, and also functionaries like the city treasurer, came second, while the nobility and the wealthy merchants only rarely made use of emancipation.[4]

The first phase of the deed consists of a ritual of liberation. The father 'emancipates and frees his son from all paternal power, authority, force and might that in any way whatsoever he might or could have over him', so that in the future 'his son might sell, buy, exchange or validate by receipt, might make a will, codicils, donations or any manner of contract, might act in law and in business and do any other thing that may be done by a free man and true Roman Citizen and pater familias'. Sometimes the recital of this formulation might also be accompanied by specific gestures: for example, the father, with the son on his knees, would take his hands and lift him up while telling him, 'you, my son, from this hour on shall be emancipated, free of any will of mine'. Or else the father would recite these words while placing a hand on his son's head and then removing it. However, the rest of the document clarifies that besides acquiring legal and juridical rights as an adult person, the son was also relieved of his obligations towards the father's household. The second formulation we regularly find in these deeds actually states that all the assets that the son will acquire from then on shall be his to dispose of entirely as he sees fit, without either his father or any of his siblings claiming any rights over them. Thus, with emancipation father and son agree to separate their economic fortunes. The son usually renounces paternal inheritance and perhaps also pays a sum of money to his father as compensation for the expenses borne for the sake of his apprenticeship or education, and above all for the giving up of claims on the son's current earnings.[5] For instance, the barber-surgeon Meda paid his father 350 lire and we have already seen that the perruquier Emanuele Fassina paid his, 600; the apothecary Campeggio actually bound himself to pay his father an annual pension of 162 lire.[6] These are not negligible sums if we consider that they are coming from young men at the start of their careers (Emanuele was only nineteen on the date of his emancipation). Sometimes, the son being emancipated receives a small portion of the inheritance; among artisans, however, this is usually very little indeed: for instance, a *giornata* of land back in the countryside, or perhaps furniture or a small sum of money.[7]

A request for emancipation does sometimes appear in connection with the creation of a new family but the relationship between emancipation and marriage is not a consistent one. Sebastiano Fassina, for example, was emancipated a year before his marriage to Paula; the emancipation of the surgeon Antonio Reyneri was actually included in the same deed that drew up his dowry contract.[8] And yet many of those who requested it were already husbands, like the barber-surgeon Enrico Stura, who had been married for six years when he negotiated his formal emancipation with his father; the perruquier Parochia and the perfumer Fornero already had children.[9] Emancipation was also taken up by men who never married, such as Giò Francesco Meda.[10] Moreover, there was no link between emancipation and the moment of leaving the father's house. Although the literature frequently depicts dependency on the father in terms of co-residence, in the majority of cases we find that the son who requires his emancipation is no longer living with the family of origin, but has moved out many years previously, often at a very early age. For instance, the twenty-two-year-old Sebastiano Fornero had been 'outside the house of his aforesaid father' for eleven years when he obtained emancipation; Giò Colombatto had actually been living independently for twenty-two years.[11] These emancipations therefore confirm that the early departure from the family of origin was a significant feature of the artisan's life cycle. And yet the *patria potestas* went on for years, even without there being cohabitation. In fact, in those cases where we know the age of the emancipated son, we see that, though he was sometimes quite young, like

Sebastiano Fornero or Emanuele Fassina, he was often in his late twenties or even in his thirties.[12] What was it then that prompted the request for emancipation after so many years of relatively autonomous living and, it could be said, adult life?

Emancipation was desirable because it removed the need for the father to be present at every transaction involving the son: for instance, the dowry deed, purchases or work contracts. This obligation became more burdensome when the son started extending his business activities and had recourse to written deals more frequently. And yet, in artisan emancipations the unfailing insistence on the fact that the son owed nothing to his father makes it plain that the real aim was to avoid the father making any claim over the 'earnings and savings' that the son was now in a position to achieve. This is why emancipation often took place after some years of independent living when the son had reached a more advanced phase of his career. In this sense, Sebastiano Fassina's deed of emancipation is exemplary: it stresses that Sebastiano's earnings belonged solely to him, being 'the fruit of his labours', and that there has been no input to these on the father's part other than the expenses of apprenticeship. These expenses have already been amply repaid in the ten years during which Sebastiano has worked with his father, 'laying out all his earnings in the common service of the household'; moreover, he offers to renounce his portion of the father's inheritance. There is then mention of the extent of the paternal household, of the large number of Sebastiano's siblings 'for whose upkeep substantial expenses are required', which contrasts with the fact that 'the inheritance of his aforesaid father amounts to very little substance'.[13] The condition of the father and of his household are therefore described as being a threat to the son's nascent prosperity. At other times it is the number of the father's marriages that is presented as a problem: for example, the tailor Ruschella mentions the number of offspring from his two previous marriages (five children alone by the mother of the son being emancipated) and that he expects more to be born from his present, third, marriage.[14]

For the artisan classes, who live primarily from their own work, what matters is not so much having to be subordinate to the father's authority and decisions, which effectively has not applied for many years. The greatest preoccupation is that the son's own earnings might be used for the upkeep and settlement of the younger siblings, or for the needs of the parents themselves.[15] This is why the father often releases the son explicitly from these kinds of obligations: Ruschella confirms to his son that items the latter has already purchased shall be his own 'and not subject to be divided between his siblings'. Clearly, it is not only the father's rights as an individual that are involved, but those of the family; in theory the son has limitless duties towards it until he becomes emancipated.

What we find therefore is a situation in which the family of origin and the one formed by marriage are not legally defined and socially perceived as the object of alternative loyalties. This is why *patria potestas* persists for years even though the son may become economically independent and sexually mature, and may himself be a husband and father. The non-exclusive character of obligations towards the family of marriage appears as a specific feature that distinguishes the pattern of family relationships prevalent in parts of southern Europe from that found in North and Central Europe. And perhaps the emphasis placed by Protestantism on the conjugal unit contributed to this difference becoming more marked.[16]

If we return to the question posed at the outset, of why the artisan classes have recourse to emancipation relatively frequently, we can see that the answer must reside in the tension between the prevalent family model among these groups and the law relating to the father's prerogatives. Among artisans, the legislative strictures that give the father rights over the earnings of his sons are viewed as particularly threatening, given the limited resources upon which the household budget depends. As we have seen, older sons leave home early on, especially in large families, sometimes even in their early teens; for instance, they move out to live with the master or with a relative who also teaches the craft, or else with other young men. They build a life of their own and establish new connections, but as soon as they begin earning any money it is expected that they contribute to the needs of the family of origin in various ways, perhaps even by taking responsibility for one or more of their younger siblings. And, it seems, they do this for a time, until the situation becomes unpalatable and they have recourse to emancipation. The son who asks for emancipation is not therefore someone who repudiates his obligations towards his family, but often someone who has performed them for a considerable length of time and now wants to contain them. Carlo Campeggio, for example, had 'laid out diverse considerable sums of money in his [the father's] service and that of the whole of his household' since he became an apothecary.[17] Unlike the patrician classes studied by Kuehn for Renaissance Tuscany, the artisan groups do not experience emancipation as contributing to the preservation of the family assets; it is not, for example, part of a group strategy aimed at withholding assets from the family's creditors by making them appear to be owned by the sons – even more so as emancipation at this social level rarely involves a transfer of property from father to son.[18] It seems rather to be an expression of individual aspirations, legally sanctioning the de facto separation of the financial prospects of the sons from those of their fathers and of the family of origin.

The practice of emancipation highlights the ambivalence of the father-son relationship, which has too often been described as unidirectional. While the granting of a son's independence by his living father is usually portrayed as advantageous to the former and entailing a release to his benefit of the authority and property rights of the *pater familias*.[19] the cases in question demonstrate a reversed situation whereby the attainment of the son's full autonomy is only made possible by the renunciation of his rights of succession or even his payment of an indemnity to the father. Instead of sons who are greedy and impatient to take their fathers' place as in the time-honoured view of succession, we find demanding, penny-pinching fathers from whom the son must defend the resources he has built up.

There is not always equity in the agreements that accompany the emancipation; they take a variety of forms but they seem to be the more unfavourable to the son the higher he has risen above his social origins. What is asked of the son does not always amount to 'a fair compensation' for what he has received in education and board and lodging.[20] Even though the rhetoric stresses equity and the terms of the agreement may often be justified by the mention of these 'advances' on the inheritance, the calculations frequently fail to be well balanced. We see this in the case of Giuseppe Reyneri. I have already mentioned his early success. He was a military surgeon at the age of nineteen, then a pupil in the Collegio delle Province, and he had just turned twenty when he was sent to Paris for specialist training in his profession, in view of his (already designated) appointment to the 'chair of surgical institutions'. It was not by his father but by the surgeon Evasio Verna that he had been trained and instructed in the most lucrative of his professional activities, that of obstetrician. In 1755, when he had reached the age of thirty and had been married for five years to Verna's daughter, he drew up an agreement with his father, 'from whom he lived apart', 'in order to practise their profession together' in the shop until then kept by his father.[21] Theirs is a very peculiar partnership, with its provision for dividing in half all the expenses and the rent for the shop but also all the earnings, including those from the consultations that Giuseppe would be called to give outside the city. Although all the stipends from his public posts were to be excluded from the division, and likewise the profits deriving from the obstetric treatments in which Giuseppe was a specialist, for him this was nonetheless a ruinous contract: his fame was such that his ordinary private work was undoubtedly much more lucrative than that of his father, an obscure surgeon. In exchange, the father was surrendering the income from the dowry (amounting to 4000 lire) brought by Giuseppe's wife, Rosa, which he had pocketed and invested. There is certainly a strong impression that Giuseppe had been compelled to accept a deal that was far from equitable in order to recuperate at least the income from his wife's dowry, which was legally due to his father. It was only in 1761 that Rosa's endowments, drawn on by Reyneri the elder over ten years before, were transferred in full to Giuseppe.[22] It seems no coincidence that the following year saw the final outcome of the strange partnership between father and son. When the accounts were closed it turned out that his father owed Giuseppe 338 lire; needless to say, the debt remained unpaid.[23] This case shows us how restricted the rights of a son could be in this legal system, albeit a son who was an adult and married, if the father was alive and the fortunes of father and son had not been separated by emancipation.

Marriage and masculinity

In Northern Italy, therefore, marriage did not have the same value as a rite of passage from subordination to authority that it seems to have had in other regions of Europe and this obviously has significant repercussions for definitions of masculinity. It is now accepted that it was not just conduct in public life that defined masculine status. How the head of the family acted in the context of his domestic duties was an essential benchmark of his masculinity.[24] To attain a full masculine identity and earn a respectable position in the community, the adult man had in the first place to free himself from his subordination to the father or other figures of authority, and show himself capable of performing a leading role in relation to individuals dependent upon him through their sex, age or status (women, minors, apprentices or workers). This was usually achieved by his forming a household of his own, which was simultaneously a productive and reproductive unit. The head of a domestic group was responsible for it not just as breadwinner but morally, and therefore had to demonstrate his ability to protect the household members from theft, usurpation of rights, and attacks both physical and verbal (insults and slander). Moreover, he had to be able to control the behaviour of his subordinates in terms not only of their work input but of their conduct too, assuring the domestic order that was the basis of order in the community. In addition, and no less important, was his capacity to have children and therefore to prove his own virility in the respectable setting of marriage. Another key function of the adult male was to pass on know-how and property to his heirs, and in particular to educate his sons to be, in their turn, men who could preserve the family name and reputation. These virtues were to be matched by the capacity to control his own passions and to be beyond reproach in his own behaviour, giving an example to his subordinates. Many studies have in fact shown how male identity is defined in opposition to the characteristics of female identity, and in particular to the vanity and emotional frailty regarded as a feature of the weaker sex.[25] A real man is therefore one who is not an easy prey either to his own feelings or to momentary temptations, but who dominates his desires and impulses thanks to the rationality and character deficient in women and even more lacking in the callow young. 'The man who is not a master of his senses is no man at all' states Marquis Orazio Spada in the mid-seventeenth century.[26]

These definitions of masculinity have led to the conclusion that marriage and fatherhood were the condition for a man's attainment of a full male identity, this literature has tended in other words to establish an equation between the task of forming, leading and being physically and morally responsible for a household, and the status of husband and father. In reality this reasoning is defective: we know very well that the household and the family are not one and the same thing in the early modern period, and recent studies such as Naomi Tadmor's have brought fresh nuances to this distinction.[27] Yet the majority of studies have concentrated on married men, these being seen as the prototype for true manhood, implying that the family, not the domestic group (or household) was the sphere in which the adult male expressed and validated his own masculinity. Other forms of leadership and guidance of domestic groups that do not correspond to the conventional nuclear family, like those that were sometimes carried out by bachelors, have been ignored. As a result, the representation of the bachelor as a failed man is recurrent. Tosh, for example, states that 'neither the bachelor nor the vagrant could be fully masculine'.[28] And yet, although the number of those unmarried remains one of the hardest issues to determine for historical demographers, population studies tell us that the proportion of men who did not marry was far from negligible during this period.[29] In seventeenth- and early eighteenth-centuries England bachelors at times formed up to 25–27 per cent of their age cohort.[30] As for Italy, we know that within the more prosperous classes a high proportion of males did not marry (more than half of the Florentine patriciate and around 50 per cent of the Milanese); and the number of bachelors seems to have been fairly high also among the populace of the Tuscan countryside.[31]

Marriage was therefore not an obligatory decision for early modern men, and society in this period was clearly accustomed to accommodating a fairly high number of bachelors. Why is it then that their condition has attracted so little attention and has been all the more so regarded as marginal? One factor to be considered is that those studies that have set up models of interpretation in the literature on masculinity have referred to the Protestant world. It is therefore possible that the weight given by these authors to married status as the basis of adult masculinity reflects the importance invested in marriage within Reformation teachings. We know that it became central in the sermons of Lutheran pastors, and the creation of a holy household was seen as the basis of Reformed society.[32] But how far can this centrality of marriage be extended to areas of a different religious faith? Marriage did not have the same standing in Catholic theology. 'A man without a wife is only half a person and has only half a body and is a needy and miserable man who lacks help and assistance'.[33] These harsh words, by Johannes Mathesius (1564), one of the numerous Lutheran pastors who wrote about marriage, have no equivalent in the literature on marriage that developed in Catholic countries in the sixteenth century.[34] Here bachelorhood, far from being scorned, was exalted as the most desirable earthly state and as a route to sanctity; what is more, it was in the Counter-Reformation period that the number of religious celibates, both male and female, grew enormously. It is possible that this positive view of the celibate state would also have been reflected on those lay individuals who, for one reason or another, decided not to marry or else to delay marriage, making their condition more acceptable than in Protestant countries. What little data we have (relating to the higher levels of society) seems in fact, with few exceptions, to confirm the existence of high numbers of bachelors among the nobility of many Italian states, as well as in some parts of Spain and France, by comparison with the Protestant nobility of England, Germany and Geneva.[35] In studies of early modern masculinity, however, these doctrinal and cultural differences have not so far been given sufficient attention.

Yet another factor overlooked until now in the literature is the difference already noted in legal contexts. In some areas (Scandinavian and German-speaking lands for example) men became legally and financially independent on marriage, which also gave them political personhood and full rights of citizenship. In this context, therefore, marriage was a privilege that conferred respectability on a man as being now a stable member of the community and able to participate in its management. As such it could come about only with a certain degree of financial security that would enable him to buy a licence and to practise independently, to rent a house and a shop, and to be equipped to provide for the children who would be born. These are conditions not achievable by everyone, and so in some regions local administrations introduced restrictions on who could marry that were based precisely on an evaluation of individuals' financial fitness.[36] It is clear that in this legal framework bachelorhood can only be seen as a phase that is ideally transitory and an incomplete version of masculinity. We have observed however that in the Italian states marriage does not necessarily entail the acquisition of economic and legal rights since, without emancipation, these could only be attained on the death of the father. Becoming an adult appears relatively disconnected from marriage, given that it was possible to be married and dependent or conversely unmarried and independent. Probably for this very reason, in the Italian states the civil authority imposed no restrictions on the right to marry; marriage was not a privilege, but free. Nor did the exercise of political and public offices require that a man be married. Marriage therefore turns out to be an inevitably less significant factor in determining male respectability by comparison with what was happening in other European countries.[37] Masculinity was defined in different ways in different parts of Europe, and these were dependent upon a correlation between political, religious and legal factors that this study can only begin to delineate.

Bachelors' professional status

The argument whereby marriage represented a watershed in the course of a man's life is dominant particularly in the literature on artisans. These studies propose a rigid model of the artisan's life cycle that sets married masters apart from bachelor journeymen. The period following apprenticeship is in fact depicted as being characterised by a close correlation between bachelorhood, subordinate work, geographical mobility and residence in the master's house, while the attainment of master status is seen as intrinsically linked to setting up both shop and household, and therefore to marriage, geographical stability and financial independence.[38] This model has been described in universalising terms in overviews of the artisan condition: 'the artisanal lifecycle and the artisanal household implied that marriage and mastership coincided';[39] 'marriage generally marked the difference between master guildsmen (who in many towns had to have a wife) and journeymen (who in many places were prohibited or at least discouraged from marrying)'.[40] And yet this paradigm has been fashioned with reference most of all to German-speaking areas. In England for example, while there was a general tendency on the part of apprentices and workers to postpone marriage until achieving the status of master, or even later, it is hard to pinpoint any rules that really required married status for masters or prohibited it for journeymen.[41] It would appear that it was mainly in Germany and the Scandinavian countries that 'guilds normally denied mastership to any bachelor'. In the latter instance these restrictions lasted well into the nineteenth century.[42]

The evidence from Northern Italy fails to confirm the postulated correlation between financial independence, marriage, the acquisition of mastership and of legal rights; instead, these factors are combined in different permutations at various points in the life cycle of barber-surgeons. I have already shown that marriage does not necessarily bring with it property rights and legal prerogatives. Moreover, even though marriage and mastership frequently coincide, in other cases the two events are independent. In the first place we find young surgeons who marry before acquiring the status of master, which is to say the licence to work on their own account. This should not surprise us. Although the literature on *compagnonnage* has emphasised the itinerant character of the journeyman's experience and the impersonal relationships that he established with diverse masters and localities, we have seen that for many young surgeons the experience of subordinate work was strictly defined by the aim of entering the heart of a neighbourhood or a web of potential clients. Certainly, there is movement, but its goal is to settle down; the young surgeons are not constantly on the road but engaged in building relationships that lead to stability and independence. Marriage itself can be an aspect of these strategies of settlement and is therefore not impossible for the young surgeon. Even though they were not fully independent, many *Giovani* were involved in a working relationship that gave them a degree of financial security: this was the case for those who worked for many years in thriving shops or managed branches of the main shop on behalf of the master, or else for those tacitly designated as his heir.[43] Moreover, it was frequent practice to share a shop with a brother, an uncle or a father: Giò Colombatto, for instance, worked for many years in the shop of his maternal uncle. Such a situation allowed him to marry early and start a family. By the time he finally inherited the shop, on his uncle's death, Giò had three children. Up until then he had not purchased a licence and, technically, was therefore only a young surgeon. Yet he had been head of a household for many years, living with his own family in a nucleus separate from his uncle's.[44] Clearly, the distinction between master and journeyman is not as neat as one would expect. In this context, the opposition between married master and bachelor journeyman that is often deemed to be intrinsic to the artisan's life cycle seems ill-founded. Nor is there always evidence of the expected correlation between marriage and the forming of a new household. Matteo Stura, for example, married Anna Catta Cizaletta at a young age, but the young couple were lodged and supported financially by Anna's parents in the first two years of their conjugal life, while Matteo worked in the shop of his older brother Enrico.[45] So, although he was married, Matteo had neither a home of his own nor a shop.

Conversely we find masters who are unmarried but are nonetheless heads of an independent shop. It is impossible to arrive at any precise estimate of their proportion. The population census of 1705 provides us with an indication of the number of barbers or barber-surgeons who have no wife living with them: these are twenty-five out of the 100 aged twenty or above; of these no more than six appear to be widowers.[46] The census data, however, are silent about the time when a master got married, it may well be that those who appear to be married did so rather late and after many years of independent practice. Biographical research highlights in fact several cases of surgeons who became masters well before marrying: Busano, for example, only married six years after having obtained his licence.[47] Sebastiano Fassina was actually appointed to one of the four posts as Municipal Surgeon to the Poor nine years before getting married.[48] He is not the only bachelor to have held this prestigious post that guaranteed professional popularity and local influence. Giò Domenico Bruco was in this post for ten years before marrying.[49] The professional histories of the bachelors, therefore, are not very different from those of the married men; the two groups demonstrate similar opportunities for success. A high number of surgeons who are still bachelors or who will be so for the rest of their days, can be found among the professional elite of the city. In the last quarter of the seventeenth century, for example, the senior surgeons in the three main city hospitals were all bachelors: Alberto Verna, chief surgeon at the hospial of San Giovanni, remained a lifelong bachelor; Giò Francesco Meda died still unmarried during the military campaign of 1692, after having been senior surgeon at the Carità hospital since 1680 (as well as Surgeon and Aiutante di Camera to the Princess Ludovica); and Giuseppe Deroy married only at the age of thirty-two, after having been senior surgeon at the hospital of Santi Maurizio e Lazzaro for thirteen years.[50] Marital status does not affect their professional achievements. Alberto Verna, for example, a lifelong bachelor, was the most highly regarded surgeon working in the city in the decades around the turn of the century; renowned in particular for his expertise in obstetrics, he was one of the few notable figures in Turin surgery who also produced printed works and was remembered in nineteenth-century medical biographies.[51]

Although they were bachelors, these surgeons clearly gained the confidence of both their patients and the authorities; they were entrusted with crucial roles not just of care and treatment, but also in the super-vision of the many young surgeons who worked for them. It should be remembered that in the shop as well as the civil and military hospitals, the surgeon always worked with a slew of assistants, who served under his commands and for whose work he was responsible. Not only do many surgeons have up to three Giovani in their shop, even when they do not live in, unlicensed surgeons are connected with the shop of an approved surgeon, working in a variety of roles that are subordinate to varying degrees 'under the direction of' or 'alongside' the master. This situation is clearly reminiscent of the household, whose head directs and oversees a certain number of subordinates, while also being responsible for their behaviour. Like the head of a family, the master answers for the professional activities carried out by his assistants; thus the expressions used by the young surgeons to define the shop echo the language used to speak of the household and family: the shop is described as 'headed by' or 'under the name of'. Now, if it is true that male status is defined by the ability to rule the household, to ensure its order and efficiency, it can be argued that the shop, along with the hospital ward and the field hospital, are comparable to a 'household'. It is clear that male identity was also at stake in the professional sphere, not just within the biological family, as has been implicitly argued. The concept of 'household' therefore has been interpreted in over-restrictive terms in the literature on masculinity.

Whether his state was married or unmarried, the surgeon had, moreover, a public role to perform; cooperation with the authorities and the law was a part of his professional duties: he was obliged to report all cases of suspect injuries that he happened to examine, in which a patient might have been the victim of an assault or a participant in a brawl.[52] He was also called upon by tribunals to ascertain the cause of deaths in suspicious circumstances, or, together with a midwife, to verify the crime of sexual violence.[53] In Turin the public duties of the Surgeon to the Poor (an appointment which we have seen to be filled also by bachelors) were likewise considerable: he had to keep a record book of all those who died within his catchment area on the basis of the reports made by the *Capi Beccamorto* (Chief Sextons), distinguishing between men and women and male and female children, and on the basis of these books the munic-ipal authorities would then compile an annual record accounting for the city's population. In addition, the Surgeons to the Poor had to examine the bodies of all those who had died from injuries or accidents that were 'sudden and unexpected', and to draw up a report for their superiors.[54] The notion that the surgeon had to wait for marriage before being charged with public responsibilities seems to be unfounded.

Recent studies have suggested that there were alternative means to marriage to which men who were still dependent, and in particular young journeymen, had recourse in order to prove their masculinity: they demonstrated their physical strength and virility through violent rituals, such as fights between rival groupings, and through drinking contests and exhibitions of sexual bravado.[55] But did this kind of posturing really bring its exponents the respect of the community as a whole, beyond the closed circle of their peers? The violent actions of young bachelors were tolerated because they were associated with the shaping of a masculine identity, especially when the violence was expressed in ritual forms, but it seems unlikely that these were reckoned as proofs of adult masculinity, given that they negated the capacity for self-control on which male superiority had its ideological foundation.[56] Moreover, they violated the principle whereby a man was deemed mature by virtue of upholding the public and moral order of the community.

The young surgeons did not escape the necessity for a life marked by moderation: they needed to build a reputation for themselves, making themselves known in a particular part of the city, winning the trust not just of the masters who gave them work but of the patients that they would one day treat independently. Biographical research does indeed reveal a strong continuity between the locality where young surgeons practised and the one where they eventually set up their own shops. The period of subordinate work was an important phase for the construction of professional and also moral trust; the young practitioner had to prove that he had the right temperament for carrying out his own trade in a reliable manner. The barber, warns Tiberio Malfi, 'must flee from showing himself an ill-tempered man, revengeful, bold and prideful most of all, uncaring for the laws of God and men. [...] he shall employ no other weapons, nor shall he delight in any, save the tools of his trade, only showing his knowledge of their use [...]. Thus in his attire and all his conduct his manner should most properly befit a peaceful citizen of restful temperament'.[57] Any association with gratuitous violence or impulsiveness would have been quite out of keeping in someone responsible for treating the victims of assaults and watching out for any violent episodes that might disturb the community; moreover, a taste for alcohol could not augur well in someone who had to have a steady hand and quick reflexes in the performance of his own work.[58] It was precisely the opposite psychological and behavioural qualities that were singled out in professional tracts as distinguishing the good barber-surgeon: sobriety, judiciousness, prudence, the ability to make considered decisions, steadfastness and robustness, given that the profession frequently demanded the use of physical force, although always tempered by reason.[59] We have already seen that these attributes were central to the way in which Calvo presented the good surgeon (and himself) at work in his treatises at the beginning of the eighteenth century.[60] The virtues which Tarduccio Salvi had encouraged in the surgeon a century earlier were rather similar: he had to be 'courageous, conscientious, fearless in things that were sure, fearful in danger, circumspect in his prognoses [...] and in certain grave circumstances he must act without compassion.'[61] One is struck by the analogy with the characteristics required of a good *pater familias*. Clearly, the performance of professional duties also played a part in the construction of a masculine identity.

Even if they were without families of their own, the surgeon at the head of a shop or the hospital surgeon had considerable scope for exercising leadership, authority and responsibility in their professional and public life. The ways in which they conducted themselves in the performance of their occupation metaphorically conveyed their greater or lesser ability to conform to ideals of masculinity.

Bachelors in the domestic sphere

Bachelors were not only independent and successful professionals, able to manage shops and subordinates, but they were frequently also capable heads of a family. We have already seen in chapter seven that some took the place of a deceased father in heading the household, possibly also taking over his shop, when they were still unmarried. They therefore found themselves in the position of performing many of the duties associated with adult male status: they appear in the population census as heads of a household and its economic activities; they carry forward marriage agreements on behalf of siblings, providing sisters with a dowry and brothers with the necessary training for setting up their own business or with the ecclesiastical wherewithal to enter religious life. They also regard themselves as responsible for the material and moral needs of members of the extended family. For example, when his brother-in-law died in 1702, Giuseppe Deroy, by then living apart from his stepmother and step-siblings, but still responsible for a twenty-year-old unmarried brother who was training as a jeweller, took his widowed sister into his home along with her four children who were still minors.[62]

The composition of the household group in these life stories appears much more varied and susceptible to alteration than in the stereotyped image of the household put forward in the conduct books for the *pater familias*, which have attracted considerable attention in recent studies of early modern masculinity.[63] Many barber-surgeons are members of conventional nuclear families, others lived in complex families where members of the kinship network also featured. But there are also cases in which it is a bachelor who heads a household composed variously of members of the original family and the kinship network, along with servants, Giovani and lodgers. This should not be surprising if we consider the vulnerability of family life in the early modern age. The demographic features of the period are sidelined by recent studies which portray marriage as a universal condition of male experience and bachelorhood as an anomaly. Not only are bachelorhood and delayed marriage frequent occurrences, but the death of a father is a fairly common event; yet its consequences for male experience have not been investigated. What is overlooked is that women's experience of being widowed, which has attracted widespread attention in the last few years, has its counterpart in the children's loss of their father. For many young men this entailed the necessity of taking on premature responsibility for heading the family and the shop, albeit frequently with the assistance in these roles of a mother and sisters with suitable expertise. These considerations therefore suggest the need to give renewed attention to demographic events, before making generalisations about the features of male experience during this period. Factors such as the deaths of parents and the composition of the family at the time of their decease, for example the number of male children to be set up in work and female children to be married off could considerably reduce a young man's opportunities for marriage.

And yet, we would be wrong in arguing that family misfortunes or special needs provided the only reason for delaying marriage. There were also surgeons with fathers still alive who married only many years after leaving their family of origin and obtaining either a licence to open a shop or a surgical post. We cannot rule out the possibility that ambition and the desire for self-advancement were sometimes the main reasons for the surgeon's decision to postpone marriage. In this way he would marry well above his original social background; we have already seen the case of Sebastiano Fassina, who became Surgeon to the Poor in 1679, but married only nine years later. He was the son of a modest barber-surgeon, yet he married the daughter of a court upholsterer who brought him a dowry three times greater than the one with which Sebastiano's sister married during the same period.[64] In such cases, delaying marriage could therefore be part of a finely judged strategy of social climbing.

In other cases, giving up marriage and with it the prospect of biological offspring seems connected to forms of artificial fatherhood. Men who are bachelors or merely childless frequently have an important role to play in relation to young members of the kinship network. Let us return to one of several examples we have encountered, that of Alberto Verna, who 'adopted' some of his brothers' children, thereby assuming the role we usually attribute to fathers: those of educator, protector, provider and transmitter of material and professional assets, resources and knowledge. The nephews thus 'adopted' would in fact be the sole beneficiaries of Alberto's will, thereby giving him artificial heirs for the vast patrimony he had accumulated.[65] Through his nephews, Alberto managed to carve out a pathway for the continuance of his own professional reputation and successes. Evasio, the eldest of his these nephews, was trained in surgery by his uncle and worked with him until the latter's death, learning from him the secrets of obstetrics and subsequently inheriting his hospital post. This same appointment was later to be handed on by Evasio to another of Alberto's adopted 'sons', Evasio's cousin Giovan Battista. So, although he was a bachelor, Alberto managed to build a professional dynasty through the creation of his own descendants.

Biographical research brings to light numerous cases in which marriage was postponed or even avoided. Demographic constraints, work arrangements, strategies for social advancement or broader strategies relating to the kinship network seem frequently to have been a component in these choices of temporary or permanent bachelorhood. These stories are in striking contrast with the negative image of the bachelor suggested by studies of masculinity in the early modern period. To judge from the various kinds of recognition that Alberto Verna and other unmarried surgeons built up, their matrimonial status did not present a problem for their contemporaries. Masculine identity was expressed in a variety of forms, not only in the role of husband and biological father. Marriage was not the only means whereby men could achieve the status of head of household: the bachelor was often the head of a domestic group, even if this was not a conventional nuclear family. Moreover, forms of artificial fatherhood seem to have been a common occurrence, at least in the world of artisans: orphaned children or children from large families formed a reserve of potential heirs and adoptive children, and they gave bachelors or childless men the chance to perform roles associated with the paternal figure. What seems to have been held particularly dear by our artisans is the continuance of professional experience and the reputation of their shop and their name, and this could also be achieved through indirect biological succession. The Italian case seems in this respect to have been quite different from that of Germany or Protestant England, where marriage became an essential component of masculine identity. We have already discussed the legal dimension that seems to set Italy apart from other European countries but confessional difference also deserves attention: it is possible that in Catholic countries the figure of the celibate priest set a positive example of male bachelorhood which made it socially acceptable to replace biological transmission with an artificial substitute. After all, the priest, the confessor and the friar were all non-biological 'fathers'.

Another aspect to consider when we examine cases of informal adoption of non-natural children is that even for many of those who were married it was hard to secure biological heirs: although repeated remarriages were extremely common in a man's life (in many biographies three marriages were the norm), the number of men without surviving children was probably as great as those of fathers with too many children. Perhaps the most extreme case I have come across is that of Michel Angelo Benedicti: he married six times in the course of thirteen years, but when he dictated his will at the end of his days he had only one surviving son.[66] The erratic and strikingly capricious nature of early modern demography that seeps through biographical analysis never ceases to shock.

It was therefore the household rather than the marriage family that formed the terrain on which the status of the adult man was played out, and it was social transmission rather than biological reproduction that provided evidence of male prowess. At the same time, masculine identity was validated through the exercise of professional and public responsibilities, not just in the role of head of household. Likewise, in the shop or the hospitals where they held responsibility, bachelor surgeons could carry out important functions of leadership, education and the transmission of knowledge. And in his dealings with sick patients and his handling of illness, the surgeon could also give proof of masculine virtues. Perhaps it is precisely because masculine roles were performed in these indirect or metaphorical forms that I have found no trace of the social inferiority of bachelors within the artisan setting.

Notes

1 With the exception of Kuehn, only historians of legal institutions have taken any interest in them. T. Kuehn, *Emancipation in Late Medieval Florence* (New Brunswick, 1982).

2 R. Szramkiewicz, *Histoire du Droit Français de la Famille* (Paris, 1995), p. 57.

3 Sabean, *Property*, chapter fourteen; W. W. Hagen, *Ordinary Prussians. Brandeburg Junkers and Villagers, 1500–1840* (Cambridge, 2002), chapter three; G. P. Sreenivasan, *The Peasants of Ottobeuren 1487–1726: A Rural Society in Early Modern Europe* (New York, 2004), chapter five.

4 S. Cavallo, 'Le emancipazioni: una fonte per lo studio dei rapporti tra padri e figli', in A.

Bellavitis and I. Chabot (eds), *Famiglie e Poteri nell'Italia Medievale Moderna* (Rome, forthcoming).

5   Only in rare cases did this not happen, for example the emancipated son of barber-surgeon Parochia remained heir to the share of inheritance that was due to him (Ins. 1727, l. 10, c. 353).

6   *Ibid.*, 1692, l. 5, c. 597; 1679, l. 7, c. 15; 1665 l. 2, c. 465.

7   Both Ruschella and Colombatto paid 300 lire to their sons, Bonardo, 684. *Ibid.*, 1692, l. 3, c. 13; 1697, l. 5, c. 1051; 1699, l. 4, c. 563. The apothecary Giacobi Brena received a credit for a more considerable sum (1500 lire) and the furniture to set up homeL *ibid.*, 1676, l. 8, c. 529. More substantial sums of money are found among merchants and professionals: see Cavallo, 'Le emancipazioni'.

8   Ins. 1688, l. 5, c. 503; 1725, l. 2, c. 261.

9   *Ibid.*, 1683, l. 3, c. 531; 1727, l. 10, c. 353; 1671, l. 2, c. 5.

10   *Ibid.*, 1699, l. 5, c. 597.

11   *Ibid.*, 1671, l. 2, c. 5; 1697, l. 5, c. 1051. We already know that both Sebastiano and Emanuele Fassina had been living independently for many years.

12   We do not know his precise age, but Meda was certainly over thirty on the date of his emancipation. Giò Colombatto was thirty-three. The surgeon Giacomo Antonio Reyneri was twenty-nine, and the perruquier Giuseppe Parochia, the son of the surgeon Giacomo, was twenty-seven and had already had his own shop for a number of years (*ibid.*, 1725, l. 2, c. 261; 1727, l. 10, c. 353).

13   *Ibid.*, 1688, l. 5, c. 503.

14   *Ibid.*, 1692, l. 3, c. 13.

15   This could even happen without the knowledge of the interested party; for example, the father could give the son's assets as security for a loan or investment of his own.

16   For family obligations in early modern England I. Ben-Amos, 'Gifts and favors: informal support in early modern England', *The Journal of Modern History*, 72 (2000).

17   *Ibid.*, 1665, l. 2, c. 465.

18   Kuehn, *Emancipation*, pp. 156–9.

19   L. K. Berkner, 'The stem family and the developmental cycle of the peasant household: an eighteenth-century Austrian example', *American Historical Review*, 77 (1972).

20   The idea of a 'fair compensation' is dominant in accounts of inheritance agreements between parents and children. Precisely in relation to the emancipations see, for example, Dolan, *Le notaire*, pp. 90–7. For a dissenting voice that talks instead about 'rigorously non-egalitarian strategies' in the transmission of assets to children in seventeenth-century Venice, see Levi, 'Comportements', pp. 202–6.

21   Ins., 1755, l. 6, vol. I, c. 525.

22   *Ibid.*, 1761, l. 7, c. 1079.

23   *Ibid.*, 1762, l. 3, c. 993.

24   For a synthesis of definitions of masculinity relevant to the pre-industrial period, see J. Tosh, 'Men in the domestic sphere: a neglected history', in Arru, *La Costruzione*, pp. 48–9; for detailed studies on England, E. Foyster, *Manhood in Early Modern England: Honour, Sex and Marriage* (London, 1999); Shepard, *Meanings*.

25   See for example A. Fletcher, 'Manhood, the male body, courtship and the household in early modern England', *History*, 84 (1999); Foyster, *Manhood*, chapter two; Ago, 'La costruzione'.

26   Ago, 'La costruzione', p. 22.

27 Tadmor, *Family*.

28 Tosh, 'Men in the domestic sphere', p. 49. See also Shepard, *Meanings*, pp. 206–7, 210.

29 On methodological problems in the study of celibacy, see D. Wrigley, E. Oeppen and R. Schofield, *English Population History from Family Reconstitution 1580–1837* (Cambridge, 1997), pp. 195–7.

30 *Ibid.*, p. 121; D. Weir, 'Rather never than late. Celibacy and age at marriage in English cohort fertility 1541–1871', *Journal of Family History*, 9 (1984).

31 R. B. Litchiefield, 'Caratteristiche demografiche delle famiglie fiorentine dal sedicesimo al diciannovesimo secolo', in C. A. Corsini *et al.*, *Saggi di Demografia Storica* (Florence, 1969). On Milan, see D. Zanetti, *La Demografia del Patriziato Milanese* (Pavia, 1983). Somewhat similar data emerges from Corsini's study of the Tuscan countryside: C. Corsini, 'Chi si sposa per primo? Rango di nascita e soluzione matrimoniale', in A. M. Falchero et al. (eds), *La Storia e l'Economia. Miscellanea di Studi in Onore di Giorgio Mori* (Varese, 2003), volume 1, p. 182. A significant limitation of these studies is, however, that they aggregate data relating to two centuries.

32 S. Ozment, *When Fathers Ruled: Family Life in Reformation Europe* (Cambridge Massachusetts, 1983); Roper, *The Holy Household*.

33 Cited in Wiesner, *Women and Gender*, p. 22.

34 D. Frigo, 'Dal caos all'ordine: sulla questione del 'prender moglie' nella trattatistica del sedicesimo secolo', in M. Zancan (ed.), *Nel Cerchio della Luna. Figure di Donna in alcuni Testi del XVI Secolo* (Venice, 1983).

35 Sarti, *Europe at Home*, p. 56.

36 Roper, *The Holy Household*, pp. 39, 138–9; Sabean, *Property*, p. 106; Ehmer, "Servi di donne"; A.-L. Head-König, 'Forced marriages and forbidden marriages in Switzerland: state control of the formation of marriages in Catholic and Protestant Cantons in the eighteenth and nineteenth centuries', *Continuity and Change*, 8 (1993), pp. 441–65; M. Lazinger, 'Una società di nubili e celibi? indagine su una vallata tirolese nell'ottocento', in M. Lanzinger and R. Sarti (eds), *Celibi e Nubili nella Società Moderna e Contemporanea* (Udine, 2007).

37 This does not mean that it was not seen as a positive factor. Malfi for example lists marriage among the attributes appropriate (but not indispensable) to the good barber-surgeon: 'It seems to me useful and very fitting for him to have a wife, because it will bring him good reputation'. (*Il Barbiere*, p. 45).

38 Crossick, *The Artisan*, pp. 7–8; J. Ehmer, 'Tramping artisans in nineteenth-century Vienna', in D. J. Siddle (ed.), *Migration, Mobility and Modernisation* (Liverpool, 2000), p. 170.

39 Crossick, *The Artisan*, p. 9.

40 Farr, *Artisans*, p. 245.

41 D. Woodward, *Men at Work. Labourers and Building Craftsmen in the Towns of Northern England 1450–1750* (Cambridge, 1995), p. 59; I. Ben-Amos, *Adolescence and Youth in Early Modern England* (New Haven, 1994), pp. 229–30; H. Swanson, *Medieval Artisans. An Urban Class in Late Medieval England* (Oxford, 1989), p. 7.

42 M. Walker, *German Home Towns. Community, State and General Estate 1648–1871* (Ithaca, 1971), p. 85; J. Rogers, 'Nordic family history: themes and issues, old and new', *Journal of Family History*, 18 (1993), p. 297.

43 See above, chapter six. Many studies have emphasised the great variety of financial bonds linking masters and journeymen: M. Sonenscher, *Work and Wages. Natural*

Law, Politics and the Eighteenth-Century French Trades (Cambridge, 1989); Rosser, 'Crafts'; Crossick, *The Artisan*, p. 8.

44 *Consegna dei Francesi 1690.*

45 Ins. 1670, l. 8, c. 91.

46 Art. 530. This we can tell from the presence of children in the household, or else it has emerged from biographical research. Of the seventeen who appear to be bachelors six are between twenty and twenty-eight years old, six are between thirty and thirty-seven, three between forty and forty-five, and two are over fifty.

47 Ins. 1686, l. 5, parte 2, c. 647.

48 ACT, vol. 294; Ins. 1689, l. 1, vol. II, c. 827–9.

49 ACT, vol. 295; Ins. 1711, l. 9, c. 699.

50 *Ibid.*, 1708, vol. I, c. 353. The appointments to senior surgeon are to be found in the minutes kept in the archives of the respective hospitals.

51 Bonino, *Biografia*, vol. 2, p. 59.

52 Borrelli, p. 974, 29 July 1616.

53 Pastore, *Il Medico in Tribunale*. This material has not been preserved for Turin, alas.

54 ACT, vol. 295, c. 46.

55 Roper, *Oedipus*, A. Shepard, 'Manhood, credit and patriarchy in early modern England, c.1580–1640', *Past and Present*, 167 (2000), pp. 98–9; Shepard, *Meanings*, pp. 211–12 and Karras, *From Boys*, chapters three-four.

56 On attitudes to youth ritual violence see Davis, 'The reasons', Schindler, 'Guardians'.

57 *Il Barbiere*, p. 39.

58 'Wine first of all harms the brain, dimming the senses both within and without, but foremost of all the sight, which above any other thing is necessary to us. Secondly, it weakens the nerves, in that it brings about shaking, a thing which in us is most reprehensible' (*Ibid.*, p. 46).

59 Wear, *Knowledge*, pp. 241, 251–2.

60 Chapter one, pp. 46–7.

61 Salvi, *Il Chirurgo*, p. 3.

62 In 1706 the domestic group was made up of: Carlo Giuseppe, thirty years old and a surgeon; Luigi (his brother), twenty-three years old and a jeweller; Teresa (his widowed sister), twenty-seven years old, and her stepchildren (from her deceased husband's first marriage) and children, Anna, aged fifteen, Giuseppe aged eleven, Cristina aged eight, and Violant, aged seven, as well as Margherita, a servant, aged twenty-five (Ins. 1700, l. 3, c. 381).

63 Fletcher, 'Manhood'; Shepard, *Meanings*, chapters one–three.

64 Ins. 1688, l. 11, c. 545; 1695, l. 6, c. 757.

65 *Ibid.*, 1710, l. 3 ,vol. II c. 771; 1731, l. 6, c. 8; 1737, l. 2, vol. I, c. 369; 1740, l. 8, c. 1385.

66 His first wife, Barbara Vinella, died in February 1682 after they had been married for six years. Two months later, in April, Michel Angelo remarried. His new wife was Anna Catta Stura, who, however, survived only until the end of October. In January 1683 he married Maria Catta Meda, who died in October that year giving birth to Michel Angelo's first child, the young Anna Catta. But the little girl survived her mother by only a few weeks. By the start of 1684 Michel Angelo had already found another wife, Margherita, who in October gave birth to Giacomo Francesco, the only child we find still living at the time of Michel Angelo's death in 1697. This fourth marriage was also the longest, lasting for ten years, then Margherita also died. Immediately, she was

replaced by a new wife, Domenica, who died, aged twenty-two, at the end of 1694. But a year later, the birth of a daughter to Michel Angelo and Teresa Maria tells us that he had remarried yet again. However, Teresa Maria also left Michel Angelo a widower, in June 1696, when she was aged only twenty-two. After having been married six times Michel Angelo died, paradoxically as a widower, in March 1697 (AAT, 18.2.11; 18.2.6; 18.2.14; 18.2.15).

10

The good surgeon

The value and meaning of the licence

nterest in the ways in which trust and reputation were created in early modern medical practice has been for the most part limited to irregular practitioners: those who had not received a canonical education and training, and who had not been certified by the licensing bodies (either the professional Colleges or the *Protomedicati*). The assumption has been that building professional credibility was especially problematic for those healers who did not have enduring ties with a clearly defined professional environment, and who lacked a regular clientele (itinerant practitioners and charlatans).[1] By contrast, there has been little attention given to the strategies used by practitioners who were stable residents, well established within a specific area and social space, in their efforts to gain and hold on to a clientele, and to persuade the public of their reliability and expertise. It it often assumed that the legal authorisation granted by the authorities (the licence) was the key element in giving legitimacy to the activities of these settled practitioners. The licence is implicitly seen as the boundary splitting the medical world into regular and irregular practitioners. In what follows I should like to question this assumption. In our own time the authorisation to practise medicine is the basis of reliability and a reflection of genuine competence. But did the licence have this same meaning in the early modern period? How important was it in the eyes of the public, and of the authorities and the practitioners themselves? And was the gulf between licensed and unlicensed surgeons really so wide? The analysis of the *Consegna* (survey) of all those practising, both legally and illegally, as barbers, barber-surgeons or surgeons in the city and province of Turin in 1695 will help us to address these questions.

The Consegna was the only form of control the authorities exerted over surgeons.[2] It was not an inspection of shops, like those carried out in the case of apothecaries; it took the form of an order that all surgeons, barbers and apothecaries who ran a shop should, within a certain number of days varying between ten and thirty, present themselves before the Protophysician or his delegates and produce their licence to practise. The order was usually issued whenever a new Protophysician (*Protomedico*) took up his post and wished to update his records.[3] Those who turned out to be unlicensed were invited to conform with the law by taking the admission examination. The 1695 Consegna is the only one to have survived in the archives.[4] It differs from previous surveys in having been undertaken in a time of war, presumably with the aim of raising income for the State by way of fines (those who did not have a licence were made to pay a fine of fifty scudi), and it was initiated by the State *Referendari*, that is the provincial heads of finance, rather than by the State medical officers. Its comprehensive character is what makes this survey of the workshops of barbers and surgeons a unique source of information.

Studies of the Italian medical profession have relied heavily on judicial proceedings, which is to say the prosecutions conducted by the Protomedicato or by the Colleges of Physicians against practitioners who had been reported by their patients or fellow practitioners for malpractice or illicit practice.[5] The 1695 Consegna provides a more thorough overview of surgery as a trade since, in principle, it includes all of the practitioners currently running shops in the city and its provincial towns and villages, not just those caught in the net of the controlling bodies. Indeed, the order seems to have been scrupulously implemented, especially in the smaller localities, for, once the deadline had passed for presenting the authorisation, those practitioners who had failed to come forward were tracked down by the guards of the local magistrates.[6] We can therefore arrive at a relatively accurate estimate of the proportions of the licensed and unlicensed among those practitioners who were geographically stable and had enduring ties with a particular town or neighbourhood.

The Consegna shows that many of those who were well established in a locality (including those who practised in the more sophisticated world of the capital) did not have a licence. Out of sixty-seven barbers, surgeons and barber-surgeons with a fixed residence in the province of Turin, as many as twenty-nine (43 per cent) were without a licence. In the capital itself, eighteen out of a total of eighty-nine were practising without a licence (over 20 per cent). Fortunately, the survey is not merely a quantitative source, and the justifications offered by the unlicensed give us some clues to their professional histories and the extent to which these differed from those of the licensed.

War and poverty are the major factors invoked, especially by those at the start of independent practice. Thus, Giuseppe Bassino, who had been working as a surgeon at Settimo for five years, argued that he 'had not obtained a licence because he had not been able to get a loan to pay for it'. And Antonio Viberto, who had been practising as a barber and surgeon for a year at Rivoli (his birthplace), 'owing to the disasters brought about both by the enemy and by friendly armies, has not been able to spare the money to obtain a licence, since he needed everything he earned to support himself and his younger brothers and sisters'.[7] We do not know what the total cost of a licence was but especially for surgeons to small localities, who made a precarious living, it was clearly a considerable expense and its acquisition required savings. But there are also cases in the capital of barber-surgeons who had taken the examination and made the initial payment of 14 lire, yet had never collected their licence because they lacked the requisite amount for the balance of the cost.[8] Some practitioners also gave war conditions as a reason; they claimed they had been unable to get to the capital to collect the licence or to take the necessary examination.[9] Other depositions shed light on the ephemeral nature of the licence, a simple parchment that could be stolen, as happened to the surgeon Maglino, a stipendiary of the town of Collegno whose workshop had been ransacked by 'the Germans', or else lost, as in the case of Acellano, in the course of his move from Rome to Castellamonte. As such cases bear out, the licence was a fairly vulnerable proof of professional competence.

While these depositions show a willingness, at least when faced with authority, to accept the value of the licence and the obligation to have one, there are others that openly challenge the idea of the necessity for such authorisation. Even in the capital we find surgeons like Giò Matteo Ferraris, who declares that he has been practising for thirty years as a surgeon and barber without 'ever having had a licence or having taken any examination, and has always carried out his trade without anyone questioning his right' (*senza contradizione alcuna*). It appears that a large number of the unlicensed were not practitioners who had failed to obtain a licence, but rather healers who had never 'sought' one. Among the most striking cases of long established surgeons who did not have a licence are two surgeons of the town of Caselle, who had been practising for thirty-five and thirty years respectively. This lack of a licence though, does not seem to have prejudiced their acceptance by the public, nor even by the local authorities. Among the unlicensed there were also practitioners in official posts. One example is Schioppo, the municipal surgeon of Orbassano. The training Schioppo claimed to have received at the Santo Spirito hospital in Rome evidently served as credentials enough for the town authorities, despite the absence of any authorisation issued by the Savoy State's medical officer.

The licence does not therefore seem to have been perceived as a necessary means of certification for surgical practice and there are doubts about who was obliged to hold it. Many unlicensed practitioners were reluctant to acknowledge that they were in the wrong; some maintained that they were not 'meant to have any licence or permit', having up until then 'only shaved and let blood' or 'applied cups' (because of the hard times brought about by the war) and that this was 'always under the orders of physicians'.[10] Interestingly, these declarations stress compliance with the prescribed subordination of the barber-surgeon to the physician, while refusing to recognise the need for a licence, at least in order to let blood. As long as the physician's monopoly on prescribing treatment has not been violated, the barber-surgeon seems to be justified in pleading innocence and relieved of any further responsibility for the treatment provided. This perhsaps gives us an insight into the real purpose of the legislation regulating medical practice; as some scholars have argued, its true concern was to defend the hierarchical principle at the basis of the tripartite medical system rather than eliminate unlicensed practice.[11]

An even more significant challenge to standard notions of what constituted the illegal practice of surgery comes from the many practitioners who declared that they were not obliged to have a licence because they worked 'under the orders', 'under the direction' or 'discipline' of, or 'in the name of', a master who had a licence. These clearly referred to the various types of (more or less symmetrical) partnerships, which, as we have already seen in chapter six, were the norm in the practice of surgery. In some cases the unlicensed practitioner was the son, nephew or brother of the master. Thus, Canis, a barber at Chivasso, said he was not obliged to have a licence since he worked 'under the discipline' of his uncle, Sacho, and 'had never run a shop'. In other cases the unlicensed practitioner was not related to the independent master whose associate he was: Antonio Bellotto, for example, 'believed he had no need of permits since he worked for the business of Giacomo Ghidella, surgeon to the Household [of Madama Reale]'.

The 'illegal' practice of the trade legitimised by an officially qualified master was often a far from temporary situation. Some highly expert surgeons practised for many years without a licence, only covered by the authorisation of fathers, uncles or associates of diverse kinds. For instance, a surgeon called Caulet had been practising for ten years in Ozegna, officially under the direction of Tapperi. In Turin, Antonio Goria stated that he had been practising for twenty-five years under the letters patent given to his father in 1649.[12] In some cases the arrangement between the licensed master and the unlicensed practitioner was such that it allowed the latter to run a shop of his own. This was the case of Giuseppe Rosso, an apothecary and surgeon at Oglianico, who, when asked to produce his licence, protested that 'the shop he runs is a subsidiary of the one owned by *messer* Nitia of Favria'.

These depositions invite us to reflect upon what the licence meant to contemporaries; they suggest that it was thought of differently than in later periods: it was seen less as evidence of the professional competence of an individual than as a kind of badge that gave collective legitimacy to all those who worked in the shop of the licensed master, or in other shops that were subsidiaries of it. In contrast with our contemporary understanding of professional qualifications, the licence was linked to a surgical practice rather than to the individual practitioner. Forneri, for example, an unlicensed barber, defended himself by saying that he was not obliged to have a licence because he practised his craft in the shop of Ratti, a barber who was licensed and owned the shop's furniture, whereas Forneri owned only his own instruments. It is therefore crucial to grasp the centrality of work coalitions to the practice of surgery in order to understand the collective value of the licence: it was not a condition for entering the occupation, nor a way of certificating individual expertise, which was often achieved many years beforehand. This, at any rate, is the picture that emerges from the biographical information frequently contained in the depositions. These show that it was the norm for there to be a gap, even a considerable one, between starting to practise and acquiring a licence. I shall refer to one of the more extreme examples: Gutuerio declares that he has been practising in Turin for a good thirty-five years, but the letters patent he presents date from only eight years earlier. Thus, even when a practitioner was equipped with a regular licence there would be a number of years of unlicensed practice in his professional history, during which time he would have worked in association with licensed masters under various kinds of arrangement or even run his own shop. For many, such a situation would have lasted for only a few years, while there were others who remained unlicensed for much longer and in some cases without ever acquiring a licence.

These findings invite us to rethink the way in which the distinctions between licit and illicit practice should be conceptualised: they suggest that the experience of working without a licence was very common, neither confined to a handful of marginal figures nor associated exclusively with either the itinerant or the 'quack' with only an eccentric medical education;[13] rather it was structural to the specific organisation of labour that was dominant within the practice of surgery. The unlicensed barber-surgeon did not belong to a separate category of practitioners; often he was merely not in charge of a shop 'in his own name', in other words not accountable for the treatment and services dispensed there. As already noted, there are clear analogies between the ways in which a shop and a household were perceived: just as in the household liability for the actions of the group were concentrated in the hands of the *pater familias*, in the shop these responsibilities were vested in the man who run the shop, though in practice this authority was exercised much more broadly and also shared with others.

The practice of working without a licence for or alongside a licensed surgeon long remains the norm and it was by no means eradicated by the reforms of the 1720s, which introduced compulsory university education for aspiring surgeons. As late as September 1738 an edict prohibited surgeons 'from sending as their replacements for treatment Giovani who were not yet licensed, under penalty of 10 scudi and suspension of their practice'. But only three months later this was revoked with a proviso that allowed the *Magistrato della Riforma* (who had taken over the authority of the Protophysician and his reformers) to give permission for working with their master to 'those Giovani who can show that they have practised for two years under the direction of a licensed surgeon, and that they are competent and expert, and that these testimonies (*fedi*) be issued by the said surgeon'.[14] This arrangement still displays a considerable amount of confusion, on the part of the authorities, between one notion of the licence understood as certification of the competence of a single practitioner and another that instead allows for a team of practitioners to carry out their trade under the aegis of a responsible individual. Although authorisation to practise was now granted to *Giovani* on an individual basis, they could only pursue their work with one specific master; moreover, it was this same master, not a central medical authority, who had to certify the expertise of his associates.

The fact that unlicensed practitioners were fined at the Consegna by those checking the surgeons' credentials, seems to suggest that practising without a licence was seen by the authorities as illegal and was prosecuted. In reality, the attitude of the authorities demonstrates considerable ambiguity. We know already that surveys (Consegne) were infrequent and irregular; moreover, although the 1695 survey seems to have been a particularly thorough exercise, it was usually relatively easy for surgeons to evade the Consegne. In 1644, for example, the authorities complained that 'in spite of the Orders that all Apothecaries, Surgeons, Barbers and similar sorts of trades should present themselves at the office of the Protophysician to give evidence of their permission and licence to practise ... no one has come forward, and yet they continue to practise'.[15] In large towns especially, the system seems to have been an inadequate means of controlling unlicensed practice: not only was it based on the practitioner coming forward rather than on actual inspections like those carried out for apothecaries, grocers and distilleries of aquavitae;[16] but in the urban setting, where professional bodies had a role, it relied on the mediation of the trade representatives.[17] These were liable to be in connivance with unlicensed colleagues, given that the latter were most often their own associates. It would seem then that whenever irregularities were identified, those same authorities in charge of overseeing medical practice displayed considerable leniency towards cases of illicit practice. In 1738, forty years after the Consegna presently under consideration, a report from the Magistrato della Riforma was complaining that there was 'a considerable number of those who practised this profession [of surgeon] without any permits'. And yet it was also recognised that 'if all of these were prohibited from practising, as well as their becoming deprived of a living, this would also be to the detriment of the public', since it would be left without medical care. Some derogations were therefore introduced to soften the requirements necessary for obtaining a surgeon's letters patent, and we find these confirmed again in 1756.[18]

For a long time then, the licence was not a prerequisite of professional ability and qualification. So what was it? If we turn our attention to those who issued the licence, it becomes clear that in the eyes of the authorities it was much more an authorisation to practise in a given locality, rather than being a recognition of competence. It is true that in many cases the licence was issued by a medical authority – either the Protophysician or the College of Physicians, depending on the balance of power between the two bodies in any particular place.[19] In other cases, however, the licence was issued by a political or religious authority having jurisdiction over a particular territory.[20] Thus, several practitioners presented at the survey licences obtained by the local archbishop, the governor of the town, or by the duke or duchess, and these were invariably accepted by those checking the authorisation. In contrast, licences issued by distinguished medical bodies elsewhere – for example, by the Protomedico of Rome, or by the University of Padua – were not automatically accepted; the practitioners in question still had to obtain a licence from the local authorities if they wished to practise, say in Turin or Vercelli.[21] Moreover, those who were military surgeons or surgeons to sections of the ducal household (posts that were granted by the ducal authority), did not seem to need a licence for any shops they ran that were open to the general public.[22] Many were simply left out of the survey.

The authority of the Protophysician was therefore far from universal, at least where surgeons were concerned. Moreover, to judge from the situation in this part of Italy, the central control over medical practice in the Italian states, which has often been described as being particularly efficient by comparison with the supposedly more deregulated English system, seems much looser than the legislation would suggest. If work with others was a fundamental aspect of the practice of surgery, as I have suggested it was, we can reasonably suspect that the cases of unlicensed practice identified as anomalous by the occupational surveys were just the tip of the iceberg. Nor does the lack of a licence seem to have had any dramatic effect on the relationship with patients. It was probably clear to the public that there was often no significant difference between licensed and unlicensed surgeons, who were, as a rule, simply practitioners at different stages of their careers. The two categories had obviously had a similar training, had worked in the same shops and had similar kinds of experience.

But if it was not the licence that gave credibility and legitimacy to a practitioner, what did? I shall investigate this question by looking at the contents of the depositions given by practitioners at the Consegna. I shall draw mainly on the declarations made in Turin, since these are on average much richer in detail than their provincial counterparts. Although those in charge of the shop were only required to give a sworn statement of the length of time they had practised in Turin, and whether they possessed a licence to practise, and since what date, many spontaneously provided more detail concerning their previous training and the stages of their careers, evidently with the aim of parading their credentials as expert and valued surgeons. Some depositions amount therefore to a kind of curriculum vitae in which the declarant emphasises those aspects of his career and his practice that he regards as embodying special professional merit. I shall read this spontaneous part of the declaration as a guide to the values underlying the professional reputation of a surgeon.

Place and trust

In his statement, the surgeon gave priority to the fact of his established position in a particular place and the length of time he had had a shop there. Thus, the declarations laid stress not so much on the number of years a surgeon had been practising, but on how many years he had been practising in Turin. Moreover, whenever possible, surgeons emphasised the uninterrupted period of time over which their shop had been in business in one specific part of the city. The phrase 'and since then [since he first began to practise] he has always kept open shop' (in such and such a place) was regularly invoked to suggest the reliability and success of the practice, which clearly enjoyed the favour of the clients and which had not betrayed their trust. The long-standing location of the practice was stated with great precision, with reference being made to the smallest territorial unit, the *Cantone*. Giò Antonio Pellero, for instance, stated that he had 'practised the profession of surgeon for thirty-five years, always keeping open shop, as he does at present, in Cantone San Gregorio, in the parish of San Tommaso'. A long and continuous presence in the same neighbourhood was thus presented as a sign of conscientious practice, suggesting that throughout this entire period the surgeon had never been involved in any trouble that might have prompted him to leave the district.

These elements recur in the depositions of both licensed and unlicensed surgeons. Indeed, it might be said that the latter attribute an even greater value to the public aspect of the practice, and to its unblemished reputation. Thus they underline the fact that they had exercised their profession 'freely and publicly' over many years, in the same shop and Cantone of the city, often specifying its location with a wealth of detail. The implication is clearly that they are well known, that they have practised under the constant scrutiny of the local population, and have done so without arousing 'any opposition' or 'any conflict' (*senza contrasti*). Matteo Ferraris, mentioned above as the most extreme case of unlicensed practice, states that he has practised in Turin for thirty years, 'freely, serving all those who required his attentions, keeping open shop in Cantone Santa Cecilia, on the premises of Count Nomis'. It would seem therefore that it was popular approval and public reputation that conferred legitimacy upon a practice, far more than did institutional recognition.

Interestingly, being the son of a surgeon was often (though not always) mentioned in the declaration (for example: 'Giò Pietro Bruco, son of the late Giò Bernardino, also a surgeon, has appeared before us'), but not as something that would in itself confer reliability upon the practice. Belonging to a professional dynasty was of value only if it was combined with the long-standing existence of a shop in a given neighbourhood, and within a fabric of social relations that would guarantee close knowledge of its performance. Nicolao Barberis, son of the late surgeon Lorenzo, stated that he 'had practised as a surgeon, freely and without any opposition, for twenty years', both while his father was alive and after his death four years earlier, 'his father having kept open shop *in the new enlargement of this town, in the Cantone San Bonifacio, on the premises of the lawyer Frichignono, opposite the Ospedale di Carità*, which shop, after the death of his father, was kept open by him, *and altogether it had been open for thirty-five years'* (my emphasis). Professional credibility had more to do with the place, the shop and its history, than with the family tradition and the persons involved.

A shop's reputation reflected upon all those who had worked in it. Hence surgeons who had only recently set up on their own or older surgeons with an irregular professional history were particularly keen to mention professional relationships, albeit dependent ones, with shops enjoying local prestige and with the city hospitals. This served to offset the absence of a long-standing shop of their own and to reinforce a professional credibility which otherwise appeared somewhat weak. Michele Faure, for instance, had been practising 'as a surgeon' for seventeen years but had obtained his licence in Turin only three years earlier. He spontaneously provides reassuring information concerning his continuous activity in the city: he had worked as a Giovane of master Domenico Deroy, and then for two years at the hospital of San Giovanni (from 1681), after which he had opened his own shop and practised his trade 'publicly' until 1692 (hence for nine years), when he acquired the authorisation to exercise independently.

The importance given to a long-established local presence might lead us to believe that the surgeon's origins had a crucial bearing upon the building up of his credibility, and that those who could boast of having been born in Turin would mention the fact with pride. In reality, place of origin had little relevance in the surgeon's self-presentation, and does not seem to have influenced the confidence he enjoyed. Some indicated their birthplace precisely, but others simply described themselves as 'a surgeon in Turin', preferring to stress their belonging to the professional setting of the city even when we know from other sources that they were not natives.[23] Foreign origins in a practitioner do not seem to have been a handicap. This emerges clearly from the high incidence of incomers among the surgeons, whether licensed or otherwise, who appeared before the Referendari in 1695. Of the sixty-nine surgeons and barbers who declared their place of birth, a good forty-eight (i.e. at least 53 per cent of the total number of shopholders) were foreigners, as against twenty-one who declared that they had been born in Turin. Many not only succeeded in settling permanently in their new abode, but also enjoyed considerable success, and the most respected shops often belonged to immigrants. Some of them also achieved recognition outside their profession, for instance through appointment to those public offices to which surgeons could aspire. It is particularly striking that they held municipal offices that implied a strong rootedness within their district, and that we would therefore regard as the preserve of Turin natives, such as the post of municipal Surgeon to the Poor and that of *Cantoniere*, who was responsible for public order in a given district of the city.[24]

Thus despite the importance, for the surgeon's reputation, of the duration, geographical stability and continuity of his shop, the occupation does not seem to have been associated with immobility. On the contrary, movement over considerable distances seem to have characterised the early years of the young surgeon's activity. We have proof that most of the surgeons who migrated to Turin had moved there not as children, with their parents and families, but as young men (in their late teens and early twenties) or as adults. Of the twenty-five men for whom the exact age of their arrival in Turin is known, twenty-two had entered the city between the ages of sixteen and thirty-one.[25] Only one arrived at an earlier age (thirteen), and two at a later one (at thirty-six and after thirty years of activity elsewhere). Furthermore, the incomers were from places which were quite some distance from Turin: thirty-one of the forty-eight non-native surgeons and barbers in the 1695 Consegna came from within the state, but only twelve from the province of Turin, the others having travelled greater distances, coming also from the more remote regions of the duchy and from the newly acquired regions such as Monferrato. Furthermore, six came from the French regions of the duchy, from Savoy or Nice, four came from other Italian states (Milan, the Republic of Venice, and the papal states on the Adriatic coast). Lastly, six of them were French (and from various regions of France). The young surgeon was clearly perfectly willing to travel to far-flung regions in search of professional opportunities, these possibly leading to permanent settlement and the opening of his own shop. Stability was something which became important at a later stage of the surgeon's personal and professional life cycle, that is, when he glimpsed the possibility of building a career in one specific locality. At this point, moving no longer appeared desirable and was to be avoided. But at an earlier stage, mobility was the rule. Even among those based in the province of Turin we find examples of surgeons moving, sometimes over considerable distances, prior to settling down definitively. Small Piedmontese communities are documented as having practising surgeons who had trained in Rome, or who originally came from outside Italy.[26] The eighteen practitioners who exercised at Vercelli included a German, a Frenchman (from Champagne) and a Savoyard, with shops established for fifteen, ten and three years respectively.[27]

It is remarkable, however, that the mobility which had characterised the first phases of the experience of many surgeons does not seem to have been a factor likely to enhance the practitioner's reputation once he has settled. The aspects of his past experience which is worth mentioning are limited to his links with the local professional world and above all with a particular area of the city and hence with a specific public. Despite the importance that training in a hospital and serving in a military hospital seem to have acquired in the construction of a surgeon's professional image, only service in the local hospitals and in the ducal armies is mentioned as an element of merit.[28] Thus local experience and professional collaboration prevailed over any links established, or honours obtained elsewhere. Gio Tomaso Surdis, who had no local licence, states that he had been in Turin for five years. He must have trained in Rome, since he presents the licence awarded him in 1680 by the Governor of the hospital of Santo Spirito, confirmed by the Roman Protophysician, but he says nothing else about the first ten years of his career - spent in Rome or elsewhere. He does however give detailed information concerning his activities since his arrival in Turin, during the period between the 'eve of St. John's Day of the year 1690' and 'the Easter of the current year', spent working 'in company' with the surgeon Giuseppe Gloria, who has a shop 'in the palace belonging to the Marquis of Pianezza in *Contrada Nuova* [the 'new district']', and the opening of his shop 'under the porticoes of the Jesuit Fathers near the fair'. Carlo Mausin had practised surgery for twenty-five years in Turin and ten in France; of the ten years spent in Paris he mentions only the four years he worked for Signor Conte, 'surgeon to His Highness [the Duke of Savoy]'. The remainder of his personal and professional career seems to be irrelevant for the establishing of a reputation in Turin. Clearly, trust was built up by making a practitioner's professional practice as transparent and verifiable as possible.

The biographies suggest that in terms of both public perceptions and the surgeon's own identity, what counted much more than any original roots was being part of the social environment in the place where he was aiming to build his career and his life as an adult. Roots were important, but what mattered was not so much having them as putting them down. Clearly, the patients of the duchy were relatively accustomed to being treated by foreign surgeons, but these would have had to gain credibility in their new place of residence. The years spent working 'with' or 'for' others paved the way for the building up of those relationships with the local area and its people that were so crucial for the establishing of the surgeon's reputation. Indeed, it is remarkable how often the district where the practitioner had worked as a Giovane, and the one where the more fortunate managed to set up their own shops, were one and the same. Both Bellino and Calvo, for example, later opened shops of their own, though at different times, in the same Cantone S. Gabriele where they had practised as Giovani. Benedicti too capitalised on the local reputation he had earned as a result of his long service in the Ghidella shop: the practice he opened in 1689 was in the Cantone opposite the one where he had worked for fourteen years with Ghidella.[29]

At the same time, surgeons who were incomers made no great efforts to preserve their original identities, and this probably helped them to become integrated. Provenance played no conspicuous part in a surgeon's social world and the connections he established in the city. There are no common origins of place between master and Giovane, or between spouses, or within the professional coalitions created by surgeons and other artisans, or with the witnesses who are called upon for visits to the notary or for baptism and weddings. In many cases these bonds are drawn rather from the fabric of the neighbourhood, or else they have their source in the occupation itself or the working environment. Frequently, these relationships are at one and the same time professional and neighbourhood based, which is to say involving surgeons, sometimes apothecaries, more often perruquiers and other artisans of the body operating in the same block or in adjacent blocks. The phenomenon is probably connected with the already observed existence of locally based professional coalitions within, but above all between. adjacent occupations, with the aim of joining forces to offer complementary services. It is these connections between neighbours, colleagues and artisans in occupations allied to surgery that loom large in the social horizons of the surgeons, rather than those dictated by geographical origins. This picture of the 'lightness' of origins is in striking contrast to the central role attributed to belonging – something understood not as what is built but as 'the weight of origins' – in the literature on migration.[30] The majority of these studies have in fact emphasised the continuity of bonds with the original family and community that is preserved by the immigrant.[31] Instead, in the case of surgeons the accent is on the willingness of the incomers to construct, within their new realities, bonds that will form a platform for a new identity, that of 'the surgeon in Turin' or, to be more precise, in a tiny part of the city. It would seem that origins are set aside and the plunge is taken into the melting pot of the city, in the search to mould stable and lasting relationships within the surroundings in which the surgeon operates.

Public offices and professional image

It made a marked difference to the reputation of a surgeon or an artisan of the body if he held a public appointment. The apex of the surgeons' economic hierarchy was occupied by those who succeeded in obtaining positions in civil and military hospitals, at the university and at court. Clearly, considerable prestige accrued through the public exposure that came with the post, and this was a form of capital then exploited within private practice, since it attracted a vast and prestigious clientele, willing to pay higher fees. Moreover, such posts were desirable because they often meant contact with the powerful figures who gravitated around the relevant institutions (hospital governors, courtiers, army officers), and with the patronage these bestowed.[32] Even the position of Surgeon to the Poor seems to have borne some of these characteristics. The four Surgeons to the Poor were practitioners paid by the municipality to treat the poor free of charge in the area of the city allocated to them (and where each of them had to take up residence); they had the additional prerogative to prescribe medicines for their needy patients, and these were then supplied free of charge by one of the four pharmacies designated by the municipality. Being Surgeon to the Poor was an appointment for life, and a highly coveted one, even though the salary, albeit not exactly low, was quite disproportionate to the work that had to be done.[33] We have an idea of the scale of these practitioners' commitment from the number of prescriptions taken by the patients in question to the municipal pharmacies: in the order of 4000–5000 a year.[34] A further reason for the attractiveness of the post lay in the fact that it gave the surgeon considerable discretion over who could benefit from the free treatment. Thus it happened that many who were in fact able to pay were treated without payment and were supplied with free medicines. They even included the councillors of the *comune* themselves, and in particular the members of their households, which is to say the servants and apprentices that employers were supposed to have treated at their own expense. This meant that the rich were discharging their contractual duties towards their own dependants onto the public medical services, as well as ignoring their moral obligations towards their neighbours, clients and needy relatives. It also happened that this service was used to prescribe costly medicines with inordinate extravagance so that the official apothecaries would benefit.[35] Public practice thereby strengthened private practice since it allowed the Surgeons to the Poor to accumulate capital in the form of moral credits and gratitude within their local domain, not merely from their neediest neighbours but all the more so from their most prosperous ones.

A prestigious professional position also generated trust among a wider public indirectly, through a mechanism that might be described as the transfer of trust: for example through the posts that surgeons and other artisans of the body held at court. The credit accorded to them by highly placed figures became a guarantee of the soundness of their abilities and services; the fact that these practitioners inspired confidence in people regarded as having superior judgment and greater power of choice raised the esteem in which they were held by a wider public opinion.

The mechanisms whereby this transfer of trust operated also involved those areas of activity which were not strictly medical, and which surgeons often pursued in parallel with their main occupation. For example, we already know that in the seventeenth century it was common to find surgeons serving a member of the ducal family as *Garzoni* or *Aiutanti di Camera*, or as *Aiutanti di Guardaroba*. Clearly the barber-surgeon's skills in the use of cosmetics, in hair care and personal hygiene were important assets which made it likely that he would be chosen for this court office. From the point of view of the surgeon, however, what made the position of Chamber attendant desirable was the privileged proximity to the body of the prince and the intimacy it allowed. The confidence the surgeon had been able to earn at such a high level, and in matters of such delicacy, could be put to advantage elsewhere, in the private practice that he was able to carry out thanks to the part-time character of his court duties (these were performed for a term at a time or even in weekly shifts, as for the lowest position of chamberboy). Holding this office was evidence not just of competence but of discretion, one of the most valuable assets in an occupation which made the practitioner privy to the physical defects and secret diseases of the patient (think for example of venereal afflictions), and made him an accomplice who helped to disguise their ugly and often shameful signs.[36] The services these court employees provided upheld the same values as those which underpinned the professional activity of the surgeon: their efforts too were devoted to the preservation of the patient's health, the enhancement of his physical appearance and the maintenance of his privacy.

The requirements of tact, discretion and ability to protect associated with the nature of the Chamber attendant's duties are also prominent factors in making sense of another recurrent association, found in the area of public offices: surgeons were often *Cantonieri*, which is to say appointed by the City Council as representatives of the municipal authority in specific areas of the city. No scholarly attention has been paid to this minor municipal office. The office was unpaid but entitled its holder to certain fiscal and penal exemptions, and it came with other prerogatives, such as the right to bear arms, a privilege artisans did not normally enjoy. In the late sixteenth century each Cantone of the city was assigned to a Cantoniere, who had to be a resident there. In 1680 there were 125 Cantoni shared out among fifty Cantonieri; in 1724 there were 140, supervised by sixty Cantonieri (plate 4).[37] Control of his ward by the Cantoniere was virtually all-embracing: the number of residents in a Cantone ranged from 100 to 300 including children, which meant no more than thirty to sixty households, a size that made it possible for him to have firsthand acquaintance with problem cases.

What duties did the office entail? First of all the Cantoniere (normally in charge of one large Cantone or two or three smaller ones) was expected to keep an updated list of the inhabitants in his ward, specifying name, title, place of birth and occupation; he was also the one who drew up the censuses of the population when orders were given for these.[38] In addition, he assisted the city councillors in making inventory of provisions in periods of scarcity. He was also responsible for safeguarding the neighbourhood from the most 'natural' and recurrent hazard, that of fire, and led operations to extinguish fires and make sure that there was no looting in the meantime.[39] Lastly, up until 1679, Cantonieri were in charge of censuses of the poor ordered in time of scarcity; this was a highly responsible task since it was on the basis of the surgeon's report that the municipality granted outdoor relief to those recognised as deserving.[40]

From 1679 the office involved important responsibilities in the maintenance of public order and peace within the small local community.[41] The Cantoniere had to keep abreast of any disorder and excesses that might occur within it, particularly 'quarrels, scandals and armed encounters'. In their turn, citizens had the obligation, under pain of being fined, to inform their Cantoniere of any murders, thefts and woundings they might know of, and he was expected to inform the city authorities immediately. Furthermore, the Cantoniere had to be alert to disturbances and offences which took place not just in the streets and public space, but within the home or the domestic environment, though he had to refrain from reporting violations wherever 'the father, kin or master of the offender should deem to condone the offence'. The Cantoniere was therefore invested with considerable discretionary power: far from simply policing episodes of violence, he was expected to evaluate the situation in which these had taken place, mitigating conflict and facilitating the settlement of disputes, and paying due tribute to the authority figure in charge of the household. His duty was that of protecting the image of respectability of the families and neighbourhood under his supervision; his was a role of mediation rather than a merely repressive one. He was also expected to keep watch on taverns, disreputable individuals, loafers, vagabonds and late night revellers: in other words to protect the community from dangerous outsiders and potential attacks. Thus his duties were extremely complex, ranging from the preservation of the orderly functioning of the community (and the punishment or expulsion of the elements which threatened its stability), to its protection from natural disasters as well as from any attack on its honour.

Like the Surgeon to the Poor, the Cantoniere was undoubtedly a figure of considerable authority in his area; the benefits of holding such office clearly reflected on his professional activity, increasing his local influence and expanding his territorial control over the district in which he lived and worked. It is likely, however, that the attraction of the office did not reside only in the capital of moral debts and obligations the Cantoniere was able to accumulate. It also helped the surgeon to reinforce a reassuring and trustworthy image of himself. As in our earlier analysis of the masculine attributes implicit in the surgeon's performance of his professional duties, in this case too we can read metaphorically the value that conscientious performance of the functions of Cantoniere could have in reinforcing the personality traits which were particularly valued in a 'good surgeon'. Not only was the Cantoniere frequently a party to the domestic secrets of the residents of his ward and, just as the barber-surgeon, was acquainted with all that normally remained hidden under wigs and clothing, but both activities required similar qualifications of strength, determination, resolve and being equipped to protect the physical and the collective body.

The mechanisms whereby professional trust was created were therefore very complex. The power of the licence in creating professional credibility has been called into question, while other attributes appear to have played a much more significant role in providing practitioners with a sound reputation: in the first place the local stability of the practice, then the practitioner's involvement in the affairs of the local community through the exercise of the office of Cantoniere. Even the social and family ties of practitioners may have had important repercussions on their work opportunities and careers. It is likely that in the cohesive fabric of the neighbourhood patients were well aware of the identity of the surgeon's friends and relatives and membership of a kinship group with strong local roots would be regarded as a positive factor. Moreover, the fact that the surgeon tended to have an extremely homogeneous network, involving members of occupations which were culturally related (jewellers, upholsterers, tailors, perruquiers, apothecaries, etc.) might have helped to reinforce his professional credentials. His kin and the people with whom he had frequent dealings shared his ability to play discreet and delicate roles; they too were intimate with the bodies of their clients and their needs for comfort, embellishment, disguise, enhancement. Participation in a culturally homogeneous milieu reinforced individual credibility.

Notes

1 On quacks, see Porter, *Health for Sale*; also R. Porter, 'The language of quackery in England, 1660–1800', in P. Burke and R. Porter (eds), *The Social History of Language* (Cambridge, 1987), and *Quacks, Fakers and Charlatans in English Medicine* (Stroud, 2000); on the Italian case, Gentilcore, *Healers*, chapter four.

2 The 1695 Consegna is incomplete: only the depositions of those practising in the capital, in the towns and villages of the province of Turin and in the city and province of Vercelli have been kept. All the examples discussed in this chapter are drawn from: the 'Registro delli chirurghi ... di Torino', for the data and declarations referring to practitioners from Turin, and the 'Registro delli cirurgici e barbieri ... della Provincia di Torino' for those concerned with practitioners in its province.

3 For a general overview of Protomedicati in the Italian states, see D. Gentilcore, "All that pertains to medicine": *Protomedici* and *Protomedicati* in early modern Italy', *Medical History*, 38 (1994).

4 Prior to 1695 orders of this kind were issued in 1624, 1638, 1642, 1644, 1651, 1660 (Borrelli, pp. 966 ff.) and in 1674 and 1676 (Duboin, vol. 10, pp. 77, 86). We do not know, however, to what extent they were implemented.

5 Pomata, *Contracting*; Gentilcore, *Healers*.

6 AST, s.r., I Archiviazione. *Speziali, Fondighieri e Chirurghi*, 'Fisco Regio per speciari e cirugici della Città e provincia d'Alba'.

7 See also the deposition of C. Rustagno, barber-surgeon at Rivoli.

8 Depositions by M. Carignani and P. A. Camagna.

9 Depositions by C. Meyner from Pianezza and G. Sandigliano from Cocconato.

10 Depositions by G. A. Rigillino from Chivasso, C. Ballegno from Orbassano and M. A. Garrone from Borgaro. See also the cases mentioned in chapter two, p. 87.

11 Pomata, *Contracting*, p. 119 and chapter three.

12 Other examples in Turin include N. Barberis, G. D. Reyneri, G. A.Varrone, M. A.Valle, who had exercised without letter patents for twenty, sixteen, eight and two years respectively, 'under the discipline' or 'direction' of their father or brother.

13 For a critique of the notion of 'irregular practitioners' see Pelling, *Medical Conflicts*, especially pp. 142–3.

14 Duboin, vol. 14, p. 734 and 'Lettera circolare ai Riformatori', 19 December 1738, p. 736.

15 Borrelli, pp. 987–8.

16 Most of the regulations concerning medicine covered these and other categories selling remedies that, it was feared, might be adulterated or rotten. Here abuse was easy to detect via inspection of the products on sale; moreover, the visitations yielded a good income in fines. Visitations of apothecaries' shops were supposed to take place every six months and numerous orders were issued to this end from 1568 onwards. (*ibid.*, pp. 967, 974, 983, 987, 993, 998; Duboin, vol. 10, p. 102).

17 Here it was the local representatives of the trades in question – the officers of the Company (*Università*) of Surgeons and of the College of Apothecaries – who were given the responsibility for telling practitioners they had to present themselves to the authorities. This was at least the procedure followed in 1695. In smaller places magistrates were expected to know who practised locally, and were thus asked to summon the men concerned. Contrary to what one would expect, checks in the smaller locali-

ties were often more meticulous and accurate than in the cities. The fact that the 1695 survey found more unlicensed men in the provinces than in the cities might, therefore, just be the result of this different level of accuracy.

18 Duboin, vol. 14, pp. 737–8, 28 November 1738 and 7 January 1739; p. 741, 25 February 1756.

19 Whereas in the capital there was only one case of a surgeon who had obtained his licence from the College of Physicians, all the rest having obtained it from the Proto-medico, in Vercelli the power of the College seems to have been more significant: ten licences were issued by the College, four by the College with the subsequent ratification of the state medical office, and just one by the sole Protomedico. In the Province of Vercelli eleven licences were issued by the College alone, one by the College with subsequent ratification by the Protomedico, and twelve by the state medical office alone. 'Vercelli'.

20 In other countries too the authorisation to practise could be obtained from different bodies and authorities. For France see Jones and Brockliss, *Medical World*, p. 16; for England, D. Harley, "Bred up in the study of that faculty"': licensed physicians in North-West England', *Medical History*, 38 (1994).

21 For Turin see the depositions of T. Surdis and P. Moran.

22 Claudio Clery, for example, when asked to produce his licence, presented his ducal patent appointing him as surgeon to His Highness's guards and was not prosecuted.

23 Achieving recognition as a citizen through involvement in the social and economic life of the city rather than through birth is not peculiar to this occupational group. Charitable provisions to the poor distinguished between those who belonged to the city's social networks and those who did not, rather than between natives and non-natives (Cavallo, *Charity and Power*, pp. 58–62, 85).

24 Among the Surgeons of the Poor we find Busano from Biella, Turco from Mondovì (who was later also appointed Surgeon to the Senatorial Prisons), Stura from Buttigliera d'Asti, Bellino from Mathi; and among the Cantonieri: Garrone from Saluzzola, Ratti from Nizza Monferrato, Parochia from Ceva, Torelli from Sale, Cerrutto from Biella, Bausset from Alessandria.

25 The information is drawn from: the *Consegna dei Francesi 1690*, the *Rollo dei Francesi … 1704* and the testimonies to free marital state of the parish of Santi Processo e Martiniano (AAT, 18.4.9–10).

26 For instance Acellano, a surgeon at San Maurizio Canavese, Schioppo, at Orbassano and the Frenchman Caulet at Ozegna.

27 'Vercelli'.

28 See for example the deposition of the unlicensed Antonio Bellotto, a Frenchman.

29 Benedicti's shop was in the Cantone of San Gallo (60), and Ghidella's in that of Santo Stefano (66) (see plate 4).

30 The literature on migration is huge: a recent synthesis is L. P. Moch, *Moving Europeans. Migrations in Western Europe since 1650* (Bloomington, 1992). See also D. Hoerder and L. P. Moch (eds), *European Migrants. Global and Local Perspectives* (Boston, 1996), Introduction; L. Fontaine, 'Gli studi sulla mobilità in Europa nell'età moderna: problemi e prospettive di ricerca', *Quaderni Storici*, 93 (1996); Arru and Ramella, *L'Italia delle Migrazioni*, pp. IX–XXII. Specifically on Piedmont see G. Levi, 'Come Torino soffocò il Piemonte. Mobilità della popolazione e rete urbana nel Piemonte del Sei e Settecento', in his *Centro e Periferia di uno Stato Assoluto* (Turin, 1985). I discuss

this literature in my 'La leggerezza delle origini: rotture e stabilità nell storie dei chiru-rghi torinesi tra Sei e Settecento', *Quaderni Storici*, 106 (2001).

31 Poussou however points to the new emphasis on 'enracinement' that appears to be replacing that on sedentary ideal in French historiography: J. P. Poussou, 'De l'intérêt de l'étude historique des mouvements migratoires européens du milieu du Moyen Âge à la fin du XIX siècle', in Istituto Internazionale di Storia Economica F. Datini di Prato, *Le Migrazioni in Europa Secc. XIII–XVIII* (Florence, 1994), pp. 20–43.

32 On the relevance of patronage to the success of medical practitioners see Jewson, 'Medical Knowledge'; Pelling, *Medical Conflicts*, pp. 234–45, 315–23.

33 On this office and the salaries it commanded see chapter six, pp. 213–19. n. 26.

34 Although these figures are only available for the year 1735 and for the 1750s, they provide an indication of the situation in earlier years: it is likely that the prescriptions were even more numerous in the period 1670–1720, given that the yearly expense in medicines for the poor was higher then than in later decades (Cavallo, *Charity and Power*, p. 77).

35 ACT, *Ordinati*, especially 1679 (21 December), fos 319–20; 1688 (15 May), fo. 123 and 1708 (8 August), fo. 174. See also 1653 (29 September), fo. 133; 1662 (29 May), fo. 74; 1672 (10 September), fo. 84; 1679 (30 September), fos 239–40; 1688 (24 April), fo. 104.

36 It is no coincidence that the ability to observe discretion through silence and the keeping of secrets is mentioned in the professional tracts as necessary attributes of a barber-surgeon. *Il Barbiere*, pp. 40–2: Salvi, *Il Ministro*, pp. 3–4.

37 ACT, vols. 294, 295, 296; AST, s.I, *Provincia di Torino*, m.1, 'Cantonieri'. The surgeon's was among the most highly represented occupations: in 1714 for example eleven Cantonieri (or 1/5 of the total) were surgeons (ACT, Coll. XII, *Rolli della popolazione*, 1714).

38 Duboin, vol. 26, pp. 944–5, 4 July 1706; vol. 13, pp. 644–5, 653, 25 October 1703 and 15 January 1714.

39 It was also up to him to ensure that property owners kept their fire equipment in good condition: *ibid.*, p. 770, 25 August 1705.

40 On these provisions see Cavallo, *Charity and Power*, chapters one and two.

41 Borelli, pp. 924–6, 22 September 1680.

Conclusion

I n these concluding pages I want to draw together the main findings of this study so as to highlight some of their broader implications along with the issues they raise for further research, both in the field of medical history and that of work and family relations in an urban setting. A question also arises in terms of what the outcome of our inquiry tells us about the 'Italianness', or Southern European specificity, of some of the practices highlighted.

In the first instance this study has re-mapped the intellectual and professional boundaries that define the experience of being a surgeon in the early modern period, and, by extension, those of the professional community to which the surgeon belongs. A close reading of surgical tracts authored by Bernardo Calvo has afforded us important insights into how an ordinary surgeon, active in the late seventeenth century and the early decades of the eighteenth, would understand the workings of the body and of medicine. The idea of a sharp demarcation between the outside and the inside of the body appears entirely alien to Calvo's conceptualisation of disease and treatment; his work challenges the distinction between physic and surgery not just in terms of the surgeon's everyday practice (the subject of much scholarly argument) but also at a theoretical level.

In the second place, my enquiry into the ways in which the body and its 'excrements' were perceived in treatises written by barbers and in other health-related literature has led me to question the assumption that, in the course of the seventeenth century, a growing divide came to separate surgery from barbering and other body care activities. Such periodisation relies on the idea of a sharp distinction between the domain of health and that of appearances, whereas this is not reflected in the accounts of contemporaries. The terminology employed both in everyday life and in the legislation shows that the distinctions between barbers, surgeons and the new occupations of perruquier and *baigneur* remained hazy. Moreover, unexpected affinities emerge between the duties of barber-surgeons and those of artisans engaged in occupations seemingly unrelated to the field of medicine. My study of the services carried out in the ducal Chambers reveals that surgeons acquired a key role in activities connected with the appearance, hygiene and comfort of the master's body, and shared similar concerns and a common discourse with the jewellers, tailors and upholsterers who worked in the same environment. Research into the professional culture of some of these occupations suggests that they were epistemologically less distinct that it would appear to a modern viewer: occupational links, I have argued, were grounded in contemporary understandings of the body and its functioning. By introducing the concept of culturally homogeneous professional milieu this study has provided a new perspective on the tendency (often observed by labour historians) of some occupations to cluster in unexpected ways. To what extent cultural affinities played a part in the formation of other types of professional networks is an open question.

The professional and social space to which 'artisans of the body' belonged also appears to have played a crucial part in shaping their consumer tastes and behaviour: in particular, their involvement in service in the court Chamber and in its gift-economy set them apart from other categories of artisans as well as from other groups of medical practitioners.

The complex identity of the barber-surgeon and the fact that he is embedded in a world of professional relations with occupations which are not normally categorised as medical prompts a view therefore of 'the medical community' as much more permeable and less clearly defined than is usually believed. These findings bear important consequences for the representation of medical occupations. On the one hand, they show yet again the limitations of the distinction between popular and learned healers that has long informed accounts in the history of medicine. In the 1980s in particular, scholars argued that evacuative practices and forms of body-care aimed to purify the inner body belonged to the domain of 'popular medicine' and were frowned upon by official, orthodox practitioners.[1] The involvement in cosmetic and hygienic tasks in the ducal Chamber by respectable practitioners who were also chief hospital surgeons in Turin and syndics of the Company of barber-surgeons, further discredits the validity of this bipolar representation of medical practice - one that has already lost currency in the last few years, without, however, being replaced by an alternative interpretive model. On the other hand, my study of Turin's surgeons exposes the flaws in the positivist distinction between regular and irregular practitioners, which is largely constructed on a representation of the medical community deriving from its corporate organisation. The weak and discontinuous character of the Company of Surgeons in Turin (an association which is hard to pin down since it appears under different forms over time and has left very few traces of its existence),[2] belies the tendency to depict as marginal and irregular those practitioners operating outside the corporate framework of professional companies and guilds. Moreover, in the capital city of Turin, practitioners who were not legally authorised existed in abundance and were fully visible, while their irregular status did not seem to matter in the eyes of patients, nor even in the eyes of the authorities. These facts allow for a reinterpretation of the value and meaning of the licence in the thinking of contemporaries. A comparison between the depositions of licensed and unlicensed practitioners shows that there was frequently a significant gap between the start of surgical practice and the later acquisition of the licence. This suggests that the unlicensed were not a separate group of practitioners, as is often assumed, and rather that work without a licence was a normal stage of the surgeon's career and that sometimes it characterised a practitioner's entire professional experience.

Working without a licence was not only very common but was a structural phenomenon within a specific organisation of labour. Looking beyond the picture of work relations projected by the corporate organisation of the medical profession and by the body of prescriptions concerning medical matters, this study has drawn attention to the various types of partnerships and forms of dependent work which were the norm in the practice of surgery. Recognition of these characteristics of the labour market also introduces important correctives to the representation of the marketplace that emerges from the recent literature on consumption and on medical services: while these studies have stressed rivalry and competition between individual artisans and practitioners, the instance of Turin highlights the range of informal sodalities and unofficial agreements between men practising the same occupations, as well as between those in related trades. These had the effect of shaping the supply of medical services. Thus the focus on intra-professional networks rather than on single individuals and occupations makes it possible to identify group strategies that would otherwise remain hidden. These considerably reduced customer choice, giving the market a much less free and deregulated character than is often assumed. Access to the independent exercise of the occupation and to professional positions was largely controlled through mechanisms of internal succession and transmission rather than being regulated institutionally or through free competition. Kinship networks, in particular, had a key role in establishing control over areas of the market for health-related services. It was often only by forming a marriage tie to an established master that many young surgeons managed to establish themselves in the trade in an independent position.

While stressing the impact of kinship on various aspects of the work experience of barber-surgeons, this study has also proposed a redefinition of the methods normally employed to trace kinship. The focus on ego-centred kinship networks, including both maternal and paternal kin, both blood and affinal relations, has made it possible to adopt a fully bilateral view of kinship ties and to highlight forms of transmission of knowledge and professional resources which would otherwise be overlooked. This approach has been particularly revealing about the role of women and that of lateral and affinal kin in the reproduction of the trade. Indeed, the biographical perspective has shed light on the strong tendency towards inter-marriage among barber-surgeons and allied body crafts. As a consequence, barber-surgeons' kinship networks contain a striking recurrence of a limited range of occupations: the close connection between aesthetic, hygienic and medical functions which typifies the practice of barber-surgeons is in fact replicated at the level of their kinship ties. This pattern of marriage and the occupational configuration of the kinship group encouraged transfer of skills and expertise within a wider pool of relationships than that of father and son; moreover it facilitated a circulation of skills and expertise between adjacent occupations. Whether the limited range of marriage choices found among artisans of the body was also a feature of other occupations is another question that it would be interesting to address in future research on different professional areas.

More generally, the biographical approach and the bilateral examination of kinship have allowed for a radical re-appraisal of the image of the early modern artisan family. Far from being dominated by patricentric and patrilineal priorities, and by the primacy of blood ties, among artisans of the body the family is 'horizontal', its core being constituted by siblings and brothers and sisters-in-law. Moreover, it is a 'diagonal' family, in which what I have defined as 'half-generation' ties play a crucial role, especially in the economic and professional spheres. It is therefore age, rather than the degrees or types of kinship on which scholarly discussion has often focused, that figures in my analysis as the key factor in determining significant and enduring relationships between kin, and also between neighbours and men engaged in similar or related professional activities.

The focus on inter- and intra-generational relationships has led us to challenge the persistent association established between age and authority in the early modern period. Life histories of artisans of the body suggest that, among the middling sort, youth was neither the rebellious nor the subordinate stage in life that the literature has portrayed, and that social mobility was often associated with early emancipation from the family of origin. The transmission of knowledge, trade, reputation, clients and other occupational resources, which we associate with parental roles, was often fulfilled outside the conjugal family, not only by members of the kinship group but also by non-kin who participated in the intense flow of exchanges frequently characterising relationships between neighbours or between a master and his pupils. This study shows therefore how the nuclear family was embedded in a web of relationships with kin that often coincided with neighbourhood ties, and that ties with neighbours frequently turned into kinship ties.

Among the members of the kinship group, unmarried men and childless couples deserve special attention in this context. Their role as artificial parents appears to be structural, rather than incidental, within this social milieu, and this has led us to question recent definitions of early modern masculinity which see a strong association between adult male status, marriage and paternity. We looked instead at the alternative ways through which adult men could prove their manhood, both in the domestic and professional domains.

If kinship is traced bilaterally, therefore, horizontal kinship ties appear to be the most vital core of the artisan family. This is in sharp contrast to the patrilineal picture of the family among the upper classes of the late medieval and early modern period, while conforming to the scattered evidence emerging from studies of the 'middling sort' family in both medieval and contemporary Italy. For example, the picture emerging from Turin is remarkably similar to the one drawn by Henry Bresc for the 'bourgeois family' of fourteenth- and fifteenth-century Sicily. There, too, we can note 'the primacy of individual initiative over family continuity', and more precisely 'a bilateral family ..., a neighbourhood solidly established by custom, which places the two parents on the same level and sees agnatic and cognatic kin and the world of neighbours as equally relevant'. It is true that in medieval Sicily the devolution of property was also fully bilateral and the patrimony was dispersed among both agnates and cognates in a more marked way than in later periods. In other ways, however, the similarities with the early modern urban situation examined here are striking: while lineage ties are weak, 'horizontal kinship ensures protection, services, militant solidarities and partisanship' between brothers-in law, siblings and cousins. Moreover the recruitment of god-parents 'is made above all within the [horizontal] family' rather than within a vertical structure of clientelism. Ties between blood and spiritual parents enlarge once again 'the sense of implicit association' among horizontal kin, facilitating transactions, providing guarantors for the honesty and trustworthiness of a partner or representative.[3] Some of the key features of the family model outlined in this work are also encountered in Christiane Klapisch-Zuber's discussion of the domestic arrangements and relationships of a fifteenth-century Bolognese mason, as revealed by his diary: among them the bilateral character of his family ties, the attraction exercised by the bride's family and the weak authority of the father over his children.[4] According to the received periodisation, however, this 'cognatic shade' is lost in the centuries that follow. Yet scattered examples of the persistence of bilateral practices among the middling groups have been noted for later periods, especially by scholars of Southern Italy.[5] As this study suggests, these practices have not been given the attention they deserve.

The significance of the 'horizontal family' is also a feature of some of the family forms described by Gabriella Gribaudi for contemporary Naples. The *camorra* family, in particular, is 'open at the local level and, contrary to the stereotype, is characterised by weak internal hierarchies'. In none of the gangs do we find any vertical family organisation of fathers and children. How to become a *camorrista* is learned from the world of the local tough-guy, not from the father. Alliances are forged, instead, with brothers and brothers-in-law, and friends then join in: 'these are gangs which develop within a defined territory, out of street-level sociability, and are true generational groups', 'here the family as a nucleus of parents and children is extremely weak, and is replaced by a loosely defined web of relationships between neighbours, various kin and friends from the street'.[6] In Naples, similar traits also typify the artisan family of the most low-class districts, in particular 'its openness to the streets that surround it, and the blurred boundary between neighbourhood and kinship: from childhood on, ties of friendship are formed around the workshop, which then often lead to marriage'. Kin are often also work partners as well as neighbours and these work relationships in turn often generate kinship ties. 'It is a family of brothers and sisters, to some extent an extended family, but anomalous with regard to the classic model; for example, it is not characterised by strong hierarchical roles'.[7]

Are we to conclude that this 'horizontal' character is a specific feature of the Italian family, at least among middling sort groups? To some extent this seems to be the case. In other respects, however, it seems premature to suggest an Italian specificity, even if this is limited to particular social ranks. Recent studies highlight the relevance of kinship ties in early modern England[8] (something that has long been denied). Moreover, Naomi Tadmor's work on the language of kinship suggests that, among the same middling social groups at the centre of this study (although not exclusively in the urban setting) a classificatory terminology was used to define kin which did not distinguish between members of the nuclear family and members of the wider kinship group, nor between blood relatives and affines. Hence parents would define the spouses of their children as 'son' and 'daughter', and brothers and sisters could refer to the spouse of a sibling as 'brother' or 'sister'. The wives of uncles were clearly addressed as 'aunts' and the husbands of aunts as 'uncles'. Given the frequency of remarriage, the usage of this classificatory nomenclature leads to the paradox of a person who refers to three different women as 'my mother'. These are important clues which, if pursued, could perhaps lead to the identification of a greater closeness between family models in Northern and Southern Europe, at least in relation to some of the elements discussed in this work: namely, the importance of kinship ties in the lives of individuals, and in particular the horizontal relationships established through marriage.

This study has mainly concentrated on the consequences that specific forms of family relations, inter- and intra-generational ties and marital choice had on young men and adult men. It has examined the relationships between men within the family – father and son, brothers and nephews and uncles – a subject still largely under-researched, and it has analysed the sources of male independence, stressing their specificity by comparison with the situation in other parts of Europe, and among more prosperous social groups. My research has particularly highlighted the need to pay greater attention to the legal framework within which father-son relationships were negotiated, and to the different expectations affecting the timing and the forms taken by the emancipation of sons in different geographical contexts. This comparative dimension of analysis has so far been missing in studies of the position of men in early modern society and it is clearly worth developing, likewise in relation to religious specificities and the ways in which different doctrinal contexts affected ideals of being a man.

Undoubtedly, the focus adopted in this study has been the male one; the implications of the strength of horizontal kinship ties for women's lives remain an issue that this work has merely begun to map out, by pointing to the crucial part played by women of the family in the workshop, as well as in the provision of body-care services in the ducal households. Here, too, my concern has been to shift attention from individual figures to groups consisting of both men and women, and to show that the employees of the ducal Chamber were families rather than single individuals. This perspective underlines the fact that women had a key role in the reproduction of the horizontal family as a cultural, working and political entity. But did their contribution also translate into real authority, economic power, entitlement to property and other rights available to their male counterparts? These are issues which it has not been possible to investigate in great depth. Similarly, did the horizontal family model involve a non-hierarchical orientation in relationships between relatives in everyday life, and therefore a softening of gender discrimination? The emotional implications of this particular type of family setting, for men, as well as for women, clearly require further consideration.

Notes

1 A. Klairmont-Lingo, 'Empirics and charlatans in early modern France: the genesis of the classification of the 'other' in medical practice', *Journal of Social History*, 19 (1986), pp. 587, 591.

2 In Bologna too, at least in the eighteenth century, surgeons did not have 'a college or even an association'.: Pomata, *Contracting*, p. 67.

3 H. Bresc, 'La famille dans la société sicilienne médievale', in *La Famiglia e la Vita Quotidiana in Europa dal Quattrocento al Seicento. Fonti e Problemi* (Rome, 1986), pp. 187–96.

4 Klapisch-Zuber, 'La vie domestique et ses conflicts', pp. 485–98.

5 See Ida Fazio's overview, 'The family, honour and gender in Sicily: models and new research', *Modern Italy*, 9 (2004), pp. 274–5.

6 G. Gribaudi, *Donne, uomini, famiglie. Napoli nel Novecento* (Naples, 1999), pp. 29–31.

7 *Ibid*, pp. 18–19.

8 See the works discussed in Tadmor, *Family*, pp. 103–16.

Bibliography

Printed sources

Arnobio, C. *Tesoro delle gioie, trattato curioso, nel quale si dichiara breuemente la virtu, qualita, e proprieta delle gioie ... Raccolto dall'Academico Ardente Etereo* (Venice: F. Ginami, 1670; 1st edn, 1602).

(L')Arte di Conservar la Sanità tutta intiera ... per Bartolomeo Traffichetti da Bertinoro, Medico di Rimini (Pesaro: G. Concordia, 1565).

Auda, B. See *Breve Compendio.*

(Il) Barbiere di Tiberio Malfi da Monte Sarchio Barbiere e Consule dell'Arte (Naples: O. Beltrano, 1626).

(Il) Breve Compendio di Meravigliosi Secreti. dato in luce dal signor Frate Domenico Auda, Capo Speziale dell'Archiospitale di S. Spirito di Roma e Canonico dello stesso Ordine (Cuneo: B. Strabella, 1666; 1st edn, Rome, 1652).

(Un) Breve et Notabile Trattato del Regimento dela Sanità ... di Roberto Gropretiio, (Venice: M. Tramezino, 1560).

Bruno, M. See *Discorsi.*

Calvo, B. See *Chirurgia Teorico-Pratica; Lettera Istorica.*

Castellani, G. M. *Filactirion della Flebotolmia et Arteriotomia con aggiunta di un trattato nel qual s'insegna il vero modo d'applicar ventose o coppe* (Viterbo: P. e A. Discepoli, 1619).

Chirurgia Teorico-Pratica di Paolo Bernardo Calvo Chirurgo Colleggiato in Torino. Trattato primo De' Tumori (Turin: G. B. Fontana, 1702).

Chirurgia Teorico-Pratica di Paolo Bernardo Calvo Chirurgo Colleggiato in Torino. Trattato delle Ferite (Turin: Guigonio, 1712).

(Il) Chirurgo. Trattato breve di Tarduccio Salvi da Macerata (Rome: Paolini, 1613).

D'Amato, C. *Prattica Nuova et Utilissima di tutto quello ch'al diligente Barbiere s'appartiene* (Venice: G. B. Brigna, 1669; 1st edn, 1632).

Del Conservar la Sanità Opera del Dottor Roderigo Fonseca Primo Lettor di Medicina nello Studio di Pisa (Florence: A. Semartelli, 1603).

Del Riccio, A. *Istoria delle Pietre,* ed. R. Gnoli and A. Sironi (Turin: Allemandi, 1979).

Discorsi di M. Matteo Bruno Medico Riminese (Venice: A. Arrivabene, 1569).

Dolce, L. See *Libri Tre.*

Duboin, E. A.*Raccolta per ordine di materie delle lege editti, manfesti ecc. pubblicati ... sotto il felicissimo domino della Real Casa de Savoia* m 23 vols (Turin: Marcio, 1818–69).

Fonseca, R. See *Del Conservar la Sanità.*

Garzoni, T. *La piazza universale di tutte le professioni del mondo* (Venice: M. Miloco, 1665; 1st edn, 1586).

Gropretiio, R. See *Breve et Notabile Trattato*.

Histoire des Perruques où l'on fait voir leur origin par M. Jean Baptiste Thiers, Docteur en Theologie, Curé de Champrond (Paris: aux dépenses de l'auteur, 1690).

Lancetta, T. *De Pestilentia Commune a Bruti … e un dialogo attinente alla missione di sangue con foglio della vena* (Venice: Guerigli, 1632).

La Scala Messanesi, D. See *Phlebotomia damnata*.

Leonardi, C. *Speculum Lapidum* (Venice: Sessa Melchiorre, 1516).

Lettera Istorica di Paolo Bernardo Calvo Chirurgo Colleggiato in Torino (Turin: G. B. Valetta, 1714).

Libri Tre di M. Ludovico Dolce nei quali si tratta delle diverse sorti di pietre che produce la natura (Venice: Gio Battista Marchio Sessa, 1565).

Lomazzo, *Trattato dell'Arte della Pittura, Scoltura e Architettura* (Milan: Paolo Gottardo, 1585).

Malfi da Monte Sarchio, T. See *Barbiere; Ministro*.

Melli, B. *La Lancetta in Pratica … opera postuma … a cui si è aggiunto un breve trattato circa la pratica del ventosare di questo stesso autore* (Venice: G. B. Recurti, 1740).

(Il) Ministro del Medico. Trattato breve di Tarduccio Salvi da Macerata (Rome: Facciotto, 1608).

Monti, H. *Trattato della Missione del Sangue contro l'Abuso Moderno … di Cavar Gran Quantità* (Pisa: L. Zeffi, 1627).

Opera Nova intitolata il Perché (Venice: Zorzi di Ruscoi Milanese, 1507).

Phlebotomia damnata a Dominico La Scala Messanensi (Pavia: Sardi 1696).

Ricettario Fiorentino di nuovo illustrato (Florence: Vangelisti, Vincenzo & Matini Piero, 1670).

Salvi da Macerata, T. See *Chirurgo*.

Scuola Salernitana del Modo di Conservarsi in Sanità (Perugia: P. Petrucci, 1587).

Svegliarino alli Signori Veneziani per Poter con Sicurezza Viver di Continuo in Sanità sino agli Anni Cento e Dieci (Venice: L. Pittoni, 1691).

Thiers, J. B. See *Histoire des Perruques*.

Torrino, B. *Consulto se sia Bene Cacciar Sangue a Fanciulli* (Turin: B. Zavatta, 1659).

Traffichetti, B. See *L'Arte di Conservar la Sanità*.

Trattato del Custodir la Sanità di Viviano Viviani Filosofo e Medico Venetiano (Venice: G. Piuti, 1626).

Verna, G. B. *Princeps Medicaminum Omnium Phlebotomia* (Padua: Patavii Manfre, 1716).

Viviani, V. See *Trattato del Custodir*.

Secondary references

Articles & chapters

Ago, R. 'La costruzione dell'identità maschile: una competizione tra uomini', in A, Arru (ed.), *La Costruzione dell'Identità Maschile nell'Età Moderna e Contemporanea* (Rome: Biblink, 2001).

Ago, R. 'Il linguaggio del corpo', in M. Belfanti and F. Giusberti (eds) *La Moda. Storia d'Italia Annali 9* (Turin: Einaudi, 2003).

Allegra, L. 'Un modello di mobilità sociale preindustriale. Torino in età Napoleonica', *BSBS*, CII: 1 (2004).

Ben-Amos, I. 'Gifts and favors: informal support in early modern England', *Journal of Modern History*, 72 (2000).

Berkner, L. K. 'The stem family and the developmental cycle of the peasant household: an eighteenth-century Austrian example', *American Historical Review*, 77 (1972).

Borello, L. 'Reliquie a Torino. Memorie sconosciute da scoprire', *BSBS*, C:2 (2002).

Braunstein, P. 'Dal bagno pubblico alla cura termale privata: tracce per una storia sociale dell`intimo', *Ricerche Storiche*, 16:3 (1986).

Bresc, H. 'La famille dans la société sicilienne médiévale', in *La Famiglia e la Vita Quotidiana in Europa dal Quattrocento al Seicento. Fonti e Problemi* (Rome: Ministero per i Beni Culturali e Ambientali, 1986).

Calvi, G. 'Widows, the state and the guardianship of children in early modern Tuscany', in S. Cavallo and L. Warner (eds) *Widowhood in Medieval and Early Modern Europe* (Harlow: Longman, 1999).

Carpanetto, D. 'Gli studenti di chirurgia', in D. Balani, D. Carpanetto and F. Turletti, *La Popolazione dell'Università di Torino, BSBS*, 76 (1978).

Castelnuovo, G. '"À la court et au service de nostre prince": l'hôtel de Savoie et ses métiers à la fin du Moyen Âge', in L. C. Gentile and P. Bianchi (eds) *L'Affermazione della Corte Sabauda: Dinastie, Poteri, Elites fra Savoia e Piemonte dal Basso Medioevo alla Prima Età Moderna* (Turin: Zamorani, 2006).

Cavallo, S. 'Proprietà o possesso? Controllo e composizione dei beni delle donne a Torino 1650–1710', in G. Calvi and I. Chabot (eds) *Le Ricchezze delle Donne. Diritti Patrimoniali in Italia (XIII–XIX secc.)* (Turin: Rosemberg & Sellier, 1998).

Cavallo, S. 'What did women transmit? Ownership and control of household goods and personal effects in early modern Italy' in M. Donald and L. Hurcombe (eds) *Gender and Material Culture: Historical Perspectives* (Basingstoke: Macmillan, 2000).

Cavallo, S. 'La leggerezza delle origini: rotture e stabilità nelle storie dei chirurghi torinesi tra Sei e Settecento', *Quaderni Storici*, 106 (2001).

Cavallo, S. 'Health, hygiene and beauty', in M. Ajmar-Wollheim and F. Dennis (eds) *At Home in Renaissance Italy* (London: Victoria and Albert Museum Publications, 2006).

Cavallo, S. 'L'importanza della 'famiglia orizzontale' nella storia della famiglia Italiana', in I. Fazio and D. Lombardi (eds) *Generazioni. Legami di Parentela tra Passato e Presente* (Rome: Viella, 2006).

Cavallo, S. 'Le emancipazioni: una fonte per lo studio dei rapporti tra padri e figli', in A. Bellavitis and I. Chabot (eds) *Famiglie e Poteri nell'Italia Medievale e Moderna* (Rome: Ecole Française de Rome, forthcoming).

Chaytor, M. 'Household and kinship in Ryton in the late sixteenth and early seventeenth centuries', *History Workshop Journal*, 10 (1980).

Corsini, C. 'Chi si sposa per primo? Rango di nascita e soluzione matrimoniale', in A. M. Falchero et al.*La Storia e l'Economia. Miscellanea di Studi in Onore di Giorgio Mori* (Varese: Lativa, 2003), vol. 1.

Cressy, D. 'Kinship and kin interaction in early modern England', *Past and Present*, 113 (1986).

Crossick, J. 'Past masters: the artisan in European history', in J. Crossick (ed.), *The Artisan and the European Town 1500–1900* (Aldershot: Scolar, 1997).

Crouzet-Pavan, E. 'A flower of evil: young men in medieval Italy', in G. Levi and J. Schmitt (eds) *A History of Young People in the West* (Cambridge, Massachusetts: Harvard University Press, 1997), vol. one.

Dambruyne, J. 'Guilds, social mobility and status in sixteenth-century Ghent', in *International Review of Social History*, 43 (1998).

Darnton, R. 'The great cat massacre of Rue Saint Séverin', in R. Darnton, *The Great Cat Massacre and Other Episodes in French Cultural History* (London: Allen Lane, 1984).

Davidoff, L. 'Where the stranger begins: the question of siblings in historical analysis', in L. Davidoff, *Worlds Between. Historical Perspectives on Gender and Class* (Cambridge: Polity, 1995).

Davis, N. Z.'The reasons of misrule', in N. Z. Davis, *Society and Culture in Early Modern France* (Stanford: Stanford University Press, 1975).

Delille, G. 'Marriage, faction and conflict in sixteenth-century Italy: an example and a few questions', in T. Dean and K. Lowe (eds) *Marriage in Italy 1300–1650* (Cambridge: Cambridge University Press, 1998).

De Renzi, S. 'Medical competence, anatomy and the polity on seventeenth-century Rome', in S. Cavallo and D. Gentilcore (eds) *Spaces, Objects and Identities in Early Modern Italian Medicine, Renaissance Studies* 21: 4 (2007).

Diefendorf, B. 'Give us back our children: patriarchal authority and parental consent to religious vocations in early Counter-Reformation France', *Journal of Modern History*, 68 (1996).

Dolan, C. 'The artisans of Aix-en-Provence in the sixteenth century: a micro-analysis of social relationships', in P. Benedict (ed.), *Cities and Social Change in Early Modern France* (London: Routledge, 1992).

Egmond, F. 'Execution, dissection, pain and infamy. A morphological investigation', in F. Egmond and R. Zwijnenberg (eds), *Bodily Extremities. Preoccupations with the Human Body in Early Modern European Culture* (Aldershot: Ashgate, 2003).

Ehmer, J. "Servi di donne". Matrimonio e costituzione di una propria famiglia da parte dei garzoni come campo di conflitto nel mondo artigiano mitteleuropeo', *Quaderni Storici*, 80 (1992).

Ehmer, J. 'Tramping artisans in nineteenth-century Vienna', in D. J. Siddle (ed.), *Migration, Mobility and Modernisation* (Liverpool: Liverpool University Press, 2000).

Esposito, A. 'Stufe e bagni pubblici a Roma nel Rinascimento', in M. Miglio (ed.), *Taverne, Locande e Stufe a Roma nel Rinascimento* (Rome: Roma nel Rinascimento, 1999).

Evenden, D. E. 'Gender differences in the licensing asnd practice of female and male surgeons in early modern England', *Medical History*, 42 (1998).

Fazio, I. 'The family, honour and gender in Sicily: models and new research', *Modern Italy*, 9 (2004).

Fletcher, A. 'Manhood, the male body, courtship and the household in early modern England', *History*, 84 (1999).

Flynn, M. 'Taming anger's daughters: new treatment for emotional problems in Renaissance Spain', *Renaissance Quarterly*, 51 (1998).

Fontaine, L. 'Gli studi sulla mobilità in Europa nell'età moderna: problemi e prospettive di ricerca', *Quaderni Storici*, 93 (1996).

French, H. R. 'The search for the middle sort of people 1600–1800', *Historical Journal*, 43:1 (2000).

Fresquet Febrer, J. L. 'La práctica medica en los textos quirúrgicos espanoles en el siglo XVI', in *Dynamis*, 22 (2002).

Frigo, D. 'Dal caos all'ordine: sulla questione del 'prender moglie' nella trattatistica del sedicesimo secolo', in M. Zancan (ed.), *Nel Cerchio della Luna. Figure di Donna in Alcuni Testi del XVI Secolo* (Venice: Marsilio, 1983).

Gai, L. 'Artigiani e artisti nella società pistoiese del basso medioevo', in *Artigiani e Salariati. Il mondo del Lavoro nell'Italia dei Secoli XII–XV* (Pistoia: Centro Italiano di Storia e d'Arte, 1984).

Gaude-Ferragu, M. 'Le coeur 'couronné': tombeaux et funérailles de coeur en France à la fin du Moyen Âge', *Micrologus*, 11 (2003).

Gentilcore, D. '"All that pertains to medicine': *Protomedici* and *Protomedicati* in early modern Italy', *Medical History*, 38 (1994).

Gentilcore, D. 'Apothecaries, 'charlatans,' and the medical marketplace in Italy, 1400–1750', in D. Gentilcore (ed.), *The World of the Italian Apothecary, Pharmacy in History*, 45:3 (2003).

Goody, J. 'The evolution of the family', in P. Laslett and R. Wall (eds) *Household and Family in Past Time* (Cambridge: Cambridge University Press, 1972).

Grandi, A. 'Il monopolio delle forbici. Il conflitto tra barbieri e parrucchieri a Bologna nel XVIII secolo', in A. Guenzi, P. Massa and F. Piola Caselli (eds) *Corporazioni e Gruppi Professionali* (Milan: Angeli, 1999).

Grendi, E. 'Associazioni familiari e associazioni d'affari. I Balbi a Genova tra Cinquecento e Seicento', *Quaderni Storici*, 91 (1996).

Griffith, P. 'Masterless young people in Norwich, 1560–1645', in A. Fox, P. Griffith and S. Hindle (eds) *The Experience of Authority in Early Modern England* (Basingstoke: Macmillan, 1996).

Groppi, A. 'Lavoro e proprietà delle donne in età moderna', in Groppi, A. (ed.), *Il Lavoro delle Donne* (Rome: Laterza, 1996).

Hajnal, J. 'European marriage patterns in perspective', in D. V. Glass and D. E. C. Eversley (eds) *Population in History* (London: Edward Arnold, 1965).

Hamraoui, E. 'L'invention de la pathologie cardiaque', *Micrologus*, 11 (2003).

Harley, D. "Bred up in the study of that faculty": licensed physicians in North-West England', *Medical History*, 38 (1994).

Head-König, A.-L. 'Forced marriages and forbidden marriages in Switzerland: state control of the formation of marriages in Catholic and Protestant Cantons in the eighteenth and nineteenth centuries', *Continuity and Change*, 8 (1993).

Hughes, D. O.'Domestic ideals and social behavior: evidence from medieval Genoa', in C. E. Rosenberg (ed.), *The Family in History* (Philadelphia: University of Pennsylvania Press, 1975, repr. 1984).

Jenner, M. 'Civilisation and deodorisation? Smell in early modern English culture', in P. Burke, B. Harrison and P. Slack (eds) *Civil Histories* (Oxford: Oxford University Press, 2000).

Jewson, N. D. 'Medical knowledge and the patronage system in 18th-century England', *Sociology*, 8 (1974).

Jutte, R. 'A seventeenth-century German barber-surgeon and his patients', *Medical History*, 33 (1989).

Kirshner, J. 'Material for a gilded cage: non-dotal assets in Florence, 1300–1500', in D. Kertzer and R. P. Saller (eds) *The Family in Italy from Antiquity to the Present* (New Haven: Yale University Press, 1991).

Klairmont-Lingo, A. 'Empirics and charlatans in early modern France: the genesis of the classification of the 'other' in medical practice', *Journal of Social History*, 19 (1986).

Klapisch-Zuber, C. 'Kin, friends and neighbors: the urban territory of a merchant family in 1400', in her *Women, Family, and Ritual in Renaissance Italy*, trans. Lydia Cochrane (Chicago: University of Chicago Press, 1985).

Klapisch-Zuber, C. 'Les coffres de mariage et les plateaux d'accouchée à Florence: archive, ethnologie, iconographie', in S. Deswarte-Rosa (ed.), *A Travers l'Image. Lecture Iconographique et Sens de l'Oeuvre* (Paris: Klincksieck, 1994).

Klapisch-Zuber, C. 'La vie domestique et ses conflits chez un maçon bolonais du XVe siècle', in P. Boglioni, R. Delort, C. Gauvard eds, *Le Petit Peuple dans l'Occident médiéval. Terminologies, Perceptions, Réalités* (Paris, Publications de la Sorbonne, 2002, Histoire ancienne et médiévale, 71).

Laslett, P. 'Family, kinship and collectivity as systems of support in pre-industrial Europe: a consideration of the "nuclear hardship" hypothesis', *Continuity and Change*, 3 (1988).

Laudani, S. 'Mestieri di donne, mestieri di uomini', in A. Groppi (ed.), *Il Lavoro delle Donne* (Rome: Laterza, 1996).

Laughran, M. A. 'Oltre la pelle. I cosmetici e il loro uso', in M. Belfanti and F. Giusberti (eds) *La Moda. Storia d'Italia Annali 9* (Turin: Einaudi, 2003).

Lawrence, C. 'Democratic, divine and heroic: the history and historiography of surgery', in C. Lawrence (ed.), *Medical Theory, Surgical Practice* (London: Routledge, 1992).

Lazinger, M. 'Una società di nubili e celibi? indagine su una vallata tirolese nell'ottocento', in M. Lazinger and R. Sarti (eds) *Celibi e Nubili nella Società Moderna e Contemporanea* (Udine: Forum, 2007).

Le Goff, J. 'Head or heart? The political use of body metaphors in the Middle Ages', in M. Feher, R. Naddaff and N. Tazi (eds) *Zone 3: Fragments for a History of the Human Body* (New York: Zone, 1989), Part 3.

Levi, G. 'Mobilità della popolazione a Torino nella prima metà del Settecento', *Quaderni Storici*, 17 (1971).

Levi, G. 'Come Torino soffocò il Piemonte. Mobilità della popolazione e rete urbana nel Piemonte del Sei e Settecento', in G. Levi, *Centro e Periferia di uno Stato Assoluto* (Turin: Rosemberg & Sellier, 1985).

Levi, G. 'Les usages de la biographie', *Annales: Economies, Sociétés, Civilisations*, 44 (1989).

Levi, G. 'Household and kinship: a few thoughts', *Journal of Family History*, 15 (1990).

Levi, G. 'Carrières d'artisans et marché du travail à Turin (XVIII–XIXe siècles)', *Annales: Economies, Sociétés, Civilisations*, 45 (1990).

Levi, G. 'Comportements, ressources, procès: avant la 'révolution' de la consommation', in J. Revel (ed.), *Jeux d'Echelles. La Micro-Analyse à l'Expérience* (Paris, 1996).

Litchiefield, R. B. 'Caratteristiche demografiche delle famiglie fiorentine dal sedicesimo al diciannovesimo secolo', in AA.VV. *Saggi di Demografia Storica* (Florence: Università di Firenze, 1969).

McCray Beier, L. 'Seventeenth-century English surgery: the casebook of Joseph Binns', in C. Lawrence (ed.), *Medical Theory, Surgical Practice* (London: Routledge, 1992).

Merlo, E. 'Gli speziali milanesi nel Settecento. Storie di antidoti e affari di droghe', in A. Guenzi, P. Massa and F. Piola Caselli (eds) *Corporazioni e Gruppi Professionali* (Milan: Angeli, 1999).

Muldrew, C. 'Class and credit: social identity, wealth and the life course in early modern England', in J. Barry and H. French (eds), *Identity and Agency in England 1500–1800* (Basingstoke: Palgrave Macmillan, 2004).

Musacchio, J. 'Weasels and pregnancy in Renaissance Italy', *Renaissance Studies*, 15:2 (2001).

Musacchio, J. 'Lambs, Coral, Teeth, and the Intimate Intersection of Religion and Magic in Renaissance Italy', in S. J. Cornelison and S. B. Montgomery (eds) *Images, Relics, and Devotional Practices in Medieval and Renaissance Italy*, Medieval and Renaissance Texts and Studies, V. 296, (Temple: Arizona Centre for Medieval and Renaissance Studies, 2005).

Niccoli, O. 'Rituals of youth: love, play and violence in Tridentine Bologna', in K. Eisenbichler (ed.), *The Premodern Teenager. Youth in Society 1150–1650* (Toronto: Centre for Reformation and Renaissance Studies, 2002).

Nutton, V. 'Humanist surgery', in A. Wear, R. K. French and I. M. Lonie (eds) *The Medical Renaissance of the Sixteenth Century* (Cambridge: Cambridge University Press, 1985).

O'Hara, D. 'Ruled by my friends: aspects of marriage in the diocese of Canterbury c.1540–1570', *Continuity and Change*, 6 (1991).

Palmer R. 'Physicians and Surgeons in sixteenth-century Venice', *Medical History*, 23 (1979).

Palmer, R. 'Pharmacy in the republic of Venice in the sixteenth century', in A. Wear, R. K. French and I. M. Lonie (eds) *The Medical Renaissance of the Sixteenth Century* (Cambridge: Cambridge University Press, 1985).

Palmer, R. 'In bad odour: smell and its significance in medicine from antiquity to the seventeenth century', in W. F. Bynum and R. Porter (eds) *Medicine and the Five Senses* (Cambridge: Cambridge University Press, 1993).

Pancino, C. 'Soffrire per ben comparire. Corpo e bellezza, natura e cura', in Belfanti and Giusberti (eds), *La Moda. Storia d'Italia Annali 9* (Turin: Einaudi, 2003).

Paravicini, W. 'Structure et fonctionnement de la cour bourguignonne au XVe siècle', in J. M. Cauchies and G. Chittolini (eds) *Milano e Borgogna, Due stati Principeschi tra Medioevo e Rinascimento* (Rome: Bulzoni, 1990).

Park, K. 'The Life of the corpse: division and dissection in late medieval Europe', *Journal of the History of Medicine and the Allied Sciences*, 50 (1995).

Pelling, M. 'Occupational diversity: barber-surgeons and other trades, 1550–1640', *Bulletin of the History of Medicine*, 56 (1982).

Pelling, P. 'Medical practice in early modern England. Trade or profession?', in W. Prest (ed.), *The Professions of Early Modern England* (New York: Croom Helm, 1987).

Pelling, M. 'Compromised by gender: the role of the male medical practitioner in early modern England', in H. Marland and M. Pelling (eds) *The Task of Healing. Medicine, Religion and Gender in England and the Netherlands, 1450–1800* (Rotterdam: Erasmus, 1996).

Pelling, M. 'The body's extremities: feet, gender, and the iconography of healing in seventeenth-century sources', in H. Marland and M. Pelling (eds) *The Task of Healing. Medicine, Religion and Gender in England and the Netherlands, 1450–1800* (Rotterdam: Erasmus, 1996).

Peruzzi, P. 'Lavorare a corte: 'Ordine et Officij'. Domestici, familiari, cortigiani e funzionari al servizio del Duca d' Urbino', in G. Carboni Baiardi, G. Chittolini and P. Floriani (eds) *Federico di Montefeltro*, vol. 1, *Lo Stato* (Rome: Bulzoni, 1986).

Pigeaud, J. 'Coeur organique, coeur metaphorique', *Micrologus,* 11 (2003).

Plakans, A. and C. Wheatherell, 'Household and kinship networks: the costs and benefits of contextualisation', *Continuity and Change*, 18 (2003).

Pomata, G. 'Practising between earth and heaven: women healers in seventeenth-century Bologna', *Dynamis*, 19 (1999).

Pomata, G. 'Menstruating men: similarity and difference of the sexes in early modern medicine', in V. Finucci and K. Brownlee (eds) *Generation and*

Degeneration: Tropes of Reproduction in Literature and History from Antiquity to Early Modern Europe (Durham NC: Duke University Press, 2001).

Pomata, G. 'Family and gender', in J. A. Marino (ed.), *Short Oxford History of Italy. Early Modern Italy 1550–1796* (Oxford: Oxford University Press, 2002).

Porter, R. 'The language of quackery in England, 1660–1800', in P. Burke and R. Porter (eds) *The Social History of Language* (Cambridge: Cambridge University Press, 1987).

Poussou, J. P. 'De l'intérêt de l'étude historique des mouvements migratoires européens du milieu du Moyen Âge à la fin du XIX siècle', in Istituto Internazionale di Storia Economica F. Datini di Prato, *Le Migrazioni in Europa Secc. XIII–XVIII* (Florence: Le Monnier, 1994).

R. A., G. P. and M. P. 'Preface', *Quaderni Storici*, 86 (1994).

Rabier, C. 'Chirurgie', in D. Lecourt (ed.), *Dictionnaire de la Pensée Médicale* (Paris: Presses Universitaire de France, 2004).

Reher, D. 'Family ties in Western Europe: persistent contrasts', *Population and Development Review*, 24:2 (1998).

Revel, J. 'La storia come biografia', in F. Cigni and V. Tomasi (eds) *Tante Storie* (Milan: Mondadori, 2004).

Rogers, J. 'Nordic family history: themes and issues, old and new', *Journal of Family History*, 18 (1993).

Roper, L. 'Blood and codpieces', in L. Roper, *Oedipus and the Devil* (London: Routledge, 1994).

Rosenthal, P.-A. 'Les liens familiaux, forme historique?', *Annales de Démographie Historique*, (2000).

Rosser, G. 'Crafts, guilds and the negotiation of work in the medieval town', *Past and Present*, 154 (1997).

Schindler, N. 'Guardians of disorder: rituals of youthful culture at the dawn of the modern age', in G. Levi and J. Schmitt (eds) *A History of Young People in the West* (Cambridge Massachusetts: The Belknap Press of Harvard University Press, 1997), volume one.

Shepard, A. 'Manhood, credit and patriarchy in early modern England, c.1580–1640', *Past and Present*, 167 (2000).

Starkey, D. 'Intimacy and innovation: the rise of the Privy Chamber 1485–1547', in D. Starkey et al. *The English Court from the War of the Roses to the Civil War* (London: Longman, 1987).

Tosh, J. 'Men in the domestic sphere: a neglected history', in A. Arru (ed.), *La Costruzione dell'Identità Maschile nell'Età Moderna e Contemporanea* (Rome: Biblink, 2001).

Vigarello, G. 'S'exercer, jouer', in *Histoire du Corps*, vol. 1. *De la Renaissance aux Lumières* (Paris: Seuil, 2005).

Visceglia, M. A. 'Corti italiane e storiografia europea', *Dimensioni e Problemi della Ricerca Storica*, 2 (2004).

Wear, A. 'Making sense of health and the environment in early modern England', in A. Wear, *Medicine in Society. Historical Essays* (Cambridge: Cambridge University Press, 1992).

Weir, D. 'Rather never than late. Celibacy and age at marriage in English cohort fertility 1541–1871', *Journal of Family History*, 9 (1984).

Weinstein, R. "Thus will *giovani* do'. Jewish sub-culture in early modern Italy', in K. Eisenbichler (ed.), *The Premodern Teenager. Youth in Society 1150–1650* (Toronto: Centre for Reformation and Renaissance Studies, 2002).

Wiesner, M. 'Wandervogels and women: journeymen's concepts of masculinity in early modern Germany', *Journal of Social History*, 24 (1991).

Books

Amelang, J. S. *The Flight of Icarus. Artisan Autobiography in Early Modern Europe* (Stanford: Stanford University Press, 1998).

Amselle, J.-L. *Logiques Métisses. Anthropologie de l'Identité en Afrique et Ailleurs* (Paris: Payot, 1990).

Arro, F. *Del Diritto Dotale secondo i Principi del Gius Romano* (Asti: Garbiglia, 1834).

Arru, A. and F. Ramella (eds) *L'Italia delle Migrazioni Interne. Donne, Uomini, Mobilità in Età Moderna e Contemporanea* (Rome: Donzelli, 2003).

Barry, J. and C. Brooks (eds) *The Middling Sort of People: Culture, Society, and Politics in England, 1550–1800* (Basingstoke: Macmillan, 1994).

Bartolini D. *Medici e Comunità. Esempi dalla Terraferma Veneta dei secoli XVI e XVII* (Venice: Deputazione Editrice, 2006).

Belfanti, M. and F. Giusberti (eds) *La Moda. Storia d'Italia Annali 9* (Turin: Einaudi, 2003).

Bellavitis, A. *Identité, Mariage, Mobilité Sociale. Citoyennes et Citoyens à Venise au XVIe Siècle* (Rome: École Française de Rome, 2001).

Ben-Amos, I. *Adolescence and Youth in Early Modern England* (New Haven: Yale University Press, 1994).

Bonino, G. G. *Biografia Medica Piemontese*, 2 vols, (Turin: Bianco, 1824–25), vol. 2.

Bourdieu, P. *Outline of a Theory of Practice* (Cambridge: Cambridge University Press, 1977).

Bourdieu, P. *Distinction: A Social Critique of the Judgement of Taste* (London: Routledge & Kegan Paul, 1984).

Brockliss, L. and C. Jones, *Medical World of Early Modern France* (Oxford: Clarendon Press, 1997).

Broomhall, S. *Women's Medical Work in Early Modern France* (Manchester: Manchester University Press, 2004).

Brusatin, M. *Storia dei Colori* (Turin: Einaudi, 1983).

Calvi, G. *Il Contratto Morale. Madri e Figli nella Toscana Moderna* (Rome: Laterza, 1994).

Camporesi, P. *Juice of Life. The Symbolic and Magic Significance of Blood* (New York: Continuum, 1995).

Carpanetto, D. *Scienza e Arte del Guarire. Cultura, Formazione Universitaria e Professioni Mediche a Torino tra Sei e Settecento* (Turin: Deputazione Subalpina di Storia Patria, 1998).

Cavallo, S. *Charity and Power in Early Modern Italy. Benefactors and their Motives in Turin 1564–1789* (Cambridge: Cambridge University Press, 1995).

Cerutti, S. *Mestieri e Privilegi. Nascita delle Corporazioni a Torino secoli XVII–XVIII* (Turin: Einaudi, 1992).

Chojnacka, M. *Working Women of Early Modern Venice* (Baltimore: Johns Hopkins University Press, 2001).

Chojnacki, S. *Women and Men in Renaissance Venice. Twelve Essays on Patrician Society* (Baltimore: Johns Hopkins University Press, 2000).

Cohn, S. K. Jr *The Laboring Classes in Renaissance Florence* (New York: Academic Press, 1980).

Cook, H. *The Decline of the Old Medical Regime in Stuart London* (Ithaca: Cornell University Press, 1986).

Cook, H. *Trials of an Ordinary Doctor: Joannes Groenevelt in Seventeenth-Century London* (Baltimore: Johns Hopkins University Press, 1994).

Delille, G. *Famille et Propriété dans le Royaume de Naples (XVe–XIXe siècle)* (Rome: École française de Rome, 1985).

Dictionnaire de Spiritualité: Ascetique et Mystique. Doctrine et Histoire, 17 volumes (Paris: G. Bochesne, 1937–95).

Dolan, C. *Le Notaire, la Famille et la Ville (Aix-en-Provence à la fin du XVIe siècle)* (Toulouse: Presses Universitaires du Mirail, 1998).

Duden, B. *The Woman Beneath the Skin: a Doctor's Patients in Eighteenth-Century Germany* (Cambridge, Massachusetts: Harvard University Press, 1991).

Eamon, W. *Science and the Secrets of Nature. Books of Secrets in Medieval and Early Modern Culture* (Princeton: Princeton University Press, 1994).

Eiche, S. (ed.), *Ordine et Officij de Casa de lo Illustrissimo Signor Duca d'Urbino* (Urbino: Accademia Raffaello, 1999).

Eisenach, E. *Husbands, Wives and Concubines. Marriage, Family and Social Order in Sixteenth Century Verona* (Kirksville: Truman State University Press, 2004).

Elias, N. *La Civiltà delle Buone Maniere* (Bologna: Il Mulino, 1982).

Enciclopedia Cattolica, 12 vols (Città del Vaticano: Ente per l'Enciclopedia Cattolica, 1948–54).

Fantoni, M. *La Corte del Granduca. Forma e Simboli del Potere Mediceo fra Cinque e Seicento* (Rome: Bulzoni, 1994).

Farr, J. F. *Hands of Honor. Artisans and their World in Dijon 1550–1650* (Ithaca: Cornell University Press, 1988).

Farr, J. F. *Artisans in Europe 1300–1914* (Cambridge: Cambridge University Press, 2000).

Fissell, M. *Patients, Power and the Poor in Eighteenth-Century Bristol* (Cambridge: Cambridge University Press, 1991).

Foyster, E. *Manhood in Early Modern England: Honour, Sex and Marriage* (London: Longman, 1999).

Frigo, D. *Il Padre di Famiglia: Governo della Casa e Governo Civile nella Tradizione della 'Economica' tra Cinque e Seicento* (Rome: Bulzoni, 1985).

Gelfand, T. *Professionalizing Modern Medicine: Paris Surgeons and Medical Science and Institutions in the Eighteenth Century* (Westport, Connecticut: Greenwood Press, 1980).

Gentilcore, D. *Healing and Healers in Early Modern Italy* (Manchester: Manchester University Press, 1998).

Groppi, A. (ed.), *Il Lavoro delle Donne* (Rome: Laterza, 1996).

Gribaudi, G. *Donne, Uomini, Famiglie. Napoli nel Novecento* (Naples: L'Ancora del Mediterraneo, 1999).

Grubb, J. S. *Provincial Families of the Renaissance. Public and Private Life in the Veneto* (Baltimore: Johns Hopkins University Press, 1996).

Hagen, W. W. *Ordinary Prussians. Brandenburg Junkers and Villagers, 1500–1840* (Cambridge: Cambridge University Press, 2002).

Hardwick, J. *The Practice of Patriarchy: Gender and the Politics of Household Authority in Early Modern France* (University Park: Pennsylvania State University Press, 1998).

Hoerder, D. and L. P. Moch (eds) *European Migrants. Global and Local Perspectives* (Boston: Northeastern University Press, 1996).

Hufton, O. *The Prospect before Her* (London: Harper Collins, 1995).

Hunt, M. *The Middling Sort: Commerce, Gender and the Family in England 1680–1780* (Berkeley: University of California Press, 1996).

Jacquart, D. *La Médecine Médiévale dans le Cadre Parisien XIVe–XVe siècles* (Paris: Fayard, 1998).

Jenner, M. and P. Wallis (eds) *Medical and the Market in England and its Colonies, c. 1450–1850* (Basingstoke: Palgrave Macmillan, forthcoming).

Karras, R. *From Boys to Men. Formations of Masculinities in Late Medieval Europe* (Philadelphia: University of Pennsylvania Press, 2003).

Keniston McIntosh, M. *Working Women in English Society 1300–1620* (Cambridge: Cambridge University Press, 2005).

Kent, D. and F. W. Kent, *Neighbors and Neighborhood in Renaissance Florence* (New York: J. J. Augustan, 1982).

Kuehn, T. *Emancipation in Late Medieval Florence* (New Brunswick: Rutgers University Press, 1982).

Lehoux, F. *Le Cadre de Vie des Médecins Parisiens aux XVIe et XVIIe Siècles* (Paris: Éditions A. J. Picard, 1976).

Levi, G. *Inheriting Power: The Story of an Exorcist*, trans. Lydia G. Cochrane (Chicago: University of Chicago Press, 1988).

Maclean, I. *Logic, Signs and Nature in the Renaissance* (Cambridge: Cambridge University Press, 2002).

McTavish, L. *Childbirth and the Display of Authority in Early Modern France* (Aldershot: Ashgate, 2005).

Menozzi, D. *Sacro Cuore. Un Culto tra Devozione Interiore e Restaurazione Cristiana della Società* (Rome: Viella, 2001).

Merlin, P. *Tra Guerre e Tornei. La Corte Sabauda nell'Età di Carlo Emanuele I* (Turin: Società editrice internazionale, 1991).

Mikkeli, M. *Hygiene in the Early Modern Medical Tradition* (Saarijarvi: Finnish Academy of Science and Letters, 1999).

Mitterauer, M. *I Giovani in Europa dal Medioevo ad Oggi* (Roma Bari: Laterza, 1991).

Moch, L. P. *Moving Europeans. Migrations in Western Europe since 1650* (Bloomington: Indiana University Press, 1992).

Mongiano, L. *Ricerche sulla Successione Intestata nei Secoli XVI-XVIII. Il caso degli Stati Sabaudi* (Turin: Giappichelli, 1990).

Muldrew, C. *The Economy of Obligation: The Culture of Credit and Social Relations in Early Modern England* (Basingstoke: Macmillan, 1998).

Nagle, J. *La Civilisation du Coeur. Histoire du Sentiment Politique en France du XIIe au XVIe Siècle* (Paris: Fayard, 1998).

Ozment, S. *When Fathers Ruled: Family Life in Reformation Europe* (Cambridge Massachusetts: Harvard University Press, 1983).

Park, K. *Doctors and Medicine in Early Renaissance Florence* (Princeton: Princeton University Press, 1985).

Pastore, A. *Il Medico in Tribunale: La Perizia Medica nella Procedura Penale di Antico Regime (sec. 16-18)* (Bellinzona: Casagrande, 1998).

Pelling, M. *The Common Lot. Sickness, Medical Occupations and the Urban Poor in Early Modern England* (London: Longman, 1998).

Pelling, M. *Medical Conflicts in Early Modern London. Patronage, Physicians and Irregular Practitioners 1550-1640* (Oxford: Oxford University Press, 2003).

Pisetzky, R. Levi, *Storia del Costume in Italia* (Milan: Istituto Editoriale Italiano, 1964-69), Vol. III.

Pomata, G. *Contracting a Cure: Patients, Healers and the Law in Early Modern Italy* (Baltimore: Johns Hopkins University Press, 1998).

Porter, R. *Health for Sale. Quackery in England 1660-1850* (Manchester: Manchester University Press, 1989).

Porter, R. *Quacks, Fakers and Charlatans in English Medicine* (Stroud: Tempus, 2000).

Raggio, O. *Faide e Parentele. Lo Stato Genovese Visto dalla Fontanabuona* (Turin: Einaudi, 1990).

Romano, D. *Patricians and Popolani: The Social Foundations of the Venetian Renaissance State* (Baltimore: Johns Hopkins University Press, 1987).

Roper, L. *The Holy Household: Women and Morals in Reformation Augsburg* (Oxford: Clarendon, 1989).

Roche, D. (ed.), *Journal de ma Vie. Jacques-Louis Menetra Compagnon Vitrier au 18e siècle* (Paris: Montalban, 1982).

Sabean, D. W. *Property, Production, and the Family in Neckerhausen, 1700-1870* (Cambridge: Cambridge University Press, 1990).

Sarti, R. *Europe at Home. Family and Material Culture 1500-1800* (New Haven: Yale University Press, 2002).

Sigerist, H. E. *Landmarks in the History of Hygiene* (London: Oxford University Press, 1956).

Siraisi, N. G. *Medieval and Early Renaissance Medicine. An Introduction to Knowledge and Practice* (Chicago: University of Chicago Press, 1990).

Shepard, A. *Meanings of Manhood in Early Modern England* (Oxford: Oxford

University Press, 2003).

Solnon, J. F. *La Cour de France* (Paris: Fayard, 1987).

Sonenscher, M. *Work and Wages. Natural Law, Politics and the Eighteenth-Century French Trades* (Cambridge: Cambridge University Press, 1989).

Sreenivasan, G. P. *The Peasants of Ottobeuren 1487-1726: A Rural Society in early Modern Europe* (New York: Past and Present Publications, 2004).

Stuart, K. *Defiled Trades Social Outcasts. Honor and Ritual Pollution in Early Modern Germany* (Cambridge: Cambridge University Press, 1999).

Swanson, H. *Medieval Artisans. An Urban Class in Late Medieval England* (Oxford: Basil Blackwell, 1989).

Szramkiewicz, R. *Histoire du Droit Français de la Famille* (Paris: Dalloz, 1995).

Tadmor, N. *Family and Friends in Eighteenth-Century England: Household, Kinship, and Patronage* (Cambridge: Cambridge University Press, 2000).

Torre, A. *Il Consumo di Devozioni. Religione e Comunità nelle Campagne dell'Antico Regime* (Venice: Marsilio, 1995).

Trompeo, B. *Dei Medici e degli Archiatri dei Principi della Real Casa di Savoia* (Turin: G. Biancardi, 1857-58).

Truant, C. M. *The Rites of Labour. Brotherhoods of Compagnonnage in Old and New Regime France* (Ithaca: Cornell University Press, 1994).

Venturelli, P. *Gioielli e Gioiellieri Milanesi. Storia, Arte, Moda (1450-1630)* (Cinisello Balsamo: Silvana, 1996).

Vigarello, G. *Le Propre et le Sale* (Paris: Editions du Seuil, 1985).

Walker, M. *German Home Towns, Community, State and General Estate 1648-1871* (Ithaca: Cornell University Press, 1971).

Wear, A. *Knowledge and Practice in English Medicine 1550-1680* (Cambridge: Cambridge University Press, 2000).

Wiesner, M. *Women and Gender in Early Modern Europe* (Cambridge: Cambridge University Press, 1993).

Wilson, P. K. *Surgery, Skin and Syphilis. Daniel Turner's London (1667-1741)* (Amsterdam: Rodopi, 1999).

Woodward, D. *Men at Work. Labourers and Building Craftsmen in the Towns of Northern England 1450-1750* (Cambridge: Cambridge University Press, 1995).

Wrigley, D., E. Oeppen and R. Schofield, *English Population History from Family Reconstitution 1580-1837* (Cambridge: Cambridge University Press, 1997).

Wunder, H. *He is the Sun, She is the Moon. Women in Early Modern Germany* (Cambridge, Massachusetts: Harvard University Press, 1998).

Zanetti, D. *La Demografia del Patriziato Milanese* (Pavia: Universita, 1983).

Theses

Lanoe, C. 'Les Jeux de l'Artificiel. Culture, Production et Consommation des Cosmetiques à Paris sous l'Ancien Régime, XVIe–XVIIIe Siècles' (PhD thesis, Université Paris I, 2003).

McClive, C. 'Bleeding Flowers and Waning Moons: A History of Menstruations in France, *c.* 1495-1761', (PhD thesis, University of Warwick, 2004).

Pediconi, A. 'The Art and Culture of Bathing in Renaissance Rome' (MA dissertation in Renaissance Decorative Arts and Culture, Victoria and Albert Museum and Royal College of Art, 2003).

Index

CPSIA information can be obtained at www.ICGtesting.com
Printed in the USA
LVOW131009090612

285148LV00004B/5/P